IDAHO
A GUIDE IN WORD AND PICTURE

THE WORKS PROGRESS ADMINISTRATION

Printed, lithographed, and bound in the United States of America by
The CAXTON PRINTERS, Ltd.
Caldwell, Idaho
48058

TO
ALL IDAHOANS WHO HELPED TO MAKE IT,
THIS BOOK IS DEDICATED

FOREWORD

ETTING out a book of this sort proved to be an
unusually difficult task because on so many matters,
such as flora and fauna, there was little published information, and on still other matters much of what had been
published was inaccurate. It is quite beyond reason to expect that no inaccuracies exist herein, but it is hoped that
the number is few. In some instances statements may be
challenged by persons who are unaware that a good many
of the traditional notions about Idaho are not supported
by fact.

To the hundreds of Idahoans who gave willingly of their
information and time, acknowledgment is now made, and
it is regretted that their names cannot be appropriately
recorded here. The Guide is indebted more especially to
Harry Shellworth, Ben Oppenheim, Ansgar Johnson, and
Dr. A. E. Weaver for their assistance in many matters;
to members of the University faculties at both Moscow
and Pocatello for their reading of certain chapters; to the
supervisors of all the National Forests of the State for
their willing aid; and above all to M. S. Benedict whose
generosity in placing his skill as a photographer at the
service of Idaho knew no limits.

The Pocatello copy was written by business men of
that city, and the two essays on Indians by Ruth E. Lyon.
The maps are the work of F. M. Tarr. It will be noted, of
course, that much interesting material, and notably in
the categories of social and cultural development, has

been omitted because of limitations of space. If funds are forthcoming for the completion of the task, these and many other items will be covered in the atlas and encyclopedia which is presumably to follow the Guide.

CONTENTS

		Page
FOREWORD		7

SECTION I

I.	AN ESSAY IN IDAHO HISTORY	17
II.	HISTORY OF IDAHO INDIANS	41
III.	ANTHROPOLOGY OF IDAHO INDIANS	55
IV.	IDAHO FROM THE AIR	73
V.	FLORA	93
VI.	FAUNA	119
VII.	HUNTING AND FISHING	153
VIII.	RESOURCES AND PRODUCTS	165
IX.	EMERGING FROM THE FRONTIER	183

SECTION II

| I. | TOURS | 193 |

General Information for Tourists 194

Idaho's Major Points of Interest 195

Tour 1

Section a, U S 191, Montana Line to Idaho
Falls 197

Section b, U S 91, Idaho Falls to Utah Line....210

Tour 2, U S 91, Montana Line to Idaho Falls....216

Tour 3

Section a, U S 30 N, Wyoming Line to
Pocatello 218

I. Tours—*(Continued)*   *Page*

Section b, U S 30 N and U S 30, Pocatello to Boise 230

Section c, U S 30, Boise to Weiser 253

Tour 4, State 27, Blackfoot to Junction with U S 93 2 m south of Challis 265

Tour 5

Section a, U S 93, Montana Line to Hailey....273

Section b, U S 93, Hailey to Nevada Line......285

Tour 6, State 15 and 44, New Meadows to Boise 293

Tour 7

Section a, U S 95, Canadian Line to Lewiston 300

Section b, U S 95, Lewiston to Weiser............308

Tour 8, State 9 and 7, Spalding to Grangeville 319

Tour 9, U S 95 Alt., Coeur d'Alene to Potlatch 325

Tour 10, U S 10, Montana Line to Washington Line 331

Tour 11, State 3 and U S 195, Montana Line to Washington Line 337

II. The Primitive Area 345

III. A Trip into the Area 353

IV. Buried Treasures 365

V. Ghost Towns 379

VI. A Few Tall Tales 393

VII. Origins of Names 405

A Selected Bibliography 415

Acknowledgments 419

Index 423

ILLUSTRATIONS

Following
Page

Idaho State Flag ....Frontispiece

Jim Marshall of Fort Hall
Fort Hall Indian
Fort Hall Indian
Fort Hall Indian 64

A lava field near the Craters of the Moon
Sawtooth Mountains west of Stanley
An aerial view of Boise 80

Bayview on Lake Pend Oreille
Lewiston
Looking northeast toward Atlanta from Arrowrock Dam
The Seven Devils 86

White pine and cedar
Matured yellow pine
White bark pine: two grotesques
Tag alder; aspen 96

Mountain ash; elderberry
Colorado blue columbine; kinnikinnick
Syringa: Idaho State Flower
Sego lily: Utah State Flower 102

Indian paintbrush; marsh marigold
Balsam and lupine 114

Bear up a tree; come on down
Elk in winter
Deer on Moore Creek
Antelope in flight 120

Mountain goat
Rocky Mountain sheep: beginning of a battle
Elk: finish of a fight 124

*Following
Page*

Hunting is good in Idaho
The limit: cutthroat and rainbow
Snake River sturgeon
Wild geese and ducks 156

Power plant at Moyie Falls
Sheep
Timber
Sluicing logs; trainload of logs 168

Panning for gold
Idaho's big potatoes
A row of onions
A lettuce patch 172

Upper Mesa Falls
Teton Peaks 200

Crystal Falls Cave: Crystal Falls
Crystal Falls Cave: a backdrop
Crystal Falls Cave: a corridor
Crystal Falls Cave: a ceiling 204

Corridor of the Kings
Cavern of the Idols
The Bride 220

Snake River Gorge: the footprints of time
Perrine Coulee Falls
Twin Falls
Shoshone Falls 242

Balanced Rock
Phantom Walls
Icicle Cove
Snowbank Falls at Blue Lakes 244

Thousand Springs
Malad Gorge
Bruneau Canyon
Map of the United States—in Middle Fork of Boise River..............248

A Boise sky
A view of Boise
Arrowrock Dam
Historic Table Rock 256

Jump Creek Canyon
A profile in Sucker Creek 260

Monoliths at sunset and Volcanic Crater—Craters of the Moon
Cave Mouth and formation of cave interior—Craters of the
    Moon
Indian Tunnel: entrance and corridor—Craters of the Moon
Lave flow and impression of charred log in lava—Craters of
    the Moon 268

Natural bridge near Arco
Mount Borah 270

*Following
Page*

The Sawtooth Mountains east of Stanley
The outlet of Redfish Lake
Stanley Lake
Roaring Lake 280

Pettit Lake
Alice Lake
Imogene Lake
Galena Summit 282

Dog team on Wood River, near Hailey
Trail Creek near Ketchum 284

Middle and third chambers, Shoshone Ice Caves
Gooding City of Rocks
Salmon Dam
Twin Falls-Jerome Bridge 288

South Fork of Payette River
Payette Lake 294

Spirit Lake
Forest trail from Hayden Lake to North Fork
Hayden Lake
Surf-riding on Lake Coeur d'Alene 302

Coeur d'Alene
U S 95 through the pines of northern Idaho
A campus view
The Lewiston Hill 304

White pine lumber
Winchester Hill
Along the Salmon River
The Salmon River from the North-and-South Highway 310

Typical National Forest lookout
Rapid River Falls 314

The Lochsa River
Pierce City, one-time capital of Idaho Territory
Through the Clearwater National Forest
Government pack string on the Selway River 322

Marble Creek
The St. Joe River
Beauty Bay, Lake Coeur d'Alene
Sunset on Lake Coeur d'Alene 326

The Sunshine Mine
Coeur d'Alene National Forest
The Mullan Tree
Fernan Lake and beyond 334

Lake Pend Oreille
Priest River country
Priest Lake
Chimney Rock near Priest Lake 340

*Following
Page*

Middle Fork of Salmon River
Junction of Middle Fork and main Salmon
Submerged town of Roosevelt—Thunder Mountain area
A monument on Monumental Creek 346

Packing in
Mountain goat country
Cougar Dave and his dogs
Journey's end 356

The old hotel at Florence
Grave of an old-timer 380

MAPS

*Facing
Page*

History Map 17

Relief Map 73

Fish and Game Map 153

Resources Map 165

Products Map 177

Transportation Map 183

Key Map to Sections and Tours 193

Section I

Section VI

Section II

Section III ....following 196

Map of Boise 253

Section IV

Section V ....following 292

Recreation Map 253

SECTION I

I

AN ESSAY IN IDAHO HISTORY

AN ESSAY IN IDAHO HISTORY

AFTER three centuries of adventurous seeking, the American continent has been explored and settled, and the last frontier is gone. The lusty and profane extremes of it still live nebulously in the gaudy imbecilities of newsstand pulp magazines and in cheap novels, wherein to appease the hunger of human beings for drama and spectacle, heroines distressingly invulnerable are fought over by villains and heroes and restored to their rich properties of mine or cattle ranch; and the villain, if left unslain, passes out of the story sulking darkly; and the hero, without cracking a smile, stands up with the heroine clinging to his breast and addresses the reader with platitudes that would slay any ordinary man. But these villains with their Wild Bill mustaches, these apple-cheeked heroines agog with virtue, and these broad adolescent heroes who say "gosh ding it" and shoot with deadly accuracy from either hand are remote in both temper and character from the persons who built the West. They are shoddy sawdust counterfeits who would have been as much out of place in the old West as Chief Nampuh with his huge feet would have been among the theatrical ineptitudes of a Victorian tea.

It is a little strange, therefore, that many of the recent books about frontiersmen have been so painstakingly off the track. It is unfortunate that opinion runs to one of two extremes. There are, on the one hand, those writers who declare solemnly that the men and women who moved westward, conquering the last reaches of wilderness and danger, were either morons who had no notion of what they were doing or low-browed rascals fleeing from the law. Those who argue, as some have, that the frontiers were settled largely by vagrant shysters must be overwhelmed by distaste for their own anemic and stultified lives; and doubtless seek through perversity a restoration to their self-esteem. Nor is the matter improved, on the other hand, by those who, lost in glorification of ancestors, declare that nearly all of the pioneers were lords of foresight and courage, shepherded by wives whose gaze was everlastingly full of visions. The fable here is especially absurd when those writing of pioneers are themselves the sons and daughters or the grandchildren.

Most happily, as a matter of fact, the frontiers were conquered by neither saint nor villain. The men and women who pushed by thousands into the West were quite like the people of this generation from whom all physical frontiers have been taken. A few of the old-timers came because they were unusually adventurous in spirit; a larger number came because they were shoved out to new anchors by privation and want; and others came as crusaders to preach the particular creeds they were trying to live by. It is quite pointless for us today to extol those generations which moved westward, laying resources in waste or building their empires: they were neither villain nor hero except in the way that any person may be when driven to face a frontier and try to find his meaning in it. They were not, with rare exceptions, even aware that they were laying the foundations for the future of a huge territory: they were trying to make a living, to survive, quite as these are the matters which engage the wits and energies of those who have come after them. And it is equally pointless to call them marauders and thieves: in a primitive struggle to survive there is no time for amenities. The men and women who blazed the trails and built forts and laid open the mines and the forests had zest and vitality, and there are no virtues more indispensable than those.

Of the persons who penetrated the unknown regions, none were more adventurous of spirit or less greedy of purpose than the explorers. It was Lewis and Clark and their party who were the first white men to enter what is now Idaho; and it seems only plain fact to declare that the epic of their journey has hardly been surpassed in American annals. From the time they left St. Louis with a keel-boat and two Mackinaw pirogues until they looked at the broad Columbia, they faced perils with resourcefulness and courage and with little complaint. Their intrepid undertaking is so bright a chapter in history that it needs no embellishment with legend, nor does it serve any purpose to canonize the memory of the Indian woman who acted in some small degree as their guide. From Manden in North Dakota they were accompanied by Sacajawea, the Shoshoni woman who had long ago been stolen by the Crows and taken eastward; and it is from the name of her captors and not because she tripped lightly on her toes that she has passed into legend as the Bird Woman. Sacajawea rendered a service to white men, and has suffered under quaint indignities ever since. It seems not to have occurred to historians that she might have had as her only purpose in accompanying the party a wish to be restored to her people, and that all of her fabulous escapes from grizzlies and rattlesnakes were perhaps not related at all to the desire of Captain Lewis to reach the Columbia. Today she stands bright and terrible in legend as the Bird Woman who understood what President Jefferson wanted and led the invaders to her homeland so that the greed of the Hudson's Bay Company could follow.

Lewis and Clark saw that fur-bearing animals were so thick they were in one another's way, but the fur companies did not follow at once. Military posts had to be built along the explored routes, and a good many Indians had to be killed or bribed or driven out. It was David Thompson who got there first. He built Kalispel House

on Lake Pend Oreille, the first fort in what was to become
Idaho, and held thriving control over all the animals in
the Columbia and its tributaries until another English
company came awake to what it was missing. But the
North West Company, managed by Donald McKenzie,
merged with Hudson's Bay in 1821, and together they
slaughtered the furred beasts and outraged the Indians
until 1846. After the merger, Hudson's Bay held a
monopoly for many years on all the trapping trade between Puget Sound and the headwaters of the Missouri.
Its district overlord, now known variously as the Father
of Oregon, Monarch of the Northwest Country, or plain
John McLoughlin, was as astonishing a mixture of virtue
and villainy as ever laid an iron hand on everything he
touched. He was, like Brigham Young, an aggressive and
somewhat terrifying genius who built empires as easily
as most men build dreams. If he could not buy his rivals
out, he exterminated them. And later, after devastating a
large part of the animals in the north, he smelled profits
southward and established Fort Boise in 1834. Two years
later he bought Fort Hall to destroy his competitors
there. Nathaniel Wyeth, another early Idahoan, says
McLoughlin had good business methods; and doubtless
he had, because his trappers took as many as eighty
thousand beaver pelts from Snake River in a season, and
his rivals quaked when they heard him speak.

When Mr. John Jacob Astor decided that he wanted
some of the profits from fur, he discovered that wanting
them was one thing and getting them was another. His
first ship around Cape Horn was wrecked, and the crew
of the second was set upon by Indians and scalped. After
an expedition to the Boise River was destroyed, the Astor
interests—the American Fur Company, of which the
Pacific Company was a part—refused to compete with
Hudson's Bay and the Indians and confined their fur trade
to areas east of the Rocky Mountains. The first successful
commercial enterprise in what is now Idaho was that of
the Rocky Mountain Fur Company under General William

Ashley and Major Andrew Henry; but instead of establishing trading posts, this company had an annual rendezvous
at Pierre's Hole (now Teton Basin) to which trappers
came to barter pelts and gather supplies. This rendezvous,
like any other in early days, was a carnival of drunkenness and brawls and sharp practice. To a Hudson's Bay
employee, Wyeth wrote: "I have again to repeat to you
the advice which I before gave you not to come with a
small party to the American rendezvous. There are here
a great collection of scoundrels." There was a still larger
collection east of the rendezvous, and in 1834 the Astor
company forced the American out of business here. It
was this Wyeth himself who organized an expedition in
Boston and made the first continuous overland trip to
Vancouver, though his supply ship was wrecked in round-
ing the Horn. He established Fort Hall and went into
business for himself, but the competitive emphasis lay
too much in ambush and guns, and he was forced in 1836
to sell. The Missouri Company meanwhile had sent
Andrew Henry to the Snake River country, and there in
1810 Fort Henry was built near the present town of St.
Anthony. It was abandoned the next year and this company was practically extinct by 1822. Manuel Liza, its
founder, was accused of enticing Iroquois trappers from
their employers and persuading them to sell to him,
though in this matter historians do not agree. It is an
unimportant matter. No one could ever be credulous
enough to suppose that these barons of greed and sharp
wits gave much attention to scrupulous methods. Large
companies became larger and small companies went out of
business; and this, here or elsewhere in the West, is the
history of trapping: there was no time for gentleness and
there was no place for weaklings.

These hardy men who followed the explorers and preceded the miners were lusty freebooters whose only law
was the law of survival. As Chittenden points out in
The American Fur Trader of the Far West, the constant
study of each group was to forestall and outwit its rival,

to supplant one another in the good will of the tribes,
and to annihilate one another's plans or to mislead in
regard to routes, and to place every possible disadvantage
in the way of competitors. It was a tremendous epic of
wits and brawn; and Nature, who abhors a weakling as
much as a vacuum, had matters quite to her taste. The
early traders were content to camp along the rivers or
lakes and remember what they used to be; but after a
little while they were all bearded savages living close to
the earth and living mightily. In comparison with them,
the trappers back along the Missouri were dandified gentlemen who were getting neurotic from want of profanity
and hardship. Washington Irving said no class of men
on earth led lives of more constant exertion and peril or
were so enamored of their occupation; and he might have
added that the Indians were often apt students of the
profane and indefatigable invaders of their land.

The trappers were enamored because they were doing
a man's work in a way that the world is now rapidly for-
getting. More than half of these hard-fisted freebooters
were killed, but those who survived went right ahead
taking life with enormous relish and spending little time
grieving over what was gone. Many of them married
Indian maids; and if the tribe said no, as likely as not the
girl was abducted and married anyway. And because these
men trapped only in late fall and early spring in regions
where the snow was deep, they had much time heavy
on their hands and no disposition to use it gently; and
because they usually set their traps with a rifle ready or
a companion standing guard, they grew accustomed to
danger and took a narrow escape in a day's stride. Henry
lost twenty-seven men on his first trip into the wilderness; and of the two hundred men Wyeth started with,
only forty were alive at the end of three years. They died
from Indians, or infrequently from disease, or even from
starvation; but when not starving or murdering they
learned they could get a valuable fur for a ten-cent string
of beads; and with their greed whetted they graduated

from experimental trickery to bolder methods that more expediently served their ends. To call them scoundrels is to misunderstand them entirely. They were men fighting against death and hunger and they fought with the weapons that served them best. And more than that. They were men standing four-square upon their ancient heritage and their primitive rights, and in their plangent power is recorded the early epic of Idaho's emergence from a wilderness of Indians and beasts.

But the story is not alone one of mighty men who slew animals by hundreds of thousands. Some of these early brigands became as savage as men have ever been, and not infrequently betrayed or butchered the red men when they approached seeking peace. Captain Bonneville, one of the hardiest of the early adventurers, gives instances, one of which turns on Jim Bridger, long since a legendary hero, who with his party sought trapping grounds in the land of Blackfeet. When they came upon the Indians, a chief drew near and extended his hand in greeting, but Bridger thereupon cocked his rifle and was knocked off his horse for his pains. Whether the story is true hardly matters: it declares the temper of the times. Another instance is a story of brutality on the part of white men that many Indians would have been abashed to think of. Bonneville sent a scout with twenty men to hunt on the margin of the Crow country. The scout and his party came to a Crow village, a notorious assortment of rogues and horse thieves, and these persuaded most of the scout's men to desert him and to sneak off with all the horses and equipment. When the scout attempted to retake the deserters, he was warned by the Crows that the scamps were their friends; whereupon, with the few men who had remained loyal, the scout went to another fort. Here, too, he learned, the white men were everlastingly hotfooting it out of camp with whatever they could steal. He went next up the Powder River to trap, and one day, while the horses were grazing, two Indians rode into camp. While they affected friendliness, the horses disappeared, and the two Indians were at once made prisoners by the white men and threatened with death. The robbers came back to bargain for the release of their comrades and offered two horses for each man freed. Upon learning that they would have to restore all their booty, they deserted the prisoners and moved off with most lamentable howlings, and the prisoners were dragged to a pyre and burned to death in plain view of the fleeing pirates.

This story may be an extreme in white brutality, but it is understandable inasmuch as these men were isolated from the East with their mail going to Vera Cruz and across to the Pacific and then out to the Hawaiian Islands and then back to Vancouver and from there inland if there was anyone to take it. They were men who were more solitary by nature, as trappers are today, than any tribe who went before them or came after, more courageous than any save the explorers, and more resourceful than any group that followed them into the forested empires. They sank quickly to a rugged elemental level of eating and sleeping and slaying their enemies; and it was inevitable that missionaries should come to rebuke their zest and confuse the Indians.

Missionaries then, as now, were of all kinds. Some of them were earnest persons of courage and kindness who wanted to convince the lusty trappers that they were headed for the devil and to lift the Indians from their anthropomorphic level. Many of the explorers and trappers had already intermarried, and some of the Indians had already heard of the Christian religion. Jason Lee had accompanied Wyeth on his second journey into the West and had held the first religious service (in what was to be Idaho) at Fort Hall in 1834. In the next year the Reverend Samuel Parker, sent out by the Dutch Reform Church of Ithaca, joined Marcus Whitman in St. Louis and traveled with members of the American Fur Company to Green River. Here the need of the Indians was so apparent that they decided to remain in the West.

Whitman returned to enlist volunteers, and Parker went on to the Nez Perce country and thence to Walla Walla where he chose a site for the Whitman Mission. While traveling across country it is declared that he taught his Indian companions the Ten Commandments and persuaded some of them to spurn polygamy and return to their first wives. Precisely in what way this settled the matter for their second and third wives is not divulged. Whitman returned, meanwhile, with his wife and the Spaldings, who established themselves at Lapwai Creek a few miles above the present site of Lewiston. The Spaldings, husband and wife, were two missionaries who in most instances were remarkably tolerant and wise: they reached beyond empty ritual and instructed the red men in home economics and agriculture and thoughtful living.

While the Spaldings up north were teaching the Indians to grow vegetables and fruits and to desert their lusty deities, a colony of Mormons pushed northward out of Utah and settled in a little valley which they named for a king in the *Book of Mormon*. They built a fort of planks and mud and settled down to make their homes. Idaho historians usually place this colony among the missionaries, but these persons came to homestead and not to argue. They were from that larger colony which had established itself in the Salt Lake Valley under that great and wise leader of men and movements named Brigham Young. But Brigham Young and the Mormons generally were not mystics or metaphysicians: they were pioneers seeking homes and an opportunity to build a kingdom beyond the reach of persecution wherein every man could have as many wives as God and his own provisions would allow. And it was a Mormon colony that founded Idaho's first permanent settlement two years later. These persons, imagining they were in Utah when they called their village Franklin, made irrigation a fact in Idaho by building a canal three and a half miles long. They also established in 1860, the year of their arrival, the first school for white children within the present boundaries of the State.

There were other important missionaries in Idaho besides the Spaldings. No one can doubt the sincerity of most of them, nor, on the other hand, can anyone with the welfare of his race at heart believe that they achieved much good. What missionaries did to the Indians, except in rare instances, was to befuddle their wits and make them more amenable to subsequent degradation. It was not only that Father De Smet impressed upon the Flatheads the notion that Sunday was a day of rest and so encouraged them to greater laziness than they had formerly been disposed toward. It was not only that Samuel Parker was abandoned to the ironic circumstances of seeing his red congregation leap up right in the middle of a sermon and take to their weapons when an elk came in sight; and it is doubtful if he helped matters later when, after having rebuked them for working on Sunday, he sat down with them to feed on the beast they had slain. Nor was it only, as the shrewd W. A. Goulder points out in his reminiscences, that too many of the missionaries "seemed sometimes purposely to have placed some pasteboard lions in their path for the simple pleasure of kicking them out of the way." It may not even be quite enough to add, as he does, that we must forgive zeal so fierce that it is not always accompanied "by knowledge required to justify and dignify its workings."

Matters would have been improved if Protestants, Catholics, and Mormons had lived in peace with one another, all seeking the same ends. But much of their work was vitiated by petty suspicions and jealousies, and it takes more than pious historians who gloss the facts and expand the fictions to make some of these early missionaries look any bigger than the persons they came to instruct. It is the first white child born in what was to become Idaho, Eliza Spalding Warren herself, who declares that her father and Whitman believed that Indians were incited to malevolence by Catholic priests; and even Spalding, greatest of the lot, recorded the spiritual limits within which he worked when he called the baptism by a Jesuit priest of "blood-stained" children (after the Whitman massacre) one of the vilest deeds in history. It may be true that he accused Jesuits of abducting unsuspecting girls for their "large and flourishing schools throughout the country"; and it may be, too, that Catholics suspected Protestants of malpractices equally petty; and both, of course, absurdly fancied that Mormons were recruiting girls for polygamous harems. It is difficult to believe that men so far from the meaning of God themselves could have brought to the Indians a larger vision of humanity and fellowship.

But if, on the whole, they did not, the fault was not wholly theirs. These simple-minded red men heard the Sermon on the Mount on one day and on the next were got drunk or robbed or attacked by persons from that race with which the Sermon had been a byword for nineteen centuries. And later, treaties added confusion to confusion as the Indians were steadily driven from their ancient homes to the poorer lands set aside for them. Soldiers were brought in, as in Clearwater district, to force them out and subject them; and these soldiers were often, as Kate McBeth points out in *The Nez Perces Since Lewis and Clark*, a demoralizing influence and helped to bring this tribe to a degradation it had never known before. Drinking and gambling and fighting were the rule of the day and the night; and added to these were the preachments of brotherhood and good will which made incredible ironies of the whole picture. "Such a mix-up of heathenism, white men's vices, and religion was perhaps never known before." It is folly, on the one hand, to grow sentimental over the Indians. They were not noble savages. They were not thriftless vagabonds. It is folly, on the other hand, to pretend that the early missionaries, no matter how well-intentioned, were able to achieve more good than harm.

And it is little wonder that after awhile some of the Indians went on the warpath, and it is amusing to read what some historians have to say of the matter. An attack by Indians, they will tell you, was an outrage, a treachery, or a plain and terrible massacre; but attacks by white warriors were courageous stands against howling and bloodthirsty maniacs. The Indians, fighting to retain what they had owned for ages, were unmitigated rascals; but the whites, fighting to possess what did not belong to them, were splendid soldiers of God. The Indians, often driven to actual starvation, and striking back desperately with arrow or tomahawk, the only weapons they knew, were yelping and unvarnished assassins; but the whites, eager to lay the camas meadows under agriculture, were approved by all the centuries of plunder in which right has been on the stronger side. And not only that: those Indians who, deserting their own traditions and people, came to the aid of the whites are today commemorated in monuments; but the few whites who went over to the Indians are held in unspeakable infamy.

The Coeur d'Alenes and Spokanes had boasted for years that they had never shed the blood of a white man. But they were driven to it by persistent invasions of their country, and in one battle they united with the Palouse and Yakima tribes and came within an inch of exterminating a hundred and fifty-five men under Colonel E. J. Steptoe. Then an expedition was sent to punish these Indians who had resisted invasion; and after many were killed and wounded at the battle of Four Lakes, Colonel George Wright rounded up all the Indians' horses and slaughtered the entire herd of eight hundred. Thereupon the Indians surrendered and the colonel took a chief and several others as hostages and made it plain that if the Indians didn't like the ordeal of being civilized he would return and destroy the tribes. The colonel then went to the Palouse country and hanged several leaders there, took hostages, and made threats that almost shook the Columbian Plateau. It has been declared that the colonel was a successful Indian fighter—and there really seems to be little reason to doubt it. "Without the loss of a man he had defeated the Indians, who sustained heavy losses, confiscated their horses and cattle, executed eleven murderers, and captured large stores of supplies."

The Nez Perce Indians had always been friendly toward the whites. The more, in fact, one reads in the shameful history of warfare against Indians, the more one is impressed not by the treachery of the red men but by their credulity. They were children. They did not know that for countless centuries wars and persecutions, greed and torture, had masqueraded in the name of civilization, and they did not foresee that the white men who came to convert them would remain to seize their lands. After the whites came into the fertile valley of this tribe, Indian ponies actually starved to death for want of forage. Government agents, meanwhile, had repeatedly promised to move settlers out of the Yakima territory, and the Yakima tribe strove to enlist the support of other tribes in a general war. The Nez Perces refused. The chief of the tribe was talked into selling the land of his people but later resisted yielding it, and President Grant returned it to the Indians. But two years later the White Father repudiated his promise, and the Indian Bureau tried to force the tribe to move to the Lapwai Reservation. The wise and friendly old chieftain, finding himself dying, asked his son never to give up the land of his birth and home. That son was the famous Chief Joseph. He sought, even after one of his subordinates was thrown into jail, to restrain his people from violence; but when the final day of departure came, some of the more courageous Indians began what a historian called a "horrible series of murders"—by which he doubtless means that they were doing their best to slay their enemies. Then a Captain Perry marched in with a small army and was outsmarted in White Bird Canyon: his detachment was cut in two and one part was almost wiped out. "Lieutenant Theller and eighteen brave comrades were caught in the trap and killed." At this point, Lolo, the Nez Perce traitor, came on the scene and rode twenty-six miles to procure aid for some whites awaiting attack in a stockade.

One historian says it is difficult to imagine how "she could suppress her feelings of loyalty to members of her own people"—and it does seem difficult.

General Howard now came with several hundred men. He had a job to do, and he learned that it was to be the most exciting job in his busy lifetime. One commentator says the Indians, now fighting with their backs to the Clearwater River, held their ground "with an obstinancy that was surprising"—and it seems a pity that they should have been so stubborn merely because white men wanted their fertile valley. It seems a pity that the bloodcurdling rascals did not all jump into the river and drown themselves. But let us suppose for a moment that an Indian historian is writing of this desperate battle and this famous retreat.

There was a band of only three hundred Indians, with their backs to the Clearwater, with twice that number of well-armed soldiers facing them, and with a poor assortment of weapons in their hands. They were fighting for their homeland where they had lived for centuries and where their dead were buried. They had been lied to by the Great Father in Washington; they had been robbed and tricked by white men ever since these came to their country; and they were now being driven to a cheap and barren home that they did not love and did not want....

The white invaders with their terrible ghostly faces and their brutal instruments of death fought with surprising obstinancy and strove with all their power to murder us; and though we were outnumbered two to one we fought with the courage of a beaten people and time after time resisted every bloodthirsty attack....

And when at last we saw that our cause was hopeless, we slipped away and set forth in the night with no home to turn to, no friends anywhere. For weeks we fled, and there were three different armies of these vengeful white invaders trailing us and trying to trap us; but we had a great chief, our Joseph, and for weeks he outwitted three armies and made them look like a bunch of lost boys. But in our long flight of thirteen hundred miles, barefooted, over rock and stick and thorn, ragged and starved and sick, hopelessly outnumbered and defeated but never subdued, we had no place to go, no road that was ours. Our feet left blood in our tracks, but day after day, night after night, we marched, wishing only to be left alone to our birthplace and our rights....

And when at last we had to surrender and accept the gall of the white man's triumph and the barren land which he himself did not want, we went forth in rags and they did not recognize us. But we were proud and still unconquered. And as we stood there, the

skeletons who had survived, our Joseph gave to those unashamed
assassins of red men the most magnificent rebuke that has ever been
flung by a defenseless people at their barbarous conquerors:
From where the sun now stands, I shall fight no more!

But that would be a very temperate account from the
pen of an Indian historian. He would see the coming of
white men as a scourge, a nameless and invincible terror.
And it is time to admit that Chief Joseph was a great
soldier and that the Nez Perce Indians gave a lesson to
their conquerors in heroism and fortitude in conflict, and
pride and dignity in defeat.

Idaho had other Indian wars, most important of which
was with the Bannacks who were guilty of resenting the invasion of their camas meadows. But meanwhile the gold
seekers had come in. With few exceptions, the trappers
were hand-picked and somewhat solitary men who sought
the farthest reaches of the frontiers and assumed a dangerous life because they loved it. Quite different from
them in many respects were the miners. Some of these
were men not driven by obsessions and fevers, but a lot
of them were minor rascals of various breeds—nomadic
knights seeking pots of gold, petty thieves and shysters,
and restless unfortunates who had succumbed to greed.
Of the thousands who poured into Idaho after the discovery of gold, a large part was a feverish and floating
horde who had already rushed from place to place with a
vision of wealth bright and terrible in their eyes. Some of
them, diverted from their quest, organized gangs and
plundered stages and stores and trains, and others were
predatory scoundrels who worked darkly and alone. Of
the banded packs, the Plummer gang in Montana was the
most dangerous, and typical of such bandits was Cherokee
Bob. After killing two soldiers in Walla Walla, he fled to
Lewiston where he became leader of an assortment of cut-
throats, and then moved to Florence. There one night he
defended his mistress, a harlot who had been thrown out
of a hall, and was slain by another bandit as notorious as
himself. There were hundreds of Cherokee Bobs in Idaho
seventy years ago.

It has been said by some Idaho historians that these
thousands who rushed pell-mell into the State were unusually intelligent on the whole, and that many of them were
educated. One historian even solemnly declares that their
discussions around campfires would often have been a
credit to dignified deliberative bodies. But these attempts
to transform the early miners into a bunch of gentlemen
who sedately panned their gold and then meditated on
Aristotle are a gross injustice to an army of hell-roaring
and money-mad men. With exceptions, they were a rough
and blasphemous crew who swore like pirates and drank
whiskey as if they had been nursed on it, though now and
then one, it is true, got off by himself to brood over such
trivial matters as destiny and fate, or took to himself a
wife and minded his own business. But the majority of
them laid into life with furious appetites, and it is a most
lugubrious irony to dress up these tough-palmed, unmoral
roustabouts to look like the men today who fetch the milk
and play bridge and lead the house dog around the block.

Some of these miners were, of course, men of prey
from the time they entered the Western country, and
others learned to be after they got there. And these grew
in number until lawlessness in varying degrees prevailed
in every mining camp, and hardly a man anywhere dared
venture forth with his bag of gold dust in his hands.
After awhile the vigilantes came, and scoundrels of all
kinds were found hanging by their necks from bridge
beam and tree. Even the farmers in the Boise Basin came
alive to fury and pursued a gang of marauders clear into
the Grand Ronde Valley of Oregon; and "if any casu-
alties occurred, they were all on one side." The outraged
citizens of the Payette Valley organized and decreed three
modes of punishment: banishment for the apprentices in
the trade, flogging for those who had begun to prosper in
the ways of villainy, and hanging for those who had become masters of murder. When the Stewart brothers in-
discreetly published throughout the area the boast that
there weren't enough vigilantes to chastise them, they

soon found themselves hanging from a brand-new scaffold.

These avengers were chiefly farmers who lived a quieter life than that of the miners for whom the brothel and gaming table were as familiar as the beds they slept in. And the irascible temper of these philosophers is to be seen in a desperate war that broke out south of Boise between the Ida Elmore and Golden Chariot Companies over boundaries of their claims. Scorning compromise, the managers of these mines hired a few dozen gentle and book-loving thugs to engage in a pitched battle and fight it out. The Golden Chariot army stormed their opponents, and the owner of this company, while too curiously peeking at his foe, was shot through the head. During the ensuing night these lusty gentlemen blazed away at one another and kept it up for three days until a squad of cavalry was sent out from Boise. And two days later, after hostilities had ceased, one of the survivors was sitting in front of the Idaho Hotel, doubtless pondering a volume of Herbert Spencer, when a feudist from the opposite camp, one Marion More, accompanied by several gentlemen who preferred the works of Hume, came up to continue the quarrel. More was shot dead, and the man who had been sitting in meditation later died of his wounds. When even the owners of mines went on the warpath and hired a small army of idle freebooters to fight their battles, it seems a little beyond the facts to suppose that the common run of the miners were gun-shy introverts whose learned discussions troubled the Royal Society of England.

They were too busy living to have time for vagaries. Perhaps they did read now and then; and if so, it may be that they saw in the Boise *News* how "Justice Walker fined himself five dollars on Thursday for becoming angry in court and swearing at an attorney," or perhaps they saw that red drawers were only three dollars a pair or that Eureka whiskey was only six dollars a gallon whereas kerosene was nine. Or perhaps they read in the

Statesman that General Crook was on his way to Harney Lake and "had gobbled a few bucks on the way" but expected to find Indians more abundant in a less hunted region; or that the "most jovially reckless gentleman who ever sat in a gubernatorial chair" was Governor Bennett, who marched into a saloon and turned to those present to say, "Is there a ——— ——— here who will take a drink with the Governor of Idaho?" After Idaho Territory had rid itself of such a rascal as Brayman, it was inclined to look upon Bennett as a man almost scrupulous in his gentleness.

Gold was discovered in the Clearwater country in 1860, and rich strikes followed in the Salmon River and Florence areas, in Boise Basin, in the Owyhee terrain, in the Coeur d'Alenes, and elsewhere. The wilderness of trappers yielded to an era of lusty mining towns, and for years the territory knew little more than the feverish industry of thousands of men exploring the earth for its treasure, and hundreds preying upon them. In 1863 the Idaho Territory was created, and the temper of the time is to be found summarized in its Governors. The President, in fact, had difficulty in finding Governors who would go to "Idaho," and some of them, like Gilman Marston, never appeared at all, "having got lost or stolen on the way out. Alexander H. Conner, from the Lord only knows where, was the next venture of the President but for some unknown reason he, too, failed to appear." Former Governor Hawley next surmises that President Grant was growing impatient over the vanishing of his appointees and insisted that the next one actually reach the Territory and look around. This man saw so many educated young fellows sitting on their heels that he shook the dust of Idaho out of his shoes and disappeared in a week. William Wallace, still another, was bolder, but is said not to have shown even ordinary cunning in his crookedness; and still another, who signed himself as Caleb Lyon of Lyonsdale, specialized in ebullient rhetoric and died while he was being investigated for misappro-

priation of funds for the Nez Perce Indians. Of still
another, David W. Ballard, Hawley says he was a good-
natured sort of fellow "who drew his salary with com-
mendable regularity and did little else to inform people
that he held high office or was alive at all." And while
the Governors were disappearing or swindling or hiding
behind their salaries, the legislature was racking its
brains over the fact that the capital was up in the Panhandle and most of the Territory was lying beyond impassable regions south of it. Or it was prohibiting marriage
between whites and Chinese, or it was taxing Chinese four
dollars a month to live in the Territory or, strangely
enough, as early as 1885, it was appropriating money for
an insane asylum. Many things must have happened during those years if so many persons were violently crazy
that an asylum was needed five years before the Territory
was admitted to the Union. And many things did happen.
The lusty ripsnorting extremes of it now lie quietly under
the almost forgotten graveyards in the dozens of ghost
towns that are today the decaying monuments to twenty
violent years.

History shifted from trapping to boom towns, and
then came the sheep and cattlemen, and the feuds broke
upon a new scene. Cattle came first, arriving in herds
from Utah and Wyoming, and for awhile Idaho was a
huge cattle ranch. Thousands of beef were driven eastward to Cheyenne and shipped before the railroads came,
and sheep with them, and another war was on. It is true
that dead sheepherders were sometimes found in lonely
places and that cowboys now and then toppled from their
steeds because of guns fired from ambush; but even the
most diligent search has not found a single heroine who
stood by during these lively times to ride down Goose
Creek or Rattlesnake Gulch and shoot the horse from
under the villain and faint in the hero's arms. The women
of Idaho seem to have missed spectacular opportunities
here. As a matter of fact, though, there were no villains
and no heroes: Idaho Territory was a huge pasture, and

two factions fought to possess it and they fought for
the love of fighting and with the weapons that served
them best.

And besides, Idaho was now growing up and becoming an empire of its own and lawlessness and exuberance
were slowly yielding to discipline. For a long while it had
been known as the Columbia River country and later as
the Oregon country, of both of which it was a part. Oregon had been admitted to statehood before Idaho had
become more than a vague geographical area of Indians
and trappers, and even when it became a Territory of its
own it included most of what is now Montana and Wyoming. It did not become a State until 1890, the forty-third
of the Union, just after the railroads and ranchers had
definitely marked its transition from the old West to the
new. After running through five magnificently vital
decades of trapping and three of mining, it emerged to
precise boundaries and comparative serenity and settled
down to the job of building its kingdom. Most of its valleys were rapidly homesteaded by sturdy stock chiefly
from the Middle Western States; its surviving thugs were
driven out or thrown into jails; and its great mines and
forests were laid open. Idaho is no longer a frontier, but
the frontier still lives in countless ways within its borders.
It is to be seen modified and disciplined and slowly changing in every one of the cities and towns; and in a few of
these the old spirit is now and then resurrected and walks
in thunderous zest down the streets.

But the frontiers are gone, no matter how vividly they
still live in memory or how poignant their slow vanishings
may be from end to end of the State. The building of railroads, the coming of the cattlemen and sheepmen, and the
homesteading of the valleys and plains have effected the
transition from the frontier to the Idaho of today. The
Northern Pacific laid its rails across the Panhandle in
1880-82, and the Union Pacific crossed the southern part
of the State in 1882-84. In the latter year the Coeur
d'Alene country was the scene of one of the wildest stam-

pedes in the history of mining, and is still the most important mining area in the State.

The development of agriculture came later. The northern half of Idaho has reclaimed much logged-off land to become one of the most productive areas in the West, and the Snake River Valley and its tributary basins have prospered under the broad sweep of reclamation projects. In 1894 the Carey Act gave to each of the States 1,000,000 acres with the provision that the land was to be irrigated; and those acres Idaho has irrigated together with many more. Under the Reclamation Act of 1902 the State has developed the Minidoka, King Hill, and Boise Projects. Lands too far removed from water or for which water has not been available have been cultivated as dry farms, given chiefly to wheat and other grains.

Idaho is still a very young State. Because its social development remains largely in the future, it has little to boast of in the arts, in education, and in names of men who have made history. Of the latter it has, of course, William E. Borah, dean at this writing (1936) of the U. S. Senate, and doubtless one of the great statesmen of his time. Since that memorable day when Borah opposed Clarence Darrow in an Idaho courtroom, he has become a national figure and his name and Idaho have become, in the world at large, almost synonyms.

II

HISTORY OF IDAHO INDIANS

HISTORY OF IDAHO INDIANS

LITTLE is known of that legendary period of Indian history prior to the coming of the Lewis and Clark Expedition to Idaho in 1805. All Indians were steadily being pushed westward, and through wars between various tribes had divided the entire Western coast among themselves. Those residing in what is now Idaho were too much broken into small and scattered groups to act as whole tribes or nations, and their history other than a few exceptional events relates to petty strifes, local disturbances, and the robbing and massacre of white emigrants who were dispossessing them of their lands. These make the facts of their history, but the story itself, like that of the Indian people as a whole, is the tragic one of a race robbed of its birthright.

When Lewis and Clark made the first historically known contact with Indian tribes of this region, the explorers were for the most part received in friendly fashion. It has been said that the Shoshonis were friendly because the party was guided by Sacajawea, a Shoshonean woman and the sister of their chief, but it is true that members of the Nez Perce tribe were also friendly and assisted the party in every way possible. Gifts were exchanged, feasts given, and the extreme good will of the Nez Perces shown by the fact that six chiefs accompanied the expedition as far as Riparia, Washington, to protect as well as guide the explorers.

Almost immediately on the trail of Lewis and Clark

came the fur traders, who in the majority of cases were also received with friendliness even though they were becoming rich at the expense of the Indians. The traders attempted to promote this friendship because it was to their advantage to do so, and the Indians responded because they had not yet realized what this invasion was to mean to them. Although the tribes were at times troublesome, there were few catastrophes at all comparable to those after the settlers began pouring into the region.

It was the trappers and traders who first attempted to substitute Christianity for the religions of the red men. Although decidedly not a religious group, these adventurers interested the Indians in their religion and paved the way for the missionaries, of whom Reverend H. H. Spalding was perhaps the most successful. Spalding cemented the friendship of the Nez Perces, already demonstrated in their dealings with the explorers, and taught the Indian men to till the soil, while his wife instructed the Indian women in the arts of housekeeping. The Catholics were a strong influence on the religious-minded tribes of northern Idaho—so much so that in 1831 four Nez Perce Indians made a trip to St. Louis to see the priests there and obtain more information on the white man's religion. Almost every denomination sent missionaries to the Indians of the Idaho territory, their various efforts often resulting in confusion because these simple people could not understand the differences in creed. Hard, too, for them to understand was the apparent lack of co-ordination between the principles preached by the missionaries and the practices carried out by the white settlers.

It was difficult for the Indians to comprehend why these white men and women could come into this land which they considered rightfully theirs by heritage, and settle on it, usurping their hunting and camas fields. Little by little the most fertile valleys and the best grazing lands were being occupied by the whites, and the Indians, while experiencing the pinch of hunger, were expected to retire gracefully to barren lands allotted them. It is true that there were predatory bands of Indians who scalped and raided for the pure love of killing, but for the most part the outrages perpetrated upon the whites came as a direct result of the Indians' attempt to stop the onrushing flood of settlers who were simply moving in without asking permission.

Although all Indian tribes of the Northwest were becoming alarmed at this invasion, the Nez Perces remained steadfast friends of the white men. It was only this friendly and peaceable attitude that saved the settlers from being wiped out in 1855 when the Yakimas tried to enlist Nez Perce support in a general uprising of the Northwest tribes. This hostility on the part of Northwest Indians was caused by the Government's attempt to arrange a treaty providing for the sale of lands of all these tribes. Fighting a losing battle as always, they finally agreed to surrender their lands, and two treaties were signed in 1855. A treaty with the Kutenai, Pend d'Oreille, and Flathead Indians gave them lands in Idaho and Montana for a reservation; while one with the Nez Perces defined for them a reservation including specified lands in Idaho, Oregon, and Washington.

These treaties were negotiated successfully, but troubles with the Indians in that region were not at an end. In 1858 settlers in the West became apprehensive when members of the Coeur d'Alene, Palouse, Spokane, and Yakima tribes attacked Colonel Steptoe of the fort at Walla Walla after he had set out to investigate the murder of two miners by Palouse Indians. Since all these tribes had been peaceable in the past, this attack made the whites realize the seriousness of the situation. A force under the leadership of Colonel George Wright was immediately sent out to punish the Indians, and the first battle was fought at Four Lakes, about sixteen miles southwest of the present Spokane. After routing the Indian band and slaughtering their horses, Colonel Wright pressed on to the Coeur d'Alene Mission where the frightened Coeur d'Alene Indians were forced to agree to terms which he set forth. Moving on to the Palouse country, he dictated terms to them as well, and returned to Fort Walla Walla with such a complete victory that the Government felt it an opportune time to remove the Indians to reservations and so protect the increasing numbers of white settlers.

Steps were first taken to confine the Nez Perces, because the treaty of 1855, never satisfactory to the Indians, had become most unsatisfactory to the whites after it was learned that gold had been discovered in this region. In 1863 the whites accordingly attempted to negotiate a treaty by which the Nez Perces would cede back these lands and accept a smaller reservation in the Lapwai Valley. Old Chief Joseph, their leader, had signed the treaty of 1855, but when the Government wished him to agree to giving up the fertile Wallowa Valley, he became less amenable and refused to give up any of his lands. A direct result of old Chief Joseph's stand was a division in the Nez Perce ranks by which two factions sprang up, known as the "Treaty" and "Nontreaty" Indians; but his rebellion against the greediness of the whites was later to bring far-reaching and more serious consequences.

Indians everywhere throughout the State were becoming increasingly restless as hordes of white settlers began usurping their lands, and Indian outbreaks became common, although for the most part they were local in character and did not develop into what could be called a war. These outrages took the form of massacres of lone wagon trains, of which conspicuous in early Idaho history is the attack on the Ward party in August of 1854. This train of twenty-three members was attacked by a band of Snake Indians about twenty-five miles from old Fort Boise; all of the men were killed, the children killed or captured, and the women taken to the Indian camp a mile away. The only survivors of the atrocity were two of the Ward boys who succeeded in escaping into the brush even though they were wounded and near unconsciousness. A rescue party from old Fort Boise reported that the details of the crime were most horrifying, and an eye-witness tells us that "no pen could describe the fiendish savagery displayed in the torture and treatment of the victims." Here was an instance of the Indians retaliating in the only way known to them.

Such attacks were common in southern Idaho during the years from 1860 to the late 70's, and it became necessary to provide military protection for the long trains of wagons moving westward across the Snake River plains. Lone settlements were at the mercy of the Indians, and particularly harassed was a small colony of Mormons who had made the first permanent settlement in the State at Franklin near the southern border of Idaho. Brigham Young had tried to achieve friendly relations with the Bannacks by feeding them and refusing to quarrel with them, but this policy made the warlike tribesmen overbearing, and in the winter of 1862-63 their menace became so great that the terrified pioneers were forced to appeal to Colonel P. E. Connor at Fort Douglas, Utah. In January of 1863, troops sent to protect the Franklin families found the Indians encamped at Battle Creek, near the site of the present town of Oxford, and engaged in battle with them. Colonel Connor answered criticisms regarding this action by saying that it was impossible to surround members of the tribe and capture them without bloodshed because of the Indians' strategic position. The Bannacks fought with ferocity and desperation, but were finally severely defeated with a loss of 224 men. This battle was an important one to the State because it put an end to severe Indian trouble in that section and was followed in the same year by treaties made in Utah with the eastern and western bands of Shoshoni Indians, recognizing their claims to lands of which part lay in Idaho.

At this time all dealings with the Indians were carried on by treaty, and each tribe was recognized as an independent nation. These treaties were more often broken

than not since Washington was far distant and Indian
Superintendents had too much territory under their jurisdiction effectively to prevent treaty breaking. With cal-
lous indifference, more and more white settlers moved
into lands that were set aside for the red men by treaty,
and the original owners were helpless to combat peace-
ably this intrusion when Government agents seemed blind
to their rights and repeatedly broke promises made.

In most cases the Government had been successful in
persuading the Indians to give up their lands and go to
reservations which had been established as rapidly as
possible. In 1869 the Fort Hall Reservation was set aside
by President Grant for the Indians of southern Idaho
with especial mention of the Shoshonis and Bannacks. In
1872 the Colville Indian Reservation in Washington had
been set aside for the Kutenai, Pend d'Oreille, Colville,
and Spokane Indians, part of whom had resided in Idaho.
In 1867 an attempt had been made to provide a reservation for the Coeur d'Alene and Spokane Indians, but the
Coeur d'Alenes refused to accept the reservation as designated, and it was not until 1873 that the Coeur d'Alene
Reservation was officially set aside. In 1875 the Lemhi
Indian Reservation was set aside for Tendoy's band of
the Shoshonis, Bannacks, and Tukuarikas, and in 1877
the Duck Valley Indian Reservation, partly in Nevada
and partly in Idaho, was set aside for the Shoshonis and
Paiutes. Successful in the matter of these reservations,
the authorities were annoyed because they had been unable to persuade the nontreaty Nez Perces to accept the
treaty of 1863 and settle on the Lapwai Reservation,
giving up the land previously held by them.

The reservation was a bone of contention for many
years. Old Chief Joseph died in 1872, but before his
death he had made his son Joseph, the new chief, promise
never to give up the Wallowa. The valley was ceded back
to the Indians in 1873, but was taken again by the Government in 1875. In 1877 a final attempt was made to
force the nontreaty Nez Perces living there to move to

the Lapwai Reservation in Idaho, surrendering completely their rights to the valley of the Wallowa. A three-day council was called at Lapwai, the disagreements culminating in the arrest of the Indians' holy man, who had firmly announced that he would not go on the new reservation. Although the angry Indians wished to make war immediately on their oppressors, Chief Joseph restrained them and it was agreed that they should move to the reservation within thirty days.

Just as Government officials were congratulating themselves on their easy victory, and on the last day allotted to the Indians before removing to the reservation, a number of their band under the leadership of Chief Joseph swooped down on the unsuspecting settlers of the Salmon River country and began a wholesale butchering that was so horrible that protection was asked of United States troops stationed at Fort Lapwai. On June 14, 1877, Captain Perry was sent out with two cavalry companies to quell the disorders, but he was severely defeated and had one company almost annihilated in the battle of White Bird Canyon on June 17. This crushing defeat made General Howard aware that more strenuous measures had to be taken. Accordingly, he assembled a force of about six hundred, and with himself as leader, set out to capture Joseph and his braves. He finally located the band camped on the Clearwater River southeast of Kamiah, and after a two-day battle in which there were many killed on each side, he managed to dislodge them from their strategic position and force their retreat.

It was Joseph's plan at this time to take members of his tribe across the border into Canada, and he began a masterly retreat over the Lolo Trail, attempting to shake off his pursuers while hampered with women, children, and the old. He was too clever a man for the white soldiers, and would have been successful in reaching the border had not General Howard telegraphed troops in Montana to intercept the Indian band. Two battles were fought, August 9 and September 13, in both of which

Joseph outgeneraled the whites and escaped. Finally, on September 29 at the battle of Bear Paw Mountain only a few miles from the border, Colonel Nelson A. Miles with twice as many soldiers as there were Indians defeated the indomitable chief and forced his surrender. An agreement was made whereby the remnant of the band was to be returned to the Lapwai Reservation, but the whites, still afraid of Joseph's power, refused to keep the agreement and transferred the band first to Fort Leavenworth and later to Indian Territory in the South. This breach of faith was not rectified until much later when, after countless petitions to Washington by the homesick band, they were returned to the Northwest and placed on the Colville Reservation.

This, the Nez Perce War of 1877, was succeeded the following year by an uprising of the Bannack Indians, who had never really settled on the Fort Hall Reservation and who were wandering at will over southern Idaho. Primary cause of the war was the Indians' resentment because white settlers appropriated the Camas Prairie and let their cattle destroy the camas root, which was an important article of diet to the Indians. It was their custom to migrate each summer to the Camas Prairie, and they never intended to give up these lands or this privilege to the white man. McConnell, in his history of Idaho, advances the interesting theory that this whole bloody war was precipitated by the ignorance of some Government clerk who in transcribing the treaty replaced the unfamiliar name, "Camas Prairie," with "Kansas Prairie." Although because of this error there was no mention of the Camas Prairie in the treaty, it was understood that the makers of the treaty intended the Bannacks should be allowed to harvest their annual crop of camas. That was the Indians' understanding, and it is little wonder that they were angry when they found the cattle of the white men uprooting the food which they prized so highly.

The Bannack chief, Buffalo Horn, was chiefly responsible for their going on the warpath. Since he had served under General Howard in the Nez Perce War and was familiar with military tactics, he was a dangerous enemy to the whites. The band first attacked settlers on the Camas Prairie, and then began a series of murders and raids on white persons living in southwestern Idaho. They avoided a general engagement with the troops following them, although they were forced into a few brief and bloody battles, in one of which their leader, Buffalo Horn, was killed. The loss of their chief did more than anything else to break up the war, although some of the Indians, hoping to make an alliance with powerful Oregon tribes, refused to surrender even though General Howard was following them closely. Finally, however, the troops succeeded in disorganizing them, and, separating into small bands for protection, the Indians made their way back to the Fort Hall Reservation.

Some members of this band along with renegades from the Nez Perce and Shoshoni tribes had found protection among the Tukuarikas, or Sheepeaters, in the Salmon River Mountains. This small band of marauding Indians, outlaws expelled from various tribes, had been a menace to the whites in that section for some time. They were wily and treacherous, though cowardly, and lived by stealing the livestock of the settlers and murdering and robbing prospectors. Finally, in the summer of 1879, they became so bold that it was necessary to take steps to punish them. Troops were sent into the rugged mountain area to capture them, a difficult task because the Indians were too cunning to fight an armed force and kept constantly on the move. Despite the fact that the Sheepeaters were mountain people and knew the tortuous country, they finally became discouraged at being unable to shake off the white soldiers and surrendered on September 1. This game of hide-and-seek was known as the Sheepeaters' War and put an end to all Indian trouble in Idaho Territory.

The country was becoming so rapidly settled that the

Indians had no place to turn were they to become hostile, and realizing the futility of continuing this losing fight against a force too strong for them, they became resigned to the inevitable and signed treaties greatly reducing the size of their reservations. Thus these proud and independent peoples who had welcomed the first explorers as friends were reduced to little better than charity wards of the Government; and the superficialities of white civilization, for which they had no liking, were forced on them. The wild, free Idaho Indian was no more, and his later history must show him as an imperfect replica of the white man, deteriorating under his imprisonment, a Reservation Indian.

According to Stephen S. Fenn, delegate from the Idaho Territory from 1875 to 1879, in a speech before the second session of the Forty-fifth Congress, a great deal of the Indian trouble had been caused by the poor choice of agents for the reservations, because these agents through greed and corruptness robbed both the Government and the Indians whom they were selected to protect. The policy of farming out reservations to different religious denominations bred dissatisfaction and legitimate anger because many of these agents designated by the denominations were hostile to members of other faiths, and, since they were often placed in regions in which the majority of the Indians had been Christianized by some other church, the good work of the missionaries was defeated and the Indians made even more hostile. Since supplies sent by the Government to be issued to the Indians never reached them and the agents cared little whether the Indians were fed or clothed, a situation had arisen which could result in nothing but ill will.

The Lemhi Reservation, set aside for a band of the Shoshonis, Bannacks, and Tukuarikas in 1875, was more or less of a cruel jest: the lands designated consisted of hills and mountains on which it was impossible for the Indians to make a living. However, the Indians on this reservation, remnants of other tribes, were always friendly to the white men under the leadership of their chief, Tendoy. Tendoy was a great statesman and orator who was respected and beloved by the whites, so much so that in 1880 he was taken to Washington, D. C., to arrange a treaty whereby his band would remove to the Fort Hall Reservation. He agreed to this arrangement but asked that the tribe not be forced to go there until they were willing to do so. Though their reservation was barren and unfertile and at times they were miserably poor and destitute, the Lemhis did not wish to give up their lands and go among the alien tribes of the Fort Hall Reservation, and it was not until 1905, twenty-five years later, that they agreed to go in answer to a plea from Tendoy who was now an old man and in ill-health. The remaining members of the tribe did go to Fort Hall in 1909, but Chief Tendoy was not among them. He had died two years before.

With the transfer of the Lemhi Indians to Fort Hall and the establishment of a small reservation for the Kutenais in 1894, the entire Idaho Indian population, consisting of what were once great and powerful tribes, was more or less settled within four reservations, and the citizens of the state which was now Idaho, having other things about which to think, proceeded to forget their existence as much as possible. The Indians were left with the problem of adjusting themselves to the white man's civilization and of combating the diseases brought to them through that civilization.

Today Idaho still has these four reservations: Kutenai Public Domain, Coeur d'Alene, Lapwai or Nez Perce, and Fort Hall. A fifth, the Duck Valley or Western Shoshoni Reservation established in 1877, lies partly in Idaho but primarily in Nevada, and is classed as a Nevada reservation. These three northern reservations, being small, are under the jurisdiction of the Indian agency at Moscow, Idaho, but the Fort Hall agency is located on the reservation of that name. Indian population for Idaho, taken from the Annual Report of the Secretary of the Interior for the fiscal year ended June 30, 1935, was 4,195 persons. Of these 627 were registered at the Coeur d'Alene Reservation, 120 at the Kutenai, 1,407 at the Nez Perce, and 1,841 at the Fort Hall Reservation.

Such statistics show that the Indians have decreased rapidly in numbers, but they do not tell the story of each Indian's disintegration under a policy which robbed him of incentive; broke up his institutions, organizations, and tribal unity; and left him facing greater poverty each year, dependent on the arbitrary rulings of the Office of Indian Affairs.

With the passing of the Indian Reorganization Act in June of 1934, a new period in Indian history has begun, and the Indian is developing in initiative and resourcefulness as he is offered the opportunity to become self-supporting. Reorganization is not complete, but progress made by the Indians of Fort Hall, Idaho's largest reservation, is such that one can look on the Indian scene with a spirit of optimism, and can hope that the Indian will yet emerge to take his rightful place in the civilization of today.

III

ANTHROPOLOGY OF IDAHO INDIANS

ANTHROPOLOGY OF IDAHO INDIANS

THE EARLIEST Indians of Idaho have left so few records of their inhabitance that it is difficult to determine just what type of culture was theirs before the coming of the contemporary Indian. Archaeologists have discovered a number of prehistoric inscriptions on rocks and two or three interesting caves containing relics, but their findings have been meager in comparison with those of other regions. Until more undisturbed material has been found, how far back the history of man actually extends in Idaho is only conjecture.

The first important discovery of prehistoric Indians in the State was that of a cave near Marsing, on the south side of the Snake River below Nampa, in which were relics indicating that man lived in caves in southwestern Idaho some four thousand years ago. This date was set because the types of weaving found in the cave made it seem probable that its inhabitants were connected with early Pueblo culture, which archaeologists have placed at approximately that antiquity. An ingenious fishhook leads to the belief that they were fishermen, and the finding of a fishing cache points to the theory that although the cave was not a permanent residence they expected to return but for some unknown reason did not.

Another interesting cave, also believed to have been inhabited three or four thousand years ago, was discovered near the mouth of the Salmon River in 1933. Many relics were found in an excellent state of preserva-

tion under about four feet of dry earth, and from all indi-
cations the owners were of a race different from those
living here when the whites first came to the Northwest.
Much importance has been attached to a brush made of
butts of coarse, fibrous grass containing a tangled mass of
red hair, of which some strands were eighteen or twenty
inches long. Mats or long braids possibly used for floor
coverings or bedding were artistically woven from a
coarse grass which is unknown in the region today. Other
articles found were a two-strand rope, three moccasins
made of elkhide with the hair on the outside, two elkhorn
wedges, a half dozen well-formed arrowheads, a large
food pestle with either writing or ornament on the handle,
a bow and arrow, a well-polished wooden needle, and
twenty-five forked sticks, apparently used for cooking,
which were made of hard wood not found in the region.
The walls of the cave are covered with picture writing
which appears to be of an earlier period than that found
elsewhere in Idaho and which does not seem to connect in
any way with present-day Indians living in the Northwest.

The State Historical Society of Idaho lists sixty-nine
locations of rock writings in Idaho, about twenty of which
are found along the Snake River. In most cases they are
found at the sites of Indian camps along trails, and vary
in quantity, some being only a few characters on single
rocks while others contain many writings on numbers of
rocks. Pictographs, or painted inscriptions, and petroglyphs, or inscriptions carved with a sharp instrument,
are both found in the State, although neither has been
"read" satisfactorily and as proof of the general system
of Indian tribal life are of little importance. Their signifi-
cance seems to be mostly local, and attempts at interpre-
tation show them as being records of visits of individuals,
battles, hunting expeditions, game areas, religion, ceremonies, dreams, warnings, and information concerning
water or trails. Although most of them are very crude,

they show varying artistic ability and seem to be the records of ancient, probably not primitive, man.

The pictographs are most often found on walls under rock shelters or in caves, and some of them have lines so neatly executed that it is thought the painting had been sketched beforehand. In design the pictographs feature curvilinear and geometric elements with numerous dots and some triangles being used. The circular figure occurs in many combinations with connected, concentric, and plain circles as well as some used in series and chains. Other representative characters are wavy lines, rakes, stars, rain symbols, ladders, deer, mountain sheep, birds, lizards, bear tracks and paws, sheep horns, hands, men on horses, and the sun. The paints, made by dissolving mineral material with gum or resin from pine and fir trees, have glazed and become bright in color, mostly red, retaining that brightness many years. Most important of the pictographs are found in the Salmon River region. On cliffs in Birch Creek are scenes of a fight which took place between the Lemhi and Bannack Indians, painted with red pigment prepared from colored earth which has so penetrated the rocks that it can only be removed by chipping. The unpublished manuscript of John Rees in the files of the Idaho Historical Society states that the scenes were near the old Indian Trail and were intended to warn passing Indians that the game lands were claimed by the Shoshonis. In a cave in Indian Head Gulch, south of Nicholia, are drawings representing the "hoop and pole game," which was probably a championship game between the Shoshoni and Arapahoe tribes.

Petroglyphs, made by abrasion, were usually placed on the southern exposure of the rocks because the other sides were more or less prone to be covered with lichen. The stones used to "peck" were of a very hard nature, often of quartz, and the depth of the incising varies probably one sixteenth of an inch. Some marks are barely visible, although others are as fresh as though they were of recent date. In some instances writings of a later period are superimposed upon the first writing, and even a third series of marking over has been reported. Most important of the petroglyphs occur in southern Idaho. Interesting petroglyphs can be seen at Indian Point, near Danskin Ranger Station on the South Fork of the Boise River, and in Lemhi County, where one announces a hunting and fishing party to be held in the Snake River Basin and a council to settle disputes on territorial hunting and fishing rights. Near Givens Warm Springs is a typical example of Shoshonean petroglyphs, locally termed "map rock." This primitive topographical map, drawn by the Indians without compass, rule, or any kind of guide, is a remarkably accurate map of the territory of the Snake River and its tributaries showing faunal features of the Shoshonean region. It is on a large lava rock weighing several tons and resting at the bottom of a talus slope with a natural travel route between it and the river. Placed correctly on the rock, the direction of all the features, including the various tributaries adjacent to lakes and mountains, is accurate.

These few records and later legends, most of which are mythological, are all that exist of Indian history before the coming of the explorers to the Northwest in 1805. When Lewis and Clark made their way westward they found living in what is now northern Idaho the Nez Perces, Coeur d'Alenes, Pend d'Oreilles, and Kutenais; and in the southern part of the State the Shoshonis proper or "Snakes," the Bannacks, and later the Sheepeaters and the Lemhis.

The Nez Perces, purest and strongest of the Shahaptian family, lived chiefly along the valleys of the Clearwater River and its tributaries and in the lower Salmon River country. They were named Nez Perces or "pierced noses" by the French, although as far as is known they were never given to the practice of piercing their noses. They were closely related to the treacherous and warlike Cayuses by intermarriage and by the absence of difficult natural barriers between them, but the Nez Perce tribe was in most cases friendly to the whites. War and hunting were their chief occupations, and salmon their most important food in earlier times although they frequently resorted to camas roots, berries, and mosses for provender. Lewis and Clark narratives tell us that the Nez Perce population was about six thousand people living in bands or villages named according to the place of their permanent winter camp, and that their houses, made of straw and mats, were closed at the ends and had doors. Each tribe had several chiefs with one considered the leader, but there were no signs of a clan system in their social organization. The introduction of horses had facilitated hunting expeditions to the neighboring mountains, and the Nez Perces became skillful horsemen with more and better stock than any of the nations. Certain ceremonial rites formed an important part of their lives, and a large dancing house was built at each permanent camp. It was the custom of early Nez Perce Indians to overcome the spirit of fatigue by a ceremony, supposed to confer great endurance, which lasted from three to seven days and was repeated yearly from the ages of eighteen to forty. Medicine men were supposed to acquire wonderful powers and become invulnerable by retiring to the mountains to confer with the medicine wolf. Their religion consisted of a belief in any number of spirits, and steam baths and sweat houses were used for the purpose of purification in their religious rites.

The Kutenais (Kootenae, Kootenai), originally living in the northern portions of what are now Idaho and Montana and in British Columbia, were a relatively small and unimportant tribe, although they formed one of the fifty-nine distinct linguistic families in the United States. They were the most northern tribe accustomed to the horse, supposedly introduced by the Shoshonis, and lived chiefly by hunting, fishing, and root gathering. As they were few in numbers and unusually well behaved, history records little of their doings.

The Pend d'Oreilles or "Earbobs," first called Kullyspell, inhabited the region around the lake of that name and along the river now called Clark Fork. They were never an important or numerous tribe and lived chiefly on roots and venison, accompanying the Flatheads on their annual buffalo hunt. The men were of good physique, skilled warriors, hunters, and fishermen, but the women, according to De Smet, were "untidy even for savages." Their religion was characteristic of other tribes of this region although they had a peculiar custom of sending the young Pend d'Oreille, as he approached his majority, to a high mountain where he remained until he dreamed of some animal, bird, or fish which was thereafter to be his medicine. A claw, tooth, or feather from the object of his dream was worn as his perpetual charm to protect him through his lifetime from all evil. Another custom which seems to apply to this tribe of Indians when reduced to severe straits was that of burying alive the very old and very young.

The Coeur d'Alenes were members of the Salishan family who lived in the region around Lake Coeur d'Alene. The Bureau of Ethnology gives the Indian name of this tribe as the Skitswish, frequently written "Ski-zoo-mish," and Lewis and Clark called them the "Skeet-so-mish." They were never very warlike or unfriendly to the whites and were quickly subdued after a mild uprising in 1858. They have been termed "industrious, self-respecting, and docile," although early French voyageurs named them Coeur d'Alene or "Heart of an Awl" and described them as being people "having spirits that were small and hard and being particularly shrewd in trade."

Various tribes of the Shoshonean family, third largest of the linguistic stocks of the United States in extent of territory occupied, were found in the upper Snake River Valley and the major part of what is now southern Idaho. Principal members of the Shoshonean family living in Idaho were the Shoshonis proper and the Bannacks, although the cognate Paiutes, Sheepeaters, and Lemhis figured in Idaho history.

The Shoshoni or Snake Indians, supposedly of California origin, were marked by more pretentiousness in dress and ornamentation than were the tribes farther south, and their dwellings were superior to those of the Utahs. They showed some facility in the manufacturing of cruder forms of pottery and were also grass weavers. It is thought that they were named Snakes because they replied to early traders' requests for their name by making peculiar snakelike motions with the index finger to reveal the art of weaving. Their apparent timidity and grave and reserved habits gave the white settlers the erroneous idea that they were rather stupid, but closer observance showed them to be intelligent and lively. They were essentially buffalo hunters, and the unfruitful nature of much of their country compelled them to lead a wandering life. In common with other tribes, they believed in spirits and laid any ills that befell them to such evil forces.

The culturally low "Digger branch of the family," called Paiutes, lived in sagebrush huts on the desert or in the mountains, and by the barrenness of the country they occupied had been led into humble methods of subsistence on small game, fish, roots, and seeds. These Indians owned no horses and although they manufactured pottery to a limited extent, practiced a rude agriculture in certain districts, and lived under a somewhat complex social system, they were considered the most degraded of the race in the United States and were scorned by the Bannacks and Shoshonis.

More belligerent, sly, cunning, and restless than the Shoshonis were the Bannacks, a brave and warlike race, probably the most warlike of the Shoshonean family. Their name, Bannack, refers to the manner in which members of the tribe wore a tuft of hair thrown backward from the forehead, and should not have been corrupted into the Scotch word Bannock. They were tall, straight, athletically built, and were always willing to engage in open combat with the whites, by whom they were termed traitorous and hostile. As their territory lay across the Oregon and California trails and the route that connected Salt Lake City with the Salmon River mines, they infested the highways and committed robberies and murders of passing emigrants. They roamed through this country at will and even after being officially placed on the Fort Hall Reservation refused to give up their migratory habits until after their defeat in the Bannack War.

The Sheepeaters or Tukuarikas were formed from outlaws of the Shoshoni and Bannack tribes who lived in the mountainous Salmon River country. Because of the barren hilly nature of this region, they were not as well off as other tribes and lived by stealing the livestock of the settlers as well as by murdering and robbing lone prospectors. These cunning and treacherous renegades caused serious trouble until they were finally defeated by the whites.

Certain scattered members of the Shoshoni, Bannack, and Sheepeater tribes placed themselves under the protection of Chief Tendoy, a Shoshoni Indian, intermarried, and formed mixed stock later known as the Lemhis. The name Lemhi, not an Indian word, was applied to them because they lived in the vicinity of the fort of that name, and they were often called simply "Tendoy's Band." Their land was unusually unproductive, but although they were probably the most poverty-stricken of all the Indians of Idaho, they were well behaved and under the leadership of Tendoy were always friendly to the white men.

Most of these tribes other than the Nez Perces and Shoshonis were relatively unimportant and their culture similar to the two more important groups. For this reason, discussion of the customs, legends, clothing, and handicraft of Idaho Indians will be limited to the Nez Perce and Shoshoni tribes.

When the first traders came to Idaho the dress of the Indians was somewhat varied. Nez Perce men dressed as nearly as they could like white men, wore their hair short, and looked like Spanish-speaking inhabitants of Arizona.

The women had long hair, sometimes banged in front and sometimes tied at the back with bits of ribbon. Their skirts were never short, and they liked bright shawls, wearing them pulled over their heads so their faces were half hidden. The Shoshonis were rather well dressed in typical plains fashion. Their blankets, made of buffalo, antelope, or deerskin dressed with the hair, were the same for both sexes, except that the women's were smaller. In summer they used elkskins without hair. The blanket was thrown loosely over the shoulders and drawn together by the hands or held by a girdle. Moccasins, made of one piece, were of deer, elk, or buffalo skin dressed with hair; in winter moccasins the buffalo skin was fixed with the hair inside. The Shoshoni tippet is described by Lewis as the most elegant Indian garment he saw, its collar being a strip of otter skin with the head, tail, and from one hundred to two hundred and fifty small rolls of ermine skin attached. At that time only children wore beads, but today necklaces are very popular among the men and women. Working clothes of the Indians today are much the same as those of the white men, although they still make some clothing of buckskin and have traditional costumes for ceremonies.

At Fort Hall bead weaving of belts, armlets, hat bands, purses, bags, and numerous other articles is done on a crude bow or loom made of native timber with strong cotton threads for the warp.[1] The older Indians, especially the Bannacks and some Shoshonis, use seed beads and geometric designs while the Bannack Creek Indians and those living along the Portneuf River use more floral designs and brighter colors of glass beads. The Washakie or Portage Shoshonis make the floral designs with one beadwork like the outline stitch and do beautiful work in embroidery and other sewing. The men on the reservation make hackamores, bridles, reins, and the like of

---

[1] For much of the following information credit is due Mrs. Minnie Y. LeSieur, a part-Indian woman of the Fort Hall Reservation.

rawhide; twist hair lines or ropes; and make bows and arrows. They use Indian hemp to make fish nets and to wrap and fasten the hooks of the fishing spears.

The principal material for useful and ornamental work is buckskin, which is tanned by the Fort Hall Indians in the old way. The tedious process includes the soaking, scraping, and fleshing of the hide; the application of the tanning preparation of brains and liver boiled and mashed into a soft mixture; and the continued soaking, pulling, rubbing, and stretching of the raw stuff until it is soft and pliable. When it is finished it is snow white and can be used in that natural color for dresses, vests, gloves, or purses. If a shade of yellow, orange, or darker yellow is desired, a white tanned hide is made airtight and strung over a shallow hole in which a fire has been made of white pine or some other kind of wood which gives a yellow color. The right side being next to the smoke, any shade can be obtained by a briefer or longer time over the smothered smoke, and the process is doubly valuable since it prevents buckskin from hardening as it would do if wet in the raw state.

Baskets, which are still used by the older Indians for various purposes, are made from twigs or slender sprouts of certain willows. Favorite material is taken from a squat variety of willow called the "frog willow," ("Yah-gwa-tsa-seeve") although the "Coo-sie-seeve" and pussy willow are used at certain times. In making the baskets the sap wood is separated from the heart by splitting the willow into three parts and trimming to the desired size. The older women are more skilled and artistic in making the design work, which is often bicolored, the colors being obtained by dye from roots, bark, or berries or by using wilted and discolored willows for brown and tan shades of geometric designs. They make long baskets with wide tops for berry picking, carrying baskets or receptacles for food, shovel-shaped fans to clean seeds and grains, and closely coiled water-jar baskets coated inside with pitch from the pine or piñon pine.

Jim Marshall of Fort Hall

Fort Hall Indian

Fort Hall Indian

Fort Hall Indian

The Indians of Fort Hall make a little money by selling these articles of handicraft from booths during county fairs and through stores the year around. All of the stores at Fort Hall sell Indian goods, as well as several in Pocatello. The northern tribes have almost no income from this source. They make a few articles such as moccasins, gloves, cornhusk bags, and beaded purses, but sales are mostly individual and articles are found only in small quantities in the towns on and adjacent to the reservations. The primary source of income and the chief occupation of all Indians in Idaho is agriculture, and persons interested in the Indian today feel that his salvation lies in persuading him to cultivate his lands instead of leasing them. The Indians of Fort Hall use and rent their lands, own stock ranches, and have co-operative cattle associations. Potatoes have been supplied to various nonreservation schools such as the Haskell Institute in Kansas and the Sherman Institute in California, and various agricultural products have been marketed within the State, although crops are not abundant because the climate and fertility of the valley are spoiled by the scarcity of water.

Since food is never plentiful because of this shortage of water, the Indians residing on the Fort Hall Reservation feel the need of utilizing every available food supply. Wild berries such as chokecherries, serviceberries, gooseberries, and currants, some years abundant, are dried by the older Indians and canned by the younger educated women. The old people dry the ground roots they get from Camas Prairie and gather sunflower seeds or grains to be made into sunflower porridge by the old methods. Chokecherries are still crushed or ground with seed grinders of stone by the older Indians who scorn modern methods, preferring to boil or roast their meats over a campfire and bake their unleavened bread in a bed of hot ashes or a Dutch oven. Occasionally an Indian gets a deer in this limited area, spears or catches a fish, or joins in a rabbit drive, the obtaining of meat being so important that any surplus is dried and made into pemmican as was the custom long ago.

Most of the old Indians cling to tribal traditions and practices, and the clan has survived as it always was. The office of chief continues to be hereditary or elective according to the members of a tribe, the present hereditary chief being assisted by a tribal business council and an advisory council set up by the Indian Reorganization Act. There is still functional ownership of tepee or other articles by the woman who made them, and an ownership of rituals and songs. The older Indians are true to their primitive religion, have medicine men and women, and continue to use the sweat house, their religious ceremonies being accompanied by traditional music which is kept secret from the white man. Marriage is allowed between opposite clans of the Shoshoni or between Bannacks and Shoshonis, but there is a strict rule against intermarriage within a clan even though the tribal marriage ceremony is disappearing. At a funeral it is the custom to give such articles as clothing, blankets, buckskin, and money to those who have recently buried some one; but as the old Indians die, many of these ancient and interesting customs are changing.

Indian music is, as it was in the past, significantly linked with Indian life. Every public ceremony and every important act in the career of an individual has its accompaniment of song with a rhythm always peculiar to the occasion. Some songs have no words, but their absence does not impair the definite meaning, since vocables are used which once set to melody are never changed. Each ceremonial dance has its own songs and drumbeats, with rhythm even in the throb of the drum, although it is erroneously thought that these dances are accompanied only by vocal "ki-yis." Most important of the Shoshoni ceremonials is the Fort Hall Sun Dance, which is held about the twenty-fourth of July each year in an enclosure usually built of willows three or four miles west of the agency. Not far from American Falls is a worn circle which marks the spot of the rites which were held there until 1917. The Sun Dance, a supplication to the Great Spirit for health and strength, lasts two days and three nights, followed by pleasure dances called variously the War, Owl, Rabbit, and Grass Dances. The latter part of January or the first part of February a religious recreational dance known as the Warm Dance is held to hasten a thaw or "breaking up of winter," and later there is an Easter Dance and egg feast.

Most important of the Nez Perce celebrations is the Ka-oo-yit, a formal feast held annually in Lewiston at the time of the white townspeople's Cherry Blossom Festival in May. The name signifies "eaten for the first time," in reference to the first food supply of the year, and its purpose is thanksgiving to the Great Spirit as the source of the power that produces food supplies. The older Nez Perces say that it was an ancient custom originally celebrated in a simple and quiet manner within a family circle or small group family, but as time passed it became a feast ritual in which all members of the tribe joined. James Mallikan, Nez Perce Indian living near Kamiah, says of the Ka-oo-yit: "In recent periods, intertribal celebrations have been inaugurated and the ceremonies have been highly festive and picturesque, carried out with pomp, featured with a magnificent display of regalia and dresses worn by the participants. Today it is a large day on the calendar of the Indians of the Northwest."

Of the more private religious ceremonies kept sacred to the Indian, of many of his folkways, and of the majority of his legends, white persons have learned little. Shoshoni mythology as a whole seems to lack a systematic cosmogony and a migration legend, and is coarser, more primitive, and more humorous than the Nez Perce collection. The role of the creator is sometimes assigned to A'po, the Father, or No' mono A'po, the Indians' Father, a deity that some informants identify with either

Coyote or Wolf, chief figures in Shoshoni mythology. According to Clark, the Bannacks considered Gray Wolf their creator, and the Shoshonis Coyote as theirs. In addition to the Coyote cycle, there seems to be a group of native stories which deal with the Dzo' avits, a race of gigantic ogres dwelling in stone houses, as well as others telling of apparently anthropomorphic cannibals.

The Shoshonis at Fort Hall tell of their belief in Nin-num-bees or "Small People," some asserting that they are spirits of departed warriors since they have an arrow-case slung on their backs and carry a bow. According to legend they are seen or heard only late in the evenings or very early in the mornings, singing, and fortunate is the patiently waiting warrior who sees them and learns the Nin-num-bees' song. He will then be victorious in battle, but if he tells of this vision it will never be repeated, and he will lose the power imparted. The children's story is a little different. "Hush," the mother tells her children when encamped in this vicinity, "this is where the Nin-num-bees live. Do not play near the large rocks or caves; the small people will take you away. Once a young girl while picking berries fell in love with one and followed him away and was never seen again."

Many legends were told to explain habits and characteristics of animals or birds, such as this one which tells why turtle doves mourn. "Long ago they were called Co-ah-wee-haw, derived from the cry of the bird which is similar in sound. They were also called 'rattlesnake's brother-in-law' (Toag'-go-in-dayts) because of a strange belief that whenever an Indian mocks one of these birds or kills its mate it tells a rattlesnake which way he is going and asks the snake to place himself by the Indian's path to bite him as he passes by. In this way the wrong is avenged. If an Indian kills one of these reptiles, the doves sit on a tree and weep, lamenting over the departed snake by reiterating their mournful cry. Because of these things, the Indians have a strange superstition against mocking or killing this bird."

The Nez Perces in legend explain why coyotes howl at the stars. "Coyote had become great. He had done many wonderful things such as stealing fire for men and giving fish to the Indians, so he came to think great of his powers and lived apart on a high mountain top. He wished to travel in the sky-world with the star which every night came close to his mountain top. Every night he begged star to take him on a journey, but star would only laugh at him. Then Coyote would shake with anger. At last star grew tired of Coyote's pleadings and said, 'Come to me tomorrow night and I will take you to the star sky.' The next night star came very near to Coyote and he sprang far up into the air to catch hold of star. Star turned and they climbed high into the sky. Beside them shone the moon. Below them the tallest pines looked like tiny spears of grass. The frost spirits lived in the sky and Coyote grew very cold as he traveled upward. Star too was cold, and moon. Coyote became colder and colder until his paws were stiff and he could not hold on. He slipped and fell. When he struck the earth he was crushed flat. He lay very still as his brothers crowded around him and howled in anger at the treacherous star. In this way great Coyote was killed, and this is why each night other coyotes point their noses toward the sky and howl in sorrow for his death."

The Shoshoni Indians have a charming legend telling the story of the Indian Spirit at Mesa Falls. "Many moons ago when the members of the tribe came to these falls to fish, a lovely maiden was helping her lover. He gracefully threw his spear; she quietly gathered the fish as he caught them and threw them on the bank. Becoming bold, he waded into the deeper water, but he lost his footing and the swift stream swept him down. She followed him; the boiling waters caught her, and she lost her life. Her lover swam out and was filled with sorrow at learning his sweetheart had drowned. Each year since then the Indians have watched in the falls for the mist-look of the maiden. At times she appears to them clad in white, smiling, with her long hair floating gently in the wind and spray. Sometimes when the wind is blowing softly her voice can be heard calling, 'Do not long for me, for I am happy here guarding these falls and watching over you.' "

IV
IDAHO FROM THE AIR

IDAHO FROM THE AIR

TOPOGRAPHICALLY, Idaho is one of the strangest States in the Union. At the beginning of the last century it was part of that indefinite geographic area known as the Columbia River country. After 1820 it belonged to the Oregon country, which roughly included the present States of Oregon, Washington, and Idaho, as well as what is now western Montana and western Wyoming and a large part of the present British Columbia. In 1846 the British Columbia area was withdrawn by treaty with England, and in 1848 the Oregon Territory was established. In the next two decades, Idaho's territorial boundaries were changed five times. In 1853 the region was divided, and the northern half was called Washington Territory; and when, in 1859, Oregon was admitted to the Union, Idaho became a part of the Washington area with its eastern boundary lying upon what were to become Montana and Wyoming. In March of 1863 Idaho was declared a Territory, and then included a large section of country lying east of the Bitterroot and Rocky Mountains. In 1864 a portion of it was withdrawn to Montana; in 1868 the remaining area east of the mountains was given to Wyoming. Idaho, in consequence, was reduced to its present strange shape, and all attempts to alter its boundaries since that time have failed. In consequence, too, it has no logic in its present boundaries except the Bitterroot Mountains and the Continental Divide between it and Montana, and the Snake River between a part of it and Oregon.

It is little wonder then that no other State in the Union
has a topographical structure so varied and sometimes so
appalling. Idaho lies among a group of States each of
which has a more definite geological integrity and a more
connatural face, mountainous though they may be; and is
homologous in the north with Washington or western
Montana, in the far south with Nevada, in the southeast
with Utah, and upon its eastern boundary with Wyoming.
It is, in consequence, a State that seems to have been
parceled from many, and offers not only unusual and dramatic changes in scenery but also remarkable shifts in
altitude. From the east, down through the great Snake
River Valley, it drops in a long broad incline from almost
six thousand feet to a little more than two thousand;
and from here, in the western part, it lifts over mountain
ranges and drops two thousand feet into Lewiston, the
lowest point in the State. And lying, as Idaho does, from
Canada to the temperate Cache Valley in Utah, and from
the frozen Teton Peaks to warm Pacific winds, it perhaps
offers, too, more extremes in temperature and weather,
ranging from freezing altitudes to the mild climate of
its southwestern valleys. Upon parts of Idaho very little
snow falls and the little that falls rarely remains long;
and upon other parts, even along rivers where farms are
many, the snow in February may lie eight feet deep. The
streets of Boise may lie bare when thirty miles northward a town is buried to its gables. Parts of the State
harvest full crops under rainfall and with no irrigation;
and other parts, with little rain and no irrigation, lie
brown and barren through the summer months. In parts
of Idaho even deer, exhausted by want of forage, may
freeze to death; in another part, at the same time, the
largest privately owned orchard in the world may be getting ready to blossom. Within southern caves in January
wild animals may lie indolently fat in warm chambers;
and in the same hour mountain goats, standing upon the
great watersheds, look across deserts of snow that have
completely buried evergreens thirty feet in height.

Idaho has huge semiarid reaches, but it also probably has more running water than any other State. It has flat formidable tablelands that defeat everything but sagebrush and coyote, but it also has more lakes than have ever been counted and nobody quite knows how many remain undiscovered and unexplored. It has broad benches slabbed out of basalt that reach like vast gray pavement from county to county; but it also has, one upon its border and two within it, the deepest canyons in the United States. It has alpine pinnacles where the ice never melts, but it also has so many hot springs that some cities pipe the water into their homes for heat. It has two of the largest remaining herds of antelope, one of which forages upon a mighty landscape that rolls away into the desolate reaches of northern Nevada, the other of which grazes in pocketed mountain valleys high against the timber line. Upon one part trees may be drenched with blossom while less than a hundred miles away the boughs of the alpine larch are breaking under their burden of snow. So diversified, indeed, is the State in its physical aspects that no one has ever tried to summarize it in one comprehensive formula.

Almost from boundary to boundary across southern Idaho falls the broad sweep of the Snake River Valley. It has a rolling and often impassably rugged floor of lava bed laid upon Tertiary sediments hundreds of feet deep. Southward are, from east to west, the Caribou, Bear River, Portneuf, Bannock, Sublette, Albion, and Owyhee Ranges, with the vast Bruneau Plateau lying between the last two. Northward are the Lemhi, Sawtooth, Boise, and Seven Devils Ranges, with the deepest gorge on the North American Continent dropping almost eight thousand feet in the latter. In the center of the State, north of Snake River and running from Wood River northeast past the porous volcanic terrain where two rivers vanish, is a magnificently desolate steppe of thirty-four hundred square miles. From its northern edge, two rivers and several creeks enter this area and lose themselves in the holes and

fissures and all but vanish from sight; and lakes form
here in the spring and disappear in the fall. Lying under
this steppe is nobody knows what; but far underground
the rivers must take their journey along subterranean
beds to burst forth at last upon the wall of the Snake
River Gorge. Upon these solidified sheets, interbedded
with the sediment of what was once a great lake, are
countless vents and cones, recently extinct craters, caves
filled with ice, and superchilled springs. The dominant
rock structure here is the Idaho batholith, a great dome
with a north-south axis two hundred and fifty miles long
and an extreme width of a hundred miles. In late Jurassic
time occurred this uplift beneath sedimentary beds of
limestones, sandstones, and shales; and some of the beds,
folded down and protected from erosion, now appear as
schists and ridges and dikes; but elsewhere streams and
glaciers have cut intricate weird patterns on the batholith top.

These corrugated lava flows of a former time have left
phenomena called sinks, and it is into these that rivers
disappear to emerge at last far away into hundreds of
thousands of springs with innumerable ones gushing from
walls of stone and with others to rise high to tumble in
waterfalls. Snake River (Mad River the French Canadians called it) has cut a gorge across most of the State,
and across the southern flank of this lava steppe it has
eroded a stupendous path. Sometimes it lies hundreds of
feet under its walls of stone and pours over cascades or
flows through shadow under the outpouring of buried
rivers; and farther in its journey, upon the Oregon-Idaho
line, it has cut through lava and flows upon a bed of
granite seventy-nine hundred feet below He Devil Peak.

The reaches of rock in this part of the State include
granite and syenites and schists, quartzites and limestones, and calcareous and noncalcareous shales. The
granite farther north, once thought to be of Archean Age
but now regarded as younger, is a coarse texture of feldspar and mica and quartz. This enormous rugged pave-

ment of stone is a geologic continuity that has intruded in
innumerable places, and unfolds, in consequence, into a
panorama of faults and gorges, corrugated ridges and
black caverns and basaltic buttes. There are huge bodies
of pink and white quartzites, deep-bedded, hard, and uni-
form; there is pink quartzite resting upon granite and
overlaid by dark blue and black calcareous slates; and on
the northern border, next to the watersheds of the Wood
and Salmon and Lost Rivers, slates and shales and limestones rest upon granite to a depth of thousands of feet.
Mount Borah, highest point in the State, carries coral
limestone on its very crest, lifted from the sea bottom
that was once three miles below. Southward the eruptive
volcanic rocks lie in superimposed flows, including the
basaltic sculpturings in the Craters of the Moon. Big
Butte and East Butte are extinct volcanoes that antedate
the Snake River basalts, and stood like islands long ago
amid the encroaching boiling floods of stone.

Such briefly is one part of Idaho as geologists see it.
From automobile or train window it is a rolling mass of
loneliness and waste, with the integrity of granite and the
changelessness of time. From the air it is much the same,
with its hard and formidable surface lying endlessly upon
the miles. A more impervious area it would be difficult to
find, or one more inviolable within its empire of aridity
and stone. Most of it can never be used, save for grazing,
and must lie here forever as it is now under the journey
of trains and the desolation of its sky. But for those who
know it and have stood within its strength, it is a splendid
and timeless area upon which a thousand centuries will
leave almost no mark of change; and they love its caves
and craters and the weird terracing of its scene. This part
of Idaho, looking as if the sky had poured boulders upon
it, or looking as if it harbored a vegetation of rock; this
toothed steppe, furrowed and gouged and spilled in pyramids, is not for persons whose homes are in tropical
growth under cloudy skies. This is the last frontier, de-

livered to rock and desolation and set apart as a monument of its own.

But it is chiefly this part of Idaho which persons see who travel across the State to the Pacific Northwest. They come in from the humid Middle West or the industrial East, where landscape seldom breaks into rugged and terrifying extremes; and they find this region awful in its aloofness and inexplicable in its calm. There is no shadow in its bald glare and no witchery in its horizons: it is candid in sunlight and alien and ageless in its mood. Persons entering the State by a valley in the southeast, and then reaching and gazing upon this rocky subterrane north and south, and then coming to and soon passing beyond the Boise Valley, doubtless think of Idaho as an appalling desert with an oasis at either end. But this region is only a very minor part of the State.

Eastward from it lie the upper reaches of the Snake River Valley, famous for its potatoes; and here, under irrigation, what was once loosely called a desert of sagebrush without exposed rock is now one of the most fertile and productive areas in the West. It runs from the western entrance of Yellowstone to the city of Pocatello; and from the sky it is discovered to be a network of canals upon the river's lower drainage basin, with farms covering it in June like a great green blanket. In October it is landscaped in hundreds of thousands of bags of potatoes standing in endless rows; in trainloads of sugar beets that almost reach across the cities; and in stacks of alfalfa hay. A desert here has been reclaimed. For half a century the earth has been excavated in hundreds of canals and ditches; and the waters of the Snake, pouring down from the mountains standing against Wyoming, have been diverted to these canals. Much of this land, once regarded as worthless for all but grazing, has changed hands at $300 an acre. Besides potatoes and beets and hay, orchards are here, too, and fields of peas; and herds of cattle and sheep. Upon the foothills flanking the mountains in the east and reaching down into the valley in long rolling prairies are the unirrigated wheatlands. These areas, also, once bedded with sagebrush and greasewood, wild grasses, and wild flowers, were regarded as worthless; and less than twenty-five years ago a man was thought to be out of his wits when he went experimentally to one of these arid hills to plant wheat and learn if it would grow. Now nearly every available acre has been plowed; and farms here, as in eastern Oregon and elsewhere, literally hang from mountainsides like pictures, green in June and golden in August. Seen from above, these rolling hills and these less precipitous mountain backbones are alive with tractors that look like huge insects turning the furrows or dragging the harvesters; and in August and September the highways show caravans of trucks hauling the grain. The two forks of Snake River come down out of subalpine valleys and pour their waters through headgates and into canals; and the whole view, when seen from far up, is one of shimmering lines of silver in the valley and shimmering fields of gold upon the hills.

A great chain of mountains, standing upon the Idaho-Wyoming boundary, fences this valley in the east. Upon the north it is rimmed by the Continental Divide. And in the west, more remotely, far over the arid steppe which water will never reclaim, is the magnificent Sawtooth Range. Here are peaks reaching altitudes of more than twelve thousand feet, among which are many tiny valleys, some holding lakes, some fertile, tilled basins, and all of them walled in by the forested slopes of other ranges. A larger basin, holding smaller ones within its area, is that in which the Salmon River and its tributaries lie. It has an area of about fourteen thousand square miles. Bounded on the west by the wild Seven Devils area, on the north by the Clearwater Mountains, on the east by the Beaverhead Mountains, it looks southward to the Sawtooth and Salmon Ranges. At no point does this elevation fall below four thousand feet, and in most of it the altitude is considerably more than a mile. Westward is the Primitive

Area. Eastward, looking across at one another, are Mount
Hyndman and Mount Borah, the two highest reaches in
the State.

Under its surface, this area is quite unlike that of the
desolate steppe south of it. The underlying formation,
dating from the Pre-Cambrian to the Mississippian Ages,
is granite overlaid by sedimentary beds, folded and eroded.
Possibly the lower stratum ranges from basalts to rhyo-
lites; the middle is of volcanic ash and sandstones; and the
two are capped by rhyolitic flows. The eroded alluvial deposits have left high level terraces of sand and gravel. And
on their surface, this alpine region and the steppe south are
sharp and complete in their contrast. One is a black and
gray area of impregnable stone. The other is a region of
tumultuous rivers and tiny sheltered basins, of a vast
rolling acreage of high meadows and forested canyons and
white zeniths. And yet upon a part of their boundaries
these two areas touch.

The Salmon River here, often called the River of No
Return, is a physical phenomenon in itself. It is the
headlong and furious stream that Clark entered in 1805
only to turn back after he had followed it fifty miles; and
it is the river that a few others, since that day, have
ventured to navigate, some to emerge with their hair
standing on end and others never to emerge at all. "The
boat trip from Salmon to Lewiston through three hundred and ten miles of the Salmon River and lower Snake
River Canyons is a scenic and sporting event without
equal."[1] The river rises in the eastern slopes of the
Sawtooth Range near Galena Summit among the lovely
lakes of Alturas, Redfish, and Stanley, all of glacial origin,
and flows northwest for thirty miles. Then it abruptly
turns eastward through a canyon, finds a small valley and
picks up the East Fork, and swings into the north. For
about a hundred miles it flows northward, gathering to its
breast two more rivers and several creeks; meets and

---

[1] U. S. Department of Interior, *Geological Survey of Water-
Supply Paper 657*, p. 23.

A lava field near the Craters of the Moon

Sawtooth Mountains west of Stanley

An aerial view of Boise

possesses the North Fork which has come down out of the Bitterroot Range; and turns suddenly westward. After about thirty miles it gathers the Middle Fork and has now traveled two hundred miles without getting any closer to Snake River, its point of delivery, than it was at its source. But now, as if having learned by trial and error, it plunges into its deep gorge, picks up two more rivers, and takes its cold subterranean way down its canyon for two hundred miles to its outlet. It hunts its sunless way from cascade to cascade, and churns so furiously that long stretches of its journey are rimmed with froth and foam.

And the country around it is no less magnificent than the river itself. Its mountainous breadth is the home of hundreds of peaks, many of them unnamed, and of more lovely lakes than have been named and explored, and of millions of feet of timber in which there has never been the sound of an axe. This is in many parts of it an undiscovered forested wilderness and presents, when seen from the air or from its own altitudes, some quite overwhelming contrasts. It has many a broad sweep of ragged peaks and high almost inaccessible pockets where mountain sheep live; but adjacent to any of these more formidable reaches, and in almost any direction, there are lakes of utmost loveliness and serenity, or impassable jungles of fir and lodgepole and pine, or meadows where wild flowers grow dense and knee-deep, or river gorges dropping sharp and sudden to the white-capped waters below. There are innumerable smaller streams hidden by shadow and jungle growth where the fish have never seen an angler. There are little mining towns dropped down into the mountainous pockets, or little hamlets like Stanley in Stanley Basin, like Cape Horn, where the frontier still lives almost isolated from the world and mountaineers are still a law unto themselves.

From the tallest peaks here there is a drop of more than ten thousand feet to Boise which, from the headwaters of the Salmon River, is less than eighty miles

into the southwest. Here, in western Idaho, are several
valleys upon the gently rolling watersheds of several
rivers, the largest of which, the Snake, lies for a thousand
miles within Idaho or upon its boundary. Falling within
the belt of prevailing westerly winds and subjected to
the ameliorating influence of the Pacific Ocean, these
valleys lying from the Sawtooth foothills to the Oregon
line have an unusually mild climate for this latitude. The
winters are temperate, with zero weather rare, and with
the snowfall for the most part little more than a sleety
mist of rain. The summers are long and cloudless, and
irrigation here is necessary, as in all of Idaho elsewhere
save in the northern part. Upon these separate adjacent
valleys there are more than a half million acres under
irrigation, much of which is given to alfalfa and clover,
to fruit orchards, and to celery and lettuce fields. There
are also dairy herds, potatoes and onions, beans and peas;
but the personality of this part of the State is to be found
in its gentle climate with its not infrequent Indian summer in midwinter, and in its thousands of acres of orchards, white with bloom in springtime and memorialized
in festivals, and blue and red and purple with fruit in late
summer and early fall. Some of these single fruit gardens
show long corridors of blossom or fruit running for miles.
When, in late spring, the westerly winds come across Oregon, the fragrance from these orchards and fields is in
the air and the sky is swept clean to its deepest
blue, with the cool northern background nebulous in white
or purple mist. The reach of these valleys is about a
hundred miles. In climate, in personality, and mood, they
are quite unlike any other part of the State.

Three hundred miles north of them is a region wholly
different. Here, in the upper Panhandle, is an area of
surpassingly lovely lakes and of great evergreen forests,
with cities standing literally within the shadow of larch
and hemlock and pine. Some of these cities are on the
margins of lakes against great forested backdrops; and
some, built within the forests themselves, look from a

distance as if the trees had grown up through sidewalk and pavement and every front yard. And again, when seen at a distance and against twilight, some of these towns look like nothing so much as a half a million lighted Christmas trees. They are all drenched with the smell of conifers and fresh-water lakes and cool mountainous reaches. After the central steppe, or the valley of potatoes, or the valleys of vegetables and fruits, it is difficult to think of this American Switzerland as a part of Idaho. Formerly this region was a huge lake, from which there still remain Pend Oreille, one of the largest fresh-water lakes wholly within the United States, and Coeur d'Alene, besides many others. The Kootenai River and the Clark Fork of the Columbia, entering from north and east, flow across the State here; the Coeur d'Alene and St. Joe Rivers flow into Lake Coeur d'Alene, and the Spokane River flows out of it; and besides these rivers there are the Priest, Palouse, and Potlatch, and farther south the St. Maries, Clearwater, and Lochsa. This area, seen from the air, is one of rivers and mountain streams, of almost countless lakes, and of great dark blankets of forest. Lake Coeur d'Alene has the nebulous reputation of being the fifth loveliest lake in the world: along its shores, as well as upon the shores of other lakes here, are some superbly scenic highways; the summer homes of wealthy persons; and the downsweeping backdrops of timber so dense that it is almost blue-black. More rain falls here than over most of Idaho; and even at lower altitudes where cities lie, snow sometimes reaches a depth of eight or ten feet. But this region, nevertheless, lying as it does within western winds, has a surprisingly mild climate for its latitude, and often is neither so hot nor so cold as parts of the State six hundred miles south. This small scenic wonderland belongs topographically to eastern Washington and is much closer in kinship with Spokane than with Boise. It is, indeed, so remote in both interests and distance from the great bulk of Idaho that a resident of the Snake River Valley feels less at home, upon coming here, than he would have felt if he had gone into Montana, Wyoming, or Utah.

And far south, against the Nevada line, is to be found another remarkable contrast. Here, within one county, is a great region larger than the two smallest Eastern States put together, and so barren and bleak and terrifying in most of it that even sagebrush and greasewood grow precariously, and what was supposed to have been in part an ancient lake bed is an overwhelming waste. Snake River cuts across its northern extremity, but even here, in bizarre desolation, with black basalt towering in vivid bluffs against pale-colored sediments, very little grass grows and only a few stunted trees. Much of Owyhee County is an area of ghost towns. Largest of these is Silver City, six thousand feet up, and citadel of this overwhelming homelessness, where snow, hurried by terrific freezing winds, is heaped into drifts large enough to bury a town.

But this northern stretch of Nevada, lying strangely within the boundaries of Idaho, is not a level tableland of desert. It is anything but that. Channeled and gouged and eroded, scabrous and cragged, it is a huge area of materials for a steppe that have never been ordered and flattened out. Snake River, rising in its South Fork at the base of the mighty Teton Peaks, crosses Idaho for hundreds of miles down a valley that is from 35 to 125 miles wide. It comes through silted regions and lava plains, over great waterfalls and down sunken gorges; and this southwestern part of Idaho looks as if the river for countless centuries had deposited its cargoes here. The flanks of the Owyhee Range, long ago, were flooded with rhyolitic outpourings and topped with enormous basaltic masses. An accumulation of these dammed the middle drainage basin of the river; a depression was formed and then filled with sediments from the eroded areas; and after the first immense outbursts came the lake beds and continued eruptions. The climate here was mild and moist then, and a huge lake is thought to have

been formed that soon reached its upper levels and then
broke and poured into lower Snake River Canyon which
had already cut deep upon its path. This whole region, laid
under the dramatic sculpturing of turmoil for a long
period, is today one of the most picturesque terrains in the
West; and it is because of the enormous shifting of valleys
and mountains ages ago that the whole area now presents
such terrifying aspects.

Today, in this region, granitic scarps and ledges are
exposed for long distances, or the rock lies in long backbones that are cut across by deep and narrow gorges.
War Eagle Mountain is diked and veined with the records
of a once turbulent time. On the plateaus falling away
from the range are old lake beds laid down on granite
foundations and covered now with tremendous avalanches
of basalt; and in other areas are shales and limestones,
compact clays of fluviatile gravels, and irregularly eroded
bluffs, all of which, in their arid colors, give to the region
an unusual picturesqueness. There are solid rock dikes
ten feet wide and hundreds of feet long. There are deep
trenches in the ancient beds with barren mesas between.
And under it all is not only the Owyhee batholith, still
masked and disguised on its surface with overlapping
volcanics, or faulted and folded into an overwhelming
panorama of monuments and terraces and deep river
tunnels; under it there is nobody knows how much imprisoned water lying in lakes below the lava a thousand
feet or more in depth.

This Owyhee country, summarized here as a desert,
is less a desert than a great natural monument of rivers
bedded in stone. Besides three rivers that drain it, there
are several large creeks, and all of these for the most part
lie deep in their narrow sunless canyons sculptured out
of rock. Of very narrow gorges, that of the Bruneau
River is said to be one of the deepest on earth. A person
can stand and look out over the torn miles and believe
there is no water anywhere within the sky line; and he

can go to what seemed to be only a broken path of shadow and look down a thousand feet to foaming torrents in river beds where the sun never strikes. Or a person can stand on the eminence of Sugarloaf Butte and realize that no one lives east, south, north, or west as far as he can see.

Just east of Owyhee County lies one of Idaho's four principal valleys, and this, too, not long ago, was a prairie of sagebrush and buffalo grass, coyotes and rattlesnakes and horned toads. Here is the State's most dramatic chapter in reclamation, and a valley now no less fertile and productive than the one famous for its potatoes or the other for its prunes. Far at its eastern end, the engineering feat of the American Falls Reservoir, largest in the State, and impounding one million and seven hundred thousand acre-feet of water, was more than ordinarily spectacular; but one reservoir was not enough. The Milner Dam, undertaken and completed through private initiative, diverted water to almost a quarter of a million acres in the areas north and south of Twin Falls; and the Minidoka Dam added another fifty thousand to make the largest contiguous irrigated area in the United States. Of this region Washington Irving once wrote:

"It is a land where no man permanently resides; a vast, uninhabited solitude, with precipitous cliffs and yawning ravines, looking like the ruins of a world; vast desert tracts that must ever defy cultivation and interpose dreary and thirsty wilds between the habitations of man."

He could hardly be expected to know this country if he were to rise today and look around him. And yet he might, too, for this Twin Falls section of Idaho has many remarkable features of its own. It was here that Snake River, before reclamation broke its might, poured its flood over cascade after cascade, the deepest of which, the Shoshone, has been called the Niagara of the West. No less impressive are two cities of rock, one of them volcanic in origin, the other of granite and calcareous limestone shaped by wind and water and sand, and both of them

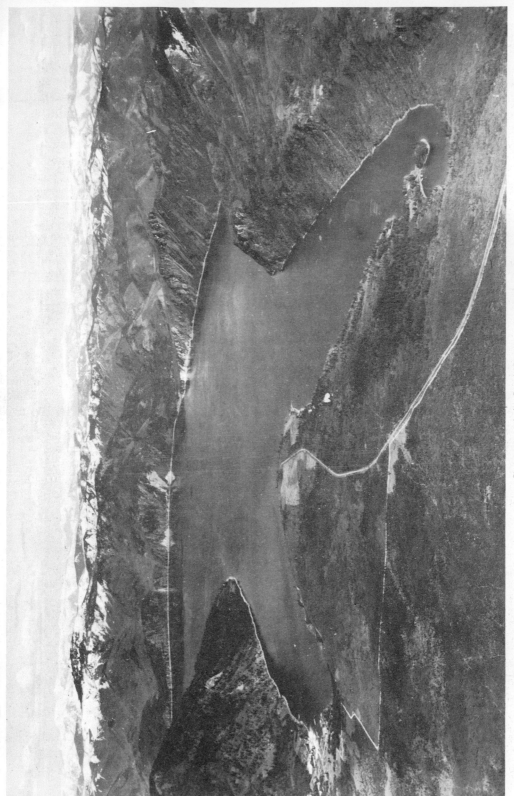

Bayview on Lake Pend Oreille

Lewiston

Looking northeast toward Atlanta from Arrowrock Dam

The Seven Devils

looking like an assortment of Gothic cathedrals that have fallen into ruins.

Three hundred miles on a beeline into the northwest from this valley of dairy herds and beans and potatoes, hay and fruit, is perhaps the most nearly unique spot in Idaho. From the mountain rim north of it, a person's gaze goes westward over Washington to a broad and apparently limitless sweep of rolling distance that Irvin Cobb declared to be the most breath-taking vision of his journey through the Northwest. Still from this rim, the gaze turns southward and drops two thousand feet to the junction of two great rivers, the Snake and the Clearwater, and to what is strangely and most unmistakably a city. Lewiston is one of the largest cities in Idaho, walled in by great mountains save for the slender valleys down which the rivers come. It is a city almost entirely of one long street, and a river running parallel on the north and a mountain abutting the buildings on the south. And at first glance there seem to be only mountains and two rivers and a city. There is much more. The industrial life of this place swings out and around in concentric arcs of increasing size. The shorter radii reach out and touch the business district and the homes; and within the next circular segment are to be found one of the world's largest sawmills, and fruit orchards so vast that more than two thousand persons live within their area; and in the next wide swing are to be found the Clearwater forests and the valley farms; and within the last huge arc are the mines. This city, the lowest point in Idaho, is spoken of as the State's only seaport because ships come up the Columbia and the Snake to its door. Together with its long narrow valleys, it is protected from extremes of climate and from winds; and because it is so sheltered and because it is flanked by huge orchards and forests, it smells like a garden in springtime, and like a harvest of fruit and mountain water and pine boughs in the fall.

Such briefly in word and picture, presented candidly in sharp panoramic contrasts, is the State which in Indian language means sunrise. It is geographically so disparate that persons living in one part of it are less familiar with much of the remainder than they are with States contiguous to their position. If Spokane in Washington is in some respects the cultural center of northern Idaho, Salt Lake City, a thousand miles away, is the cultural center of the southeast and east. For Idaho is a State which is divided in many ways against itself; and if it gains thereupon in diversity of picturesqueness and in sharp differences in grandeur and scene, it loses in industrial and cultural integrity. Without homologous structure and centralization of interests, it spreads diffusely into all the States roundabout, and has, more than many others, an obscure indecision within the symbolism of its name. Idaho for some may mean chiefly the magnificent forested areas and the subalpine lakes from which one of the chief agricultural regions is twice as remote in distance and interests as Seattle or Portland. Or for some it may mean chiefly the thousands of bags of potatoes that are standing row on row in the fields when the distant mountain maple is scarlet and the cottonwoods along the river bottoms are like piles of yellow bloom. For others Idaho may mean chiefly the small towns isolated in the tops of mountains to which in wintertime the only means of travel is by airplane. In these subalpine basins persons live throughout the year within the smell of high white peaks and pine and spruce, and within reach of thousands of wild animals of many kinds. For others Idaho may mean the rolling unirrigated grainlands where the summers are hot and too often rainless, and water, in a State that has so much, has to be hauled for both man and beast. Here there is quietness like that on graveyards. Or Idaho may have meaning chiefly in wetness and sound where one fall after another takes the mighty pouring of the Mad River through its canyon or where thousands of springs burst from the walls of stone. Or Idaho may mean the hushed desolation of ghost towns where cities that once housed thousands of persons are now only the forsaken quiet of a few shacks. Many of these towns, now given over to decay and specters, were among the dramatic spots on the last frontiers. And Idaho may, for still fewer persons, mean chiefly that deepest and in some respects most awful gorge on this continent. And this, the Grand Canyon or the Seven Devils Gorge, is only one of the many phenomenal spots to which Idaho highways lead.

V

FLORA

FLORA

T HE DOUGLAS FIR (not a fir at all, and often known as Douglas spruce, red pine, Oregon pine) is fourth in size of the trees of earth but does not in Idaho reach the proportions found on the Pacific Coast. It is one of the stateliest of trees, with a straight tapering shaft and a magnificent bulk of foliage; and in nurseries it is the fastest growing of all evergreens. Its wood is the toughest of all American conifers. In Idaho it is one of the commonest and commercially one of the most valuable trees, growing at medium elevations with white fir, lodgepole, and yellow pine. Its rich green foliage, pointed buds, and beautiful pendant cones distinguish it from all other trees. Like it, the western larch is, in point of size and height, among the seven most majestic trees on earth, but this one is not common in Idaho. The larch may reach a height of 250 feet, the fir 300, but such heights are unusual. The larch is unlike any other conifer in having almost no foliage after it reaches some size and in dropping its leaves when winter comes. A mature tree has in summertime a bushy top high in the air and a mighty spire of trunk as straight as a lodgepole. Very slow in growth, a larch only nine inches in diameter may have been standing for fifty years: one tree examined was only eighteen inches in diameter but had been a tree for a quarter of a millennium and had taken eight years to gather its last inch. It is this tree that gives the parklike grandeur of ancient estates to the forest in which it is found. Limned against light, its foliage has a silken spidery loveliness because its unsheathed needles grow in tufts or tiny spray brooms.

Even slower in growth is the Rocky Mountain red cedar, a patriarch of the American forest and very similar to the red cedar of the East. One of these in Logan Canyon in Utah is three thousand years old, perhaps the oldest tree in the intermountain area. A favorite with John Muir, who made a study of it, this lonely baron, he said, wastes out of existence when killed about as slowly as granite. "Even when overthrown by avalanches, they refuse to lie at rest, leaning stubbornly on their big elbows. . . . " Often this tree is an ancient and windswept titan standing alone on dry soil or rocky mountainside. The Giant Arborvitae (giant cedar, canoe cedar) favors moist bottomlands in the upper Clearwater and northern lakes region. It grows to such mammoth size that it often outtops the surrounding forest; and was a favorite with Indians who ate its fruit, used its soft wood for totem poles, or excavated its huge trunks for canoes. Its lovely evergreen robing, hanging in lacy sleeves, is much daintier than that of pine or fir. The dwarf or mountain juniper is widely distributed on upper mountain slopes and rocky ledges. More of a bush than a tree, it is loaded with blue-gray berrylike cones in wintertime, and these are a favorite with wild birds.

Of the several pines found in Idaho, two species are unusual. Western yellow pine is another titan of the Western forests and one of the most beautiful trees, with its golden bark, its deep black seams, and its straight stateliness. The most extensive pine forests in the world are of yellow pine in the Northwest, wherein the bulk is estimated at two hundred and fifty billions of feet. Hardier than most trees and amazingly adaptable to rigorous conditions, this tree grows to great size in arid foothills of volcanic origin, or on mesas of the Southwest, where it is the chief source of lumber, or in the comparatively rainless area of western Nebraska, or on swampy slopes of the Cascades, or high in mountains against the

timber line. Because it is a huge tree at maturity, it was
called bull pine by frontiersmen; because it is so heavy
it will barely float in water, it has been called ponderosa
by lumbermen. Ponderosa pine is its trade name over
the Nation. In even greater favor for lumber is white
pine, a much smaller tree. Because its lower limbs die so
young that the lower trunk is almost without knots, the
wood of this tree with its white soft texture has been
eagerly sought. It is now planned to preserve areas for
the study of hydrophytic and mesophytic growths of
western white pine, western cedar, and western hemlock.
One such area, the Roosevelt Grove of gigantic cedars,
has already been set aside in northern Idaho. Here are
magnificent trees a thousand years old bedded down in
alpine flora of mosses, lycopods, ferns, and evergreens.
The white pine is found only in the northern part of the
State and is perhaps the commonest tree seen from the
highways.

Lodgepole pine is the commonest evergreen tree in
Idaho and one of the most uniformly straight of all trees
that grow. And because it tapers so little, it has long
been in favor for the building of mountain cabins, many
of the most unusual of which are to be seen in Yellowstone Park. In Idaho this tree grows in dense stands in
flat and protected areas and forms many a beautiful corridor along the scenic highways. A strange tree, and
one of the most unconquerable of alpine conifers, is the
white bark pine which occurs only in the north part of
central Idaho and in western Wyoming. It grows high,
often rimming the world and often getting flattened into
a mass of boughs and ice; and even at lower levels mountaineers sometimes build their beds on the wide flat
branches lying on the earth. At their topmost elevations
these hardy trees are dwarfed and beaten down but seldom killed and they often look like young trees when in
fact they are remarkably old. Muir says he measured
one that was only three feet high but had been a tree for
four hundred and twenty-six years: one of its supple

twigs was only one eighth of an inch in diameter but
was seventy-five years old and so tough that Muir tied
it into knots. Usually found with it is limber pine, a
crooked stunted tree that seeks dry rocky hillsides and
other severe sites. There are two species of piñon pine
found only in the extreme southern part of the State:
both are small round-topped dwarfs at dry low elevations,
and though of little commercial value, their seeds are
edible and are sometimes marketed.

Pines are identified by their needles gathered at the
base in bunches of from one to five and by the thick
woody scales on their cones; spruces by their sharp pointed single needles and by cones with parchmentlike scales.
The most beautiful spruce in Idaho is the Engelmann, the
white spruce of the Rocky Mountains. It grows at high
levels and sometimes is mantled with snow during most
of the year; but in late spring it is lovely in bluish-green
foliage, and in autumn its showy brown cones scatter
their black-winged seeds. It shares in some degree the
popularity of the blue spruce as an ornamental tree and in
Idaho is fairly common within its range. The blue spruce
is found only in the extreme southeastern part of the
State.

Firs are identified by their blunt grooved needles and
by their almost invisible cones that stand erect on the
upper branches of the tree. The balsam fir is when found
in its native area a beautiful tree, broad and symmetri-
cally branched, and sometimes running to more than a
hundred and fifty feet in height. The bluish-green foliage
is often intensified by the bright indigo of the flowers;
and the purple cones complete the striking picture of this
fir when left standing alone by loggers to reseed the half
acre of its home. At lower elevations is the white fir,
usually close by streams, upon which it often forms beautiful borders. This tree is called black balsam in Utah; its
bark is darker in color than that of balsam fir, and its
foliage is a dark blue-green. Both of these firs, but especially the balsam or alpine, yield a thick juice that In-

White pine and cedar

Matured yellow pine

White bark pine: two grotesques

Tag alder

Aspen

dians and old-timers used for the healing of bruises and cuts. Lowland white fir is found in the intermountain region only in western Idaho, in the Weiser, Payette, and Idaho National Forests, from which it has spread far to the north and west. It is difficult to tell from alpine fir but it grows at lower elevations, has a wider crown, and usually a broad spread in its limbs.

The alpine larch scorns low altitudes and prefers the highest tablelands, where it chooses the most bleak and windswept ledges and exposes itself to every peril of temperature and storm. Often close by is the mountain hemlock, sometimes called black hemlock, or even spruce or fir or pine, the tree which Sargent declared to be the loveliest of the cone bearers in American forests. A mature tree may be four feet in diameter and a hundred feet in height, with gracefully drooping branches, each with a feathery sheath of gently arching evergreen needles, and beautifully colored cones. This tree grows "along the margins of alpine meadows in groves of exquisite beauty, pushing the advance guard of the forest to the edge of living glaciers." In Idaho it is found only in the north and chiefly at the upper tree limits of the Clearwater area. Transplanted to Eastern States, this lovely tree withers to the size of a dwarf and loses all its grace. The western hemlock is also a tall tree with lacy branches. Its shorter needles do not clothe the limbs in a tight sheath but spray out in tufts. This tree has been known to reach two hundred feet in height and nine feet in diameter.

For some persons the loveliest of all evergreens is the mountain laurel, though in Idaho the species is usually only a low shrub. When a tree, it has a dense round head, red or yellow bark, flowers in large compound corymbs; and in June and July may hide its brilliant leaves with clusters of flowers spreading in masses often a foot across. But this beautiful heath is being stripped from its native hills by nurserymen and collectors, as well as by vandals who gather masses of loveliness to wither in heated homes. The

Pacific yew, commonly called mountain mahogany, covers thousands of hillsides in Idaho and forms a favorite feeding ground for deer in late spring. The Indians of Alaska cut paddles and bows out of it, but today it is valuable only as coverage for watersheds, though in autumn its brilliant berries are the banquet of birds.

Shrubs: Of deciduous trees the Rocky Mountain ash is a hardy wanderer but almost dainty in appearance, with its graceful elderlike foliage and its tropical aspect. It has remarkably showy flowers and fruit clusters, and after its leaves are gone the broad disks of scarlet berries cling until winter is almost done. This tree is not an ash but belongs to the apple family and is sometimes called apple chokecherry. Its buds are cream-colored before they open, and its small white flowers are of exquisite fragrance. All of Idaho's native deciduous trees are small except the aspen and cottonwood, the latter of which is found in pine belts of the north along streams, and in southern and eastern Idaho along rivers and upon moist bottom lands. There are several species but it is difficult to tell them apart. From a distance, and against the sky in autumn, the foliage of the cottonwood looks like great masses of yellow sunset.

Commoner is the quaking aspen, which grows in dense jungles upon thousands of semiarid hills and upon lower mountain elevations facing the sun. Some horticulturists say it is the most widely distributed of North American trees. It thrives equally well in Chihuahua and Alberta; and throughout the Rocky Mountains it now covers great areas that were once swept by fire; and over the entire West has been the most important tree in determining the kinds and distribution of evergreens. In springtime its foliage is such a delicate green that it looks rain-washed; and in autumn, after the frosts, it covers countless hills and mountains with clearest lemon yellow. But most gorgeous of all Idaho trees in autumn coloring is the mountain maple. Sometimes a tree, often a shrub only, especially when growing on rocky slopes facing the sun, this maple

ranges widely and thrives in the shade of evergreens. It
fills ravines with dense growth and after the first frosts it
stands in fields of brilliant scarlet.

There are numerous species of willow, including the
western black, the diamond, the mountain, and the sand-
bar, of which the latter is probably commonest. It grows
in thickets along streams, delays erosion, often prevents
the cutting of new channels, and helps to hold floods in
check. Found often with it is the white (tag) alder, an
impressive tree in later winter when it hangs its yellow
catkins while other deciduous trees are still asleep. Usually in company with it is the red or river birch with its
dotted bronzed bark and its fountain of leafy spray.
Nothing about the red birch is more noteworthy than the
speed with which it grows. In drier locations are the
serviceberry and chokecherry, both of them widely distributed throughout America. In Idaho the jungles of
both in late spring are gardens of blossom and fragrance;
and in late summer (if the season has not been too arid)
they hang with fruit. Some botanists have said that the
chokecherry, once tasted, is forever scorned, even though
birds and Indians are fond of it; but many Idahoans
know better than that. They know that it makes jelly
second to none in its pungent and exotic flavor, and years
ago they learned, too, that wine made of it is, when prop-
erly aged, very rich and heady. Persons along the St.
Lawrence River must have discovered its uses also because it is earnestly cultivated there. The serviceberry,
too, is a favorite in Idaho. It is lovely in bloom, and its
fruit, a large, juicy, and full-flavored berry, eagerly
sought by Indians and birds and by early settlers, is still
preserved today. The Indians used to dry the berries for
winter use, or they pounded masses together into loaves
weighing fifteen pounds, which they later ate by breaking
off chunks and soaking them in water. A third fruit used
by pioneers is that of the hawthorn. This short tree or big
shrub with its great spread of branches and its deadly
thorns grows equally well on dry hillsides or along

streams. It is a flowering bush in late spring and is lovely again after frost has turned its foliage into burnished sheaves.

Of smaller shrubs, none are more striking than those which produce both flowers and fruit. Growing high in moist subalpine slopes and meadows among the Douglas fir, is the thimbleberry with its large five-lobed leaves and its perfect roselike blossom which measures two inches across. Sometimes it is found in company with syringa and ocean spray and spiraea and snowberry; and all these, with a wealth of flora tangled in thickets around them, make gorgeous gardens in higher altitudes. The berry is about the size of and in flavor is much like the red raspberry, though some find the fruit thin and dry. And perhaps it is, in comparison with that fruit which some declare to be the most luscious wild berry that grows. The huckleberry (and it is not the insipid blueberry which east of the Rocky Mountains is usually called huckleberry) grows in patches of hundreds, often thousands, of acres on high cool mountainsides. Usually it yields abundantly though the fruit hangs singly and not in clusters; and countless Westerners make pilgrimages in August to gather the berries for preserving and for wine. The shrub that bears this fruit is widely scattered in the forests of the State and is so highly regarded along Ditch Creek in the Salmon River country that this area is protected from grazing. The dwarf bilberry (or low whortleberry) is common in the central mountains and the northern lakes region. It is a small shrub from three to seven inches tall, hidden in the grass in meadows or on gentle slopes, with the small green leaves bunched near the top. In springtime lovely little pink-and-white bells appear among the leaves and later become blue berries covered with an attractive bloom. In autumn the leaves of this shrub turn a deep red. The grouseberry or grouse whortleberry is found on higher slopes of the Western mountains just below the tree line. These dwarfed bushes are less than a foot in height but often cover their favorite altitudes with great patches and sometimes grow rampantly even in deep forests. Its leaves are small and finely toothed, and its flowers are tiny red goblets of single bloom. By the middle of August the plant is dotted with bright red berries of pleasant flavor which are held in high esteem by grouse.

Of a different sort is the devil's club, a stalwart shrub four or five feet tall with spiked stalks. The maplelike leaves sprout from the stalk on a long stem about twelve inches below the red berries and form a dense coverage upon the ground. In the Selkirk Mountains the thickets are almost impenetrable. The ivory baneberry prefers humus soil by mountain streams in shady locations. The white flowers appear in two-inch racemes at the top of slender stems and are of sweet odor. When the berries ripen and become heavy they overwhelm the stems supporting them and soon fall. They are said to be poisonous like the seeds of other members of the buttercup genus to which this baneberry belongs. The red-osier dogwood, widely distributed along streams in both open and wooded areas, is a pleasant shrub both in bloom and in fruit. In early fall, spherical clusters of bluish-white berries show against leaves turned scarlet, golden, or purple. To this shrub the Indians gave the name kinnikinnick, the bark of which they smoked in preference to that of any other plant. This shrub seems also to go under the name of bearberry.

The twinberry, a famous little trailing evergreen of the honeysuckle tribe and a delicate relative of the elder, has a botanical name that honors the great Carolus Linnaeus who always wore a sprig of it when he was painted or photographed. Loving cool woods and mountainous marshes of both hemispheres, it is found in Idaho chiefly in the Seven Devils area and northward in the cool forests. Pairs of pink bells sway at the tip of long slender stalks and are much in favor for the delicacy and charm of their fragrance. Its berries are of purple-black color and are bitter to the taste. Quite different are the two species of elderberry, found at lower elevations on dry slopes and growing in single or multistemmed shrubs. The bright red or black berries are widely used, and especially in Utah, in the making of preserves and pies and wines. The elderberry is a low shrub with opposite compound leaves, flowers in clusters, and typical pithy twigs. For California Indians the elder was the tree of music because the straight young stems easily accommodated themselves to the flute makers.

Snowberry, sometimes called corralberry or wolfberry, is also widely scattered. An erect shrub from one to four feet tall, and with slim glabrous branches, it grows along streams and in less densely wooded areas. The mountain snowberry is a southwestern shrub that follows more arid hillsides, but the creeping snowberry with its pungently delicious fruit prefers the wetter region of the northern lakes. The salmonberry, too, grows in moist woodlands. It has solitary and perfect reddish-purple flowers and a golden fruit much like the raspberry. This shrub grows from two to five feet in height. The small cranberry favors bogs in the northern lakes region. It is a typical boreal plant, and upon the retreat of glaciers it migrated from its high refuge to the swamps formed by the damming of streams. It now ranges throughout the glaciated territory of the northern hemisphere. It has feathery green mats of foliage that hug the ground, tiny reddish-pink flowers at the end of threadlike reddish stems, and curling elongated sheaths on the ground runners.

The swamp black currant (prickly currant) is a very beautiful bush in blossom. Dainty racemes of yellowish flowers shaded with red are the center of scattered color among the dainty leaves. In full sunlight this shrub is so attractive as to command instant attention. Found in Idaho in moist woods and along streams, it has small dark berries that are in favor as a sauce with venison. The hackberry grows on arid rocky bluffs or in low hot valleys, particularly along the Snake and Salmon River Canyons. It is a low shrub with drooping branches and a reddish-

Elderberry

Mountain ash

Kinnikinnick

Colorado blue columbine

Syringa: Idaho State Flower

Sego lily: Utah State Flower

brown berry of thin sweet meat. The wood of this plant is so tough that the breaking of even a small twig is difficult. There are also wild currants with their piquantly flavored yellow or black fruit, and wild gooseberries, both of which were in favor with frontiersmen.

The Pacific flowering dogwood, discovered as recently as 1902, inhabits the woods of the upper Clearwater region. In spring it is a glorious vision of white bloom, and it escaped attention for so long only because it grows in remote places. The beauty of this shrub is less in its small tubelike flowers than in the four large petallike scales or bracts that surround them. In the Eastern species, these bracts inclose the flowers during the winter, but in the Western species the bracts instead of embracing the flowers are borne beneath them. This shrub in autumn is covered with crimson berries. The burning bush (wahoo, prickwood, spindletree), a close relative of the climbing false bittersweet, is a curious little tree that looks much like the wild plum except for its bark. Its flowers are in purple petals of four; and its fruit of four flat lobes in a purple husk that opens to show a scarlet interior, together with colored twigs and leaves, gives to this bush its name. In midwinter there is no more vivid spot of color in the landscape.

The purple heather is one of the principal charms of mountain meadows and upper crests in the central part of the State and in the Bitterroot Mountains. A low evergreen shrub, often growing in clumps several feet in width, it has numerous alternate leaves minutely serrated that crowd the branches and are so nearly stemless that they seem to sprout from the limbs themselves. The flowers are usually magenta pink, though variations occur. The lovely white heather was named Cassiope by Muir, with whom it was a favorite. Found on high summits, this low-branching evergreen with slim ascending stems often less than a foot high is cloaked in an overlapping sheath of leaves arranged in fours. From the axils of the leaves, tiny bowls of white bloom, sometimes gently flushed like a pale pink lily of the valley, nod on graceful threadlike stems. The twin-flower, found from the Seven Devils area northward, is a dainty trailing evergreen vine unsurpassed in its demure loveliness. This member of the honeysuckle family has tiny pinkish flower bells that droop at half-mast and are of such sweetly penetrating fragrance that the smell of their bloom is often evident in trains passing along mountains where the plant is found. The American vetch is another graceful and lovely vine found in moist woods and thickets. It clings tenaciously to any available support and sprouts in vivacious green leaves and in washed purple flowers in clusters of long slender bloom.

Moss and Ferns: The flora of Idaho, especially in much of the forested area, is a dense undergrowth of moss and fern. Of the latter the running pine is common in shady places. In Europe the spores of this strikingly denticulated prostrate creeper are gathered for lycopodium powder. The ground cedar is another creeper with a wide geographical range. It creeps, or thrusts upright branches that spread in fans, with the inner row of leaves along the stems looking like the tips of leaves only. Less lovely but more widely distributed in Idaho is the scouring-brush, one of the commonest of the large horsetails. Its rough silicious fiber used to be widely favored in the scouring of pots and pans and it is still put to such uses in remoter places. Known variously as scrub-grass, snake-rush, gun-bright, snake-grass, and winter-rush, it is used in Holland to prevent erosion, and was shipped to England as scouring material and took the name of Dutch clean-rush. Swamp horsetail flourishes in marshes and along streams. In Sweden it is fed to cows to increase their butterfat, and in Lapland it is one of the chief foods of reindeer. In parts of America it is sometimes cut for hay, and in Idaho cattle are said to prefer it to grass, and in the menu of muskrats it is a favorite.

Much lovelier, perhaps loveliest of all grape ferns, is the Virginia, often called rattlesnake fern because its spored tips resemble the tail of a rattler, or "sang sign" in

Kentucky, where it is declared to keep the tip of its leaf forever pointing at a ginseng plant. Of another sort is the brake (bracken) which grows in rank abundance and is especially common in the northern part of the State. It has enormous leaves, sometimes, as in New Zealand, twenty feet long, and often fourteen feet long in the Northwest. Eaten only by goats, impervious to drouth, and growing to a height of six or seven feet, this fern makes parts of Idaho look densely tropical. Indians used its rhizomes for food, and in parts of the world it is still eaten as asparagus, but what with one plant sometimes covering an area of eighty square feet, it is often an unconquerable pest now on logged-off lands. Hunters and trappers formerly used these plants as a mattress.

Quite different is the common maidenhair, a graceful fern with very thin leaves which Indians laid upon strips of cedar to make beds for drying wild berries. This fern prefers shady banks with water seeping out of the soil. Still more delicate in its tracery and more widely distributed in Idaho is the Rocky Mountain Woodsia, a long, slender, and remarkably symmetrical fern. The male fern is found in Idaho, too, and the lady fern as well: long ago, herbalists thought these two represented the sexes somehow, though precisely in what manner, inasmuch as the two ferns live side by side in peace, is not known. Their sex, one authority declared, was "just figurative." In Idaho the lady fern grows high in the mountains, as on Packsaddle Peak, and looks out from under boulders. Of another species is the clover fern, a small and lovely plant that folds up at night and goes to sleep.

There are countless other ferns which help to make undergrowth jungles in forests. Alaskan club moss, a creeping plant with erect tufted branches, grows at great altitudes, even reaching above the timber line. Leathery grape fern is remarkable because of its size: it often looks more like a tree and is found over much of the Northwest. The spinulose woodfern is the kind that helps to give loveliness to wooded regions, together with fir club moss, bladder fern, wood fern, and oak fern. Historically interesting is the parasitic licorice fern which grows on maples and red alders. Some early settlers used it to flavor tobacco, and children today like to chew the rhizome for its licorice. The sword fern is a handsome plant that looks vaguely like fifty or sixty knife blades with their handles buried in a single shaft. A favorite for decoration, carloads of it are shipped annually from the Northwest to be used in the East as wreaths.

Flowers: Because so much of Idaho visible from railway coaches and highways seems to be arid region save where irrigated, it may not uncommonly be supposed that the State is relatively flowerless. This is by no means true. Many States, especially in the Middle West, are almost wholly under cultivation, and the wild flowers they once had have been driven to corner copses and ditchbanks and roadsides. In Idaho, where so extremely small a part of the area is under cultivation, wild flowers have suffered from no enemy except human beings and cattle and sheep. From intensively grazed sections most of the wild flowers have largely disappeared, but in other sections, and particularly in the north, there are huge gardens of thousands of acres of almost continuous bloom. The varieties, too, are so many that it would take a small book merely to list their names. In the following pages only a selected list is given, and chiefly those that are commonest or rarest or loveliest.

The State flower of Idaho is the syringa, a native variety of mock orange that was discovered by Captain Lewis. It is a tall bush from six to twelve feet in height that is found on mountainsides, forest borders, and along streams; and in parts of the state, especially the northern, its white bloom in June and July sometimes reaches for unbroken miles. The stems of this shrub the Indians used for bows, and the macerated leaves they used for soap. The squaws used the stems to cradle their infants. These stems were also used by Indians for tobacco pipes, and to excavate the pith they cannily allowed grubs of beetles to eat their way from end to end. A more famous flower in the records and legends of early explorers, and an important food of Western Indians, was the camas, which made many a meadow blue. Its blossoms spread in dense gardens in wetter places, and these from a distance look like lakes of blue water. Its liliaceous edible bulb was steamed for twenty-four hours or longer in a kind of fireless cooker of heated stones. Indians fought wars for possession of camas meadows; and the Bannack War itself was caused in part at least by white invasion of camas fields. The flowers, from a dozen to thirty on a pedicel, are blue or white and bloom from April to July. Idaho has memorialized this flower in the name of a prairie and a town.

Of other flowers chiefly affecting mountain meadows none is lovelier than the columbine, which blooms from May to August. Erect, with branching stalks three feet tall, its flowers are to be found in scarlet, yellow, blue, or white, sometimes looking, when thrust up from a tangle of ferns, as if they were disembodied loveliness growing on the air. There are several species of beardtongue or blue pentstemon, slender flowers of remarkably delicate beauty with their crowded whorls of blue petals. Those in high meadows bloom in July and August, and those along streams earlier. The western buttercup may also grow in fields or even among sagebrush. Especially striking is a meadow when the golden buttercup and the blue camas carpet the earth. The tall larkspur is usually from two to four feet in height, and if not crowded its basal leaves form a green bower from which rise long spikes of stalk with rich purple-blue flowers poised on the stems like so many floral butterflies. Linnaeus gave it the name of Delphinium because he fancied a resemblance to a dolphin.

The mountain daisy (also called fleabane), a compound flower of striking size and coloring, is one of the most conspicuous in high valleys. The large golden-yellow cen-

ters are surrounded by graceful purple rays of varying
tints. Much smaller, and always closed on cloudy days, is
the blue gentian: the moment the sun strikes them, the
petals, hardly more than scallops at the top of a deep
flower goblet, open and flare out to show their regal
purple. The alpine Androsace is a tiny member of the
primrose family, so daintily inconspicuous in both size
and coloring that it often escapes notice. The small narrow leaves clump thickly against the ground in a rosette
of green from which rise tendril stems almost as fine as
hairs, supporting the tiny five-petaled white blossoms.
The peacock sego grows twelve or fourteen inches high
and has purple spots on the broad petals of the white
bloom. Common in meadows, too, is blue-eyed grass with
its tiny flowers fading in a day and with its buds forever
opening to bloom again.

Deep in the forests are several species of orchid,
rarest of which is the phantom, a waxy white plant in stem
and leaf and petal, save for a golden spot within the
flower's throat. Blooming in May and June, and spectral
in its loveliness, its fragrance is as unusual as the flower
itself. Spotted coral root belongs to the parasitic orchids,
of which three species are found deep in moist woods in
the northern lakes region. The flowers are brownish purple, and the root resembles a branch of coral. Latest of
the orchids to bloom is the hooded tresses with its twisted
bloom that looks vaguely like a braid of hair. The flowers
are white or yellowish and are easily identified by the
dense curved line of blossom on the spike.

In comparison with the delicate sorrel of the East, the
mountain sorrel is a titan, with its heart-shaped leaves
bursting into huge showers of foliage. It prefers the
depths of forests but often is found on shaded mountainsides and along streams, blooming in May and June. It is
a menace to cattle because of their fondness for its lush
and succulent foliage.

Found in moist thickets is another group of lovely
plants. The wild lily of the valley, found in Idaho only

or chiefly in wet shade in the northern lakes region, has
very small white blooms on stems eight to sixteen inches
high, and a red berry. False Solomon's-seal is a graceful
decorative plant. Each stem, terminating in a pyramid
of waxy bloom, rises in a curve from the earth. The
blooming period is April and May, and late in the summer the flowers produce an edible red berry. A single
lovely rose-purple bloom hanging at the end of a rosy
stem gives to calpyso its common name of fairy slipper.
The tiny slipper-shaped flower, two of its petals forming
an upward-flaring ribbon at the back and with the toe
decorated with yellow fuzz, has been long fancied as a
fairy's foot.

If it were not for its sharply penetrating fragrance,
wood nymph (one-flowered wintergreen) would escape
notice. It belongs to the Pyrola family and is a genus of
its own. The leafless stems, rising from green rosettes
and hidden by moss, support five-petaled yellowish-white
flowers which against contrasting background look like
five deep scallops drawn together and closed. Mourning
groundsel was named because of the massacre in the
Yukon of a party of Eskimos, but is called black-tipped
groundsel by St. John. The plant is one of central stalk
about a foot in height, sprouting from a rosette of long
streamerlike leaves, and putting forth an irregular spray
of six spidery yellow flowers which bud out from as many
slender stems. A deep chalice of green sepals holds a big
orange-yellow center, and from this radiate pale yellow
rays like so many insect legs at loose ends.

The alpine beauty has drooped under the names given
to it. Called Clintonia by some after a New York politician
named Clinton, and queencup by a Canadian royalist, it
suffers in Oregon under the name of alpine beauty. Its
commonest name in Idaho has not been learned. It grows
abundantly in Idaho and often covers the earth with its
remarkably beautiful leaves and its solitary lilylike
flower. Called western bluebell by Walcott and languid
lady by St. John, the martensia, a cousin of the forget-

me-not and the heliotrope, grows in large clumps under
favorable conditions. The leaves are stemless, two or
more cupping together at a single place in the stalk to
curve outward and downward in a sort of pointed horse's
ear. From the juncture of leaves and stalk droops the long
pendulous blossom on slender curved stems as if the inverted bell were emptying itself of fragrance.

Scattered more widely are many submontane species.
Named horrendously avalanche lily by some, lamb's
tongue by others, easter bells in Utah, dog-toothed violet
in the East (against which Burroughs revolted, only to
suggest nothing better than fawn lily), and trout lily by
fishermen who have seen it blooming at the opening of the
season, this flower is, in spite of the many folknames
it has suffered, one of the commonest and loveliest in
Idaho. It pushes up at the edge of melting snow, rarely
at altitudes below four thousand feet, and flowers into
yellow blooms of exquisite fragrance. Sometimes it is
found in company with violets, buttercups, and spring
beauties (queencups). The smooth yellow violet is a
charming golden flower that is found chiefly in central
and northern Idaho, but the yellow bell (yellow fritillaria) is found in Snake River Canyon as well. Its flowers,
yellow or orange tinged with purple, nod on stems four
to six inches high. The wild hyacinth, also found throughout the State, has blue funnel-shaped flowers in clusters,
and edible bulbs that were used by Indians for bread. The
white or Rocky Mountain rhododendron is a beautiful
plant which does not have, like the Eastern species,
a glossy evergreen foliage. Its leaves are deciduous. Its
flowers are bunched along the leafy twigs instead of being
concentrated at the ends of branches in clusters. These
are fragrant and creamy, suffused with pink, and recall
the waxen charm of orange blossoms.

The showy fleabane is one of a large number of flowers
that achieve fullest development in Western States; and in
Idaho this brilliant member of the aster family gives a gay
attire to lower slopes in June and July. The flowers thrust

up in groups with one central perfect bloom surrounded by half-open buds, with daisylike yellow centers in the lavender blossoms. The wake robin or western trillium, a member of the lily family with its pure white bloom darkening to deep purple, is especially abundant under the big cedars on Pine Creek. The Clarkia, named for the explorer and first found along the Clearwater River, is a low annual with slender racemes of lilac flowers that deepen to rose. After being discovered it was introduced into Europe and has been widely cultivated there; and what was once almost a botanical anomaly now has several varieties and is known from London to Moscow, with ranges in color through salmon pink and magenta to purple. The wild hollyhock is a tall stately flower that sometimes covers whole mountainsides and drenches the air with fragrance. It is especially abundant in Wyoming on the eastern slope of Teton Pass, and in northern Idaho.

Among aquatic or semiaquatic flowers are several lilies. The tiger lily, blooming in June, prefers wet rich soil and can be found in valleys at high elevations. It is strikingly handsome with its orange blooms spotted brown and borne in spreading panicles of as many as twenty flowers. The water or yellow pond lily grows along lakes, where its huge leaves float on the water and its solitary yellow flowers bloom from May to August. Wokash is the Indian name. Some tribes made flour of the seed; and with the Klamaths the gathering of the wokash was preceded by a harvest dance. Almost a hundred years ago observers reported having seen hundreds of bushels of lily seed stored along marshes in tule sacks. The umbrella plant, growing along streams or in wet rocky areas, is named for a leaf so large that it can almost be used for a parasol. It gives forth blossoms in early spring. More lovely are its leaves, which were sometimes eaten by Indians, a circumstance from which it takes its common name of Indian rhubarb. The crimson monkey flower is another that borders streams. It blooms in July and August. The flowers are in pairs on tall graceful pedicels, and the color is usually rose red. Its succulent stems have been used as a substitute for lettuce.

Water plantain, common on shores in the Palouse country, is a perennial with small white or pale pink flowers. The twisted-stalk, a member of the lily-of-the-valley family, is a tall branched plant with greenish-white flowers and bright red oval berries which hang singly from fine arching stems. The giant hellebore is still larger. A member of the lily family, it has very showy green flowers that strongly resemble the lady's slipper. The lower portion hangs as if on a hinge and moves easily, and so gives to the plant its folkname of chatterbox. Out of mud and muck the arrowhead sends up large vividly green leaves shaped like an arrow, and delicate whitish blossoms sketchily petaled with yellow centers. The buckbean (bogbean) has a genuinely beautiful blossom which, like the forget-me-not, has a stem and foliage incapable of setting it off as it deserves. The flowers are white with pink and purple shadings and have a cut-petaled loveliness rivaling that of the bog orchid. In full bloom they resemble tiny stars with all points curved down. This plant grows in lakes and ponds; the skunk cabbage in swamps.

Of green and golden beauty with a heavy sweet fragrance like that of tube roses, the skunk cabbage has done well to survive under its name, or under an Indian legend that gives to it a war club and an elkskin blanket. The wapatoo is an edible tuber growing in mud of the northern lakes, above which it lifts arrow-shaped leaves and curious waxy white spikes. The history of the Northwest gives the wapatoo root as the principal food, during a terrible winter on the Oregon coast, of those wanderers who followed another man's dream of empire (and an Indian girl) to the sea. Indian pipe (ghost plant) has weird flowers that develop in warm midsummer after rains. When most plants have done blooming, the flowers of this one rise from the forest floor, living on decaying vegetable matter and looking ghostly white. As the seeds mature, the flowers turn upward and blacken. The plant gets its name from the way the petals of the long blossoms shutter so closely together as to seem like layers on a small cylinder and in appearance quite like the bowl of a pipe.

Of flowers of hill and mountainside a considerable number deserve mention. Some say the fireweed was named because it springs up quickly in burnt-over areas, and some because a patch of it sets a hillside aflame. It grows three to six feet in height, and is often found with the paintbrush, a bushy blossom that looks as if it had been washed in crimson. Often in company with them is the goldenrod, which, Muir declared, is enough to cure unbelief and spiritual aches; but on dry farms in southern Idaho it is an unmitigated pest. It thrives luxuriantly in earth so parched that grain withers, and after an unusually arid summer turns many a hillside golden. Varieties of lupine are found with these tenants, each a bunched plant topped with blue clusters that fill the rainless air with fragrance; but these, like the goldenrod, are sometimes an ineradicable pest. The golden cinquefoil, with petals resembling in form but not in substance those of the wild strawberry, is often found in sagebrush areas, where it looks almost as much out of place as the lilies; but the harebell prefers shady hillsides, especially in aspen groves. Drooping in frail melancholy loveliness on its slender stalk, it is often hidden by grass and fern or is rendered inconspicuous by its showier neighbors.

Ranging far and wide are the lilylike fairy bells, a flower with berries of golden or orange that give to the plant its folkname of gold-drops. It bears its flowers singly or in clusters of two or three, and these are bell-shaped and white and sometimes quite hidden under broad leaves. It blooms in April and May. The Oregon grape is not a grape but a barberry, though jelly made from its fruit has the flavor of grape. It has evergreen leaves, used much in decoration; numerous fellow flowers that bloom from April into May; and clusters of dark blue fruit. Its root has medicinal value and in the Northwest is dug and shipped by the ton. This barberry, the State flower of Oregon, grows in Idaho in woodlands or on rocky low mountainsides or even under high cool banks where the sun seldom shines. First found in Siberia, but common along the American coast line from Alaska to California, Siberian miner's lettuce got its name because it is sometimes used in salads. Its flowers grow on long pedicels and are white or pink and bloom from March to June in open woods. It also grows luxuriantly along the shaded banks of streams. The buckbrush (sticky laurel), really a shrub, grows on wooded hillsides, sometimes in thickets that stretch for miles. It has gorgeous white blossoms that hang with the profusion of lilacs. In some places it is called wild lilac, in some, chaparral, and either name is more appropriate than the one by which it is usually called in Idaho. Slender shooting star (bird bill) is widely distributed in Idaho. It is a flower of bizarre delicacy, so frail in appearance that it is a wonder how it survives in the situations it chooses. It has leafless threadlike stems that support rose-pink flowers shaped much like a bird's bill, with downsweeping petals that leave the center. The flower is commonly known as shooting star. Buff pussytoes (rush everlasting: either name is silly), a member of the aster family, has a great many varieties. In most of the species the plant has a long slender shoot that spreads in leafy runners over the earth to form dense foliage. The compound flower heads bloom upright and are supposed to suggest pussy toes in their soft lobed form. Another beautiful flower, unimaginatively named, is the pearly (or pearl) everlasting. It has clusters of small white flowers with large yellow centers, long and narrow and lazily tapering leaves, and the plant contour of the aster family to which it belongs. The flowers are often gathered and dyed to use as Christmas wreaths. Found chiefly in Owyhee County, the mountain lily is a pure white and very fragrant flower that blooms in early spring.

It belongs to more arid regions, as do several others of exceptional loveliness. The desert lily, most beautiful of

Marsh marigold

Indian paintbrush

all the Mariposas, is so close in appearance to the Eastern
lily as to deceive all but trained observers. But it forms an
exquisite picture and may be found blooming in the most
arid places, its peacock hues sometimes hiding under the
dry hot sage. If there is enough rainfall it will put forth
from ten to twenty blooms, each expanding in twos and
threes. There are few more incongruous sights than a
garden of these incomparable flowers right in the bleakest
wastes of sagebrush country where nobody would expect
to find anything but the horned lizard and the coyote. Some
think that the loveliest of the Mariposa tulips is the sego
lily, which, too, is found on dry hillsides as well as in
meadows. It blooms in May and June; and on its stalk a
foot and a half high it looks in a wind like a gorgeous white
butterfly held by its feet. This is the State flower of Utah
and was one of the most welcome sights to greet the Mormons when they emerged, almost a century ago, into the
arid desolation of Salt Lake Valley. But the Mormons
did more than to look at it and marvel. Sego (seego) is a
Shoshoni name for food; and the edible bulb of this flower
the Mormons ate and found good. The graceful sego lily
has petals softly fuzzed toward the center, and some have
given to it the odious name of cat's ear or pussy ear. The
violet-shaded tripetaled desert lily has the light poised
grace of three butterflies resting with closed wings. The
purple lily grows on dry hillsides in Owyhee County and
on the lower reaches of mountains in the center of the
State. The flowers of this fritillaria are of dark purple
mottled with yellowish green and are very slender on
comparatively leafless stems.

Another desert dweller, the stonecrop, gets its unlovely
name from its habit of growing among rocks in tiny
pockets of soil. Its leaves in bushy rosettes and its
flowers in yellow clusters are striking in May against
their background of dry earth and gray stone. Called
variously soap grass, squaw grass, and elk grass, the gorgeous plant which is more commonly known as bear grass
is a thorough rebuke to the unimaginativeness of the

human mind. The foliage itself is remarkable, growing in dense hummocks; and when the plant sets up its huge creamy plumes, it is, from June until August, one of the most unusual visions in semiarid places. This tall flower has received its unlovely names because bears eat its roots, because some persons have used its roots for soap, because squaws used the plant for basketry, and because elk eat its leafage. It is abundant along the Lolo Trail where it was first discovered by Lewis and Clark.

Old maid's hair, owl-clover, and balsamroot are three others unfelicitously named. The first, also called prairie smoke, is typical of the great prairie regions of the United States. Its red, budlike flowers sprout in groups from a crimson stalk, and in late summer the silky plumed heads shimmer like pale purple mist in the distance. Owl-clover, a member of the figwort and not of the clover family, is also widely distributed. It lifts in great patches of pink color among the grasses, and though different from the paintbrush in its manner of growth, like the paintbrush it blooms in bracts which flower at the tops of long wiry stems. The lean spidery foliage streams upward close to the stems, giving to the latter the appearance of being sheathed. Balsamroot grows on dry hillsides and in Idaho is abundant on the Snake River plains. The large leaves, blue green on top and white underneath, have the shape of arrowheads; and flaunting above them are the vivid yellow flowers. The roots were eaten by Indians, as well as by early Mormons, and in Utah the plant is sometimes called Mormon biscuit. One of the commonest of the cacti, the prickly pear is found on arid slopes, its large multi-petaled flowers of light sulphur yellow rising above the green shining discs of the plant. In late afternoon sun the flowers fade to salmon. The stamens, which may be either yellow or red, are so sensitive that when a bee settles on them they curl inward and downward, at once enclosing the insect. The plants with red stamens are by far the most striking.

VI
FAUNA

FAUNA[1]

THE WILD life of Idaho, like that of any Western State, is so various that only the more important or interesting or destructive species can be covered here, and these only briefly. In its high mountains, and in less degree in its semiarid regions, Idaho has thousands of wild animals, both herbivorous and predatory; in its marshes and along its innumerable streams it has hundreds of thousands of small animals and wild fowl; and in areas affected by such creatures it has many varieties of reptile and amphibian. According to the State Game Department, those beasts and birds which are italicized ought to be exterminated if Idaho is to realize its possibilities as a hunting and fishing playground.

For some persons who have studied him, the grizzly is the most splendid of all the wild animals of earth. A large beast of prodigious strength, this bear sometimes weighs a thousand pounds but in Idaho probably averages about six hundred. The number of grizzlies in the world is not large, because few animals are so remorselessly tracked to their death; and in Idaho, when signs of one are discovered, word usually goes forth to some big game hunter who at once comes in to hunt the big shy fellow to his death. Though supposed by some to be a menace to deer and elk and sheep, the best authority declares that he is a solitary baron who lives almost entirely on mice

---

[1] Fish and wild game fowl will be found in Chapter VII.

and rats and rabbits and wild fruits. This pilgrim of remote places, long a subject of romantic legend, would, if allowed to, go his calm and powerful way alone; for he is of gentle rather than ferocious nature and will often sit for a long while to meditate on the beaver or the water ouzels at play.

The black (or brown) bear, too, nearly always minds his own business. A lazy and shiftless fellow, he runs to quiet blinking indolence and fat. When fleeing from danger he is almost as noiseless as a rolling ball of cotton, but when gorging on huckleberries he is likely to make a great racket. Sometimes, for change of diet, he will lie on a log overreaching a stream and drop his paw for an unwary salmon or trout. The grizzly will spend time and ingenuity in fashioning a winter home to suit his taste, but the black bear is content to use any cave or hole he can find. He will even crawl under the stumpage of an overthrown tree and allow the snow to build a roof over him. This animal seems to be an enemy of small cattle and sheep, as well, possibly, of smaller wild game, and in parts of the country a bounty is laid on his head. Fairly common in Idaho, he ranges over practically all of the mountainous terrain and is quite frequently seen.

Of a different sort is the *cougar* (American panther, mountain lion, and in South America the puma). This huge cat is an implacable enemy of wild game, especially of deer and elk, and in stalking its prey is a beast of amazing patience. Often it will lie in wait for twenty-four hours or longer, crouched and motionless, until the victim comes within forty or fifty feet. The cougar can leap a distance of forty feet, and for a short sprint is said to be the fastest animal alive. After leaping to a deer it drives talons into the flanks and fangs into the neck and with one powerful effort twists the head back and breaks the spine. How many deer one cougar will kill annually, nobody knows, but fifty-two, or one a week, is a safe guess. Largest of the cats, and sometimes nine feet from tip to tip, the cougar is at home in the jungles of

Bear up a tree

Come on down!

Elk in winter

Deer on Moore Creek, seventeen miles from Boise

Antelope in flight

Panama or ten thousand feet above the sea. It is said to
be able to vanquish the black bear in a struggle, to drive
the jaguar out of its territory, and to slay a full-grown
elk. Possibly it has never, except when wounded or
trapped, attacked a human being. It is a beautiful animal, lithe and clean and intelligent. About forty are killed
annually in Idaho.

And the *timber wolf* and the *bobcat* should go with it.
The first, often weighing a hundred and fifty pounds, is
almost the same as the dreaded beast of European folklore. Formerly on the Western plains in great numbers,
it has been driven into mountains where it is not often
seen, and members of the United States Biological Survey declare that no wolves remain in Idaho. At this statement, old-timers, and especially in Owyhee County, look
down their noses. There are very few, however, and these
few are infrequently seen. One of the most difficult of all
animals to trap, the wolf has developed a most uncanny
knowledge of trappers and their ways and will step warily
aside from even the most cunning set. It has ferocious
courage, but its cousin the coyote is a skulking wretch
that fights, like most human beings, only when he has to.
The coyote is one of the commonest of wild animals in
Idaho, and thousands are trapped annually. An old-timer
in Owyhee County who has taken as many as 724 in a
single season now prefers to tie a piece of chain to the
handle of a broom and to overtake them on a fast horse
in snow a foot deep and to clout them on their skulls.
Trappers who have devoted years to these noiseless nocturnal wanderers tell amazing stories of the coyote's
cunning.

The *bobcat* or *lynx* (much the same animal, though
the former is stockier and less savage) is one of the
craftiest of hunters. It is about three feet long and may
weigh twenty-five pounds. A wide ranger in the deep
forests and along river bottoms, it feeds chiefly on mice
and rabbits, though it can, when it has a mind to, kill the
fox and the deer. In Arkansas it is said to have been so

vicious an enemy of hogs that hog raising in certain parts of the State has been abandoned; and in Idaho it is with the cougar the worst enemy of cattle and sheep. It is a credulous simpleton that never harms a human being, and it is valuable in destroying rodents, but sportsmen declare it has too much relish for wild game to be tolerated.

The moose (the name is Indian for twig-eater) is said by some to be lord of the American forests. The great range belt of this animal is, of course, through Canada and Alaska, but many are still found in the states, and quite a number in Idaho. It is a large beast that may stand, if a bull, almost seven feet to the top of his shoulders, and ten feet to the top of his antlers, and may weigh fourteen hundred pounds, though bulls of this size are rare. His antlers are two broad, curved slabs of bone with as many as twenty prongs on the two of them. A bold and terrible warrior, he will attack anything when provoked, using as weapons his antlers and sharp forefeet. He is said to have slain full-grown bears by driving the beasts through with one blow of his foreleg. Bulls engage one another, too, in the mating season and sometimes get their antlers inextricably locked and both perish. The moose likes to frequent lakes and take a cool bath daily and make great noise among the lily pads; and because its neck is so short and its height so great, it has to seek these or other propitious places to feed.

The elk (wapiti) is much commoner in Idaho than the moose, and thousands of them range in the high mountains. The name elk was given by early Virginia colonists, who called the beast an olke. Smaller than the moose, a bull elk may weigh a thousand pounds, but six hundred is an average. This animal, too, is a fearless warrior when in mating season he goes bugling through the forests, and like the bull moose, he often gets his horns interlocked and dies a prisoner of his own fury. The elk's chief enemies besides man and the cougar are the millions of insects that assail him, the most deadly of the latter being the deer tick (not yet a menace in Idaho), which often so weakens an animal by bloodsucking that it dies in late winter of starvation. Thirty years ago elk ranged in great numbers, but they were slain by thousands by greedy hunters who were after the two canine teeth, which were marketable and are still.

In Idaho there are about twenty thousand elk and about five times as many deer. These, about evenly divided between blacktail and whitetail, range over all the forests of the State, with the former more abundant in the south and the latter in the north. During summer months many of them leave the mountains for lowlands and not uncommonly pasture in wheat fields, leaping the tallest fences with ease. Like other wild herbivorous mammals, the deer is a creature of amazing vitality and may run for a hundred yards after being shot through the heart. Like the elk, it is cunning when pursued and will enter a river and wade up or down it and perhaps swim across and back and again enter the mountains. In the rutting season the stag is another fierce warrior, but after his antlers fall he is shy and reticent and goes off by himself to brood and wait for another set of horns.

The antelope (pronghorn or prongbuck) is more graceful than even the deer. The two herds in Idaho, one in the Pahsimeroi Valley and the other in Owyhee County, are said to be the largest in the world. Of all animals in North America, the antelope is said to be the swiftest; and so assured of its immunity to capture is this otherwise defenseless creature that it will often remain to gaze at interlopers when elk or deer would be crashing madly through the timber. It has a curious and most enviable sign of danger: when alarmed it declares its perturbation in a patch of white hair on its rump that stands straight up and in bright sunlight shines like a mirror. But its one invincible protection is speed. Adults are said to have outdistanced automobiles going forty miles an hour; and fawns only three weeks old can leave coyotes far behind. The antelope buck fights when in love, too, but less fiercely and less fatally than the bulls and stags. Its courtship tournament takes the form of massed attack by young males on an old and weary leader.

Ranging much higher than moose, elk, and deer are the mountain goats and sheep. These alpine climbers prefer the windswept altitudes lying between the timber line and the perpetual snows; and in those high and remote places they have few enemies but themselves. The males of these cliff dwellers also fight savagely during mating season, sometimes engaging in combat on narrow ledges from which the more unfortunate one is hurled to his death on the shelves below. It takes quite a fall, however, to kill one of these rugged and incredibly nimble creatures. When pursued they think little of leaping off precipices twenty feet in height, and have been known to drop twenty-five feet and to sprint off unharmed. How many wild goats and sheep there are in Idaho it is difficult to learn, but there is a fairly large number and the number is increasing.

Smaller Animals: On the streams are several animals of unusual value and interest. The beaver, largest of the rodents, and formerly so persistently trapped that it is now protected in most States, is an engineer and builder of dams, a mason, and a feller of trees with no equal except man. Once a beaver dam is placed, it is likely to resist flood and weather for an indefinite time, even though it may be a hundred feet in width and four in height. The beaver is a powerful animal for his pounds and will tow against a strong current and without apparent effort a log weighing a hundred pounds; or two working together will maneuver large boulders into place. When felling a tree he sits on his broad flat tail or thrusts it out behind him as a prop, grasps the trunk with his forepaws, and then bites above and below and pries the chips out with strong teeth. These teeth, if unused, grow so large that they become intractable and cause the animal to starve to death: they have to be whetted constantly and kept worn down. The beaver's long ladle of a tail has many uses: as a rudder when swimming, as a chair to

Mountain goat

Rocky Mountain sheep: beginning of a battle

Elk: finish of a fight

sit on, as a trowel in plastering, and as a mortar board on which to carry mud. He uses his paws with the agility of a monkey and tunnels, burrows, plasters, or grasps sticks. He lives on the inner bark of deciduous or broad-leaved trees, preferring aspen, cottonwood, and willow, and always stores for winter use much more than he can ever eat. Nothing about him is more remarkable than his persistence. A person can tear out a section of dam every morning for week after week; he can set fire to it and burn it to the water and mud; he can dynamite it and blow it over a half acre; he can even hang a lighted lantern two feet above the dam—but by daylight of the next day the dam will be built again.

Like the beaver in appearance, save for the tail, though much smaller, is the muskrat. This interesting creature, more closely related to mice than to rats, is aquatic like the beaver and lives in burrows with a sub-water tunneled entrance, and feeds chiefly on bark and roots. Unusual is his fastidious cleanliness: after choosing a root he will find a secluded spot and scrupulously scrub his foot before eating. His pelt, with long overhairs and dense underfur, is practically waterproof. Musquash is his Indian name. Though known to venture far from water, the muskrat is for the most part a solemnly busy fellow who sticks to his home and stupidly tunnels into dams and releases ponds as much to his regret as to the farmer's. For in Idaho this creature is more trouble than he is worth. He breeds four or five times a year in litters of six or more and raises Cain with many small irrigation projects.

A much greater rascal is the *otter*, which in legend is said to be able to kill a deer, and which in water can easily capture the fastest fish that swims. When not murdering, this bloodthirsty creature likes to build slippery slides on clay banks and spend hours toboganning into the water, climbing out and sliding down as if he had nothing else in the world to do. Though among aquatic animals, he travels far and swiftly, ranging up and down rivers in search of prey. The mink, also an enemy of fish, possibly in Idaho does more good than harm. He is an amazingly quick and relentless killer. More agile on land than the otter, the mink can climb trees with the ease of a timber squirrel or travel a long reach of shoreland in a night. He eats rats, mice, and squirels, but is also fond of eggs of birds and waterfowl. If unable to obtain any of these, he will eat salamanders and frogs and snakes.

The fisher, largest and deadliest member of the weasel clan, and the only animal on earth that knows how to slay a porcupine without injury to himself, probably no longer exists in Idaho. But the weasel is common. If this creature were as large as a cougar, nobody would dare to venture out-of-doors, because he is second to none, including the badger, in courage, and is possibly the most bloodthirsty villain on earth. And except in the matter of traps he is as crafty as a fox. Weasels invade many a hencoop and leave the hens paralyzed with fright with a part of their number slain; and when cornered they will attack any animal and even fly into the face of a human being, though they are only a little larger than a squirrel. They render some service by preying on mice and rats and lizards and insects, but they also prey on songbirds, sucking the blood of each and demanding that the blood be fresh. And when they have a chance they always slay from ten to a hundred times as much as they need. The fur of this pest is, of course, the commercially valuable ermine.

Like the weasel, the badger has more courage than he knows what to do with and will attack anything that annoys him. A chunky, close-to-the-earth fellow, he is a tenant of prairies, and here, usually in pursuit of squirrels, he digs with astonishing rapidity, disappearing from sight in less than a minute and going as deep as necessary for his prey. There are few more dramatic spectacles than a fight between two males. They engage in combat with such deadly fury that a human being can approach and kick them and they will remain unaware of or wholly indifferent to his presence; and now and then they get their jaws locked in a death grip and die together. A badger is a creature of such enormous vitality that often one shot through with a rifle and carried all day behind a saddle will crawl off when thrown to the earth.

Quite unlike him is the skunk, a denizen of wooded areas and strangest member of the weasel family. It has a defense so effective that safety from its enemies has allowed it to grow slothful and fat. A gaudy creature in appearance, its colors are intended not to disguise it but to warn its enemies of its presence. The skunk is very common in Idaho, and aside from the worth of its pelt it is valuable in its feeding on grasshoppers and crickets. It is also fond of the juicy larvae of bumblebees and yellow jackets and will almost demolish a colony in one visit; and upon approaching an apiary cautiously and scratching on the hive to invite the bees outside, it will, indifferent to fury and stings, eat as many as it can pick out of its fur and then proceed to the larvae inside. It will also eat lizards and earthworms, gophers and mice and rats.

The skunk may be valuable, but the *porcupine,* which inhabits the same areas, is, according to Forest Service officials, an unmitigated nuisance. Instead of eating injurious insects and rodents and so placing itself in the esteem of man, this creature, safe under its bristling armor, feeds on succulent plants and on the bark and cambium of trees, especially the yellow pine and Douglas fir. Many small seedlings are completely devoured, and older trees are girdled and killed; and in some areas, heavily infested, not a single tree has been left undamaged. To make matters worse, this dull-witted creature is nomadic and wanders far and aimlessly, sometimes stupidly reaching high altitudes where there is no food at all. It lives in great rocky dens when not prowling, and because it has no enemies except the fisher (which is rare) it breeds unmolested.

The *gopher* (salamander, camas rat) has, unlike the

porcupine, a great many enemies, but it multiplies rapidly in its burrows and devastates whole areas with its tireless industry. Considerably larger than the field mouse, and in appearance and habits much like its cousins, the mole and shrew and vole (meadow mouse), it lives chiefly underground and devotes most of its time to eating. It is estimated that a mole will eat fifty pounds of earth-worms in a year and will starve to death if denied food for forty-eight hours. The gopher also eats worms, but it throws up huge mounds in alfalfa fields; destroys dams and dikes with its tunneling; and lays countless fields open to erosion and flood. The shrew is the smallest of all flesh eaters and is a fierce mouselike little fellow that lives along streams and lakes and preys on insects and fish. Much commoner in Idaho is the gray ground squirrel. Though friendly and cheerful, it has enormous relish for succulent herbage including wheat and alfalfa, and in every year thousands of them are poisoned or shot. This is a prairie animal, but the red squirrel (often called pine or timber squirrel) lives in the forests. It is a hand-some and impudent fellow who noisily resents intrusion but is easily tamed and becomes the pet of men in the lonely forest lookouts. Just as pertly incredulous, and quite as favored in the hearts of those who know and love its ways, is the chipmunk.

More interesting than the gopher or mole because more intelligent is the pack rat (trade rat, cave rat, wood rat, bush rat, drummer rat, and mound builder). It is an erratic nocturnal prowler that always looks astonished and guilty and has reason to because it is everlastingly up to mischief. Hating famine as much as fire, it lays in huge stores not only of food but of everything it can carry, including spectacles and clothes and all sorts of glittering gadgets. In New Mexico eight carloads of nuts were once recovered from pack-rat storehouses. This busy pest is sought by nearly every predaceous bird and beast in its region because of its tender flesh. Because of its foul odor and mousey appearance it is not held

in esteem in Idaho as a table delicacy, but in parts of the
world, as in Mexico, the flesh of the pack rat is regarded
in quality as second to none. Upon entering a house it
will walk about, thumping the walls and ceiling with its
stiff hard tail as if determined to waken every sleeping
thing; and on being discovered it offers an astonishing
mien of stupidity and cunning, of apology and insolence.

Without even a small part of the pack rat's intelligence is the snowshoe rabbit, whose only defenses are
fecundity and speed. There are several species of rabbit
in Idaho, all of them looking equally haunted, and all of
them forever in flight from their enemies, not the least
of which are the confusing headlights of automobiles.
There are thousands of them, and it is remarkable that
there should be because of all creatures of mountain and
desert none is so remorselessly sought. Coyotes and
wolves and weasels overtake them; horned owls and
hawks pick them up with ease; reptiles creep up to them
while they are dozing; and bot, warble, and fluke, fly and
louse and tick and tapeworm are all among their deadly
enemies. These creatures with their big terrified eyes
and wildly beating hearts are one of the commonest animals in the West, even though, in addition to their natural enemies, human beings drive them by thousands into
pens and club them to death.

The rockchuck (often mistakenly called woodchuck)
favors as its home piles of slide-rock near succulent meadows. All three species of marmot are found in Idaho, and
this is the only state in which all three are found. The
hoary keeps to the highest peaks; the brown (woodchuck
is the common name) prefers deep forests, and is often
called the thickwood badger; and the yellow (rockchuck)
chooses the rocky flanks. The woodchuck is the most
widely distributed of all animals its size, but is much less
frequently seen in Idaho than the rockchuck, members
of whose huge clans are often run over by cars. During
the day a sentinel is placed on a lookout, and at any sign
of invasion it gives a cry of warning that can be heard

for a mile. Its chief enemy is the eagle and coyote—and
man, for more and more commonly the rockchuck devastates cultivated fields. It shares its castle with others
who are too lazy to establish one of their own: with the
rockchip, for instance, a potbellied little elfin that sits
humbly at the feast and is content to eat what the lord
of the manor does not want. It is declared, but some deny,
that the marmot is the only wild animal that carries in
all its stages the deadly tick of spotted fever.

Reptiles: In comparison with Southeastern or Southwestern States Idaho is free of reptiles, and yet it is said
that rattlesnakes are so numerous in parts of Idaho County
that a recent expedition into the area had to be recalled.
Of these, there are the Pacific and the prairie: the two
are almost indistinguishable, though the former is
smaller and climbs higher. Both are dangerous and quick
to strike. The prairie, rarely exceeding six feet in length,
is rumored to put more energy into a fight than any other
reptile in North America. Legend, however, exaggerates
the ferocity and courage of snakes, and of this one it can
be said that unless stepped on or cornered it will get out
of sight as quickly as it can. The rubber boa (silver
snake, worm snake, or two-headed snake because both
ends are blunted) is a true boa and well named, for rubber is quite exactly what it looks like. It is a glistening
and polished and indolent fellow with a gray back and an
immaculate yellow belly. In disposition it is like the Old
World sand boa; in eating it constricts its prey in the
manner of its kind. This snake is shy and is rarely seen.

The Pacific bull or gopher snake is a handsome viper of
yellowish brown and splotched black, and is of moderate
size. In prairies and mountains it grows larger than on
the coast and may achieve a length of four and a half
feet. When disturbed it hisses furiously and shakes its
tail and tries to look as formidable as any bull snake
should, but it is only eager to get out of sight. This one,
too, is uncommon in Idaho. The gopher or indigo snake
preys, as its name declares, chiefly on gophers and mice,

and is of considerable value. Blue-black in color, it has
the polish of a new gun barrel and is a prismatic marvel
as it moves swiftly through shadow and sunlight. Much
commoner in Idaho and frequenting the same areas is
the striped racer, a very slender dark brown or black
reptile with numerous yellow lines on its sides. It is fast,
either in vaulting bushes or moving over ground. The
yellow-bellied racer (blue or green racer) is olive green
with a yellow belly, and sometimes reaches a length of
four and a half feet. It lives among bushes and climbs
them with ease in search of bird nests. As with other
racers, folklore invests it with remarkable boldness, but
the most notable thing about all of these sleek fellows
is the speed with which they flee from anything larger
than themselves. Ground snakes in Idaho are rare, but
water snakes of several varieties are common and are
among the chief enemies of fish. One of these snakes
will eat as many as fifty rainbow fingerlings at a meal.

Idaho seems to have no skinks, but there are several
kinds of swift. The sagebrush swift is small but bril-
liantly colored and lives on prairies or on mountains to
an altitude of nine thousand feet. It is much more uncommon than the western, which prefers arid regions
and makes frantic haste when discovered. The stansbury
is larger, attaining a length of six inches. All the swifts
are terrestrial lizards of remarkable agility that live in
subarid zones and spend their lives chasing insects. The
collared lizard is one of Idaho's gaudiest natives: its chief
color may be yellow or pale gray or bright green, lavishly
decorated with white or yellow dots. Behind its green
head and the orange of its throat is a brilliant collar of
two jet-black bands which are the margins upon a white
or yellow necklace. Its legs may be dotted red. It is rare,
and when found is usually sunning itself on a stone. Similar in habits and fairly common is the leopard lizard, also
flamboyant, though his color harmony is of red and
brown. This cannibal, like the other, rises to his hind
legs when chasing prey. Of the horned lizard (often

called the horned toad) there are at least two species.
These flattened-out creatures with their conical horns and
formidable spines look much more dangerous than they
are and frighten by appearance rather than by power.
They live in areas of lava and seem happy only when the
heat is intolerable. When captured they feign death; or
they may puff up prodigiously; or they may seem to void
all their organs and be only lidless eyes and horned skin.
Some of the horned lizards can, Ditmars declares, squirt
blood from their eyes to a distance of three or four feet,
though precisely of what value such a spectacular maneuver is in terrifying their enemies seems not to be
known. Lizards feed on ants and grubs and grasshoppers
and crickets.

Birds: Without birds, authorities declare, humanity
would perish from the earth and its trees would perish
with it. Without swallows, purple martins, swifts, and
nighthawks, not to speak of countless others whose appetites are less gluttonous, the atmosphere would be a fog of
midges and mosquitoes and gnats. It would be a dark and
trembling mass of larger insects without kingbirds, flycatchers, phoebes, and peewees. Trees would wither from
larvae and plant lice if it were not for the warblers and
vireos that search every trunk and leaf; for thrushes and
orioles and catbirds and wrens that devour caterpillars
and beetles and locusts and spiders; for woodpeckers that
bore for the beetles. The earth would be overrun with
moths if it were not for the red-eyed vireo and birds like
it. In meadows and on hillsides human beings would wade
ankle-deep in chinch bugs and cutworms and wireworms
and beetles and locusts if it were not for robins and sparrows and larks. The land would be taken by weeds if it
were not for the finches and doves, any one of which will
eat almost a thousand weed seeds for breakfast alone.
We'd need an army of pied pipers if hawks and owls were
to develop sudden distaste for mice and rats. When, not
long ago, agriculturists of Hungary persuaded a deluded
people to exterminate the sparrow, the country was over-

run with insects. In the island of Bourbon the martin was destroyed, and grasshoppers took possession of the land. And Utahans still remember when the Salt Lake Valley was saved by gulls. Idaho was once a refuge where birds were numbered in millions, but cat fanciers, tiring of too many pets, now take the beasts on fishing trips and turn them loose. The United States Biological Survey says the common cat, gone wild, is one of the three most destructive animals in Idaho. A domestic cat goes wild in a few weeks, and many parts of the State, once ringing with birdsong, are now in the possession of English sparrows and cats. But the State is still so rich in bird life that a few years ago the Cleveland Museum of Natural History sent an expedition here to discover how many varieties there were. Authorities estimate that there are fifty million cats in the United States that kill hundreds of millions of birds annually, but parts of Idaho, such as the Primitive Area, are still huge bird sanctuaries.

The bald eagle, emblem of a great Nation, has been divested of much of its legendary glory and represented for the ineffectual carrion eater that it is. Though a huge handsome fellow with in some respects the most impressive majesty of all things that fly, it is not a fierce lonely hermit with the aloofness of distance and altitudes. On the contrary it is an unconscionable and lazy rascal that lives chiefly by stratagem and theft. When sitting on a cliff he looks olympian, but in plain truth is a piratical parasite that will even eat the carrion which the vultures disgorge. And if, driven to hunt for himself, he goes about seeking prey, he prefers, some authorities declare, the wounded birds that have gone into hiding to die. Or he may skulk around to learn if the osprey has not left some of its fish, or he may descend to eat with the ravens and crows. The *war eagle*, on the other hand, is a fierce creature that rarely touches food that it has not slain. It likes lonely inaccessible places, from which it goes on marauding expeditions to seek the young of mountain goat or sheep, and like the bald eagle, it mates for life. A huge folklore has been built around the amorous single-mindedness of this aerial wayfarer. It is enough to know that where the war eagle has been exterminated, mountain sheep and goats rapidly increase.

The turkey vulture or buzzard has a wing spread of six feet. It is a rather ornate scavenger with its black and brown plumage, its naked crimson head, its white beak, and its flesh-colored feet. Soaring high with imperceptible movement of its wings, falling or rising in great effortless arcs, or sailing round and round, it seems to float rather than fly, and in grace and majesty of flight is the master of all birds. It has been suggested that, like the wood ibis, this lord of the air soars incessantly in an effort to digest its gorge. A serene philosopher that wars with nothing, it eats what most birds scorn and has been led by its peaceable nature to have distaste for fresh meat. But of carrion it is said to eat so gluttonously as to be unable to leave the ground; whereupon, philosopher still, it waits calmly until digestion has diminished its weight. If disturbed while feeding it will blow hisses through its nostrils or grunt or sometimes resort to the mean trick of disgorging its stomach upon the intruder. Its nest is so foul of smell that it has rarely been studied.

Of hawks, Idaho has too few of the right and too many of the wrong kind. To the latter belong most of the falcons. Swifter than the eagle, swiftest, indeed, of all birds that kill, is the falcon, that bird which men have observed for ages with envious interest, noting the graceful certainty with which it achieves what it undertakes. No bird that flies is more daring than the *peregrine*. This marauder follows game birds in their flight north or south and destroys them in vast numbers, especially ducks, which it kills with spectacular deftness. Rising from the frantic bird, it folds its wings and drops, striking with powerful talons; and then swoops to catch the dying bird in mid-air. Often pigeons will rise swiftly in an attempt to elude the peregrine, and both hunter and hunted will vanish beyond human sight. The smallest of falcons, the sparrow hawk, never eats anything bigger than a grasshopper and is a most valuable bird.

The marsh or mouse hawk is less spirited in flight than some of his kind and is content to skim the earth for small mammals and frogs. But in mating time he exerts himself and has some tricks of his own. Said to mate for life, he goes about the matter with most impressive earnestness and will fall part way down the sky, turning somersaults in his descent; or, failing in this, will pursue a long course parallel with the earth, somersaulting again and screeching with fervor. Of a different sort is the *sharp-shinned hawk,* a fierce little edition of the Cooper: this fellow's speed and audacity and appetite are the terror of songbirds. When birds are seen in desperate flight from a twisting and gyrating and relentless predator, most likely this is the hawk in pursuit. His large cousin, *Cooper's hawk,* lives chiefly on small game birds and is one of the most villainous rascals in the air. A still larger cousin is the *goshawk,* or blue hen or partridge hawk, one of the most destructive creatures on wings. Though it eats rodents, it prefers grouse and quail and ducks, and is so greedy that it always slays more than it eats. It has been known to kill as many as five grouse for one meal. It is very common in Idaho. Another useless pest is the *osprey,* which feeds on fish. Dropping like a plummet, this hawk strikes the water and disappears, and the sound of its vanishing can be heard for half a mile. In sharp contrast with this scoundrel is a hawk which many Idahoans unwisely kill. This, the western redtail, is a large serene bird that lives almost entirely on mice and squirrels. The *pigeon hawk,* or American merlin, lives chiefly on birds.

Of owls in Idaho, the *great horned* is the largest except one, and the deadliest. It is two feet in length and has tufted ears and yellow eyes. Perhaps not even the peregrine falcon is a more remorseless enemy of ducks and geese and game fowl, and especially inasmuch as the

horned owl eats only the brains. Said by some to have
the most bloodcurdling scream of all wild things, and
called by others melodramatically, the tiger of the air, this
voracious fellow is afraid of nothing and will even attack
a skunk. So bold is it that stories are told of duck hunters who, sitting quietly in a bog, have been swooped
down upon by this creature and almost knocked out. It
does not, of course, attack human beings, but does sometimes mistake their head or their hat for an animal of
smaller size. The snowy owl is a far northern bird that
sometimes comes to Idaho and adjacent States to engage
in a meditative butchery of crows. For some unknown
reason crows regard this white visitor from arctic regions
as an enemy and attack it in great numbers; and the owl
quietly awaits the more indiscreet birds and strikes and
drops their dead bodies one by one. The snowy owl is
diurnal and preys largely on smaller birds. The great
gray or spectral owl is the largest owl in the world. This
dusky creature, mottled white, is abundant in the far
north, but in Idaho is rarely seen. Quite common, on
the other hand, is the American barn or monkey-faced
owl, which has the face of a toothless old hag with a half-
witted but strangely sly mien. During the day it has a
melancholy face full of grief, but when darkness comes it
gives off its ghastly scream and sallies forth to slay the
shrews and bats, beetles and frogs. Its favorite delicacy
is the head of a mouse, and as a destroyer of pests it has
few equals. The short-eared (marsh, meadow, or prairie) owl is about the same size as the long-eared and
barn. Unlike most owls, it does not live in woods, does
not confine its hunting to the night, and does not nest
above the ground. Some have said this owl will attack
a man: the most it will do if disturbed and lifted from its
roost is to click angrily and try to look much larger than
it is. The flight of all owls is practically noiseless, and
this one is perhaps the most uncannily soundless one of
the tribe. The long-eared (cat) owl is nocturnal; and inasmuch as it prefers to sleep and hunt and give no time

to home building, it appropriates the nest of crows. It feeds chiefly on mice. The *barred* (hoot, wood) *owl* is the one that fills the woods with the desolate who-who-too which many old-timers believe to be an infallible sign of change in weather. This lazy maurader steals the nest of hawk or crow and eats more fish and small birds than mice. The saw-whet (Acadian) owl is much smaller, measuring only about eight inches, and is a handsome burnished fellow with a lot of white in his plumage. Haunting the deepest forests and feeding almost entirely on mice and insects, it is as lazy as its cousins and chooses for its home a woodpecker's hole. The screech (mottled, red, or little horned) owl is a trifle larger than the saw-whet, and though it appears usually in a dress of red trimmed in white or buff, it may, for reasons apparently unknown, change its colors and wear black and gray. It, too, feeds on insects and mice. By day it sleeps and is seen only when some mischievous blue jay chases it blindly through the daylight for other birds to torment.

There are other worthless butchers in Idaho, though few of them murder with the zestful wantonness of the peregrine falcon. Of shrikes the State has, unfortunately, two: the *white-rumped* and the *northern*. The latter is a large bird almost a foot in length with dark wings and tail and a barred gray breast. Both of these vandals make havoc of songbirds, often gathering many of them and impaling them on the thorns of rosebush or haw. Commonest of the *cormorants* in Idaho is the white-crested, which, inasmuch as it is peculiar to America, is not the Greek bald raven. Cormorant is a corruption of Latin meaning marine crow: the creature was so named because of its voracious appetite. Perhaps its only breeding place in Idaho is at the head of the American Falls Reservoir, where attempts are being made to destroy it; for the cormorant feeds on fish and dives with remarkable speed and skill. The *kingfisher*, equally notorious, darts down to seize unwary victims and then hammer the life out of them on a rock. It thereupon swallows the fish whole and headfirst and utters a rattling chuckle that some have fancied to be a laugh of exultation. The kingfisher has a compact, oily, water-resisting plumage, bluish gray above, tipped with white on the wings and tail. It is easily recognized by its long crest. The *cowbird,* often called buffalo bird on the plains, and long despised for its parasitical insolence, lays its eggs in the nests of other birds, chiefly warblers, vireos, and sparrows. Though this bird lives chiefly on insects and weed seeds, its destruction of other nestlings places it definitely among the enemies of humankind. The same fate ought to await the sagacious *crow,* which preys too much on the eggs and young of other birds to be tolerated for the insects it eats.

The *great blue heron* (often called blue or sandhill crane) is perhaps of all useless birds the one most ardently defended. This tall gawky creature stands in a river like a grotesque assortment of angles and impales fish as they come along, gives them a knock or two to finish them off, and then tosses them into the air and swallows them headfirst. The *black-crowned heron,* somewhat flamboyant and less gawky than its cousin, has an ornament of two or three long graceful white feathers that reach from its head and across its back like a plume. The sandhill crane is, unlike the solemn heron, a clown. When the cranes arrive in the spring they indulge in a lot of tomfoolery and hop and skip and give off triumphant croaks, and are said in ardor to be equalled only by Indians in a war dance. This is the male's method of wooing his tall outlandish bride. These birds prey on fish, too, and stand for hours in marshes and bogs with their long necks thrust above the foliage to scan the landscape; and if fish are not available they enter fields and stand in alert wonder on one leg and wait for moles and mice. When cranes migrate, streaking through the sky in serpentine fashion, the leader croaks orders that are repeated from crane to crane down the line. The *white pelican* breeds in Idaho in huge colonies and feeds gluttonously by scooping up fish as it swims along. In Yellowstone Park they fish systematically, according to Knowlton, and move backward and forward at equal distances apart.

There are five species of grebe in Idaho. These birds, closer in evolution than others to the reptiles, are the most skillful of all swimmers and divers, having many surprising natatorial feats. Holboell's has a red neck; the horned gets its name from brown crests; the pied billed has a black band around its beak; the eared has black head and neck and earlike tufts of golden brown; and the western is easily recognized because it is the largest of them all. The pied billed, most abundant of all American species, is the one most frequently seen in Idaho; and here as elsewhere it is usually known under its folkname of helldiver. The grebe's nest is a strange affair of weeds and mud and moss built into a floating structure that sinks perhaps three feet in depth. Upon this raft the mother broods a part of the time, though for the most part the eggs are steamed into life by the heat of the sun upon the drifting cradle.

The avocet is a small wader with very long legs and a slender body and a long curved bill. Although the best swimmer among the waders, it is no less at home on land. It pays little heed to man unless he becomes a nuisance, and then nonchalantly flies away, trailing its long legs as if they were broken. The loon is not half so simple-minded as legend declares it to be. Largest and handsomest of the diving birds, it is less aquatic than the grebes but is, nevertheless, a remarkable diver, and at fifty yards is usually quicker than the gun. The common loon, possibly the only one found in Idaho, is a high and solitary wanderer that does not often make its presence known. The American bittern (marsh hen) is another lone nomad which, though often heard, is infrequently seen. Its love song is quite the sort of dismal lamentation that one would expect from so solemn a hermit. Now and then this speckled other-world creature is to be seen

standing in a bog in an apparent state of doleful indecision—and for an hour it may be as motionless as a
stump. But if a person watches long enough he will see
it suddenly snap and gulp as if swallowing all its pent-up
morbid reflections and then bellow horribly as if dying of
nausea and finally go forth with mincing deliberation as
if stepping off distance. But it is only seeking molluscs
with its toes, having first gone through contortions to
rebuke its melancholy and arouse its appetite. The
racket it makes has been variously compared with that
of bellowing cattle, with the gurgle of an old wooden
pump, and with the driving of a peg into a bog; and it
has passed in folklore under such names as thunder-
pumper, stake-driver, butter-bump, and bog-bull. Some
have said that the bittern makes its noise with its bill
in water, but its horrible croaking is only because it
must swallow a great deal of air before giving off its
pump-song.

Of terns or sea-swallows, Idaho has the black, Cas-
pian, and Forster. Terns usually remain close to the sea
or lakes but occasionally venture far inland. Among the
loveliest of birds, they rarely eat fish or anything else
that human beings think birds should leave alone; and
their chief enemy seems to be women who like feathers
in their hats. Both Wilson's and the northern phalarope
are found here. These sea snipes are smaller than a
robin, and the most remarkable thing about them, according to one commentator, is the surmise that the phalarope has the "most advanced female among the feath-
ered tribes." He means that she has stolen the colors,
does the wooing, and disports herself in various sorts of
club work while the male sits on the eggs. Laying the
eggs is, as a matter of fact, the only necessary chore
which the male does not do. Idaho has the Virginia and
sora rails, though the latter is not bagged here, as in the
rice fields, by tens of thousands. Rails are so timid that
they are said to swoon from fright, or if shot upon water
sometimes sink from terror never to emerge. As thin as

a rail is no misnomer: these birds are little more than noiseless movement and feathers and legs. The American coot (mud hen) is an aquatic bird that likes to show off in its diving where water flanks the marshes. It, too, is a shy bird, though some say that not even a starving beast would eat its flesh, and others argue that the coot when fed on wild celery is equal in flavor to the canvasback. Gregarious in all but the mating season, the coot then attacks trespassers with shrill and chattering zeal.

The black-necked stilt is by some persons called longshanks because of its reedlike legs. It wades like the avocet, seeking worms and larvae, and in nesting time is as nervous as the coot, keeping up a dismal click-clicking sound that frightens everything but itself to death. In Idaho there are the Bartramian, least, pectoral, spotted, western, and solitary sandpipers. These birds, usually called woodcocks, are among the most palatable of wild fowl, and have in consequence been eagerly sought by hunters from the Gulf to Labrador and from coast to coast. They feed on worms, declaring their presence by the round bored holes they leave; and inasmuch as worms come to the surface after dark, these birds are largely nocturnal. Like the males of crane, plover, and owl, the woodcock makes a clown of himself in mating time and exhausts his energy in swift-winged antics. During amours the pectoral can inflate his neck until it bulges like a goitre, and the spotted can swell out in his plumage until he is twice his customary size. Of plover there are the golden, black-bellied, and killdeer. Because they are fearless and take a quick sprightly run before flying, they offer an easy target and are diminishing in number with the exception of the killdeer, whose flesh is musky and insipid. In moving over ground, the killdeer has the daintiest alacrity of all birds. The bird which is often called upland plover is the Bartramian sandpiper. The American or Wilson's snipe is another table delicacy and is no longer common. The male is amusing when wooing a mate. He swoops upward, singing for all he is worth meanwhile, and drops and rises again to his former level and drops and rises again and again; until at last, as if exhausted or discouraged, he comes to the earth through a series of collapses and falls and recoveries and short spasmodic flights.

The great white or American egret has in all seasons entirely white plumage that in mating time is a splendor of drooping plumes. A large bird, shy, and more taken by wanderlust than ever because women seek its beauty, the egret is not often seen in Idaho or elsewhere. Nor is the ibis, though several species have been observed here. The quail, however, is common, as is the long-billed curlew also, especially on the shores of lakes. Gulls are rapidly increasing, and most fortunately, inasmuch as they are a deadly enemy of the grasshopper and cricket, though of course they prey on fish, too. The western herring gull, the only one whose head in winter is streaked with dark, is not common in Idaho, nor is the Bonaparte, which is perhaps the most elegant of the family. But the ring-billed is now to be seen in hundreds on the rivers and lakes. Very rare, on the other hand, is the common American or whistling swan, though formerly it was in Idaho by thousands, and Swan Valley was named for it. Those who years ago saw a flock of these great white birds rise from the water say the vision is the most memorable one of wild life. Neltje Blanchan uses the symbol of a regatta, with the birds moving like yachts under full sail; and he declares that the trumpetlike sound of their voices is equalled in power only by the French horns "blown by red-faced Germans at a Wagner opera." The musical ability of the swan seems to be confined entirely to the minds of poets.

Smaller Birds: Of smaller birds of field and woods, some of the commonest will be summarized first, then some that favor tree or stream, and then some that are loveliest, followed by some that sing most sweetly.

Of birds here, the western robin is perhaps not most

frequently seen but is most commonly recognized because
everyone who knows birds at all is familiar with this bird
that is not a robin but a thrush. Almost as abundant in
prairie and field is the mourning dove, whose melancholy
love notes have long endeared them to distracted lovers.
Blackbirds, especially the Brewer, were formerly to be
seen in enormous flocks, but cats have driven them out
of many parts of the State. The Brewer male is a handsome fellow with a remarkably liquid gurgling in his
querulous call; but the female looks like a smaller male
who long ago faded in sun and rain. The female redwing
also looks like a shoddy edition of her lord. The yellow-
headed blackbird, rare in the East, is to be found in huge
colonies in the West. The male is handsome in a dress
that is lustrous black save for a white patch on the wings,
and the brilliant yellow of the head, neck, and breast.
The absurd thing about him is his song: he spreads his
tail, inflates his throat, and after a harsh and experimental tuning-up gives a longdrawn choking squeal. His
attempts are accompanied by contortions that suggest
anguish—and may be, for possibly he realizes how shame-
less it is for a lovely bird to sway on a willow and look
over a beautiful world and summarize his joy in so lamentable a squawk. These birds prefer flag swamps, tule
beds, and reed brakes.

Of swallows, there are, of course, several species: the
bank, smallest of the family, which digs surprisingly deep
holes in the earth; and the barn with its forked tail and
iridescent upper parts and sepia breast; the cliff, identified
by its glossy black back and chestnut rump and by its twit-
tering as it flies; and the violet-green, loveliest of the swallow clan, whose metallic green plumage has purple lusters,
a silky white breast, and a violet-purple tail and nape.
Found here, too, are the white-bellied and the rough-
winged. Of sparrows, the most common, unfortunately, is
the *English,* a worthless parasite that drives most birds out
of their sanctuaries. The western vesper, often seen singing from post to post, is a common ground bird in sage-

brush areas, but the western song sparrow keeps close to shrubbery. The white-crowned has a head striped black and white; Gambel's crown has a delightful whistling morning song; and Brewer's, sometimes called sagebrush chippy, is very common in arid regions. Common also are chickadees, all varieties of which are easily identified by the white stripe above their eye. Of juncos or snowbirds there are several varieties, often in large flocks, and all of them very friendly and pert. The song of the Rocky Mountain junco is a sweet little tinkling trill. The snowflake, snow bunting, or snow lark, so named because it often rides on the breast of a blizzard, inhabits the Arctic zone but comes southward in the fall. Of flycatchers, there are at least four varieties, all invaluable, and all covering a wide range except possibly the olive-sided, which keeps to the evergreens.

Of birds that keep close to trees, there are none in Idaho that are better known or more amusing than the red-shafted flicker: it differs from Eastern species in having scarlet patches on the sides of its head, and brilliant red instead of yellow on its tail and shafts. The male has an absurdly elaborate courtship. Choosing the most indifferent female he can find, he hops and bows and prances and struts, all the while urging his suit with a hiccoughing song; and when she takes to wing, he follows and repeats his performance almost without variation again and again. The pileated woodpecker is found everywhere in northern wooded regions; the hairy, with the scarlet patch on the back of its head, in high forested latitudes; and the white-headed among the pines. The latter is a Western bird that differs sharply from all other members of the family: it is entirely black except for a white wing patch, head, and neck, and a red nape. The downy has a black back with a white stripe down its center, and the male of the Arctic three-toed has white wing dots and a yellow crown.

Rarer, and to many persons of greater interest, is the Lewis, a wild and suspicious bird that remains in the high forests. It has a blue-gray collar and dark red around its bill and eyes. The pigmy nuthatch is abundant in all evergreen forests. These birds herd in flight from tree to tree and keep up a rapid-fire call. The slender billed has a wretched song that sounds like hah-hah-hah, a nasal exclamation that suggests perpetual astonishment. In folklore called tree mice because of their darting flight, the nuthatches were named for their habit of thrusting nuts into cracks and hammering at them with their bills. The pine siskin, common in coniferous forests, is a member of the finch family and has a call note exactly like that of the goldfinch. Yellow patches show on wings and tail when these are furled in flight. The brown creeper can be recognized easily in autumn by its manner of going nimbly up the trunk of a tree until it reaches the first limbs and then flying to the foot of another tree and repeating. Clark's nutcracker, the only American representative of the European bird, is a high dweller among the pines. A large bird with black wings, it is sometimes mistaken for a crow but its body is of pale gray. The *red-naped sapsucker* is the Western counterpart of the eastern yellow-bellied: it has a red patch below the black of its head, and under parts tinted yellow. Commoner is *Williamson's* with its yellow belly and narrow scarlet throat patch. These rascals delight in the sap of fir and pine trees, and any tree they take possession of is doomed. The red crossbill is found only in dense evergreen growth where, scorning migration, it stays as long as there is food. This bird has a plump, dull red body, brighter on the head and rump, browner on the back with dusky markings, and dusky on the wings and tail. In cutting to the seeds of pine cones, it climbs with bill, feet, and wings and hangs or swings in every conceivable position. Two birds with a preference for water instead of trees are worthy of mention. The greater yellow-legs (called also long-legged tattler, snipe, plover) is a noisy citizen of marshes and estuaries, but not common here. It is more than a foot in length and has long, slender, chrome-yellow legs, a black back dusted with ash and flecked with white, and a long, thin, greenish-black bill. Much more frequently seen is the water ouzel or American dipper, a buoyantly impudent fellow with a fine song. Having waterproofed feathers, this bird flies easily under water and stays there solely by means of its wings; but is quite as interesting when seen bobbing up and down, touching its breast to the water, or tripping lightly.

Most wild birds are lovely but some are more gorgeous in their color or pattern, and of these none in Idaho is more conspicuous than the scarlet tanager. Infrequently seen, this handsome fellow, dressed in crimson and black, olive and green, is, like the phantom orchid, all the most impressive for its rareness. The Western species was first seen in Idaho by Lewis and Clark in 1806. In striking contrast is the American raven, rare east of the Mississippi but abundant in the West. It is a large bird, sometimes more than two feet in length, and though often confused with the crow, is larger, has a more beautiful flight, and a blacker luster burnished with purple. Where the raven is plentiful, the crow is seldom found. In sharp contrast again is the ruby-crowned kinglet, a lovely little fellow in yellow and white and gray with a scarlet crown. Its antics when angered or excited are unusually amusing, and its song, a prolonged warble punctuated with wrennish chatter, is excellent.

The black-headed grosbeak, counterpart of the eastern rose-breasted, has black head and wings, a tail marked with white, a burnt-orange breast, and a horn-colored bill. Its song is of bell-like clearness, smooth and mellow, with careful high notes. In Idaho are also the western evening, and the Rocky Mountain pine at higher elevations. In contrast again is the dainty perfection of the western bluebird with its rich azure blue of head and neck, purplish chestnut on the upper back, bluish-gray lower breast, and black bill and feet. It is smaller than the Eastern species and, unlike it, does not sing. Similar in color, but with more green, and with white on the belly, is the mountain bluebird. Exquisite, too, are the hummingbirds with their tiny feet, their quick tempers, and their busy and fearless dispositions. The black-chinned, with its black throat patch, is the nearest Western relative of the ruby-throated. The male in courtship cuts dazzling figure eights above his lady and implores her with long windy whistles. The broad-tailed is larger but in plumage resembles the ruby-throated. The red-backed rufous, commonest in the West, is of cinnamon red; and the calliope, smallest bird in America, is a dainty fellow only three inches long with a bronzed-green back and a lilac throat patch. Hardly less exquisite is the lazuli bunting, a bird only five or six inches in length, with a rich lapis-lazuli head and neck, green-blue uppers, a chestnut-brown breast, and broad white wing bars. The male has a pleasing little song much like that of the Indigo finch and is common in foothills and canyons.

Of the same size is the American redstart, found chiefly in the East but occasionally seen in Idaho. The male is of glossy blue black with white belly and flanks and flame-colored sides and under wings. In folklore it goes under the names of fire-tail and live coals. The Bohemian waxwing is slightly larger, as is the cedar also. The second of these travels in huge flocks throughout the year and is fond of cedar thickets, where it feeds on the berries. This bird is immaculately groomed, with a pronounced crest tapering back and up from the forehead, and with sleek silky feathers. Its song has been compared with the pianissimo of the whistle belonging to an Italian peanut vendor. The kingbird (bee-bird or bee-martin) is of bluish gray with a flaming crown that is seen only when the crest is erect. This fiery fellow, only eight inches in length, is an inveterate enemy of crows, hawks, and owls, all of which it seems to attack for the sheer fun of it. On the other hand, it is routed by the tiny hummingbird. The kingbird, nevertheless, has been known, Myers declares, to drive cats and dogs down the street, pecking them on the back and tail. The yellow-billed cuckoo (rain crow, rain dove, storm crow, chowchow) has a black bill with a yellow under mandible, white-tipped tail feathers, a satiny olive-gray or lilac back touched with iridescent green, and cinnamon rufous wings. His song is a succession of spasmodic gurgles. Very common, and endeared to all who know him, is the Rocky Mountain jay, the most pertly impudent (and yet entirely friendly) bird in the forests. He delights in standing on limbs to watch campers, eyeing them with astonished interest and often coming close for a more thorough scrutiny. In Idaho, too, are found the woodhouse, black-headed, and piñon jays. Bullock's oriole resembles the eastern Baltimore in size and shape but is more prodigal in the orange on its head and neck. Like the Baltimore, it is the finest staccato singer among the birds, and is rivaled in limpid tone only by the thrush. But the Western species is a shy hermit, and his clarion song is not often heard.

Of wild melodists the rock wren, common in most parts of the State, is not least, and is thought by Dawson to have the most sprightly and musical tune of any bird west of the Mississippi. It is about six inches long, and both sexes are of pale brownish gray above with a cinnamon rump and dull white under parts. The canyon wren, also common, has a famous clarion song given in a quick descending scale and ending in a little upward trill. It is brown except for white throat and breast, and is distinguished from the rock wren by its clear cinnamon-brown tail zigzagged with fine black lines. It is, as its name implies, a resident of canyons. The one listed by Myers as the western house wren is apparently the one given by Coues as Parkman's. The male is worthy of note because of his joyful song and his patience: after he has sung and labored over a nest, his spouse comes on the scene and flies at him angrily and rebuilds the nest to suit her fancy; and the male sings almost without pause and clearly without resentment as he watches her work. The common purple finch warbles like a vireo but his throat is larger and his melody fuller. The male house finch has a bubbling gurgling canarylike song that he pours forth at all seasons of the year. When his lady ignores him he sits on a twig above or below her and sings his heart out.

The pale goldfinch, with his black cap and white markings, is peculiar to the Rocky Mountains and is also tirelessly cheerful. His courtship song during short flights is in abandon second only to the bobolink's, but not so sweet in melody as the song sparrow's. As if suspecting that his song is not all that it should be, he will deliver a succession of rapid chirps and then deliver his whole being into a rhapsodic per-chic-o-ree-per-chic-o-ree. The bobolink, a species of marsh blackbird, occurs chiefly in Eastern States and is seen in the West only during migration. The breeding plumage of the male during spring and summer is a flawless black, white, and buff. Later, it lays off its full dress for a homespun brown and becomes the reedbird or ricebird of the South. The bubbling delirious ecstasy of its song is heard only in mating season, for the song changes with the feathers and becomes a monotonous syllable. When mating, the male begins with clear whistles suggestive of waltz time but presently reaches a mad outpouring or irrepressible joy in which the motif explodes and is lost in a burst of melodious fireworks. Of warblers, there are several species in the state, including the orange-crowned, the blue-eyed yellow (wild canary), the Townsend, Audubon's, MacGillivray's, the pileolated, the western yellow-throat, and the black-throated green, all of which are fairly common and sweetly liquid songsters. The elegantly slender western mockingbird, a scold and a mimic, is ash gray above with a shopworn white belly, a black tail, and black wings patched with white. During mating season the males sing night and day, perched high in treetops where they prance along the boughs or leap ecstatically into the air.

But for some, the birds of sweetest song in Idaho are the solitaire, thrush, thrasher, and lark. Townsend's solitaire is a fly-catching thrush that is found only in

the Western States and is a bird of mountain solitudes.
Its strong and beautiful song has about it a freshness and
a clarion quality as deep and mellow as the sound of a
bell. The sage thrasher, too, also found only in Western
States, is a splendid singer; and often long after dark, or
like the mockingbird in moonlight, he pours out his
melody where there are few to hear. This bird can be
recognized by triangular dusky spots on its grayish-
brown plumage, strung in such close series that they look
like chains. The varied thrush is the only representative
of ground thrushes in the Western Hemisphere. Its upper
parts are of slate, its under of orange brown fading to
white. It has a weird and wholly individual song that is
long drawn out with notes in various keys. Of the song
of the famous Audubon's hermit thrush, Coues says:
"Sweet, silvery, bell-like notes which, beginning soft, low,
and tinkling, rise higher and higher, to end abruptly with
a clear ringing intonation." Some have said this is the
sweetest singer on wings. But for those who have lived
long on the Western prairies there is no song so haunting, so invested with all that the prairie means, as that of
the common meadow lark. Years ago its limpid and
varied and mellowed refrain rang from every countryside,
but today it is much less frequently heard, not only because it nests on the ground but also because of thousands
of domestic cats that have been freed to run wild. Ex-
quisitely liquid, too, is the song of the warbling vireo,
which used to be almost as common as the lark.

VII

HUNTING AND FISHING

IDAHO GAME LAWS

The Idaho fish and game license carries a long synopsis of the fish and game laws of the State. Because conditions change from season to season, because areas are opened or closed as game and fish become too abundant or too depleted, no summary given here would be trustworthy six months from now.

Ordinarily there is a long open season on trout in all parts of the State, though many streams now closed may be opened soon, and others now open may be closed. The season on birds is even more variable. Local conditions of many kinds affect the production of wild fowl, and often it is not known until late in the summer what areas will be opened to hunting in the fall, or for how long a season. Less variable are the restrictions placed on big game, though even in regard to elk and deer, goat and sheep and antelope, areas are opened or closed from year to year. Antelope, formerly protected, are now available in the Pahsimeroi Valley, but will not be, of course, as soon as the number has been reduced to the grazing resources.

In general the bag limit on larger animals is one; on fish, from ten to forty pounds per day; and on game birds from four to eight per day. Unlawful ways in either hunting or fishing also vary somewhat from area to area. Inquiry in regard to this as well as all other matters should be made of the game warden in the region chosen.

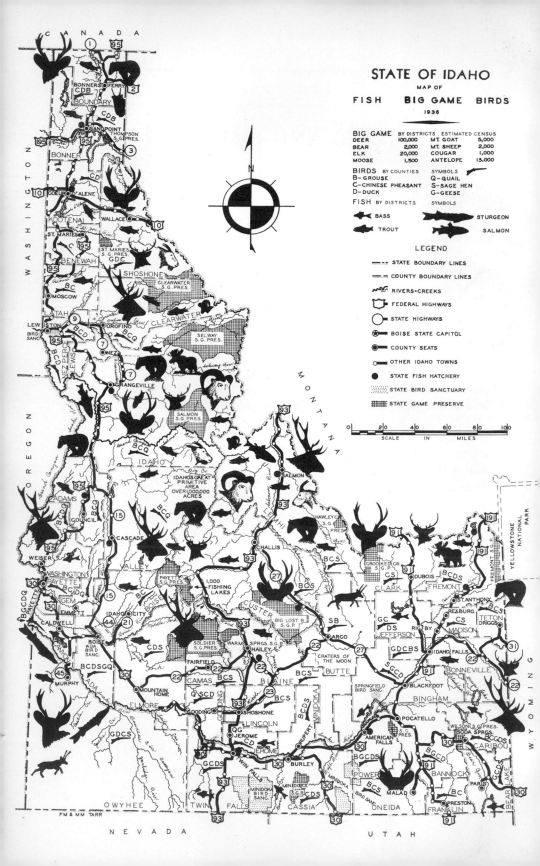

STATE OF IDAHO
MAP OF
FISH BIG GAME BIRDS
1936

BIG GAME BY DISTRICTS ESTIMATED CENSUS

DEER	100,000	MT. GOAT	5,000
BEAR	2,000	MT. SHEEP	2,000
ELK	20,000	COUGAR	1,000
MOOSE	1,500	ANTELOPE	15,000

BIRDS BY COUNTIES SYMBOLS
B - GROUSE Q - QUAIL
C - CHINESE PHEASANT S - SAGE HEN
D - DUCK G - GEESE

FISH BY DISTRICTS SYMBOLS

BASS STURGEON
TROUT SALMON

LEGEND

- ‒‒‒‒ STATE BOUNDARY LINES
- ‒‒‒ COUNTY BOUNDARY LINES
- RIVERS-CREEKS
- FEDERAL HIGHWAYS
- STATE HIGHWAYS
- BOISE STATE CAPITOL
- COUNTY SEATS
- OTHER IDAHO TOWNS
- STATE FISH HATCHERY
- STATE BIRD SANCTUARY
- STATE GAME PRESERVE

SCALE IN MILES
0 20 40 60 80 100

FM & MM TARR

HUNTING AND FISHING

NO STATE in the Union is a more undeveloped natural playground or has more to offer in hunting and fishing and remote primitive areas than Idaho. Most of the State is mountainous, almost half of it lies under forests and game preserves, and all of it except the few cultivated valleys is a huge network of wilderness and lakes and streams. Without the funds of some States, its game and fish department has been severely handicapped in stocking the streams and protecting wild life; but great strides have been made in the last few years, and an ambitious program now could foresee the development of the enormous potential resources. In the Stanley Basin area alone there are approximately one thousand lakes, and at present all but 15 per cent of them are barren; but it is planned to stock all these and barren lakes elsewhere just as rapidly as production can be increased. In parts of the State it is intended to place different species in different lakes so that fishermen can take a weekly trip and fish a different lake and a different kind of trout each day. Old hatcheries are being modernized, new ones are being built, and more determined steps are being taken to exterminate the worst of the predatory birds and beasts. Millions are spent annually now in Idaho on fishing and hunting but the present sum is doubtless only a small part of what will eventually be spent. Idaho's opportunity to become one of the great playgrounds of the Nation is second to no other opportunity facing it today.

A large and constructive program in Idaho at the present time would be especially opportune. All parts of the United States, according to recent articles in the *Saturday Evening Post,* have been largely depleted, particularly in regard to fish, of which for the entire country in 1935 fewer than one hundred millions were put into the lakes and streams. In the same year more than fifteen millions of fishing licenses were sold. This means only six trout to the angler, even if predatory birds and beasts were all exterminated; but as a matter of fact these enemies take more fish from water than the anglers themselves. The annual fish and game turnover in the United States is more than a billion dollars; and that is three times the value of its wheat and five times the value of its sheep. The average value of a domestic sheep in Wyoming, for instance, is five dollars, but this State computes the value of an elk taken by a nonresident hunter at anywhere between five hundred and a thousand dollars. And not only are anglers and huntsmen among men increasing rapidly but women, too, are taking more and more to the rod and gun.

In big game hunting, Idaho is said to have in its Chamberlain Basin and Selway the finest area in the country. In this vast region deer are especially numerous, as well as upon the Middle Fork of the Salmon River and the headwaters of Payette and Boise Rivers and the Kaniksu and Priest River sections in the extreme north. But deer are found in all the National Forests, in some of which they are now protected throughout the year, and are by far the most abundant large animal in the State. Moose are largely confined to the Selway and Lochsa Rivers in the northern part, and to the Island Park area west of Yellowstone. Elk are most numerous in the Clearwater, Selway, Lochsa, and St. Joe Rivers in the north, and in the Chamberlain Basin. There are some on the Boise and Payette Rivers and in the Seven Devils region but these areas are closed. The two great herds of antelope are to be found in the Pahsimeroi Valley and adja-

cent terrain and in the southwest corner of Owyhee
County. In the former there is now a short open season
because of damage to farms and in an effort to scatter the
herd. Mountain goats are found chiefly between the head
of Priest Lake and Canada (this region is now closed), in
the Selway and Lochsa areas, in the Bitterroot Mountains,
and upon the Middle Fork of Salmon River. Mountain
sheep cover much the same range with the exception of
the Priest Lake terrain. Cougar, of which two score or
more are taken annually, affect chiefly the Priest Lake
district, the Selway, and the Middle Fork. In the winter
of 1935-6, twenty-two were taken upon the Payette River.
George Lowe of Kooskia is now the most successful cougar hunter in the State. Bear are fairly numerous in all
the National Forests except those in the extreme south,
though grizzlies are few, with a small number remaining
in the Selway and above Priest Lake. The foregoing are
the principal but by no means the only areas in which the
larger game animals are to be found.

Game Fowl: The chief bird is the Chinese (ringnecked)
pheasant, which is fairly common in nearly all of the valleys. This handsome fellow, invaluable as a destroyer of
insects, is eagerly sought by sportsmen the world over. Its
number is being increased in Idaho. Next in abundance is
blue grouse (Franklin, dusky, gray, pine, or fool hen)
which is found only in the forests. This bird has back and
wings of blackish brown, finely zigzagged with slaty
pencilings, and a yellow comb. It is so indifferent to danger
that it often passes under the colloquial name of fool hen.
Of other grouse in Idaho, the Franklin spruce is often mistaken for the other chiefly because of its stupid foolhardiness, though, too, it is like the other in its coniferous
preferences and in its food. Resembling the blue in appearance is Richardson's but the latter is uniformly darker and has more black on its throat. The pintailed grouse
(prairie chicken, native pheasant) is rapidly disappearing
along with the sage hen, the chief enemies of which are
sheep and coyotes. The sage hen, however, can still be

found in huge flocks in parts of the State, especially in
eastern Idaho. This bird, largest of the American grouse
family, mates in springtime with stentorian hullaballoo,
walks with an absurdly cocky gait, and flies with swift
energetic wingbeats or coasts down the wind. Formerly
on the Western prairies it was numbered in millions. The
quail or bobwhite is increasing in the State and is now
fairly numerous in the western counties and in Nez Perce
and Clearwater Counties up north. The Hungarian partridge, more widely distributed, seems likely to hold its
own against hunters, inasmuch as it is easily flushed and
gets away with astonishing speed.

The State has tens of thousands of wild ducks, many
of which do not migrate, and among which the mallard
is commonest. This handsome bird, easily recognized
by anyone who knows ducks at all, is the wild parent of
the barnyard fowl. It is a valuable bird, not only for
game, especially after a season in the grain fields, but
for its destruction of insects as well. The green-winged
teal is distinguished by a rich chestnut head and upper
neck, broken by a glistening green patch behind either
eye. The green-winged, only a migrant here, has a
black-bordered white crescent in front of either eye, and
wing coverts and outer webs of some of the scapular
feathers of sky blue. The cinnamon, a South American
bird, has a black bill, a mauve-chestnut head, neck, and
under parts, darkening to black on the belly. Teals are
common in Idaho. Barrow's goldeneye has a pansy-pur-
ple sheen on his head which lengthens to a fringed crest.
The white spots in front of each eye the triangular in this
species, circular in the American golden. This duck is a
wide ranger.

The well-known canvasback has a reddish-brown head
and neck, black crown and chin, and a silvery back. Of
this famous table delicacy, Coues says there "is little
reason to squeal in barbaric joy over this overrated and
generally underdone bird; for not one person in ten thousand can tell it from any other duck on the table" unless

Hunting is good in Idaho

The limit: cutthroat and rainbow

Snake River sturgeon

it has been fattened on celery. The redhead, in fact, is
often sold for it in the East, a bird smaller but very similar in appearance, and hardly distinguishable in flavor.
This is chiefly a bay or sea duck, though often found inland upon lakes. The male of the shoveller (spoonbill) is
a jaunty fellow in mating season with a metallic green
head much like the mallard's, an amethyst abdomen and
a white breast; but after wooing he sheds his gay clothes
and looks much like his wife. He is easily identified by
his spatulate bill. The ring-necked scaup, first discovered
by Lewis and Clark in 1806, has a lustrous iridescent
head above its collar, and lower belly and sides finely
waved in black. The lesser (or common winter) scaup is,
like its cousin, the greater, a sea duck but prefers fresh
lakes and has gone as far inland as the Dakotas. The
flesh of these scaups is as offensive as their horrible cry;
and so is that of the merganser, one of the worst enemies
of fish. It has a head and neck of burnished mallard
green, white under parts tinged with salmon, and a shining black upper part, graying to ash on the rump and tail.
Known in Idaho as the common fish duck, and unfortunately common, this vandal, fishermen declare, ought to be exterminated. And with it ought to go the ruddy duck, a bird
that has survived enough preposterous names to produce
a civil war: it has been called dumpling, deaf, fool, sleepy,
butter-bowl, blather-scoot, spine-tail, dopper, mud-dipper,
paddy-whack, stub-and-twist, and both dinkey and dickey.
Belonging to the ducks with stiff tail feathers, its upper
parts are a rich rufous chestnut, with white sides, silken
white under parts, and a black patch on its head. It is an
expert underwater bird with the skill of the cormorant
in using its rudder. The bufflehead is a small fellow, related to but distinguishable from the goldeneye by the
broad snowy patches behind each eye, running to the
back of the head and uniting in a nape. The head is an
iridescent splendor of violet-purple and green. This duck,
also a survival of a score of names (butter duck, butter-
ball, woolhead, conjuring duck, spirit duck, butterback),

has no peer as an expert diver, and vanishes like lightning at the spit of a gun. The pintail has also suffered outrage. Known variously as sprigtail, piketail, peaktail, spindletail, litetail, splittail, it ranges widely and is numerous. The male has a dark sepia head, a neck glossed with green and purple and adorned below with a white and above with a black stripe, and long black feathers in the center of the tail. The wood duck has almost been shot out of existence. The male's plumage is almost spectacular in its range of colors, with green, purple, and violet on the head, snowy white embroidery on the wings, and a voluptuously lustered black-and-bronzed purple and green on the back.

Those are among the chief species that come to Idaho in thousands. The principal spot which they affect is Lake Lowell, where often they form a margin of color many feet wide for miles; but they are also abundant on the lakes of northern Idaho and particularly in the Hoodoo region; on the lakes in southeastern Idaho, chiefly Grays and Mud Lakes; and upon Snake River from Milner to the Oregon line. In wintertime the ducks on this river customarily average fifteen hundred to the mile. Geese are not so common by any means but are increasing. The black brant, distinguished by its clean white collar, open only at the back of the neck, and the darker under parts, is abundant on the west coast and more and more frequently comes inland. The Canada, the common wild goose and the best known in North America, has become famous for its V-formation in flight and for its honk. The head and neck are black with a broad white throat strap. This is the commonest species in Idaho. Ross's snow goose, all white and only about as large as a mallard duck, and the lesser snow goose, a little larger, and the greater snow goose with its white plumage stained brown on its head, are all seen, but not commonly, in migration.

Fish: To say that fishing in Idaho or anywhere else in the United States is excellent upon those streams easily reached by highway would probably be a gross misrepresentation. Fishing here, as elsewhere, ranges from depleted streams to streams that are heavily stocked and rarely visited. Expert anglers can catch their limit nearly anywhere in the State, but the less skilled must expect to travel the unimproved highways or take mountain trails to spots where trout are both abundant and foolish, and not fastidious about their food. Such streams and such lakes number hundreds in nearly all of the more mountainous areas.

The commonest trout in the State is the rainbow, which is distinguished (if at all) from the steelhead by its smaller size, its brighter coloring, and its larger scales. It takes a fly so readily that there is no need to pursue grasshoppers over the hillsides or to buy fanciful and deceptive gadgets; and it is so gamey that it will satisfy the most exacting angler. Its simple-witted indifference to a hook and line make of it delightfully easy prey for the inexperienced greenhorn. Its flesh is excellent. The rainbow is widely distributed but is especially common from Big Springs to the Oregon line in Snake River; in Big and Little Lost Rivers; in Silver Creek out from Hailey, noted for its fly fishing; in Salmon River and in Williams Lake near Salmon City; in Boise River and all its tributaries; in the Payette River and Lakes and in the whole Payette district; and in the Clearwater, St. Joe, and Coeur d'Alene Rivers in the north.

Second in abundance is the cutthroat or native trout. In color it is of a silvery olivaceous, deepening to dark steel, with the upper part of the side and the caudal peduncle covered with round black spots, with under parts silvery white, and with red blotches of the lower jaw usually constant. In general it is to be found in nearly all of the rivers and streams but more notably in Snake River; in Henrys Lake which for its size contains more fish than any other body of water in the State; in all branches of the Salmon River but particularly in the Middle Fork; in the higher tributaries of the Boise and

Payette Rivers; in the St. Joe and Clark Fork Rivers; and in Coeur d'Alene, Pend Oreille, and Priest Lakes and all their feeders.

The eastern brook or speckled trout is third, the fish most in demand by Eastern anglers. This fish likes quiet waters and is at its best in high mountain lakes. It takes a fly readily and is a vigorous if not spectacular fighter; and if taken from cold water its flesh is excellent, though owing to its large amount of oil it does not remain firm as long as the meat of other trout. In Idaho it is to be found chiefly in Buffalo River and in a private pond there which contains some extremely large specimens; near Big Springs, though this is not a brook-trout area; in the Sawtooth region and especially in Redfish and other lakes; in the higher lakes of the Grangeville district; in a few tributary streams and in the higher lakes in the Clearwater area; and from Coeur d'Alene northward, wherein is the heaviest planting in both lakes and streams. This is a more cannibalistic trout than either rainbow or cutthroat and does not in Idaho enjoy the same esteem.

Fourth in abundance is the Dolly Varden or bull trout, a voracious and cannibalistic lout that is not reared in Idaho hatcheries and is not introduced into any of the barren lakes that are being stocked. Its flesh is not so good as that of other trout, it is an erratic and annoying feeder that often scorns even salmon eggs, its favorite bait, and it raises havoc with salmon spawning. It is a native to nearly all the mountain streams and to many of the lakes.

Probably next in order are bass, catfish, and perch. The first is found in the warmer waters of the Boise Valley and westward, especially in Lake Lowell, where bass spearing is a favorite sport; in Snake River along the Owyhee Range; and in practically all the larger northern lakes. The catfish is found in Snake River from Swan Falls to Weiser; in Lake Lowell; in the Crane Creek Reservoir; in various sloughs in the Boise-Weiser area; and in a few lakes and streams near Coeur d'Alene. The perch is found in the American Falls and Minidoka and Magic Reservoirs; in Lake Lowell; in Snake River from Crane Falls to Payette; in the Lost Valley Reservoir near Tamarack; in the Payette Lakes; and in the Hayden, Black, Cocolalla, Coeur d'Alene, and other lakes in the north. Bass, catfish, and perch are dead-water fish.

At the other extreme is the steelhead, in regard to which in Idaho there is tall argument. Some say that this fish is nothing but a seagoing rainbow, and others say it is not a rainbow at all. In any case, it is migratory in habit, going to the ocean after it has grown to adolescence in fresh-water streams or lakes, and returning later to spawn. It comes from the sea to Idaho between December and early spring, and is taken by fly or by bait or spinner or with spear. It is the gamiest of native trout, and the flesh, when not out of condition from spawning, is excellent. The largest one ever taken on a rod weighed twenty-two pounds, but a steelhead of that size is rare. This fish in Idaho is found chiefly in the Salmon River and its branches, where it is sometimes known as salmon trout; in Weiser River; and in the Clearwater River, which has the greatest run. The steelheads taken in Idaho are usually yearlings, about seven to ten inches in length, before they have gone to the sea.

Several species of salmon spawn in Idaho, but no attempt has been made to commercialize them, and they are rarely taken except by spear. The chinook is the largest and most important of all the Pacific species, and this one comes to the Salmon River and its tributaries, arriving in early fall. The offspring remain about a year and then return to the ocean, where they stay for from four to seven years before they seek fresh water to spawn and die. In this State those speared do not often exceed twenty pounds in weight, though some have been taken that weighed more than fifty. The big redfish or sockeye salmon formerly spawned in the Payette and Redfish Lakes areas but is unable to reach them now. It does still come to the lower Payette waters, and may be found

below Sunbeam Dam. The landlocked species is a fresh-
water fish and does not thrive in the absence of fresh-
water smelt, which is its chief food. The Schoodic salmon
from eastern Maine has been planted in Payette Lakes and
in several lakes in the Sawtooth area. It is a game fish
of excellent flesh, and many anglers rate it as a fighter
above any species of trout.

From an entirely commercial point of view, the most
important fish in the State is a species of Rocky Mountain
whitefish in the larger northern lakes. This fish smoked
is in great demand. Several hundred families are now
almost entirely supported by this small industry, which
promises to grow considerably, inasmuch as the State
hatcheries plan soon to put not twelve but seventy millions annually into these lakes. Fisherman are compelled
to fish for these and not use a net, and are at present
limited to a daily catch of fifty pounds. In Bear Lake
there are said to be three species of whitefish peculiar
to it.

Of other fish in the State, a few are worthy of mention. The Loch Leven, said to be peculiar to the Scotch
lake of the same name, has been confused with the brown
or Von Behr trout, and in the United States there has
been much hybridizing of the two. Loch Leven occurs in
Idaho in such waters as the upper reaches of the South
Fork of the Snake, and in Montana in the Madison River.
In Lake Waha twenty-two miles south of Lewiston, and
apparently found nowhere in the world except here, is a
curious and interesting trout which in quality of meat is
said to be unsurpassed. This lake has no outlet. In Snake
River, along Owyhee County especially, sturgeon are
abundant, and sturgeon fishing in Idaho is one of the most
exciting sports. Specimens have been taken that weighed
almost a thousand pounds, but the average runs to no more
than a fraction of that weight. In Bloomington Lake in
southeastern Idaho and in Trinity Lakes on the South Fork
of Boise River, California golden trout have been planted.
It is planned to add this rare species to other waters.

VIII

RESOURCES AND PRODUCTS

RESOURCES AND PRODUCTS

I DAHO'S resources are to be found in its minerals (both ferrous and nonferrous), in its forests, in its water, both for power and irrigation, and in its land. In addition to these, it has vast wealth, for the most part unexploited, in its wild life and in its potential playground. The two latter are discussed in other chapters.

Land: Measured in production in terms of dollars, agriculture (including dairying) is first, livestock is second, timber is third, and minerals are fourth among the State's industries. Of 53,960,000 acres, 39 per cent is forested, 36 per cent is primarily grazing, and less than 8 per cent is cultivated. Of the total, 36 per cent is within National Forests; 21 per cent is public domain; 6 per cent is owned by the State; 1 per cent is in Indian reservations; 10 per cent is unsold land withdrawn for reclamation projects, parks, and game preserves; and the remaining 26 per cent is in private hands. Of that under grazing, nearly all is indefinitely beyond reclamation or other than grazing uses. Of the Indian lands, 57,000 acres remain unallotted. Of the less than 8 per cent under cultivation, a little more than half is irrigated, and the remainder is dry grainlands chiefly, though there are areas in northern Idaho with diversified crops where rainfall is ample. Of the forested areas, a considerable part is now logged off or burnt over or otherwise denuded, and most of it is valueless save for reforesting. Of the unirrigated acreage under grain, a good deal suffers crop losses for

want of rain, and within recent years many of these
farms have been abandoned to the weeds. Much of the
36 per cent which is used primarily for grazing has been
overfed and needs careful restoration. Of the total area,
there is said to be more than a million acres with ownership unaccounted for.[1]

Water Power: Closely related to land in this State are,
of course, the resources in water, most of which remain undeveloped. Aside from its thousands of fresh lakes, Idaho
has scores of rivers, and countless large creeks, many of
which are of major importance in both length and volume.
Of greatest value, both available and potential, is Snake
River with its many tributaries. Both the Salmon and the
Clearwater Rivers have huge possibilities in power but are
inaccessible to irrigation save in small basins. The water
in the northern part of the State, both rivers and lakes, is
chiefly of value for transportation and power, inasmuch
as rainfall there makes irrigation largely unnecessary.
The southern part of the State, on the other hand, has not,
for all its streams, enough water for its use. Plans are
afoot to divert rivers out of Montana and Wyoming and
possibly to bring the lower flow of Snake River into the
Boise Valley; and the Bruneau Project promises to turn
the arid region east of Boise into a garden. But at
present, Payette Valley is the only part of Idaho south
of the Salmon River that has enough water for its need.
Elsewhere, it is true, there is enough water to irrigate
more land than is now under cultivation if that water
were all delivered to reservoirs and then wisely apportioned and used. Reclamation in Idaho has been largely
experimental, and in most instances too sectional, and in
consequence rival interests have seriously vitiated efforts
that have been made. The Snake River Valley itself
should be one enormous reclamation project with the
various units subserving one another downstream and
with all of them integrated into a related pattern.

---

[1] University of Idaho Agricultural Experiment Station, *Bulletin
207.*

Though the State's distance from markets places indefinitely in the future any development of large power sites, this chapter would be incomplete without a summary of the possibilities. There are at present more than sixty hydroelectric plants powered by natural falls in the rivers or by falls made by the reclamation dams. These together develop about 292,000 horsepower in comparison with the 2,704,000 horsepower that remain untouched. Snake River itself has a greater annual flow than either the Colorado or the Rio Grande and has a drainage basin ninth in size in the United States. If all its water could be used, it would irrigate four million acres of land and develop three million horsepower. Nearly 70 per cent of the irrigable land within its basin has been supplied with water, but only 7 per cent of its water power has been put to use. A few of its more important unexploited power sites now follow.

Below the mouth of the Salmon River the absolute minimum flow is 7,000 second-feet, and this has in floodtime reached 130,000 second-feet. A flood of 300,000 second-feet is not by any means impossible downstream from its confluence with the Salmon. The only developed plant on the Snake between Weiser and Lewiston is at Ox Bow where an average of 1,800 kilowatts is produced. During this stretch between the two cities the flow is well sustained, the gradient is steep, the gorge is in most places comparatively narrow, and the rock formation would apparently support a dam of almost any height. Some fifteen sites in this canyon and in canyons adjacent have been investigated; and one alone, involving a combination of the Snake and Salmon waters and a fall of 540 feet, would, on the basis of 50 per cent of the time, develop almost a million horsepower. The fifteen sites, varying in estimated power from 18,000 to 910,000, are all within 104 miles. But development here must await a great industrialization of the Pacific Coast.

North of these sites is the Clark Fork of the Columbia, which doubles back, just south of the Canadian boundary, into a Z-canyon where the river almost literally turns upon its edge and pours through a gorge only eighteen feet wide. This river rises in the Silver Bow Mountains about eighteen miles southwest of Butte, Montana, and is fed by more than a hundred tributaries before it crosses Idaho. It has many falls, and often passes through boxed canyons so narrow that they can be spanned by footlogs. It drops nearly five hundred feet in the last fifty miles of its course. In addition to all these circumstances that favor power sites is the fact that its flow on entering Idaho is almost two thirds that of the Snake in its journey through the Seven Devils Canyon.

Upon the Snake and its tributaries in Wyoming, Idaho, Oregon, and Washington, there are 284 sites that have been listed, 249 of which are in Idaho. The latter have a potential production of 2,974,630 horsepower. These sites are scattered along the Snake and the chief streams that feed it, notably the Salmon, and are to be found at the natural waterfalls, which are many, or at the boxed canyons where dams are feasible. There are even power possibilities at some of the springs which burst from mountainsides. Most remarkable, and potentially most valuable, are those between Milner and King Hill. But Idaho's power, like much of its mineral wealth, belongs for the most part to the remote future.

Livestock: In the early days of its settlement, Idaho was a huge cattle ranch with enormous prairies rich in natural feed. It still has millions of acres under grazing, and livestock is still second in size of its industries; but the State's future here is not, save for the indefatigable optimists, unusually bright. All of the areas have been overgrazed including those in National Forests, and some of them have been temporarily destroyed. Wild grasses cannot be fed off year after year without reseeding, and some of them cannot be cropped closely in drouth years without being killed. This is especially true when areas are grazed by sheep. Efforts are being made at the present time to find a hardier grass that will stand both

Power plant at Moyie Falls

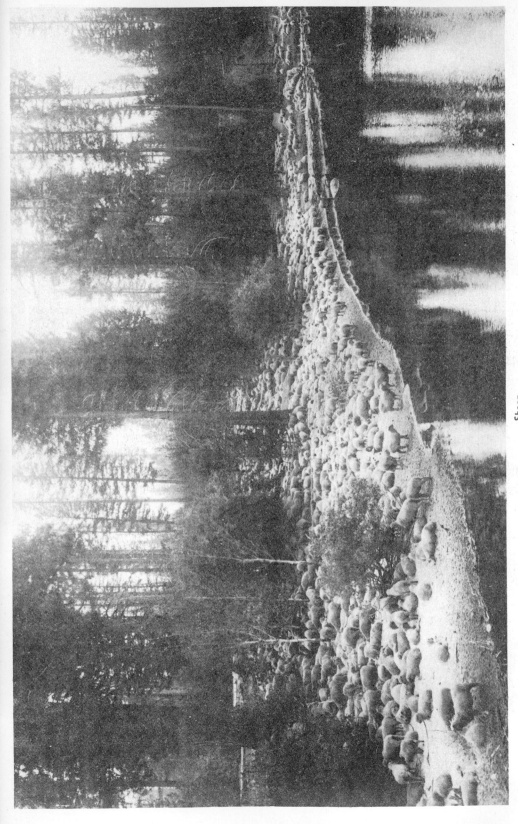

Sheep

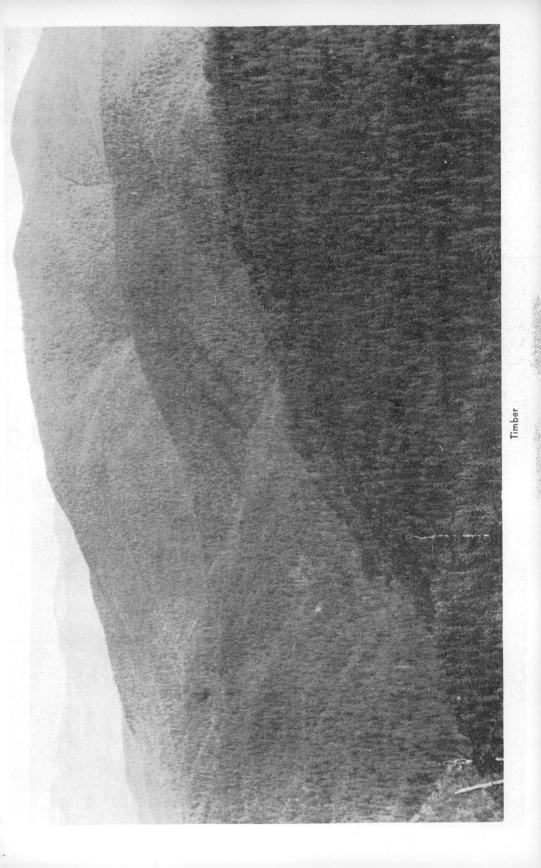

Timber

Sluicing logs

Trainload of logs

aridity and punishment, and in the crested wheat grass it is possible that one has been found. But even so, it would take many years to restore lands to their former luxuriance, and meanwhile the problem of grazing becomes increasingly acute.

Timber: The production of lumber has steadily moved westward, and within another two decades the Rocky Mountain and Pacific States will doubtless be producing the major part of the lumber supply of the United States. Maine, New York, and Pennsylvania, once famous for the amount and quality of their lumber, now produce less combined than Idaho. In 1870 the Northeastern States supplied 38 per cent of the Nation's output: today that circumstance is almost exactly reversed. But Idaho has little to boast of in regard to the intelligence with which it has protected its forested wealth. Only forty years ago nearly all of its timbered acres were public domain, but today the State owns only about a million acres, with the consequence that by 1910 ten persons owned a large part of the State's forests—more than four million acres of the best. "As a general proposition, it can be stated that the most accessible timber is very largely privately owned."[1]

Almost half of Idaho lies within forested areas. About a million acres are owned by the State, about four million by private interests, and about nineteen million by the Federal Government. Of standing timber, 8.8 per cent is owned by the State, 30.3 per cent by persons, and 60.9 per cent by the Federal Government. Of that within National Forests, about half must be classed "as indefinitely or permanently inaccessible." Within national forests, Idaho has a larger area than any other State in the Union, with California second and Montana third.

The State is estimated to have about 81 billions of feet of old-growth timber. Of this, more than three fourths is found in the Panhandle, lying between the Salmon River

---

[1] *Idaho Forest and Timber Handbook.*

and the Canadian boundary. More than 10 million of the
13 million acres in northern Idaho lie under timber.
Of the commercially valuable trees, western white pine,
17 per cent of the total stand, is first. This tree is found
only in the northern part. Western yellow pine, more
widely distributed, is next in commercial value, and is
about 20 per cent of the stand, and Douglas fir, which,
together with larch, is 28 per cent of the growth, is third.
The remaining 35 per cent is chiefly lodgepole, white and
alpine fir, Engelmann spruce, juniper, hemlock, and white
bark pine.

Though a part of the State's resources in timber is
perhaps permanently inaccessible and though a more considerable part must remain beyond reach for a long time
to come, the lumber industry is of almost indispensable
value to the State and especially to certain sections in
the north. It is most unfortunate, therefore, that millions
of acres in private hands are being denuded and sold as
logged-off lands, because these depleted regions are for
the most part valueless as agricultural land not only on
account of a too-acid soil but also because most of the
areas are too mountainous. "The best available information at hand would indicate that all told probably not more
than a million acres of additional land can be developed
out of the forest areas in North Idaho."[1] Nor is that all:
these denuded and valueless areas offer extremely difficult problems because of soil erosion and the destruction
of watersheds. "If all the forest lands of the State were
under high-class management, the lumber industry could
not only be sustained in its present volume, but could
doubtless be appreciably increased."[2] At the present rate
of depletion, the private stands will be exhausted within
thirty years, and the more valuable species long before
that. In addition to the exhaustion by private interests,
huge losses are delivered from fire and insects, and these
ravages are sometimes of epidemic proportions. Fire and

[1] *Idaho Forest and Timber Handbook.*
[2] *Ibid.*

insects may eventually be controlled. The reforestation of barren lands must depend on Idaho vision and initiative, and especially on the leadership in towns that will take their place among the ghosts if the industry which chiefly supports them is not to be sustained.

The annual lumber cut in the State is about a billion board feet, of which the two pines furnish about 68 per cent and the larch and Douglas fir about 21 per cent. There are about three hundred mills, but 93 per cent of the lumber is sawed by twenty-seven, of which the one at Lewiston is at present perhaps the second largest in the world. Besides lumber, rough and finished, the production is heavy in mine timbers and ties, lath, and shingles.

Minerals: Idaho is twelfth in production of minerals with an annual output of more than thirty millions of dollars, falling chiefly on lead, silver, gold, zinc, and copper in the order as given. The approximate total value of the metals mined in the State since 1860 is $1,300,000,000. Its mineral resources cover a wide range: it has fifteen metallic and twenty-three nonmetallic minerals which occur in quantities sufficient to be regarded as exploitable assets, and these are to be found in thirty-five of the forty-four counties. If valuable clays are included, then possibly every county in the State possesses substantial mineral wealth.[1]

The production of minerals in Idaho has in all sectors except the Coeur d'Alene been governed primarily by the discovery of ore and only secondarily by such factors as price and demand. In most areas the quantity of workable ore found in any one productive period has been small, and at present only silver and lead of the ferrous minerals are of importance or seem likely to be in the immediate future. The richest area at present is the Coeur d'Alene in Shoshone County far up in the Panhandle. The deposits here are found in a comparatively small region in the drainage basin of the South Fork of

---

[1] Rush J. White, *The Mineral Resources of Idaho.*

the Coeur d'Alene River. The ores are fine grained and intimately mixed, and about forty-five species have been recognized. Lead and silver have been increasingly productive; and though copper here at one time yielded huge revenues, it is now only a minor product from the silver-lead ores. Recently, large zinc mines have been opened, and this metal promises to be of considerable importance. Lemhi County is known to have large deposits of valuable ores, but the nearest railway station is far distant from many of these. Idaho County in the lower part of the Panhandle, Valley County just south of it, and Owyhee County in the extreme southwestern part of the State are known to be very rich in minerals. All of these, however, are far removed from railway and truck lines, and exploitation will be indefinitely delayed.

Gold is found in most of the counties and is one of the most widely distributed of the metals. Idaho now ranks only seventh in gold production because during the War many of its mines were closed and have not been reopened. In the Clearwater Mountains of northern Idaho, placer mining has yielded about fifty millions of dollars, and prospects here are favorable to future production in large-scale operation of low-grade deposits. Near here, in the Orofino district, gold is found in veins, but has not been developed because of the uncertainty in regard to geologic shifts. Near Florence there are at least seven gold veins of importance, but want of transportation has delayed development. And elsewhere in the State rich veins are known or suspected, but gold mining save as a by-product will have to wait on transportation and a more definite knowledge of the geology of the underlying regions. This is especially true of the Middle Fork of the Salmon River area, which some mining specialists have declared to be probably the greatest potential undeveloped gold area in the world.

Idaho ranked first in production of silver in the United States in 1934, and the largest producer of silver in the Nation today is the Sunshine Mine in Shoshone County.

Panning for gold

Idaho's big potatoes .

A row of onions

A lettuce patch

This is the richest area, but there are others of unusual promise. The Alturas Quadrangle on the western slope of the Sawtooth Range needs further investigation by geologists and engineers. Large deposits, and especially of low-grade ore, are believed to lie in the Vienna District in the Sawtooth National Forest.

In production of lead, Idaho ranks next to Missouri and turns out one fourth of the total in the United States. Its annual output is about three hundred million pounds, or approximately enough for the automobile industry in an average year. In Shoshone County are the three largest individual lead mines in the country: the Bunker Hill and Sullivan, the Morning, and the Hecla. Most of the unexploited lead deposits are in the Panhandle, though in Lemhi County there are large veins which show evidence of continuity, and there may be valuable deposits in the southeastern corner of the State.

Idaho now ranks about tenth in production of copper, but huge untouched deposits suggest that within the State this metal may increase in importance. Most of the copper ore here is relatively rich in gold or silver or both, and in some instances, notably in Custer and Bonner Counties, the silver content exceeds that of the copper in value. Because of the surplus now on the world's market, most of the copper mines in Idaho are idle. Chief producer is Copper Giant in the Panhandle on the south slope of Howie Mountain, and the principal untouched deposits seem to be in the Seven Devils area. This area runs for a hundred and twenty miles and varies in width from two to forty; and copper lies throughout. The development of this region is remote.

The chief coal deposits seem to be in the Teton Basin of eastern Idaho. The chemical analysis of the coal here reveals it to be equal in quality to that mined and shipped into the State from Utah and Wyoming, but geologic faults have discouraged operations. Bituminous coal of commercial importance has also been found in Bonneville, Fremont, and Clark Counties. Boise and Owyhee Counties have beds of low-grade lignite, but except for a little trucking out to local markets, no attempt has been made to exploit coal in Idaho.

Idaho's greatest mineral wealth probably lies in its enormous deposits of phosphate rock in eastern and southeastern areas. The reserves here are greater than those known to exist in any other part of the world. They underlie 268,000 acres and constitute 85 per cent of the phosphate wealth of the United States. The beds in Idaho and Utah, Wyoming and Montana, all contiguous, are estimated to exceed six billions of tons of high-grade deposit, of which five sixths are in Idaho. The only exploiter at the present time of any importance is the Anaconda Copper Mining Company, which ships the raw rock to Montana and treats it with sulphuric acid and sells the finished product at a price which is prohibitive to nearly all farmers. At the present mine price for the rock, Idaho has more wealth in its phosphate beds than in all the other minerals produced in the State during the last seventy years, multiplied by ten. Development here will have to wait on the exhaustion of beds in Florida and Tennessee, but meanwhile the State's leadership has been urged to move in every possible way to protect its interest in these fields.

There are huge limestone, sandstone, and shale deposits in Bannock County which are being used in the manufacture of cement. Near Boise there is an almost incalculable reserve in sandstone of a quality unusually well adapted to quarrying and building, and in the six western counties are vast beds of diatomaceous earth, valuable in the manufacture of brick and insulation. Various parts of the State are rich in clays of decomposed granitic stone, and in the Clearwater area are the finest fire clays in the West. Extensive asbestos deposits are found in Idaho County; graphite in commercial quantities is known to exist, notably in Blaine County; and in northern Idaho County, talc is found in significant abundance. All of these, like the salt beds in southeastern Idaho, remain undeveloped because of prohibitive freight rates. Idaho also has deposits of antimony, arsenic, tungsten, cobalt, and nickel, and some of the highest-grade deposits of barytes west of the Mississippi. There are deposits of feldspar in northern Idaho, of monazite in the southwest, and of sulphur in the southeast. In central Idaho on Meadow Creek, the red cinnabar is so abundant that over a fairly large area any shovelful of earth will yield mercury, but the deposits are low-grade and not commercially profitable at this time. Bentonite occurs in exploitable quantities in southeastern Idaho, and various bodies of iron ore remain untouched.

Although structures occur which presumably would be satisfactory, sedimentary formations are practically all of nonmarine origin, and there are no authentic instances in which petroleum has been found in fresh-water formations. The outlook, on the whole, for commercial bodies of petroleum in Idaho seems to be unfavorable, though there has been considerable drilling near Driggs and near Weiser. In the latter vicinity, a little gas was found but no oil.

Gems: Semiprecious stones, often of unusual quality, are to be found in nearly all parts of the State. Agate, jasper, and opal, as well as agatized and opalized woods, are in the lava flows of the southern part; sapphires, rubies, and garnets are in the central and western parts; and beautiful opals of gem fineness are in the Columbia lavas of the north.

Jasper, often closely resembling bloodstone, and ranging in color through green, red, and purple, is to be had in Ada County within a half mile of Boise. The western part of Owyhee County yields jasper of similar quality together with agates of all types and colors. In this county, too, are rich two-toned green quartz plasma, fine clear rock crystals, and agatized wood; but this area has been chiefly one of opals. In 1893 from one opal mine were taken seven thousand carats in the rough, and the ragged hills upon Snake River are still a favorite with opal

hunters. In Gem County, appropriately named, are lovely
fire opals in the lava of Squaw Butte about five miles east
of Emmett. Close by these are water agates of pale blue.
On Willow Creek, about halfway between Boise and Emmett, is a deposit of agatized and opalized wood of excellent quality, and farther up the creek opal varying in
color from deep red through salmon pink to white out-
crops over an area of approximately thirty acres.

In Washington County are agates of many colors,
some of which when cut into thin layers show a rainbow
iridescence. On Mann Creek, northeast of Weiser, is a
deposit of silicified wood of bright yellow color that resembles natural oak. It is extremely hard and free from
flaws, and takes a beautiful luster under polishing. Adams
County has sapphires, a few rubies, and many fine pink
garnets in the area of Rock Flat near New Meadows.
Flawless blood-red rubies have been found here which
weighed two carats after they were cut and polished. The
garnets here are chiefly pink, but some either green or
deep red have been found in the Seven Devils region westward. Over in the center of Idaho between the Salmon
and Lost Rivers is a gem hunter's paradise. At many
places in the upper Lost River Valley transparent quartz
crystals seam the geodes which have weathered out of the
lava. Scattered over the whole area are agates of every
kind known; and red, yellow, or green jasper is abundant.
Near the East Fork of the Salmon is a beautiful variety
of quartz in alternate layers of blood-red sard and white-
and-brown onyx. Near Challis is a deposit of rich black
limestone containing coral that takes a high white polish.
South of Challis are said to be the best specimens of
mordenite known.

And these summarized here are only some of the
larger gem fields. There is amethyst near Hailey; opals
and opalized wood in Lincoln and Gooding Counties; fire
opal near Moscow in Latah County; and the large White
Bird fossil deposit in Idaho County in which maple leaves
fourteen inches in diameter have been found. Persons in-

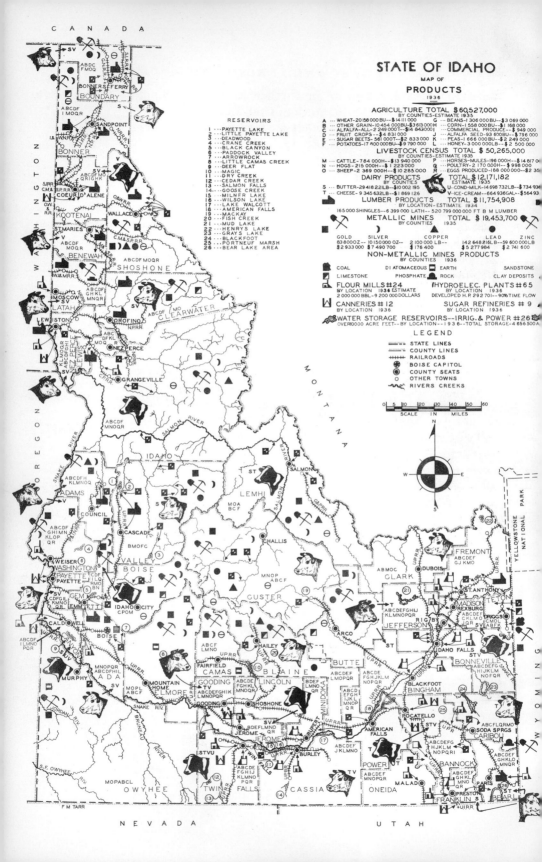

STATE OF IDAHO
MAP OF
PRODUCTS
1936

AGRICULTURE TOTAL $60,527,000
BY COUNTIES-ESTIMATE 1935

A...WHEAT-20,156,000 BU--$14,111,000
B...OTHER GRAIN-10,454,000 BU-$3,613,000
C...ALFALFA-ALL-2,249,000 T--$14,843,000
D...FRUIT CROPS --$4,831,000
E...SUGAR BEETS-561,000 T--$2,833,000
F...POTATOES-17,800,000 BU--$9,790,000

G...BEANS-1,306,000 BU--$3,069,000
H...CORN-1,558,000 BU--$1,168,000
I...COMMERCIAL PRODUCE--$ 949,000
J...ALFALFA SEED-93,600 BU--$ 796,000
K...PEAS-1,666,000 BU--$ 2,249,000
L...HONEY-3,000,000 LB--$ 2,500,000

LIVESTOCK CENSUS TOTAL $ 50,265,000
BY COUNTIES-ESTIMATE 1935

M...CATTLE-784,000 H--$13,940,000
N...HOGS-215,000 H--$ 1,223,000
O...SHEEP-2,369,000 H--$10,285,000

P...HORSES-MULES-196,000 H--$14,817,000
Q...POULTRY-2,170,000 H--$ 998,000
R...EGGS PRODUCED-188,000,000--$2,350,000

DAIRY PRODUCTS TOTAL $ 12,171,182
BY COUNTIES

S...BUTTER-29,418,221 LB--$10,002,195
T...CHEESE- 9,345,632 LB--$1,869,126

U-COND-MILK-14,698,732 LB--$ 734,936
V-ICE-CREAM--664,936 GAL--$ 564,93

LUMBER PRODUCTS TOTAL $11,754,908
BY LOCATION-ESTIMATE 1934

165,000 SHINGLES---6,399,000 LATH-- 520,799,000,000 FT B M LUMBER

METALLIC MINES TOTAL $19,453,700
BY COUNTIES 1935

GOLD	SILVER	COPPER	LEAD	ZINC
83,800 OZ--	10,150,000 OZ--	2,100,000 LB--	142,648,216 LB--	59,600,000 LB
$2,933,000	$7,490,700	$176,400	$5,277,984	$2,741,600

NON-METALLIC MINES PRODUCTS
BY COUNTIES 1936

COAL   DIATOMACEOUS EARTH   SANDSTONE

LIMESTONE   PHOSPHATE ROCK   CLAY DEPOSITS

FLOUR MILLS #24
BY LOCATION 1936 ESTIMATE
2,000,000 BBL--9,200,000 DOLLARS

HYDROELEC. PLANTS #65
BY LOCATION 1936
DEVELOPED H.P. 292,701--90% TIME FLOW

CANNERIES # 12
BY LOCATION 1936

SUGAR REFINERIES # 9
BY LOCATION 1936

WATER STORAGE RESERVOIRS--IRRIG. & POWER #26
OVER 10,000 ACRE FEET--BY LOCATION--1936--TOTAL STORAGE-4,656,500 A.

LEGEND

STATE LINES
COUNTY LINES
RAILROADS
BOISE CAPITOL
COUNTY SEATS
OTHER TOWNS
RIVERS CREEKS

RESERVOIRS

1 ---PAYETTE LAKE
2 ---LITTLE PAYETTE LAKE
3 ---DEADWOOD
4 ---CRANE CREEK
5 ---BLACK CANYON
6 ---PADDOCK VALLEY
7 ---ARROWROCK
8 ---LITTLE CAMAS CREEK
9 ---DEER FLAT
10 ---MAGIC
11 ---DRY CREEK
12 ---CEDAR CREEK
13 ---SALMON FALLS
14 ---GOOSE CREEK
15 ---MILNER LAKE
16 ---WILSON LAKE
17 ---LAKE WALCOTT
18 ---AMERICAN FALLS
19 ---MACKAY
20 ---FISH CREEK
21 ---MUD LAKE
22 ---HENRYS LAKE
23 ---GRAYS LAKE
24 ---BLACKFOOT
25 ---PORTNEUF MARSH
26 ---BEAR LAKE AREA

SCALE IN MILES
0 5 10 20 30 40 50 60

terested in exploration or in further knowledge should seek the officials of the Idaho Gem Club in Boise.

Exports: A picture of what a State *has* in resources can be given in its exports. Of agricultural products, hay is first in value, but nearly all of it is fed within the State. Of livestock in 1934, a subaverage year, the exports were about 200 carloads of horses and mules, 4,000 of cattle, 5,000 of sheep, and 1,500 of hogs. Idaho is fifth in production of wool. Next to hay is wheat, of which a large part is milled within the State. Of an average production of 22,000,000 bushels, 8,997 cars were shipped out in 1934. Of potatoes, the average annual shipment is about 30,000 cars. Sugar beets are next but very few of these are shipped. The State's average production of these is about 4,500 cars or about 5 per cent of the total output for the United States. Beans, a crop coming rapidly into favor, is next in value and is 13 per cent of the Nation's total of the white bean production and together with peas run to about 3,600 cars annually. Apples come next with 3,500 cars, and after them come barley, oats, and corn in turn, though most of these are consumed within the State. Alfalfa seed is next. For years Idaho won on an average more than 45 per cent of all the prizes offered at the Chicago seed shows, and its Grimm alfalfa seed is now shipped to many parts of the world. Of the remaining agricultural products, lettuce is of importance with about 300 cars annually, onions with nearly 3,000 cars, celery with 100, cherries with from 100 to 200, prunes with about 3,000, peaches with 300, and miscellaneous fruits and vegetables in smaller quantities. Of dairy products, the State exports annually about 800,000,000 pounds of cheese, the same quantity of condensed milk, and the bulk of nearly 30,000,000 pounds of butter.

The export of mining products varies considerably. In 1934 Idaho shipped about $15,000,000 of silver and lead and minor metals, and 737 carloads of phosphate rock. Of timber in the same year, it shipped 11,678 cars of logs, 1,297 of fuel, 110 of ties, 379 of pulpwood, 9,502 of lumber, shingles, and lath, and 357 of boxes and crates.

Some notion of the fertility of the State's cultivable land can be gathered from the following statistics from the *U. S. Yearbook of Agriculture.* Some of these are based on a five-year average and others on a single year that was regarded as typical. Idaho is first among the States in per-acre yield in beans, peas, and clover seed; second in alfalfa seed and potatoes; third in wheat, hay, and apples; fourth in barley; sixth in sugar beets, eighth in oats, and tenth in corn. In corn it is first in acre-yield of all States west of the Mississippi. A notion of its comparatively small productive area can be had from the fact that in potatoes it ranks second in yield but seventh in production; in beans first in yield and fourth in production; in clover seed first in yield, ninth in acreage, and fifth in production; and in hay, its principal crop, third in yield, sixth in acreage, but second in total (1935) valuation. Of peas and clover seed, for both of which it has small areas only, it is first in production and yield.

Imports: A picture of what a State does *not* have in resources can be given in its imports. In general, inasmuch as Idaho is not an industrial area, its imports are chiefly manufactured goods, with 16,350 carloads unloaded in 1934. Petroleum products amounted to 7,612 cars. In spite of its own cement factories, it imported 13 per cent of its consumption in this item. Other large imports were hardware of all kinds, including 75 carloads of tractors, 44 of wagons, and 16 of other agricultural implements; 500 cars of canned goods, 130 of soap, 104 of beverages, 116 of lime, and 500,000 tons of coal. Idaho is one of the few States in the Union that spends more for automobiles than for food.

Summary: In regard to its resources, Idaho is in large part an undeveloped State. Vast sums, it is true, have been taken from its earth in mineral wealth and from its forests in manufactured products; but more minerals doubtless remain hidden than have ever been touched, and much more timber will remain inaccessible than has ever been logged. Agriculturally, it can never hope to be more than a minor producer, even if all its cultivable land is eventually brought under water and its northern logged-off areas are tilled. In dairying it can continue to grow, but in livestock it may remain indefinitely on a low-profit basis. Because of huge deposits of minerals in other parts of the world closer to cheap transportation, its future in mining cannot reasonably expect to exceed its past. It would seem, therefore, that Idaho's greatest development in the future must rest upon its potential wealth as a national playground. In this respect its development has hardly started and its resources are almost second to none.

XI

EMERGING FROM THE FRONTIER

Idaho is still so close to the frontier that its social development is still for the most part in its formative stages. A detailed account of the beginnings as well as of the results achieved will be found in the Idaho Atlas and Encyclopedia. Within the limits of this book there can be summarized only a few items that are especially relevant to a guide or of more lively interest to persons unfamiliar with the State.

STATE OF IDAHO
MAP OF
TRANSPORTATION
1936

LEGEND

⬡ — FEDERAL HIGHWAYS
━━ — PAVED GRAVEL HIGHWAYS
◯ — STATE HIGHWAYS
━ — GRADED COUNTY ROADS
━ ━ — STATE BOUNDARY LINES
── — COUNTY BOUNDARY LINES
─ ─ — NATIONAL PARK BOUNDARY LINES
+++++ — RAILWAY SYSTEMS
⊾ — NAVIGATION BETWEEN ARROWS
✈ — DIRECTION COMMERCIAL AIRWAYS
━ — PRINCIPAL BUS LINES
⊗ — BOISE STATE CAPITAL
◎ — COUNTY SEATS
◯ — OTHER IDAHO TOWNS

0   20   40   60   80   100
SCALE   IN   MILES

HIGHWAYS—STATE FEDERAL—PAVED GRAVEL—
3400 MILES. FEEDER ROADS—GRADED IMPROVED
—522 MILES. LICENSED AUTOMOBILES— 96,778
LICENSED TRUCKS—21,084. P.U.C.I.—INTERSTATE
TRUCK COS. 30—INTRASTATE TRUCK COS— 68
RAILWAYS—13 RAILWAY SYSTEMS WITH 62
BRANCH LINES. TRACK 2946 MILES. GROSS
BUSINESS OVER 18 MILLION DOLLARS.
AIRWAYS— INTERSTATE—UNITED AIR LINES—
NATIONAL PARK AIRWAYS. INTRASTATE— AIR-
PORTS LIGHTED 15. UNLIGHTED 52.
REGISTERED PLANES 40. PILOTS 53.
NAVIGATION— ST. JOE, KOOTENAI AND COEUR
D'ALENE RIVERS, COEUR D'ALENE & PRIEST LAKES.
BUS LINES— OPERATING MOST ALL FEDERAL
AND STATE HIGHWAYS. P.U.C.I. INTERSTATE—
16. INTRASTATE 7.
STATISTICS   1935

CANADA

WASHINGTON

OREGON

MONTANA

WYOMING

NEVADA   UTAH

F. M. TARR, W. T. RILEY

EMERGING FROM THE FRONTIER

TRANSPORTATION: Transportation problems in Idaho in comparison with those in most of the other States are unusually difficult. The northern part of the State is remote, with natural barriers, both river and mountain, intervening, and in consequence is still inaccessible within Idaho except by highway. Difficulties have arisen, too, out of the fact that the most important railway artery was laid more than a half century ago at a time when the Snake River Valley, down which for the most part it takes its way, was unclaimed by irrigation and unsettled. In southern Idaho, cities have grown at a considerable distance from the main line, and the Twin Falls area is still served only by a branch.

In 1929 Idaho had six airports of a sort. Today it has sixty-seven, thirty-three of which are municipal. The National Parks Airways and the United Airlines Transport are the two chief intrastate lines, and operate as feeders from main routes. The former serves between Great Falls, Montana, and Salt Lake City, Utah, and crosses eastern Idaho with service during season to West Yellowstone. The latter serves between Salt Lake City and Seattle. The Panhandle is crossed, of course, by any lines serving westward from Montana to the coast. Within the State during the winter there is a great deal of airline freight service to snowbound towns.

Because so many of Idaho's towns are off the main railway arteries, transportation by motor coach and freighting by truck have developed rapidly in recent years. At present there are licensed to operate within the State twenty-three passenger lines, seven of which are intrastate, and ninety-eight truck lines, of which thirty are intrastate. Eight per cent of the State's population and one fourth of its area are not served in any degree by railways, but nearly every town and village in the State is now served by bus and truck systems.

Although Idaho is twelfth in size it is only forty-first in valuation and forty-third in population. Of its 83,354 square miles, more than three fourths is held in forests, parks, and State lands, with less than 24 per cent accessible to taxation. With such considerable handicaps, it is small wonder that the State had as late as 1919 only 5 miles of paved road and only 108 that were surfaced. Today it has more than 1,800 miles of paved or oiled road, more than 1,600 that are of crushed rock or gravel, and nearly 600 that are graded. Of Idaho's 4,800 miles of roadway, less than 800 remain unimproved.

There are five main highway arteries, of which the most important is U S 30, entering in the southeast from Wyoming and entirely traversing the southern part of the State to connect at Weiser with Oregon lines going to Eugene or Portland. U S 91 and 191 cross the eastern part of the State and together are the main-traveled route between Salt Lake City and either West Yellowstone or Butte. Branch lines off this artery are the only approaches to the southern entrance of Yellowstone Park and to the Grand Teton National Park. U S 95 is the only complete north-south highway in the State: its southern terminal is Weiser and the end (in Idaho) of U S 30, and its northern terminal is the Canadian boundary. Across the northern part of the State are U S 10 and State 3 and U S 195. All of these highways connect western Montana cities with Spokane. U S 93, the western transcontinental artery between Canada and Mexico, almost exactly bisects that part of Idaho lying south of the Salmon River.

In 1935 there were 2,946 miles of railway track in Idaho, owned by 13 systems and their 62 branch lines. By far the most important of these, the Union Pacific, serves practically all of Idaho except the Panhandle. The northern part is served by the Chicago, Milwaukee, St. Paul and Pacific, the Great Northern, the Northern Pacific, and the Spokane International.

The streams of Idaho are not navigable save in some degree in the northern part. The Kootenai River in the extreme north is navigable between Nelson in British Columbia and Bonners Ferry, with both freight and passenger boats serving between these points. Pend Oreille River is navigable between Clark Fork and Albini Falls at Newport. From Sandpoint boats operate up the river to Priest Lake and from there up Priest River to the upper Priest Lake. Upon Pend Oreille Lake, with a length of sixty miles and an extreme width of twenty, there are both passenger and freight boats. Upon Lake Coeur d'Alene, with extreme dimensions of twenty-two miles by eight, there are boats of many kinds; and the Coeur d'Alene River is navigable for twenty miles between Harrison and Cataldo. Lewiston is known as Idaho's only "seaport." Both freight and passenger lines come up the Columbia and then up the Snake to Lewiston; and upstream from the city motor launches carry sightseers and supplies to the famous Box Canyon.

Racial Elements: Because Idaho is not an urban State (more than 315,000 of its 445,000 persons live on farms), it has no cities, like most of the States to which immigrants are attracted. Its population is chiefly transplanted native American stock from the Eastern and Middle Western States, and today, in consequence, only a relatively small percentage of its people are segregated into colonies. In the State's early years of settlement, of foreign-born stock only Chinese apparently came in appreciable numbers, and such prohibitions and persecutions were laid upon these that practically all of them disappeared or were exterminated.

According to the figures of the 1930 census, of foreign-born persons or those of recent foreign extraction, the greatest number in the State is of Scandinavian stock, though of the 28,000 Scandinavians, the majority seems to have come from Minnesota and Wisconsin. In the foreign-born category there are about 20,000 English, between 17,000 and 18,000 Germans, and almost 14,000 Canadians. Next in order in this category, but in considerably smaller numbers, are the Scotch, with 4,991; the Swiss, with 4,220; and the Irish, with 4,003. There are 3,730 Russians, 2,737 Italians, 2,689 Welsh, 2,128 Spaniards, 1,421 Japanese, and 1,278 Mexicans. Indians number 3,638, nearly all of whom are on reservations. The Negro population (as of 1930) was very small, with only 668. Pocatello has a small Negro colony. Of the Chinese, once so abundant, there were only 355 recorded; and of Filipinos there were only 97; of Koreans, only 21; of Hindus, only 7; and of Hawaiians, only 5.

In the eight largest cities, the native white population varies from 86.7 per cent in Coeur d'Alene to 95.8 per cent in Caldwell; the nonnative white residents of these cities are almost entirely foreign-born. Of the 30,454 foreign-born white persons in the state, 71 per cent have been naturalized. Twenty-six and three-tenths per cent of the total population is foreign white stock, of which 75 per cent is native white with one or both parents foreign-born. In northern Idaho, there are very few Negroes or Orientals among the foreign-born, but in southern Idaho, as in Pocatello, most of this population component is Mexicans and Chinese. Nowhere in Idaho is there a large foreign section.

Of the 3,890 Indians in Idaho (the figures are for 1933), only 574 were not on reservations. These live chiefly in cities and towns near the reservations, and it perhaps ought to be noted, in this respect, that Indians

like Negroes are classified as racially intact even though
they may be largely white. Many Chinese came to Idaho
in early days to work the placer mines. As placer mining
declined, those who were not driven out went into laun-
dries or truck gardening. There is a small Chinese colony
in Boise today, and an old Chinese temple which is still
used; but in the remainder of Idaho there seems to be no
colony nor more than 250 Chinese. Though the Scotch in
Idaho are largely assimilated, the native stock in Boise
is still so strong that the birthday of Burns is celebrated.
But the largest, and by far the most significant, colony
in Idaho is that of the Basques in Boise, said to be the
second in size in the world. It is a misnomer, of course,
to call this one a foreign colony. Many of the Basques of
Spain, after efforts to translate them into good Castilians
had failed, took to the sea, and some of them arrived on
the western coast of the United States. Because they
were highlanders, they ventured inland, seeking the
mountains, and one body of them established a colony
at Jordan Valley, Oregon, more than half a century ago.
After the coming of the sheep industry to eastern Oregon
and southern Idaho, the center of the colony drifted to
Boise, and these people now number about 7,000 in the
State, with 1,500 of them in Boise itself. Loving solitude
and the hills, the early Basque men here became shep-
herds, though a few of them came after awhile to be
persons of wealth and leadership in their own right.

The Basques are known as a devout and proud and
conservative people. Aloof rather than gregarious, they
still preserve in Boise the outlines of their native culture
and customs, though less exclusive very recently than they
used to be. They have yielded their native dress but their
chief game, Jai-alai or handball, is still their own, and
admission to their special functions is still by invitation
only. On Grove Street is their De Lamar Hotel, a hostelry
popular with the colony. Formerly they had a resident
priest but now they attend St. John's Cathedral.

Education: Idaho is a large State with a small population, and in consequence its progress in education has been slow. Today it has a university with a southern branch, 2 normal schools for the training of teachers, 4 senior and 3 junior colleges, and 195 high schools of which 33 are in class A independent districts. About 145,000 persons, or one third of the population of the State, annually attend the elementary and high schools. The State's educational system is controlled by county superintendents, the State Superintendent of Public Instruction, the State Board of Education, and the Board of Regents. Boise, Emmett, and Lewiston have special charters which make their districts independent of the control of the State Board. In 1933 legislation provided for equitable distribution of school funds, and placed Idaho in this respect with New York and Missouri.

Inasmuch as the State has no large population centers, its high schools are small and widely scattered. There are 195 units with 30,000 pupils. Of these 195 accredited high schools, only one has more than 1,600 students, while over 80 per cent of them have fewer than 200 students, and 62 per cent have fewer than 100. At a time when Idaho was more prosperous than it is today, every community with a half-dozen families thought it ought to have a high school, and in consequence these that mushroomed out of misguided civic pride overnight are today hanging precariously to their life. Idaho needs few things more urgently than a farsighted consolidation of its school districts. Among the high schools are seven which are maintained by churches: the Greenleaf Academy at Greenleaf, the Northwest Nazarene Academy at Nampa, the Ursuline Academy at Moscow, St. Teresa's Academy at Boise, the Academy of Immaculate Heart of Mary at Coeur d'Alene, Our Lady of Lourdes Academy at Wallace, and St. Gertrude's High School at Cotton.

The State university at Moscow, founded in 1892, had no more than five hundred students as late as 1916, but has grown so rapidly in recent years that nearly everything except the fir trees has been used for laboratory or classroom. The buildings were intended to accommodate a few hundred students, and today the enrollment is above three thousand. The students are crowded, the faculty is overworked, and the enrollment is rapidly increasing; but the solution seems as remote as ever. As the situation stands now, Moscow and northern Idaho are fighting for urgently needed buildings and facilities to take care of a rapidly growing student body, and Pocatello and southern Idaho are fighting to make the Southern Branch a four-year college in its own right. Idaho is too poor to support one campus as it ought to be; and in addition to a divided university it has two normal schools, each surviving under rather threadbare circumstances. Knowing how bitter sectionalism can be, some Idahoans shrug and predict that Idaho will persist until it has a college or university in every principal city even though taxes mount until they precisely equal the gross income.

The northern unit maintains fifteen departments, of which agriculture, engineering, forestry, and mines are outstanding. It also embraces experimental farms at Moscow, Sandpoint, Caldwell, and Tetonia; field laboratories at Boise, Twin Falls, and Parma; agricultural and home economic extension offices in Boise, Pocatello, Burley, Rupert, and Moscow; and a wide range of public service which touches all the industries and professions of the State. The Southern Branch at Pocatello became an integral part of it in 1927, and now has an enrollment of about six hundred students. It is only a junior college except in its school of pharmacy, in which its greatest strength lies. The two normal schools, one at Lewiston and the other at Albion, have about six hundred students between them.

The Industrial Training School was established in St. Anthony in 1903, and now provides training and supervision for nearly two hundred boys and girls annually. This school seems to have been fortunate in its leadership, and is in consequence one today of which the State

can be not unreasonably proud. The school for the deaf
and blind was finally placed in Gooding in 1910. Though
it cares for more than a hundred persons, its buildings are
so congested and its facilities so inadequate that it has a
long waiting list of applicants who must remain indefinitely without care. In Caldwell is the College of Idaho,
in Gooding is Gooding College, and in Nampa is the
Northwest Nazarene College. All are accredited four-year
schools. The last, supported and controlled by the Nazarene Church, is the only one of its kind in the Northwest.
There are junior colleges in Boise, Rexburg, and Coeur
d'Alene.

In the emphasis it has placed on education, in its scorn
of illiteracy, and in its resourcefulness in stretching dollars to their farthest reach, Idaho has been educationally
progressive. It is still one of the most backward States
in the care it gives to those unfortunates who do not fall
within the normal curriculum. In progressive Eastern
States the less extreme cases of emotional instability are
not incarcerated until efforts have been made to restore
them to serviceable citizenship; but Idaho is a young State
and has not yet got around to a more charitable and en-
lightened view of its neurotic persons.

Paleontology: In 1928 Dr. H. T. Stearns of the United
States Geological Survey sent to the National Museum a
small collection of fossil bones which had been taken from
Snake River Valley, and an examination of these led to
one of the important discoveries in the field of vertebrate
paleontology of recent years. The Smithsonian Institution
organized an expedition under J. W. Gidley to study the
area, and after several prospects were studied a field
party was sent out, including C. P. Singleton, discoverer
of the Pleistocene fossil region at Melbourne, Florida.
Three tons of fossils were unearthed by the expedition.

Fauna represented by bones of uncommon size proved
to be of unusual interest. Two kinds of bison existed in
Pleistocene time: one was much like the beast of the

present, but the other much overtopped it in size and in development of horns. These were about two feet long and more than six inches in diameter at their base. It is conjectured that they must have had a spread of not fewer than seven feet. Even so, this huge fellow was not undisputed master of the plains: roaming with him was a great musk-ox sort of an animal which exceeded in size by thrice his bulk the living musk ox of the North country. There were, too, large herds of mammoths and mastodons which were more enormous by far than their living relatives, the elephants of Africa and India. Besides these, there were big heavy ground sloths, related to the present tree sloth of South America; camels exceeding those of the Old World in length of limb and neck; and horses and bears. Among smaller animals recorded here in remnants were wolves, coyotes, gophers, and hares.

Results of the expedition were so gratifying that it was continued another season. Resuming work about five miles from Hagerman, the scientists discovered the bone deposits of hundreds of animals, a large part of which belong to an extinct species of horse. This spot was apparently once a boggy terrain, possibly a drinking place. The bones are so disarticulated, intermingled, and scattered that they suggest a slow accumulation over many years rather than the sudden overwhelming of a herd in one catastrophe. Among the deposits, too, are remains of fish, frogs, swamp turtles, beavers, as well as an abundance of vegetation. But the principal yield was the remains of a hitherto unknown species of horse belonging to the rare genus *Plesippus*, a beast intermediate between the Pleistocene horses and three-toed forebears of a more ancient time. Three or four skeletons were almost completely restored.

Other remnants uncovered were of beaver, otter, mastodon, peccary, rodent, frog, swamp turtle, and fish. There were also extinct species of mammals, including cats, sloth, and two species of camel. Their age seems

to be Upper Pliocene. In 1932 an expedition spent two
months in this vicinity and exposed a portion of bone-
bearing layers of five thousand square feet, which are
declared to be the largest accumulation of fossil horse remains ever discovered. Turned up this time were five
more or less complete skeletons, thirty-two skulls, and
forty-eight pairs of lower jaws. Many of the deposits were
taken out in large blocks of several hundred pounds each.
Still another expedition came in 1934, but the quarry had
caved in. To open the deposit, dynamite was used, and the
charge blew out a mastodon skull from a level considerably above that of the horse bones. This expedition gave
the name of *Plesippus Shoshonensis Gidley* to the new
species of horse.

Of petrified trees, the most unusual deposit found in
Idaho is in a wall of basalt on Santa Creek six miles north
of Emida. The ends of the carbonized logs can be seen
in the black lava near the water's edge. These are the
remains of a dense forest that grew in Miocene time when
possibly two hundred thousand square miles of the Pacific
Northwest were buried by lava flows to a depth varying
from a few to more than five thousand feet. The trees here
were so completely and quickly buried that air was excluded
and the wood was transformed into high-grade charcoal,
with growth rings, medullary rays, and the minutest cell
structures perfectly preserved. These logs are extinct
species of oak, redwood, beech, and cypress, none of which
is native to this area at the present time. In the lava fields
near Idaho Falls was until recently a large juniper nearly
seventeen hundred years old. A study of its almost perfect
rings has yielded considerable information in regard to the
wet and dry cycles during its period of growth.

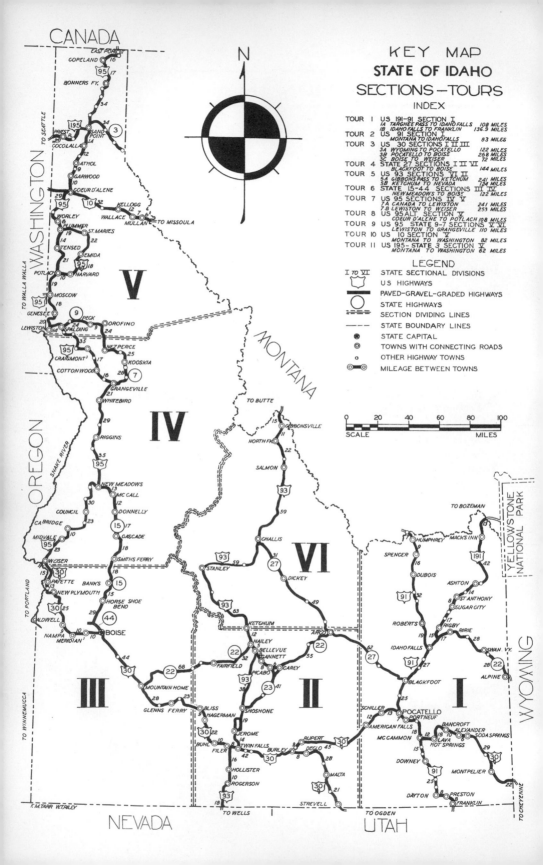

SECTION II

I

TOURS

Idaho's Major Points of Interest 195

Tour 1
Section a, U S 191, Montana Line to Idaho Falls 197
Section b, U S 91, Idaho Falls to Utah Line 210

Tour 2
U S 91, Montana Line to Idaho Falls 216

Tour 3
Section a, U S 30 N, Wyoming Line to Pocatello 218
Section b, U S 30 N and U S 30, Pocatello to Boise 230
Section c, U S 30, Boise to Weiser 253

Tour 4
State 27, Blackfoot to junction with U S 93, 2 m. south of
Challis 265

Tour 5
Section a, U S 93, Montana Line to Hailey 273
Section b, U S 93, Hailey to Nevada Line 285

Tour 6
State 15 and 44, New Meadows to Boise 293

Tour 7
Section a, U S 95, Canadian Line to Lewiston 300
Section b, U S 95, Lewiston to Weiser 308

Tour 8
State 9 and 7, Spalding to Grangeville 319

Tour 9
U S 95 Alt., Coeur d'Alene to Potlatch 325

Tour 10
U S 10, Montana Line to Washington Line 331

Tour 11
State 3 and U S 195, Montana Line to Washington Line 337

GENERAL INFORMATION FOR TOURISTS

Motor vehicle laws: Maximum speed **35 m.** outside of restricted areas. No nonresident license; but nonresidents remaining more than sixty days must register. No fee. Spotlights not to exceed two allowed. Hand signals must be used. On mountain highways no coasting on downgrade is allowed; and right of way must be given to traveler on upgrade. There is no State highway patrol.

Liquor laws: Alcoholic liquors can be legally purchased only from State Liquor Stores or authorized special distributors. Purchaser must have a permit (50c) which may be obtained in State Liquor Stores; this is not transferable. It is illegal to open a package containing liquor or to consume liquor (except beer) in a public place. Beer of more than 4% alcohol by weight is illegal.

Poisonous insects, etc.: Though parts of Idaho lie in the tick fever area, fatalities are very few, and most persons disregard the risk. There are rattlesnakes in parts of the State, but this reptile is not in general regarded as a menace. Of large wild animals there is none that will attack a human being unprovoked.

Clothing: Warm clothing is desirable in the high mountainous areas even in summer months.

Addresses of National Forest Headquarters: Boise Forest, Boise; Caribou, Montpelier; Challis, Challis; Clearwater, Orofino; Coeur d'Alene, Coeur d'Alene; Idaho, McCall; Kaniksu, Sandpoint; Minidoka, Burley; Nezperce, Grangeville; Payette, Boise; Salmon, Salmon City; Sawtooth, Hailey; St. Joe, St. Maries; Targhee, St. Anthony; Weiser, Weiser.

TOURS

IDAHO'S MAJOR POINTS OF INTEREST

THIS is a *selected* list of items and includes only those which would be worth the time of anyone to see. Following each is the tour number on which it is to be found. See the key map.

I. CAVES
a. Crystal Falls - - - - - 1a
b. Minnetonka - - - - - 3a
c. Formation - - - - - 3a
d. Shoshone - - - - - 5b

II. CANYONS
a. Middle Snake River - - - 3b
b. Bruneau - - - - - - 3b
c. Seven Devils - - - - - 7a
d. Salmon River - - - - - 5a
e. Malad River - - - - - 3b

III. AREAS
a. Primitive - - - - 5a; 3b; 6
b. Selway - - - - - - 8
c. Island Park - - - - - 1a
d. Payette - - - - - - 6
e. Seven Devils - - - - - 7b
f. Sawtooth - - - - - - 5a
g. Heyburn Park - - - - - 7a
h. Priest Lake - - - - - 11

IV. SPRINGS
a. Soda - - - - - - - 3a
b. Lava - - - - - - - 3a
c. Big - - - - - - - 1a

V. LAKES

a. Bear - - - - - - - 3a
b. Sawtooth - - - - - - 5a
c. Payette - - - - - - 6
d. Coeur d'Alene - - - - - 7a
e. Pend Oreille - - - - - 11
f. Priest - - - - - - 11

VI. WATERFALLS

a. Mesa - - - - - - - 1a
b. Twin - - - - - - - 3b
c. Shoshone - - - - - - 3b
d. Moyie - - - - - - - 7a

VII. ROCK FORMATIONS

a. Craters of the Moon - - - 4
b. Malad Gorge - - - - - 3b
c. Cassia City of Rocks - - - 3b
d. Gooding City of Rocks - - 5b
e. Balanced Rock - - - - - 3b
f. Crater Rings - - - - - 3b
g. Jump Creek Canyon - - - 3c
h. Sucker Creek Canyon - - - 3c

VIII. HIGHWAY ENGINEERING

a. Galena Summit - - - - 5a
b. French Creek Hill - - - - 7b
c. White Bird Hill - - - - - 7b
d. Winchester Hill - - - - 7b
e. Gilbert Hill - - - - - 8
f. Lewiston Hill - - - - - 7a
g. Fourth of July Canyon - - 10

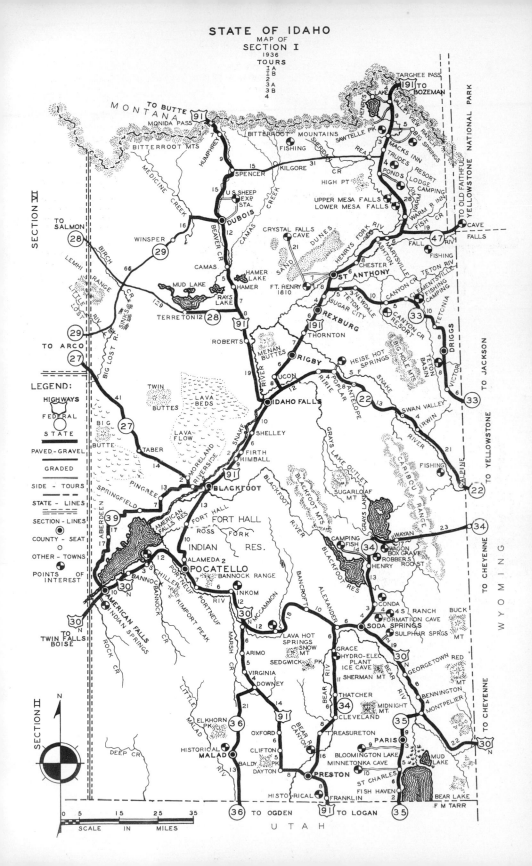

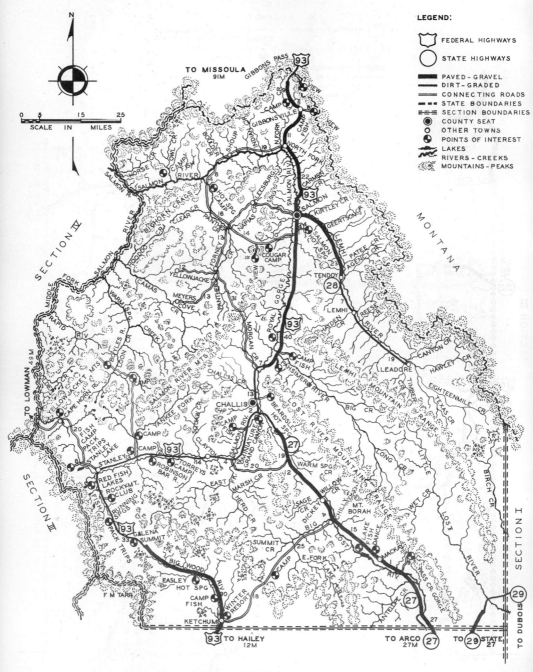

STATE OF IDAHO
MAP OF
SECTION VI
1936
TOURS
2
4
5 A

LEGEND:

⬡ FEDERAL HIGHWAYS
◯ STATE HIGHWAYS
━━ PAVED – GRAVEL
─ ─ DIRT – GRADED
═ CONNECTING ROADS
- - - STATE BOUNDARIES
=== SECTION BOUNDARIES
◉ COUNTY SEAT
○ OTHER TOWNS
⊕ POINTS OF INTEREST
LAKES
RIVERS – CREEKS
MOUNTAINS – PEAKS

N

SCALE IN MILES
0   5   15   25

SECTION IV

TO MISSOULA
9 M

GIBBONS PASS

93

VIEW

CAMP

GIBBONSVILLE

N. FORK

NORTH FORK

SALMON RIV.

CARMEN

93

SALMON

KIRTLEY CR.

GEERTSON CR.

HOT SPG.

CLEARCR.

BIGHORN CRAGS

PANTHER CR.

NAPIAS CREEK

LEESBURG

MORGAN CR.

SALMON HOT SPG.

PATEE

LEMHI

AGENCY CR.

23

TENDOY

28

COUGAR CAMP

VIEW

YELLOWJACKET

MEYERS COVE

BELLA

FORNEY

CAMAS

ROYAL GORGE

40

CAMP FISH

5 A

LEMHI

HAYDEN CR.

REESE RIVER

LEMHI MOUNTAIN

TO LOWMAN 49 M

MIDDLE FORK

SALMON RIVER

WARM

RAPID

RIV.

LOON CR.

YELLOWJACKET MTS

CAPE HORN MTS.

SALMON RIVER MTS.

YANKEE FORK

CHALLIS CR.

13

CHALLIS

LOST RIVER MOUNTAINS

BIG CR.

LEADORE

19

CANYON CR.

HARLEY

EIGHTEENMILE CR.

TIMBER CR.

TEXAS CR.

LITTLE

MONTANA

SECTION III

20 FISH CAMP PACK TRIPS

STANLEY LAKE

STANLEY

93

14

TORREYS

ROBINSON BAR R.

EAST FK.

CLAYTON

SALMON RIV.

GRAND JEANCR.

19

CAMP FISH

27

WARM SPG.

BEARDSLEE

SNAKE CURVE

20

LOST RIVER RANGE

RED FISH LAKES

ROCKY MT. CLUB

RUNNING SPGS.

FISH

PACK TRIPS

GALENA SUMMIT

33

93

MARSH CR.

HERD CR.

SAGE CR.

DICKEY

BIG LOST

WILLOW

MT. BORAH

LAKE FISH

DANCE

WET CR.

LOST RIVER

BIRCH CR.

SECTION I

TO DUBOIS

BIG (WOOD RIV.

EASLEY HOT SPG.

F M TARR

CAMP FISH

KETCHUM

WINTER RESORT

18

SUMMIT CR.

25

CAMP

E. FORK

LOST RIV.

MACKAY

ANTELOPE CR.

PASS CR. GORGE

27

29

27

93

TO HAILEY
12 M

TO ARCO
27M

27

TO STATE
27

29

STATE 27

29

TO DUBOIS

SECTION II

STATE OF IDAHO

MAP OF

SECTION II

1936

TOURS

3 B
4
5 A
5 B

LEGEND

FEDERAL HIGHWAYS		STATE BOUNDARY LINES	
STATE HIGHWAYS		SECTION BOUNDARIES	
HIGHWAY-PAVED-GRAVEL		PARK BOUNDARIES	
HIGHWAY-DIRT-GRADED		COUNTY SEAT	
CONNECTING ROADS		OTHER TOWNS	
MOUNTAINS-PEAKS		POINTS OF INTEREST	
		RIVERS-CREEKS	
		LAKES-RESERVOIRS	

TO SALMON CITY 229M
TO CHALLIS 82M
TO DUBOIS 61M
TO BLACKFOOT 54M

SECTION VI
SECTION III
SECTION I

KETCHUM
BALD MT
GARFIELD MT
ELK MT
IRON MT
ARCO
BIG LOST RIV
RED DEVIL MTS
DEER CR
HAILEY
HOT SPRGS
BELLEVUE
PIONEER MTS
EAST FK
MARTINS RANCH
CRATERS OF THE MOON NATL MONU
BUTTERCUP MT
SMOKY DOME
FAIRFIELD
CAMAS
WILLOW CREEK
LOOKOUT MT
DRY CR
TO FISH CR
CAREY
VIEW
LAVA FLOW
CITY OF ROCKS
MAGIC RES
SILVER CR
LITTLE WOOD
SHOSHONE ICE CAVES
RICHFIELD
BIG WOOD
LYE LAKE
HOT SPRING
GOODING
BLISS
MALAD GORGE
HAGERMAN
SHOSHONE
DEVILS CORRAL
TO BOISE 95M
SNAKE RIV
THOUSAND SPRINGS
CLEAR LAKES
JEROME
TWIN FALLS-JEROME BRIDGE
SHOSHONE FALLS
TWIN FALLS
HANSEN BRIDGE
WILSON LAKE RES
MILNER DAM
BURLEY CAVE
WIND CAVE
LAKE WALCOTT RES
SNAKE RIV
RUPERT
BALANCED ROCK
BLUE LAKES
AUGER FALLS
SNAKE RIV
MILNER "CALDRON LYNN"
SNAKE RIV
MIGRANT ROCK
MASSACRE ROCKS
TO AMERICAN FALLS 10M
BUHL
FILER
GODWIN SIDING
TWIN FALLS
HANSEN
TRADING STA 1863
DECLO
BURLEY
REGLAN
RAFT RIVER
CASTLEFORD
DEVILS KITCHEN
BLOW-HOLE
PHANTOM WALL
HOLLISTER
NAH SUPAH HOT SPRINGS
WILD HORSE SPRINGS
HOT CAVES
GOOSE CR
ALBION
IDAHOME
MT HARRISON
CLEVELAND LAKE
CASSIA
AMSTERDAM
MINIDOKA NATL FOREST CAMPING FISHING
OAKLEY
MT INDEPENDENCE
INDEPENDENCE LAKES
BLACK PINE PK
ROGERSON
BOSTETTER PUBLIC CAMP
PENTSTEMON CAMP
OAKLEY DAM
GOOSE CR RES
SILENT CITY OF ROCKS
JOHNSON CR
CLEAR CR
RADIUM HOT SPRINGS
SHOSHONE CR
SALMON CR DAM-RES
F M TARR
TO WELLS 61M
TO TREMONTON 67M

SCALE IN MILES
0   5   15   25

N

NEVADA
UTAH

STATE OF IDAHO

MAP OF

SECTION III

1936

TOURS
3 B
3 C
6

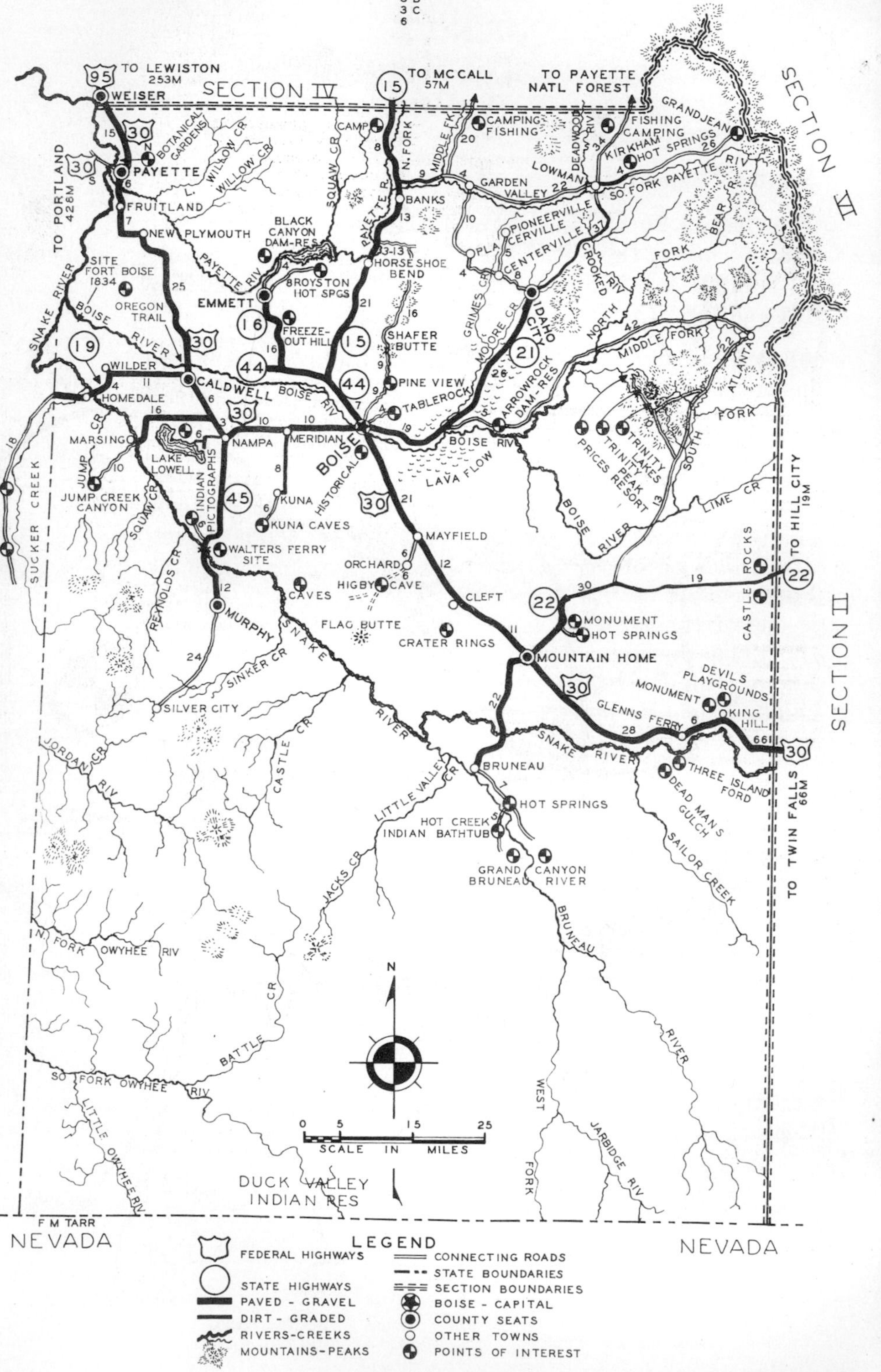

TOUR NO. 1

(West Yellowstone, Montana)—St. Anthony—Idaho Falls
—Pocatello—Preston—(Ogden, Utah). U S 191 and U S
91. Yellowstone Route.

Montana Line to Utah Line **244.9 m.**

The Oregon Short Line of the Union Pacific System and
the air route of the National Parks Airways roughly parallel U S 191 and U S 91. Union Pacific Stages follow U S
191 and U S 91 to Salt Lake City, Utah.

All types of accommodations along the highway, including
improved campsites; usual price range.

Section a. Montana Line to Idaho Falls, 108 m.

U S 191 coming out of Montana enters Idaho over
Targhee Pass (7,078 alt.) **10 m.** west of the western
gateway to Yellowstone Park and proceeds for almost
fifty miles through the heart of the Targhee National
Forest. This beautiful area of rivers and heavy timber
is one of the principal tourist regions of the State, and
this drive through Targhee Forest is one of the finest in
Idaho. The dense growth east or west of the highway is
chiefly lodgepole pine, though other trees of importance
in this forest are alpine and Douglas fir and Engelmann
spruce. In late spring and throughout the summer this
region is a continuous garden of wild flowers. Inasmuch
as the lower elevations are above six thousand feet, this
region is one of cool summers and of very deep winters,
with skiing often possible over the buildings. Though a
favorite with visitors from many parts of the world,
this northeastern corner of Idaho is still an excellent fishing area. Its streams are annually stocked not only by
the State but also by several sportsmen's associations,
some of which have clubs here.

VALLEY VIEW RANCH **4 m.** (L) is a group of cabins
on a mountainside that overlooks Henrys Lake in the west.
Meals are available here, and several cabins at very nominal

rates. Here, too, is the junction (R) with an unsurfaced road that is a cut-off to southern Montana.

HENRYS LAKE stands at the center of three mountain passes: the Red Rock, the Reynolds, and the Targhee. South of it is Sawtelle Peak. Lying upon distance against a western range, it has been invested with many a legend, and is chiefly interesting when viewed within its background of folklore. Only five miles in length, it is fed by innumerable rivulets that come out of the mountains flanking it. This, one of the unusual spots in Idaho, is said to be an interesting example of a remnant dating back probably to Pliocene times when all of these valleys were filled with water. Its mysterious floating and disappearing islands, now largely restored to a somewhat mythical past, were composed of spongy substance covered with grass, and are said to have attracted the fancy of Chief Joseph of the Nez Perces, who saw the working of a supernatural agency in their changing forms. Legend declares, too, that for many years Indians refused to explore these islands. After awhile they resolved, with ingenious courage, to use them as burial grounds inasmuch as they vanished "six sleeps in each moon" and ought on that account to put any ghost irrevocably beyond the reach of care. The Indians decided (the tale is still largely legendary) that by the time the erected scaffolds had sunk into the bogs, the soul of a dead Indian would be safely within the happy eternities. These islands became, in consequence, one of the strangest burial grounds of the world, and alternately vanished and reappeared with their cargo of dead. Perhaps of more importance today for those unaffected by legends is the fact that fishing in the lake and its near-by streams is unusually good and that ducks abound in the marshes. A State hatchery is to be found at the northern end.

U S 191 now passes through a narrow valley and enters the chief area of resorts. At **5 m.** is the junction with a trail.

Right on this trail is SAWTELLE PEAK, from which is visible most of the Targhee Forest and a slice of southern Montana (for horseback trips to this peak, see **Trudes Resort).** This trail is 8 m. long. On Mount Reynolds, west of Sawtelle Peak, are acres and acres of marine fossils.

At **12 m.** is the junction with an improved road.

Left on this road the BIG SPRINGS RESORT 5 m. (6,450 alt.) comprises a central lodge, flanked by a number of cabins. No other resort in this area stands upon so beautiful a site. BIG SPRINGS, which are only a few yards from the Inn, are almost a phenomenon in themselves. Gushing from the base of a mountain, they are the source of the South Fork of Snake River, and pour out such volume that a full-grown river is under way within a hundred feet of the springs. The average flow of 185 second-feet never varies in temperature from 52 degrees F. Upon the bottom of the stream and visible from the bridge is an interesting flora, and upon the mountains roundabout are lodgepole pine, Douglas fir, and Engelmann spruce. A favorite pastime with visitors here is to stand on the bridge and feed bread to the schools of rainbow trout. During the summer an average of twenty loaves a day are bought at the Inn for this purpose.

SACK'S CABIN (admission is free) across the springs from the Inn, is a very remarkable lodgepole cabin. Built over a period of years with painstaking care by a German carpenter creatively endowed, it has attracted the interest of thousands of persons and filled them all with wonder at what genius can do with logs and slabs and a few simple tools. All the woodwork inside and all the furniture is handmade and of most unusual craftsmanship.

From the Inn a road climbs 2 m. to BIG SPRINGS LOOKOUT and a tower which affords an excellent view of the surrounding country. The Targhee Forest maintains several public campgrounds within its boundaries, and one of the best is here at Big Springs.

MACK'S INN **13 m.** on U S 91 is the most famous resort in this region. Popular with visitors from many parts of the world and particularly with celebrities from Hollywood, it has a central unit of buildings comprising cafe, stores, and a hotel, flanked on nearly every side by rows of cabins. The North Fork of Snake River is its northern boundary, and here from the bridge visitors again delight in scattering bread to the fish. Just southwest (R) is another public campground, and down the river below it are summer homes. Across the river, both east and west, are private clubs. Some of the cabins here are noteworthy in their workmanship, but the most interesting feature of this resort is perhaps the interior of the cafe.

TRUDE **16 m.** (6,327 alt.) is on Elk Creek in the Bitterroot Range. On the highway is the dance hall, and set back from it are the main lodge and the cabins which overlook a private lake in which is said to be the largest eastern brook trout in the country. Swimming and boating are available here as well as fishing in private waters; and unlike the other resorts, Trude outfits for horseback and pack trips into adjacent areas, including Sawtelle Peak and Yellowstone Park. This resort, like Mack's, has been a favorite with a wealthy clientele.

POND'S LODGE **20 m.** is on the Buffalo River and has, like the others, a central inn and a number of cabins. The former lodge, which burned to the ground in 1935, was notable for its interior rustic woodwork. Just N of the resort (L) is the Buffalo public campground.

Left from Pond's Lodge a graded road leads to ISLAND PARK **4 m.** (6,290 alt.) and to natural campsites in a wilderness of evergreens.

From U S 191 a few miles S of Pond's, the Teton Peaks are visible. The highway again enters a forested area, and the gorge of the North Fork comes into view on the right.

At **39 m.** is the junction with an unimproved road.

Right on this road are UPPER MESA FALLS **1 m.,** where unimproved campgrounds are available. This waterfall (sometimes called the Big) has a vertical drop of 114 feet.[1] Unlike so many of the falls in Idaho it has not been vitiated by reservoirs, and in consequence the full flow of the North Fork is delivered over its wide escarpment. This plunge of water against a high mountainous backdrop is well worth seeing and in picturesqueness the campsites here are rarely excelled. Across the river on the opposite bank the lovely symmetrical trees are Engelmann spruce. Just below the falls at a point where the river plunges again is a curious formation of stone that resembles a group of heathen idols. The cascading rapids downstream are especially impressive when the river is at its flood in late spring.

At **39 m.** on U S 191 is a sign marked GRANDVIEW POINT.

A sharp turn (R) from the highway leads to an eminence which affords a fine view of LOWER MESA FALLS. This second drop is

---

[1] The height of all waterfalls in Idaho are taken from the *Geological Survey Water-Supply Paper 657.*

Teton Peaks

Upper Mesa Falls

sixty-five feet, and beyond it the mist of the Upper Mesa Falls is visible in the distance. Though only a little more than half the height of the other waterfall, the Lower Mesa excels it in its greater concentration of water into a more furious downward pouring. In this distance of a mile and a half the North Fork of Snake River drops almost two hundred feet. Just south of Grandview Point is an unusually inviting but unimproved campground.

U S 191 now descends by winding grade to leave Targhee Forest.

WARM RIVER INN 48 m. (5,284 alt.) is the last of the tourist resorts in this area. Like the others, it has a central lodge with outlying cabins, but unlike them it stands almost upon three rivers: the Warm, Robinson, and Snake. A short distance out (R) is a large dance hall which offers dancing on Saturday evenings. The highway now climbs out of Warm River and on the right 49 m. is the Reiman Ranch whose lodgepole buildings suggest what an enterprising farmer can do toward beautifying the place where he lives. Remarkably ingenious is Reiman's own hydroelectric plant on the river below.

At 50 m on U S 191 is the junction with State 47.

State 47, a graveled road, connects U S 191 with the southwest corner of Yellowstone National Park Along this road are many good campsites and unusually fine fishing. The best streams are Bechler and Falls Rivers, Boundary, Porcupine, Rock, and Ash Creeks, all accessible from the highway.

At 9 m. on State 47 is the YOUNG RANCH, which outfits pack trips into the surrounding mountains.

BECHLER RIVER STATION of Yellowstone National Park, at 19 m., is in the center of a good hiking area of Yellowstone Park and has excellent campgrounds. Right from Bechler River Station is a trail to CAVE FALLS 4 m., a lovely waterfall on the Bechler River, which gets its name from a large cave on the river bank from which the most striking view of the falls may be had. An improved camp has been provided at Cave Falls.

ASHTON 54 m. (5,256 alt.; 1,003 pop.) is the home of the famous dog derby. This event, held annually on February 22, attracts drivers from Canada and many of the Northern States. Begun in 1917, and since then copied in many parts of the country, this race was at first from West Yellowstone to Ashton, a distance of sixty-four miles. In that race a blizzard almost buried the drivers and their teams and they did not reach Ashton until the following day. Windriver Smith had a bulldog in the lead; the second man out drove a bunch of mongrels gathered from the farmyards of neighbors; but the winner had an assortment of lusty young hounds that had been used on mail teams out of Ashton. The record for the present three-lap course of eight and one-third miles is one hour, fifty-one minutes, and forty-one seconds. The favorite dogs now are red Irish setters.

Upon leaving Targhee Forest and Warm River, U S 191 enters the upper Snake River Valley and goes almost down the center of it for nearly a hundred miles. From here to Blackfoot it lies across one of the richest agricultural areas of the State. The chief crops throughout its length are potatoes, sugar beets, peas, and hay. At Ashton and from the highway east and west there are visible on a clear day the magnificent Teton Peaks (L) in Wyoming, reaching far into the sky like great towers of stone and glass furrowed with snow. The highest of these peaks standing upon the Teton Range in the Grand Teton National Park reaches an altitude of 13,747 feet.

ST. ANTHONY 68 m. (4,958 alt.; 2,778 pop.) was named for St. Anthony Falls in Minnesota. This town is the seat of Fremont County, and the center of the seed-pea industry of eastern Idaho. There is nothing of unusual interest in the town itself, but west of it are two of the most remarkable natural phenomena in the State.

Right from St. Anthony an unnumbered and unimproved road goes westward past the Industrial Training School, and from this point signs will direct the traveler. These SAND DUNES 6 m., Idaho's tiny Sahara Desert, lie in a belt more than a mile wide and thirty miles long. It is quite beyond the power of words to describe the wind-drifted golden banks that vary in height from ten to a hundred feet. They flow over the landscape like a great arrested tide with most of them unbelievably perfect in their symmetry and contour. They are a beautiful picture at any time of day, and even under a cloudy sky; but their soft and shimmering loveliness is to be seen most impressively under a gorgeous sunset, when the flame of the sky falls to the burning gold of the dunes, and the whole earth here rolls away in soft mists of fire. Under the first light of morning they awaken from an unfolded landscape of shadow and gloom to faintly luminous witchery and then steadily into dazzling piles of light and dark. And from year to year and mile to mile they shift uncertainly under the sculpturing winds, and are never twice the same.

CRYSTAL FALLS CAVE 28 m. is only one of the many caves in this desolate volcanic area. Idaho has hundreds of caves, and a few of them are known beyond the State's boundaries; but this one, seen by hardly more than a score of persons and known by name to fewer than a hundred, is perhaps the most remarkable one of all. Those who venture out to explore its interiors should be prepared for poor and unimproved road; should go equipped with warm clothing and gas lanterns or powerful flashlights and about fifty feet of rope; and ought to arrange to venture in a party of several, because for the careless or the unwary this is a comparatively dangerous journey.

The entrance to Crystal Falls Cave is by way of a ragged gulch bedded with piles of stone, but the opening itself is large and vaulted and leads easily to the first chamber. This room is huge and rough with torn ceilings and walls and with countless tons of rock heaped upon its floor. At its farther end is a rugged passage-way that leads down, but not steeply, to the enormous first corridor of the cave. The ceiling here at the beginning is perhaps a hundred feet in height and descends in sweeping curves to the walls, but after a little the ceiling comes down to thirty or forty feet, and the corridor runs for a quarter of a mile in an almost perfectly vaulted archway of remarkable formation. After penetrating for a hundred yards the explorer comes to a frozen river that lies upon half the length of the main chamber. This river of ice, of unknown depth, is eight or ten feet wide and reaches down the center of the cave with a great sloping stone shelf running parallel on either side. The explorer can take his way carefully along the glazed surface of either ledge, or he can descend with the aid of a rope to the river and walk on the ice.

At the ends of this river are the most amazing features to be found in these interiors. The end first reached is a great waterfall of ice that drops thirty feet to a tiny chamber of extraordinary beauty. Close by this chamber, toward the cave entrance, is a jagged basin some twenty feet across and thirty feet in depth, and the explorer can descend without the aid of ropes and then turn to the right and follow a short and narrow passage to the other chamber. Upon coming to the other chamber he will probably hold his breath at the unsurpassed loveliness of what he sees. This waterfall of ice looks as if a river had plunged and had been suddenly frozen, because the contour of the descending flood is perfect, even to the spilled frozen flanking structure that looks like tumbled chandeliers and draperies of glass. The floor of this small chamber is of ice with perfect cones bedded in it, formed by the dripping of water from the ceiling. On either side of the fall is a

Crystal Falls Cave: a backdrop

Crystal Falls Cave: a corridor

Crystal Falls Cave: a ceiling

valley was first explored by Andrew Henry of the Missouri Fur Company in 1810. Trappers were the first to settle here, and Beaver Dick Leigh and his Indian wife Jenny were the first to build a home in this region. The fort, erected in 1810, was the first on Snake River or any of its tributaries. It consisted of several cabins and a dugout; but after Henry and his companions trapped here and traded with the Shoshonis for a year they abandoned the fort, and it was used by Wilson Price Hunt while his men built cottonwood canoes to venture down *La Maudite Riviere Enragee* (the accursed mad river, the name given to the Snake by French *voyageurs* after they had come to grief upon its falls and cascades). For nearly a century the site of the old fort was unknown, but in 1927 a rock was unearthed which bore the inscription:

Al the cook, but nothing to cook.

This stone, together with two others inscribed "Gov't Camp, 1811" and "Fort Henry 1811 by Captain Hunt," are now in Rexburg.

A monument to Fort Henry now stands on the bank of Snake River where U S 191 crosses the bridge to Rexburg.

As **75 m.** is the junction with State 33.

State 33 leads through the TETON PASS (alt. 8,429) to Grand Teton National Park and to the southern entrance of Yellowstone National Park. Fishing along the entire length of State 33 is good, and unimproved campsites are frequent. At Canyon Creek **18 m.**, (R) from State 33 on a graded road, is the PINCOCK HOT SPRINGS **5 m.**, which has private baths and a large indoor pool but no hotel accommodations. Fishing is very good in TETON RIVER **30 m.**, which abounds in rainbow trout. At TETON CANYON **40 m.** is the only improved campground, 9 m. (L) from State 33. From VANTAGE POINT in this canyon there is a magnificent view of Teton Peaks and the surrounding country.

On State 33 is DRIGGS **41 m.**, county seat of Teton County. Here is the largest bed of coal known to exist in the State. Geologists estimate that about 11,000,000 tons lie in beds a few miles west but the fields remain almost wholly unexploited. At **44 m.** is TETON BASIN, formerly called Pierre's Hole, a famous rendezvous in early days for trappers and traders who gathered here in a rousing carnival of sharp maneuvering and drunkenness. Probably no spot in the West knew a larger congress of rascals and scoundrels. It was here that 42 adventurers encountered a roving band of 200 men, women, and children of the Gros Ventre tribe, and, reinforced by Indian allies, engaged in terrific battle. Arrows and spear points, and more infrequently, stone axes and tomahawks are still found on the battlefield. A winter carnival of skiing and dog-racing draws a crowd each year.

VICTOR 49 m. is the nearest railway station of the Oregon Short
Line R. R. of the U. P. system to the Jackson Hole Country and the
Grand Teton National Park. It is 6 m. from the Wyoming Line.

On U S 191, where it crosses the Snake River at the
northern edge of Rexburg, there is a monument to Fort
Henry (See **above**).

REXBURG 80 m. (4,861 alt.; 3,048 pop.) was founded
in 1883 under instructions from the Mormon Church.
Named for Thomas Ricks, one of its founders, it soon
established mills and a school, and five years later a college. Characteristic Mormon resourcefulness and social
integrity have made of Rexburg the principal town in the
upper Snake River Valley north of Idaho Falls, and have
symbolized their industry in the tabernacle here. In
nothing is this city more typical of Mormon planning than
in the breadth of its streets.

RIGBY 94 m. (4,949 alt.; 1,531 pop.) is another town
which, like most of those in eastern Idaho, has been
planned and developed chiefly through Mormon initiative
and enterprise. It is another center of a potato, sugar-beet,
and seed-pea area.

Right from Rigby on State 48, an unimproved road, are the
MENAN BUTTES 8 m., which stand at the confluence of the North
and South Forks of Snake River. Great quantities of sediment carried
down from the watersheds to this point are here spread out because of
the stream's decreased velocity into a broad delta with the river
cutting across it in several channels. Just beyond are the buttes,
broad of base with gently sloping sides and broad tops, rising six
hundred feet above the surrounding plains. Each has a well-
defined extinct crater in its top, about a mile in diameter and two
hundred feet in depth. The beds of ejected materials fall away in
all directions at sharp angles and flatten at the base. Sand and
gravel contained in the strata of which the craters are built indicate that these volcanoes were erupted explosively through an old
river or lake deposit. The cones are of the same age and moderately
recent. Quarried at their base is a black volcanic rock of cemented
fragments and explosive dust which is used locally in buildings.
These great bleak sentinels have been little explored, and only
rarely do persons descend to their crater beds. Between the two
are rocks bearing Indian petroglyphs of men, bison, cranes, rabbits,
and horses. Because of the fact that the horse, unknown to Indians

long ago, is represented here, no great antiquity is claimed for these writings. South of these buttes are two smaller ones, covered with juniper, which were once a favorite camping ground for Indians of this valley.[1]

At **103 m.** on U S 191 is a junction with State 22.

Left on State 22, a paved road, is RIRIE **12 m.** State 22 is the highway from Idaho which leads to the southern entrance to Yellowstone Park. Ririe is one of the most recent of Idaho towns and perhaps as close as any other to the mood and vigor of the frontier. If the visitor wishes to come as close as it is possible to come today to the rowdy spirit of the old West, he should plan to attend the Friday night dance in the new Ririe dance hall. State 22, still surfaced, proceeds to the hamlet of POPLAR **16 m.**, out of which two country lanes lead (L) to the HEISE HOT SPRINGS **3 m.** just across the South Fork of Snake River by ferry. This resort, the most popular in this part of Idaho, offers hotel accommodations and indoor and outdoor pools. E of Poplar the highway enters the foothills of the eastern mountain range; crosses the rolling belt of the Antelope dry farms, with the South Fork coming down its gorge on the left; and then falls by easy grade to the river and a tiny valley (Conant), and climbs hills again to swing leftward to the river bridge. It now follows the stream to SWAN VALLEY **37 m.**, so named because once a haven of swans. At this point it forms a junction with State 31.

State 22 proceeds up the gorge of the South Fork of Snake River to ALPINE **69 m.**, the Idaho-Wyoming line, and its junction with Wyoming 89 which goes southward to its junction with State 35 and U S 30 N at MONTPELIER (see **Tour 3, Sec. a**). From Alpine an unsurfaced road has recently been completed up the magnificent Grand Canyon of the South Fork in Wyoming to Jackson. In this stretch of twenty-five miles the river has cut across a great many sedimentary formations, with the canyon now ranging in width from one hundred to one thousand feet and in depth from one thousand to four thousand. The scenery here is rarely equaled, and the river and adjacent streams have seen few fishermen. This is the most spectacular route to the southern entrance of Yellowstone Park.

An alternate approach to Yellowstone is State 31 which proceeds from Swan Valley (L) by benchland up Pine Creek and over a pass and down into VICTOR **23 m.** After leaving Victor it climbs over a series of cutbacks to Teton Pass (in Wyoming) at an elevation of 8,500 feet, and then drops for six miles over another breathless series of cutbacks into the Jackson Hole country. The view from Teton Pass is one of the most remarkable in the West.

---

[1] Statements about these buttes (also sometimes called the Market Lake Buttes) are based on *United States Geological Survey Bulletin 199.*

IDAHO FALLS 109 m. (4,709 alt.; 9,429 pop.), the
seat of Bonneville County and third in size in the State,
is the cultural and industrial center of the upper Snake
River Valley. The most remarkable fact about this beautiful and thriving town is its hydroelectric plant, one of
the largest municipally owned in the United States. The
plant consists of two sections, one at the west end of
Broadway, and the other three miles up the river. Both
are open to visitors. The lower unit is also used to pump
water from three deep wells which have a combined flow
of 13,500,000 gallons every twenty-four hours. For the
citizens of Idaho Falls, socialism is a word that may be
anathema, but the fact remains, nevertheless, that this
is Idaho's most socialistic city, and promises to become
in consequence eventually tax-free and the most prosperous one in the State. Its electric power rate is one of the
lowest in the Northwest, and its city tax rate is only a
little more than a third of the average for Idaho as a
whole. Above all overhead and maintenance and depre-
ciation costs, this municipal plant nets the city an annual
profit of more than a hundred thousand dollars for liqui-
dation of its debts and expansion of its civic programs.
Idaho Falls will soon be free of indebtedness, and under
wise leadership it will eventually be free of taxes, and
these two circumstances will give to it an enormous advantage over other Idaho cities. And this city, finding
that its one venture into municipal ownership paid huge
dividends, next built a modern hotel, the BONNEVILLE,
and has discovered it to be an asset also. Discovering that
it had unused profits from its power plant, it built a hall to
house the fire and police departments, a radio station, and
an engineering and drafting department in addition to the
customary offices. This hall was erected at a cost of
$200,000 without bond issue or increase in taxes.

It is the shipping center of this part of the State. The
normal acreage of its seed-pea industry is fifty thousand,
and this is minor in comparison with hay or potatoes or

beets. Idaho ranks fourth in production of honey, and Idaho Falls is one of the largest centers of this product. The potato-flour mill is one of the few in the world, and uses annually about ten million pounds of culled potatoes that would otherwise be wasted or used only for hog feed. This plant, which ships to various parts of the world, produces as much as 2,500,000 pounds of flour in a season.

Left from Idaho Falls on an improved road is LINCOLN 3 m. in which is one of the largest sugar factories of the West. It has a capacity of sixty-five million pounds annually.

At the junction of Elm Street and Boulevard is Triangle Park, in which are to be found rare species of shrub, flower, and tree. Facing Snake River and off Broadway (L) is ISLAND PARK which contains a few historic relics, an aquarium, a few wild animals, and small rearing ponds for fish. KATE CURLEY PARK, covering a city block, is on Lee and Emerson; and CITY PARK is southward (L) just beyond the city limits. Here are an artificial lake, used as a swimming pool, and a small zoological garden of native wild animals. Admission is free here, as it also is to the pheasant farm just north of Highland Park. This city's golf field, one of the few eighteen-hole courses in the State, is irrigated by an underground system and has an excellent turf. HIGHLAND PARK on U S 191 just north of the city, is equipped with kitchens, tennis courts, and a children's swimming pool and playground.

The historic TAYLOR TOLL BRIDGE, of which only the stone abutments remain, was built across Snake River in 1866-7. The timbers were hauled from Beaver Canyon, eighty miles north, and the iron was obtained from old freight wagons and from a wrecked steamboat on the Missouri River. The stage station and post office here were formerly called Eagle Rock because a great stone out in the river was for many years the nesting place of an eagle. On Willow Creek north of the city are the scarred but victorious remnants of the first orchard in this part of Idaho. One huge old pear tree has become a towering patriarch that looks over even the cottonwoods along the creek.

Idaho Falls is at the junction with U S 91 (see **Tour 1, Sec. b** and **Tour 2**).

Right on U S 91 is a lava field known as HELL'S HALF ACRE 14 m., in which until 1928 was a remarkable old juniper (cedar) tree that began its growth in 310 A. D. It was still alive when cut down and an examination of it discovered 1,618 rings which, according to geologists, recorded alternate cycles of rainfall and drouth.

Section b. Idaho Falls to Utah Line, 136.9 m.

Valley route with surfaced road throughout. Customary accommodations. The Greyhound Lines and Intermountain Transport Co. buses follow this highway between Butte and Salt Lake City.

South out of Idaho Falls U S 91 proceeds through Idaho's most famous potato area. On the left is the mountain range that spills westward from the Wyoming-Idaho boundary, and on the right the fertile valley reaches away to the volcanic lava plains.

SHELLEY 10 m. (4,624 alt.; 1,447 pop.) is the center of the most prolific potato region in the State. The warehouses here export annually about two thousand carloads of Idaho russets that are known for their quality wherever potatoes are known. At the close of the harvest in October a Spud Day celebration is held, with choice potatoes on display and with baked potatoes served to passengers on every train and motor coach going through the town.

Right from Shelley on an unimproved road are THE LAVAS 4 m., a weird assortment of small caves and fissures and solidified rock flows with dwarfed trees hanging precariously to the edges, with lovely ferns thriving incongruously in the deep pits. The remoter depths are said to be the haunts of coyotes and wildcats and rattlesnakes; and are waiting, in consequence, for someone bold enough to explore

them. Because of the presence of so many arrowheads and other
Indian relics in the tables and pockets here, it has been surmised that
an ancient Indian village was inundated by the eruptions. These
lavas are upon the eastern margin of that huge area of which the
Craters of the Moon National Monument is the core. In the west the
Twin Buttes are visible on a clear day.

BLACKFOOT 27 m. (4,505 alt.; 3,199 pop.) was
named for the Blackfeet Indian tribe. The Indians were
called Siksika (meaning black of feet) because their
feet are said to have been blackened by constant wading in
the ashes of the regions which had been devastated by fire.
If a town can be summarized by a single quality, then perhaps the most notable characteristic of Blackfoot is the fact
that its indefatigable librarian has made of this city not
only probably the most book-conscious one in the State
but has also lifted its taste in reading far above the usual
levels. This circumstance is all the more remarkable when
the books in this small library are compared with those in
other public libraries in Idaho, and when it is remembered
that all the books in all the public libraries in the State do
not add to more than half a million. So awakened has this
town become to the cultural possibilities to be found in a
good library that it recently made an extensive drive to
enlarge its resources in reading.

At Blackfoot is the junction with State 27. This improved road is the most frequent point of diversion to
the Craters of the Moon (see **Tour 4**).

Left from Blackfoot is an unimproved road which leads into the
Blackfoot River country and adjacent terrain. The length of this
tour depends on the taste and time of the adventurer. The distance
is more than sixty miles if he penetrates clear to the Grays Lake
area (also accessible by way of Soda Springs: see **Tour 3, Sec. a**).
This road leads to mountains, rivers, and lakes, and to fishing and
wild game. Near the head of WOLVERINE CREEK 30 m., which
empties into Blackfoot River, are campsites, an open-air dance pavilion, and a fish hatchery owned by sportsmen of this region. GRAYS
LAKE 60 m., lying between the Little Valley Hills and the peaks of
the Caribou Range, can be reached over fair road if the traveler
wishes to penetrate wilderness and find campsites that overlook
a large part of eastern Idaho.

FORT HALL **40 m.** (4,445 alt.) is an Indian agency for the Bannack, Shoshoni, and other tribes. Annual dances of unusual interest are held here: the Sun Dance about July 24, followed by the War, Owl, Rabbit, and Grass Dances, each with its own characteristic songs and drumbeats. The Warm Dance, held in late January or early February, is a religious ritual, intended to hasten the end of winter. Later there is an Easter Dance accompanied by an egg feast. The Indians on the reservation are excellent artisans, the women engaging in many kinds of intricate bead work upon such articles of clothing as moccasins and vests. These, as well as other handicraft, are for sale in the stores in Fort Hall.

The Fort Hall Reservation lies chiefly eastward from the agency. The Indians here are engaged in agriculture, and have their own reservoir for the impounding of water to irrigate their lands (see **Tour 3, Sec a**). They have not been so successful in their agricultural enterprises as the Indians in northern Idaho, chiefly because the lands assigned to them are less fertile.

Close by U S 91 is a lava monument (L) which commemorates old Fort Hall.

Right from the Agency, on a dirt road built recently by the Indians, is the site of old Fort Hall .25 m. An old well, once the center of its enclosure, and the triangular rifle pits, now bedded with grass, are all that remain of the fort. Floods have washed away the adobe plaster with which Hudson's Bay Company covered Wyeth's cottonwood stockade, and the poles themselves were filched by old-timers to build cabins and bridges and roads. This fort, built in 1834, and becoming at once the chief refuge in this great area of Indians and sagebrush, was the only inhabited place between Fort Bridger and Fort Boise. Emigrant wagon trains, coming out of the lonely deserts and valleys eastward, could see from afar its cool whitewashed walls, its red flag lettered H. B. C. (Hudson's Bay Company, but meaning, old trappers said, Here Before Christ); and once within its walls they could forget for awhile the vast empty landscapes out of which they had come. Until its destruction by flood in 1863, Fort Hall was the rendezvous of Indians and Spaniards and French Canadians, priests and doctors and missionaries, besides hordes of nondescript adventurers of all kinds. Some came to rest, some to pray, some to celebrate on liquor distilled from wild honey, some to heal wounds made by Indian arrows, and some to bury their dead. Abandoned in 1855, the fort was a wayside inn for wagon trains until a flood demolished it eight years later. Close by the highway is a lava monument commemorating it.

Fort Hall covered a half acre of ground, and was surrounded by a wall five feet high and nineteen inches thick. Within the stockade were dwellings and stores and barns, all overshadowed by a two-story blockhouse or bastion. Standing in the center of the battle-ground of the Bannacks, Blackfeet, and Crows, and unprotected on all sides, it was in constant danger of attack, but weathered the years and its enemies to disappear at last and be forgotten. For a long while thereafter its actual site was unknown. In 1906 Ezra Meeker went over the Oregon Trail with ox team and dogs, but he was not able to determine the site until ten years later when the old well and rifle pits were found. Flood and erosion had completely changed the contour of the land upon which it had stood.

POCATELLO 52 m. (see **Tour 3, Sec. a** for this city and for the highway from it to McCammon twenty-five miles south. Here U S 30 N and U S 91 are the same.)

At DOWNEY 92 m. (4,860 alt.; 553 pop.) is the junction with State 36. From this town U S 91 and State 36 run parallel into Utah. State 36 avoids the beautiful Logan Canyon and goes over less mountainous terrain.

Right from Downey on State 36 is MALAD CITY 21 m. (4,700 alt.; 2,535 pop.), the seat of Oneida County and once the seat of this entire part of the State. The Malad River was named by French-Canadian trappers, though whether they were made ill from drinking the water or from overgorging on the flesh of beaver seems not to be known. Few towns in Idaho have had a more turbulent past. A pictorial history of Malad City would show a panorama of stage robberies, lynchings, and murders. It was over this Montana Road that gold was freighted from northern mines to the smelters in Utah, and it was in this town that the coaches of the Overland Stage came to a stop. Malad today is remarkable chiefly for the crazy irregularity of its streets, many of which were laid at random upon old paths and cow trails; and for its historic log cabins still scattered among its homes. The East Malad Mountain rises to a height of 9,332 feet and shelters the town from extremes of weather. Sixteen miles southeast in Weston Canyon is the Pass of the Standing Rock, named by John C. Fremont, who camped here on August 29, 1843, while searching for the Great Salt Lake.

From Malad City it is **13 m.** to the Utah line and **57 m.** to Brigham City in Utah.

PRESTON **125 m.** (4,718 alt.; 3381 pop.) is the seat of Franklin County and the center of this irrigated part of the State upon the watershed of Bear River.

Left from Preston is the Emigration Canyon Road (once the California cut-off used by forty-niners to avoid the long detour by way of Fort Hall), which leads into the mountains and canyons of the Cache National Forest. Fishing is good in this area, many fine campsites are available, and the drive up Bear River is the most beautiful in southeastern Idaho. A few miles northeast of Preston on State 34 is the Bear River Canyon. Four miles out, a monument marks the site of Colonel E. P. Connor's attack on the Bannack Indians on January 29, 1863. The battle took place at the mouth of a small stream (later named Battle Creek) which the Indian chieftains, Bear Hunter and Sagwitch, had chosen for their winter home. The Indians defended themselves with embankments of woven willows, but in spite of their ingenuity and their courage they were so badly defeated that Franklin settlers who visited the battleground the next day declared that "you could walk on dead Indians for quite a distance without touching ground." Arrowheads and spear points are still found near the monument.

U S 91 proceeds through the fertile valley lying between the watersheds of Bear and Malad Rivers.

FRANKLIN **133 m.** (4,497 alt.; 531 pop.) was the first permanent white settlement in Idaho. This town was founded in 1860 by a party of Mormon emigrants who thought they were in Utah, but were just across the line. They were industriously unaware that they were establishing the first school, or the first irrigation system in Idaho when they diverted the waters from Maple Creek to this section of Cache Valley. Back East, the indefatigable Brigham Young had bought a steam engine and had it shipped up the Missouri River to Fort Benton and then overland to Franklin by wagon and team. When it is remembered that this engine weighed ten thousand pounds, the long trek for hundreds of miles by wagon and oxen over mountains and rivers is to be seen as a small epic in itself. The engine, one of Idaho's few persistent historic survivals, was used first in a sawmill in Franklin; then moved to Soda Springs and back again to Franklin; and after awhile abandoned and forgotten. For many years it gathered rust by the roadside until citizens decided it was a relic and placed it in the FRANKLIN HALL where it and other historic items can be seen.

At **133 m.** U S 91 crosses the Idaho-Utah Line **20 m.** N of Logan, Utah.

TOUR NO. 2

(Butte, Montana) — Dubois — Idaho Falls. U S 91.

Montana Line to Idaho Falls, **83 m.**

Surfaced throughout, this is the main traveled highway between Butte and Salt Lake City, but it lies for the most part over flat, semiarid, and rather desolate country and offers little of beauty or interest. The route is paralleled by the Oregon Short Line of the Union Pacific System and by the Greyhound Lines and Intermountain Transport Co. buses. Accommodations limited.

U S 91 enters Idaho from Montana **132 m.** S of Butte, Montana, over the Bitterroot Mountains (6,823 alt.) and the Continental Divide, but the gradient is easy even though the highway passes from the eastern to the western watershed. For several miles the road goes through mountainous country and the western end of the Targhee National Forest.

SPENCER **17 m.** (5,883 alt.; 107 pop.) is in a formidable area of bleak landscapes that lie entirely across Clark County and far into Jefferson County on the south. This region is the northeastern flank of that vast lava terrain upon central Idaho of which the Craters of the Moon are a picturesque summary.

Right on this improved road which swings southwest and meets State 27 at **82 m.** is Arco (see **Tour 4**).

DUBOIS **33 m.** (5,148 alt.; 312 pop.) is the seat of Clark County and the largest town within a radius of thirty miles in any direction. This capital of a wasteland was named for former U. S. Senator Fred Dubois. Far out in the west on Birch Creek (but not worth a visit) is the ghost town of Viola: at one time two thirds of the lead produced in the United States came from here, but now only one log cabin and a slag dump remain.

1. Right from Dubois, State 29 leads to LIDY HOT SPRINGS **20 m.** sometimes called, and not without reason, The Oasis, where there are indoor and outdoor swimming pools supplied by hot mineralized water, a dance hall, and camping sites.

2. Left from Dubois, a fair road leads to the U. S. SHEEP EXPERI-MENTAL STATION **6 m.**, which is visited by a great many travelers over this highway.

At **57 m.** is the junction with State 28, an improved road.

Right on State 28 is MUD LAKE **12 m.**, a large body of water that harbors thousands of migratory ducks and geese. This lake has no outlet; and though Camas Creek flows into it and though it gathers much rain and snow from its watersheds, it is slowly disappearing. This circumstance is less surprising when it is remembered that this large area, and especially westward, is one of vanishing streams. Northward, the Beaver and Medicine Lodge Creeks lose themselves completely in the lava fields; and westward, two rivers disappear. Throughout this region are fissures and porous formations, and under these there are doubtless subterranean channels along which the buried streams flow for nobody knows how far. This region is underlaid for the most part by great deposits of basalt that has been poured out at different times from many widely distributed craters. These erratic flows have piled up the basalt to high levels and have in consequence produced broad but shallow and undrained depressions into which the streams are discharged. Some of these remain indefinitely as tiny lakes. North of Mud Lake is an extensive lava plain with fantastic buttes; and southwest are the Antelope and Circular Buttes, two volcanic cones that stand above the surrounding country. The flora in this area is chiefly of white or sweet sage, rabbit brush, and Russian thistle, with chaparral above 4,500 feet. Around the lake on the sloughs adjacent is a luxuriant growth of marsh grass and tule.

ROBERTS **65 m.** (4,775 alt.; 297 pop.) was known until recently as Market Lake. The former name owes to the fact that in frontier times there was a lake here upon which there were thousands of ducks and geese. These were so abundant that early settlers came here to gather their meat, and somewhat facetiously called the place Market Lake, and spoke jocularly of going to the market for a supply of food. The name was changed to honor a railroad superintendent.

U S 91 continues to Idaho Falls **85 m.** (See **Tour 1, Sec. a).**

TOUR NO. 3

(Cheyenne, Wyoming) — Montpelier — Pocatello — Twin Falls—Boise—Weiser—(Baker, Oregon). U S 30 N and U S 30. Oregon Trail Route.

Wyoming Line to Oregon Line **462 m.**

The Union Pacific Railroad roughly parallels this highway throughout, and the Union Pacific Stages follow it between Pocatello and Weiser.

Usual accommodations throughout.

Section a. Wyoming Line to Pocatello, 122 m.

This section of Tour 3 follows the Bear and Portneuf Rivers with no difficult grades. Surfaced highway.

U S 30 N enters Idaho and the Bear Lake Valley at Border on the Idaho-Wyoming line in the extreme southeastern part of the State. This part of Idaho is an area of lofty ranges, of lakes, of rivers and creeks, and of small valleys upon the great watersheds. Very little of it lies at an elevation less than six thousand feet, and this altitude makes for deep winters and cool summers, with an average temperature of forty-six degrees. The valleys are given to agriculture under irrigation, the uplands and mountains to grazing. The chief crops are grain and potatoes and the hardier fruits, with grapes abundant farther south by Utah. The Caribou National Forest is on the right, the Cache National Forest on the left, but most of the old-growth timber has been exhausted, and the somewhat denuded watersheds offer the same problems in erosion and overgrazing that are to be found in many parts of the State. Bear Lake Valley is the only part of southern Idaho that is not drained by Snake River.

MONTPELIER 22 m. (5,941 alt.; 2,436 pop.) is the largest town in this area. Founded in 1864, it was first known as Clover Creek and later as Belmont; but when Brigham Young came here and decided that he liked it, he named it after the capital of his native State. This town is the gateway to one of Idaho's most remarkable regions.

Left from Montpelier, State 35 leads to one of the chief recreation areas of eastern Idaho.

PARIS 9 m. is notable because it has the finest buildings of any small town in Idaho. On the left is a typical tabernacle of the Mormon Church. The dominant sect in eastern and southeastern Idaho is Mormon, and the most attractive architecture throughout this region is to be found in its tabernacles and temples. The Paris free campgrounds are equipped with tables and stoves to accommodate five hundred persons; and through the grounds runs the water of Paris Creek, very cold even in midsummer, and extremely clear.

South of Paris at 12 m. on State 35 a right turn from 35 past the store goes up a canyon to lovely BLOOMINGTON LAKE 9 m. This lake, lying under huge cliffs, covers twelve acres and is of clear cold water of unknown depth which gushes from innumerable springs far under. Excellent campsites are available here. In the appropriate season this lake is framed like a tremendous jewel among an unusually luxuriant wealth of wild flowers, including larkspur, columbine, dogwood, and mountain ash. In 1931 the U. S. Forest Service planted in this lake 1,000 California glacial or golden trout, a rare species that is not found in many places.

South of Paris at 17 m. on State 35 a right turn leads up St. Charles Canyon and enters Cache National Forest and proceeds to the MINNETONKA CAVE 10 m. At 0.5 m. a left turn enters the Minnetonka campground, and those wishing to explore the cave will leave their automobiles here and go up the mountain by footpath. It is a little more than a half mile, and a steep climb, and on a warm day it is advisable to take drinking water along. Gas lanterns and not flashlights are absolutely necessary equipment in exploration of the cave, as well as rugged clothing. The journey to the farthest chamber and return requires from three to six hours.

The entrance to this cave is most appropriately what the entrance to any remarkable interior should be. The visitor at the top of the trail comes to a sheer wall of rock which stands against the backbone of the mountain. Midway in the wall at its bottom is a door which opens upon a tunnel that reaches downward by easy descent for a hundred yards. Its ceiling is extremely rugged with great thrusting abutments hung together in a huge amorphous roof. Some of the stone here looks like polished green marble but farther down it yields to white mounded bluffs bottomside up.

Seventy-five yards down the corridor the right wing climbs away
into a large chamber, the floor of which meets and is welded with
the ceiling. At one hundred yards the tunnel swings to the left.
The floor of it is now an acreage of boulders that scale upward
ragged ton by ton. At the top of this climb is a grotesque serrated
ceiling with some brown columnar stalagmites on the right, and just
beyond these the stone looks as if great vats of whipped cream
had been spilled and turned to rock. The low stratified roof also
has small overflows that suggest animistic symbols on an ancient
temple.

The path now goes steeply upward over huge glazed stones
scattered in a jungle under a stupendous roof in which eternity is
commemorated in underhung ledges and reefs. Visitors should
pause here in their ascent and send one person ahead to the summit
with a gas lantern. For the beautiful stalagmites resemble nothing
so much as a cemetery on a hilltop under moonlight. The monuments vary considerably in size: some of them obviously seem to
stand over the bones of the great and some over the humble, and
all of them together, when seen under the glow of a hidden
lantern, make one of the loveliest pictures to be found in the cave.
Beyond the principal graveyard stands a huge bronzed monument
that has been called King Tut, and at his side is another, doubtless
his wife; but these look more like the images of heathen gods. The
ceiling here was once very beautiful, too, with stalactites hanging
down in an inverted garden of small columns, but vandals have
knocked most of them off and they now lie scattered on the floor.
This cemetery is under a high vaulted ceiling that is overwhelming
in the Gothic majesty of its sculpturing.

Nothing is more notable about this cave than the way in which
it becomes progressively more breath-taking. After the visitor has
passed these monuments on a hillside, he proceeds through a narrow
and indescribably ragged passageway to another stupendous chamber. In its first fifty yards its floor is a broad steep incline which
is paralleled by an equally hunchbacked ceiling. Then the corridor
widens and the ceiling lifts away. After another fifty yards the
explorer ought to observe the large stones under his feet: of apparently soft texture and of soft color, they look like blocks of
yellow congealed cream imbedded with nuts. Still floored with
these huge cream puffs or with scattered monuments that look like
case-hardened granite, this chamber continues and then drops down
into an awful gorge more than a hundred feet in depth. A more
terrifying interior it would be difficult to find; but the descent
from huge stone to stone is not dangerous, and after it is made
the visitor will find himself at the bottom of a barbarous tunnel
that is hardly more than a dozen feet wide but reaches sheer
through gloom a hundred feet to its ceiling. From the floor, the
explorer should note on his right the enormous flat shelf that is
actually laid out upon stone beams. The underside of this shelf
is a slab of pavement that is as perfect as the plastered wall of
a house. The walls in this tunnel are spiked and toothed, with each

Corridor of the Kings

Cavern of the Idols

The Bride

looking like a plateau of small crags turned upon its edge, or with
a plateau of crags inverted to make the ceiling.

At the far end the trail climbs very sharply from shelf to shelf
and comes to another gigantic chamber with boulders as large as
houses strewn over its floor and with enormous rifts running like
half-buried beams through its ceiling. Some water falls here upon
the large round stones that look like solidified kalsomine built of
river cobble rock. Water can be heard in other invisible parts of
this chamber. The right flank, vanishing into darkness, suggests
other interiors beyond, but none have been found. To the left, and
just beyond the water, is a mammoth blade of stone that looks like
the cleaver of some prehistoric giant; and beyond this, still to the
left, the path again falls sharply over rock hummocks shelved
downward in a world of anarchy and enters a long serpentine
corridor, the floor of which makes easy walking in contrast with
the floors already covered. This chamber leads after a hundred
yards to the Bride. The Bride herself is a huge stalagmite seven
feet high with her creamy trousseau draped virginally around her;
and the Bridegroom hangs from the ceiling by his heels. There is
a small stream of water under the floor here and plainly audible,
and quite likely it could be reached by removing some of the smaller
stones. The cave now runs to the left another hundred yards and
terminates, so far as is now known, in two divided chambers that
drop down into vaulted archways at their far end.

Such briefly is this enormous cave lying under the backbone of
a mountain. Undisciplined and vandalic, and the quiet but magnificent synopsis of a once turbulent time, it is in its barbarous
sculpturing the most impressive of all the known caves in the
State. Nobody knows how much of it remains undiscovered and
unexplored. Only a few persons have entered it. And these, after
several hours of difficult journeying, are usually ready to turn
back when they reach the Bridal Chamber and seek sunlight and
ponder on what they have seen. The elevation of this cave is
7,500 feet.

On State 35 is BEAR LAKE 18 m. and its many half-deserted
resorts. This body of water, lying half in Idaho and half in Utah,
was until a few years ago a very beautiful lake of deep blue with
excellent beaches and recreational facilities. There were many fine
summer homes along its shores. But the Utah Power Company
was allowed during years of drouth to install pumps and build
canals and take great quantities of water out of the lake to be diverted down Bear River to the turbines of the plant in northern
Utah. In consequence, the lake has sunk more than twenty feet,
its beaches have become quagmires or wide stretches of sand, and
its resorts have almost gone bankrupt. Lately, it is true, the lake
has risen several feet; but even if it were to be restored to its
former level, Bear Lake can never recover its former glory as
long as its water is at the mercy of capricious interests. Farms in
this valley have suffered, too.

FISH HAVEN 23 m., formerly a beautiful spot, is only a shabby ghost of what it used to be—and it used to be the most important Idaho resort on the west side of the lake. It still offers cabins, bathing, boating, and hiking; but the chief hiking is now from the resort to the lake, a quarter of a mile away. Just south of it, in Utah, is the Lakota Resort, which has sunk under a similar fate. Nor have the many summer homes fared any better: they still stand, but they overlook not the lake as formerly but the wide barren margin that the retreating waters have left. At the north end of the lake is the pumping plant of the Utah Company and north of this is Mud Lake, a much smaller body of water that is a favorite with thousands of migratory wild geese and ducks. At the northeastern corner of Bear Lake is the BEAR LAKE HOT SPRINGS RESORT with its hotel empty, its large swimming pool used only by week-enders, and its boats junked.

There are trout in the lake plus several species of whitefish, but fishing here is poor. The lake, except for its recent naked flanks, is still beautiful, and the best vantage point is in Utah. At 28 m. is an unobstructed view of the colorful mountain range that is the eastern backdrop of the lake, with a second and higher range beyond, and a third, still higher, beyond the second. Under morning sun the lake is a very deep blue, but in late afternoon it is pale gray or green with the mountains on the far side throwing soft lavender shadows. Its backdrop as the sun sets looks like a long bank of deep purple fog.

In Utah at **30 m.** a right turn leads to Logan.

U S 30 N goes west out of Montpelier and follows Bear River, which in its 165 miles of length is one of the most circuitous streams in the United States. It rises in northern Utah, flows for 30 miles through Wyoming, and enters Idaho near Border. For 40 miles now it seems decided, but W of Soda Springs it pursues every possible direction before leaving the State to enter Utah and seek the Great Salt Lake. Most picturesque is its gorge as viewed from the coaches of trains near the Utah-Idaho line. In crossing southeastern Idaho the highway crosses one of the richest areas of buried wealth in the world, because four fifths of the phosphate on the North American Continent lie here and in adjacent areas in Utah, Wyoming, and Montana.

At **46 m.** is the junction with a poor road.

Right on this road, which leads up a canyon 2 m., is the SULPHUR SPRINGS. The rock around this spring is so nearly pure sulphur that is will burn with a steady flame. Eastward a mile on U S 30 N is another left turn up a canyon to Swan Lake. An arc of stone here five hundred feet wide and forty feet high has impounded a reservoir clear across the mouth of Swan Lake Creek. Deep in the water here, petrified timbers are visible. A half mile above this lake is another of about its size, and at the head of the creek which helps to feed these lakes are springs which taste strongly of sulphur. The only fish in these lakes is a tiny minnowlike creature that seems never to grow larger than trout bait. In the wall impounding the lower lake there is a small cave.

SODA SPRINGS 51 m. (5,777 alt.; 831 pop.) is the second oldest settlement in the State. Fort Conner, the southwest part of the present townsite, was established in 1863 by General Conner and a little band of Marrisites, dissenters from the Mormon Church. The old or lower town has but one of the original buildings, the schoolhouse, still standing. The present townsite joins the original on the east. Soda Springs was named for the many springs, highly charged with carbonic acid gas and most of them cold, that gush out in this area. This whole region, in fact, is a wonderland of its own, though some of the springs, like the Steamboat, have been inundated by storage waters since the completion of a dam. The STEAMBOAT SPRING, two miles west of the town, still boils up through forty feet of water and explodes at the surface. Analysis has shown that there are twenty-two different degrees or kinds of mineral content in the springs in this region, and all of them are said to have remarkable curative power. There was formerly a bottling plant at the Ninety Percent Spring near Stampede Park, and though this no longer operates, thousands of persons do come here annually to drink the waters. Favorite of all with visitors is the HOOPER SPRING a mile north of town. Close by it is the CHAMPAGNE SPRING, and northward is the MAMMOTH SODA SPRING, which is almost precisely of the same size as the Mammoth Hot Springs in Yellowstone Park. Just south of the town, where Little Spring Creek crosses the road, is the spot where a family of seven emigrants was massacred. Just west of the town is the cemetery in which these persons were buried with their wagon box serving as a coffin.

1. Right on country road is STAMPEDE PARK 2 m., where in August an annual stampede and rodeo is held. This park is a natural amphitheater, bordered by peaks and flanked by peculiar stone formations and rock crystals. The road to the park winds through cedar and pine trees and is known as the Red Road because of the colorful rock formations which were sculptured long ago by the springs. The spring flowing into the park is known as Eighty Percent.

2. Left is MOUNT SHERMAN standing against the sky at an elevation of 9,669 feet. Its summit is accessible over eighteen miles of fair road and over trail in the last mile. From this peak, Salt Lake Mountains are visible in the south, the Teton Peaks in the north. There is excellent fishing along Eight Mile Creek which the road follows.

3. Right from Soda Springs on State 34, a graveled road, are many points of interest. SODA MOUND, beautifully landscaped, is on the left just beyond the railway track. On the left 3 m. out is a round hill at the foot of which was for a long time a nameless grave, now known to be that of Charles Robinson, an early trapper. A right turn at 4 m. out follows the Trail Creek road to the FORMATION CAVE (sometimes called the Limestone Cavern) and to the 4 S Ranch. The cave is reached by a left turn off the Trail Creek road at .25 m. from its junction. This very lovely cave is about three hundred yards long, about twenty-five feet in its average width, and about fifteen feet in its ceiling. It has been formed by hard mineralized waters, and in consequence its ceiling is studded with beautiful stalactites that look like gray and white foliage in stone—and some of them do have stems, tule, and leaves—or like delicate honeycombs or like hard fine lace. The sandy floor has some stalagmites but it is the ceiling that is a vision of loveliness.

The 4 S RANCH, the most important dude resort in this part of the State, is 4 m. from the junction with State 34. It covers thirty-five hundred acres, with excellent pastures adjoining the Caribou National Forest and with excellent accommodations. It offers fishing and hunting in season, camp sites, footpath and horseback trips, and swimming.

At 7 m. on State 34 is a right turn to CONDA, one of the principal phosphate plants of the Anaconda Copper Mining Company. This town, two miles off the road, is a model in planning and in the modern equipment of its homes. On the left of State 34, but at some distance, are the MAMMOTH SPRINGS, the source of Soda Creek. On the left at 10 m. is CHINA HAT HILL, beyond which are a second hill and a third. Between these two is a lovely nameless lake with neither outlet nor inlet but with many springs visible on its bottom. It is an unusual body of water in appearance because it is set down low and fenced around with steep walls. There are no fish in its water. At 13 m. State 34 crosses Blackfoot River, and just beyond the bridge a road leads (R) into the Caribou Forest. On the left is the BLACKFOOT RESERVOIR, the water of which is used by the Indians of the

Fort Hall Reservation. This reservoir in its beautiful setting and with hill-islands half buried looks more like a mountain lake. It is heavily stocked with fish.

HENRY 20 m. is a ghost town on the Little Blackfoot River. At 21.5 m. a left turn off State 34 skirts the northern end of the reservoir and leads to campgrounds, excellent fishing, and to a curious phenomenon. The latter, 14 m. from the junction, is a great hole in the side of a mountain, and this is visible from the road at 13 m. To reach the hole it is necessary to cross a meadow afoot. According to an old-timer, it was in the night of the second day of November, 1917, that he was awakened by a terrific sound that brought him out of bed with his hair standing on end. He went outside, expecting to see the sky falling or the earth splitting open; and on the next day discovered that a hunk had dropped out of the mountainside not far away. This hole is about 150 feet across and about 75 feet in depth on its upper side. In the bottom of it is water of unknown depth that formerly was lucid but is now covered with a brown or green scum that looks like heavy wallpaper. A part of the sheer walls are of earth, a part of stone; and the strange thing about it is the fact that this enormous piece of mountain dropped and disappeared from sight into a body of water, the depth of which nobody has been able to learn.

The main road still goes northward. At 24 m. a left turn cuts between two shelves of rock that are known as ROBBER'S ROOST. On the left a mile farther is MEADOW CREEK VALLEY, and at 28.5 m. there is a road which goes (L) along the west side of GRAYS LAKE. The southern end of the lake 30 m. is a tule marsh, for the lake itself is a large but very shallow body of water that is flanked with bogs and meadows to which come tens of thousands of wild ducks. At 33 m. the rock by the side of the road (R) is BEAVERTAIL POINT: it was here that an Indian massacre occurred and it was here that the men were buried. Two of the graves are on the Point, and a third is by the ruins of a cabin just beyond and close by the road. The latter is the grave of John Day for whom this lake was first named and from whom later the distinction was taken for nobody knows what reason. All three men were buried in wagon boxes.

At 35 m. is a junction: the left turn goes up the lake, and the right goes over the mountains and to Freedom, Wyoming, connecting there with a road that leads northward to the Jackson Hole country, Grand Teton National Park, and the southern entrance to Yellowstone Park.

U S 30 N goes westward out of Soda Springs. The flora in this part of Idaho is chiefly aspen, lodgepole pine, limber pine, and Douglas fir among trees; maple, serviceberry, mahogany, chokecherry, snowberry, wild currant, and wild rose among shrubs; and geranium, harebell, cinquefoil, lupine, violet, daisy, larkspur, aster, paintbrush, and wild carrot among the flowers. To the left at **57 m.** is SODA POINT, to which Fremont referred in 1842 as Sheep Rock because of the great number of mountain sheep seen here. It is an important geological formation inasmuch as its jutting of lava caused Bear River to turn southward and eventually enter Utah instead of following the natural watershed of this region.

At **58 m.** is a junction with State 34.

Left on State 34 is GRACE **6 m.**, where there is a large hydroelectric plant that is annually visited by many persons. Two miles south of Grace is VOLCANO HILL, and a few hundred yards east of the hill is ICE CAVE, which is structurally a curious phenomenon. The entrance pitches down for fifty yards but thereafter the floor is fairly level to the far end. About halfway through is a skylight. But the remarkable thing about this cave is its structural symmetry: fifty feet in width and about twenty-five in height, it runs in an almost perfect corridor for half a mile and looks like the upper half of an enormous barrel. And the walls and ceiling (because this was once the outlet of volcanic pourings) look as if they had been plastered with hot lava. The far end terminates in piles of lava, once molten, and is known as the DEVILS KITCHEN. Though there is not much ice in it, this interior has been known as the ice cave since its discovery many decades ago.

LAVA HOT SPRINGS **85 m.** (544 pop.) is one of the most phenomenal spots in the State, but Idahoans have been too busy taking the rough edges off an empire to give it much interest. Natatoriums, it is true, have been established there, two by the State and one by the town; and there is a fully equipped sanitarium. This town, situated on the lovely Portneuf River at the base of great cliffs, has waters which, in both volume and therapeutic value, are said to be among the most remarkable springs known. For centuries the Indians paid tribute here to the Great Spirit for the curative properties of these hot springs and set this spot aside as neutral ground to be shared in peace by all tribes. The daily flow from the hot springs here, each with a different mineral content, is 6,711,000 gallons. The springs have an average of 962.33

parts of mineral content per million. It is locally claimed
that the mineral content of these springs is higher than
that of any other hot spring in the North American Continent or in Europe.

Both the State and City natatoriums have large indoor
pools, the better one of which is the first. The State also
has an outdoor pool, called the Mud Bath, which is amazingly characterized by the varying degrees in the temperature of its waters. It is not a large pool, but a swimmer can stroke from almost cold water into hot water
and through various degrees of cold and warmth between
the two extremes. This circumstance owes to the fact
that thirty springs of varying temperature pour into this
pool. Three springs, the Ha-Wah-Na, the Sulphur, and
the Iron, have a total dissolved content of minerals of more
than nine hundred and fourteen hundred respectively.
Just below the balcony of the Riverside Inn runs the clear
cold water of the Portneuf River with hot springs steaming almost at its edge.

Against the town to the south is a great mountain
that is almost a solid pile of unquarried building stone,
which because of its strength and lightness has been
characterized by engineers as one of the best yet found.
It can be seen in two cabins across the river from the
Mud Bath, and in cigarette trays in the Inn. Interesting,
too, are other rock formations of Paleozoic limestones,
shales, sandstones, and quartzites. Upon the river within
the radius of a mile are fifty small waterfalls; and the
smoke holes of old volcanoes are within hiking distance.
The canyons and glens offer camping retreats, and fishing
in the river is good for a stream so accessible.

At **97 m.** is the junction with U S 91. (See **Tour 1, Sec.
b.**) U S 30 N turns north here and follows the Portneuf
River and Canyon, the second of which is rich in historic
lore. With its abrupt walls and innumerable crevices, cut
in limestones and shales, it was a favorite hide-out for
Indians and for white men of prey. It was here in 1865 that

a stage carrying several passengers and $60,000 was betrayed by its driver to a gang led by Jim Locket, a notorious villain. Two passengers were killed and their bodies buried in a gulch near the scene of the crime. Another robbery occurred not far south of Pocatello in a grove of trees near the Big Elbow of the river. The robbers, ten in number and said to have been terrifically villainous of aspect, held up the Wells, Fargo stage, murdered six of the seven passengers, and made off with $110,000 in gold dust.

INKOM 109 m. is the home of the largest cement plant in Idaho. For its materials the factory draws on the mountain of lime rock that stands against the village.

POCATELLO 122 m. (4,464 alt.; 16,471 pop.).

Railroad station: Oregon Short Line, end of W. Bonneville St.
Bus station: Union Pacific Stages, Fargo Building, S. Main St.
Airport, municipal: (McDougall Field). Nat. Park Airways, 6 m. N. W.
Golf courses: Ross Park (municipal), south of city, 9 holes. University course, back of Red Hill and near university, 9 holes.

It is the seat of Bannock County, the second in size of the Idaho cities, the principal gateway by railway, highway, and air to the Pacific Northwest, and one of the largest railway centers west of the Mississippi.

It stands upon an area which formerly was a portion of the Fort Hall Indian Reservation, and was named by the builders of the Union Pacific Railroad for a friendly Indian leader who helped to secure tribal consent for the transfer of needed rights of way and building sites within the reservation to the then Utah Northern. Although the latter had been practically completed by Brigham Young, the Mormon leader, from Salt Lake City to Butte in 1879, Pocatello did not take form until 1882, when, with a collection of tents, it became the junction point of these two rail properties.

Because of its fortunate position as the center of intermountain arterial transportation, the growth of the city has since then been both substantial and constant.

In addition to its rail facilities, it is directly served by Federal highways U S 30 N and U S 91, and has twice daily air mail, express, and passenger service. Because of its extensive railroad plant (the largest between Omaha and the Pacific Coast), it has an East and West Side, each with substantial downtown business and residential sections. On the East Side are the wholesale district, city and county buildings, three of the city parks, some of the better homes, and the spacious campus of the University of Idaho, Southern Branch. In FRAZIER HALL, on the University grounds, is the recently established historical museum, featuring Idaho records, relics, and specimens. Through the West Side of the city flows the romantic Portneuf River, prolific producer of beaver, royal giver, and entertainer of many famous mountain men. On this side of the city, too, are additional city parks, IRVING JUNIOR STADIUM, the SENIOR HIGH SCHOOL, the BANNOCK COUNTY MEMORIAL BUILDING, more of the finer homes, and the larger apartment houses of the city.

South, and a little way beyond the city limits, is ROSS PARK with grassy slopes, shady retreats, a swimming pool, a zoo, playgrounds, picnic grounds, and one of the finest golf courses in the State. Five miles farther south, at Black Rock at the very beginning of the Union Pacific ascent of the great Continental Divide, one stands at the principal of the rail outlets to the Pacific Coast which eminent engineers have been able to locate on the west slope of the Intermountain Rockies.

Southwest, and adjoining the city, is the MINK CREEK RECREATIONAL AREA, including many improved picnic grounds, the POCATELLO GAME PRESERVE, containing one thousand head of elk and many deer, JUSTICE PARK, CAMP TENDOY, and KINPORT PEAK. At the summit of Kinport is a roster of names of all who have climbed to this eminence for a view of the surrounding country. Beyond is Arbon Valley and its fertile, rolling "dry" lands which produce nearly a million bushels of grain annually.

At Pocatello is the junction with U S 91 (see **Tour 1, Sec. b).**

Section b. Pocatello to Boise, 268 m.

This section of Tour 3 lies through the Snake River Valley and roughly parallels the river during most of its length. The road is hard surfaced throughout. Customary accommodations.

U S 30 N goes north and west out of Pocatello. Upon the right **6 m.** is the airport, and running north on the west side of it is a country lane.

Right on this lane is the MEADER TROUT FARM 1 m., well worth a visit. Visitors are welcome but they must leave before sundown, for at this hour several huge savage dogs are freed to patrol the properties during the night. This plant has several ponds, and any time after spring spawning hundreds of trout (chiefly rainbow) of all sizes are to be seen here, with so many in any pond that the water is black with them. These fish are fed chiefly with horseflesh, and in every year dozens of wornout hacks are slain and ground up and stored in the cold rooms of the farm's hydroelectric plant.

To the right now, but not visible, is Snake River, which is tributary to the Columbia, but larger. Flowing a distance of 1,000 miles and forming 42 per cent of the Columbia River system, it drains 109,000 square miles, including western Wyoming, all of Idaho except the north and the extreme southeastern corner, the northwest corner of Utah, the northeast corner of Nevada, eastern Oregon, and the southeast corner of Washington. The extreme length or breadth of its basin is 450 miles. For more than half its distance it flows through a gorge, and has already upon it and its feeders 80 reservoirs with a combined storage capacity of 5,700,000 acre-feet. In addition to these, there are 96 known but undeveloped sites with an estimated storage capacity of 7,746,000 acre-feet, and 70 hydroelectric plants which use less than one tenth of its potential power. It is fed by 56 rivers, of which 17 are regarded as major tributaries, and by 74 large creeks. Its source is in the southeast corner of Yellowstone Park at an elevation of 9,600 feet. It flows southward through Wyoming to the Hoback River, where it swings westward into a deep canyon which runs to the Idaho-Wyoming line. Its first 61 miles in Idaho lie in a canyon, but at Heise it opens upon the Snake River Valley, and for 200 miles to Milner is not deeply intrenched. At Milner it cuts a gorge for 200 miles to emerge again at Enterprise and flow over a plain to Huntington, where again for 189 miles it lies far below the surrounding terrain. At Lewiston it enters Washington and flows 141 miles to its junction with Columbia River at Pasco.

In the earliest geologic period most of the Snake River Basin was covered by a shallow sea in which were deposited great quantities of sand and mud. These have hardened into quartzites. After the sea receded there was little invasion by marine waters but there were tremendous upliftings of granitic materials which were consolidated into the Idaho batholith and its smaller but related masses of rock. Following this there was an epidemic of volcanic upheavals and explosive eruptions accompanied by flows of lava and ash. Erosion came next and slow patient sculpturings by glaciers, but the region was not yet ready to accept its alluvial deposits, and tremors and gigantic quakings shook Idaho from time to time, and basaltic uplifts rose like black monuments on the landscape. Within recent centuries earthquakes have been infrequent and never severe, but there are still deep and troubled rumblings, and not inconceivably in some future time this valley may again steam and tremble under boiling tides. After peace came Snake River settled down to the business of eroding its gorge. In the upper valley here it goes too lazily to achieve much, but beyond Milner it gathers speed and anger and has been most impressively busy.

On the right at **20 m.** the AMERICAN FALLS RESER-
VOIR comes into view, the first and largest of many
between Pocatello and the Oregon line. Though it has a
capacity of 1,700,000 acre-feet and through a network of
canals and diversions serves 600,000 acres, it is less spectacular by far than many which are to be seen elsewhere.
The dam is a mile wide and has a maximum height of 87
feet. The reservoir it created is 12 miles wide, 26 miles
long, and covers an area of 56,000 acres. The cost of the
dam was $3,060,000, but the cost of the whole project it-
self ran to three times that sum. It is a concrete structure with a rolled earth-filled embankment at either end.

AMERICAN FALLS **25 m.** (4,330 alt.; 1,280 pop.) was
once a favorite camping spot on the Old Oregon Trail.
Or at least the former site was, for American Falls was
moved when the reservoir was created, and the thrust of
an elevator out of the lake marks the area where the town
once stood. A railroad, a power plant, and a highway
were also moved. This town is the center of a huge dry-
farming wheat belt and the gateway to reclamation projects that reach for 170 miles westward. Just below the
dam here is the bridge of the Union Pacific, and just below the bridge is Idaho Power Company's largest hydroelectric plant. Close by the plant is the TRENNER ME-
MORIAL PARK, dedicated to an engineer who helped in
the development of this region. A rocky terrace made of
lava from the Craters of the Moon, a fountain and a
landscaped lawn, a lava monolith, and a miniature power
station make of this park not only a point of interest but
also a pleasant contrast to the arid country roundabout.
The park is illuminated at night. Here, too, is one of the
State's largest fish hatcheries, with a capacity of 2,500,000
fingerlings in a season. Of unusual interest to persons
who fancy old historic trails is the fact that a part of the
Oregon Trail can still be seen within the townsite and for
a short distance south.

At **27 m.** is the junction with an unimproved road.

Left on this road are INDIAN SPRINGS 1 m., where pools and baths
are available. This resort is one of the most popular of the hot
mineralized springs of the State, not only because of its reputed
therapeutic value but also because it is easily accessible.

At **35 m.** is one of the most famous landmarks and
monuments in the State. To understand what happened
here in 1862 it is necessary to forget the telephone
lines and highways, the towns and dams, and remember
that this bleak road is a part of the most famous trail
the North American Continent has known. It is necessary
to imagine an arid region of sagebrush and loneliness, of
unexplored mountains and deep rivers, with a flat and un-
obtrusive and desolate wagon road taking its endless way
over the gray miles. It was here, on August 10 in 1862,
that a train of eleven wagons, drawn by ox teams and
carrying twenty-five families from Iowa, took its journey,
with the dust in the ruts felly-deep and with nothing in
the distance save the obscure outline of ragged stone and
beyond this the hot luminous haze of a far valley. These
eleven wagons were the vanguard of many more, all of
them headed uncertainly for Oregon. The ox teams moved
slowly over a country that seemed interminable; and
those who have followed the trails that pioneers blazed,
who now travel by train and air and automobile, find it
difficult to realize even obscurely the thirst and weariness,
the intolerable drag of the journey week after week, the
bleak sameness of earth and sky and sun. It is hard to
realize that one of these ox-drawn wagons was an hour
covering a mile and a half, or that the short distance
from American Falls to the rocks ahead filled a large part
of a day. This caravan had spent nearly the whole summer crossing Nebraska and Wyoming and Idaho to this
point, and these travelers were weary at heart, and the
fabulous valleys of Oregon seemed as remote as ever.
There were landmarks, some of which they had passed,
some of which they were now looking for in the pale
distance. Without maps, without anything but a peak
or a notched butte in a week's journey, they knew only

that they had come hundreds of miles, had hundreds still to go.

The driver of the first wagon, sitting high on the seat, was doubtless looking ahead, trying to distinguish between the blue gray of the desert and the gray blue of the sky. Behind him in the crawling wagons, reaching back for a quarter of a mile, were men and women sitting in stupor, with tired flesh and tired eyes; were solemn children who had sat in these loaded wagons week after week, going they hardly knew where; and drivers gazing back over the enormously unreal distance out of which they had come and wondering about the distance ahead. This was a hot day in August with not a tree in sight and with no breeze. The yellow earth was turned up by the wheels in lazy blinding clouds that rolled back from wagon to wagon and settled upon the freight until the travelers could write their names in dust an inch deep. The driver on that front seat was looking at the Snake River Gorge, now appearing on the right, and at the blurred piles ahead of him, and was perhaps remembering that camp in this night would be pitched on bottom lands of the river. He probably was not suspicious. When he came to the crest of a hill and looked down a long slope to great piles of stone on either side of the trail, his gaze reached beyond to the river, now a visible oasis in a landscape of scalding sun. For fifteen minutes the wagons plowed in their furrows down this hill toward the bluffs and it was not until the leader had passed into the small gorge, with refreshing shadow on either side, that a sudden movement in the stones above brought every man to a trigger. . . .

The sudden confusion and panic, the awful horror of the next few minutes, it is almost impossible to realize. The bare chronicle reads that nine were slain, six were scalped, many were injured, and a few miraculously escaped. The chronicle declares that wagons were plundered and burned and the beasts were driven off; and that on the next day the next wagon train reached this spot and buried the dead. And here, on a site now known as MASSACRE ROCKS, sixty-five years later, a monument was erected.

At **37 m.** there is a Pioneer Monument (L).

At **38 m.** is the junction with an unimproved road.

Left on this road is EMIGRANT ROCK **3 m.**, a stone twenty feet high on which are registered the autographs of early travelers. Some of the names carved into the rock or even some of those painted on with black axle grease as long ago as 1849 are still visible.

For eight more miles U S 30 N follows the river and then climbs to arid plains that have not been reclaimed by irrigation. On a clear day the Lost River Mountains are visible in the north, and on the south is a spur of the Goose Creek Range. The hilltops now offer a broad panoramic view of the Snake River Valley and the haze of Burley and Twin Falls areas. At **49 m.** the highway crosses Raft River.

RUPERT **73 m.** (4,200 alt.; 2,250 pop.) is one of the few towns in Idaho that were planned and not allowed to grow aimlessly. Laid out by the engineering department of the Reclamation Service and named for the engineer who planned it, Rupert looked ambitiously into the future and arranged itself around a central plaza. Like the cities lying westward, it is of recent origin, having sprung almost overnight out of this vast semiarid region into which water was poured. At the turn of the present century this whole area from American Falls to Buhl **142 m.** was a domain of sagebrush and coyotes, bunch grass and brome grass, cheat grass and lizards. Swiftly, section by section, it has been transformed into a huge irrigated garden, and many towns have mushroomed within it and kept growing. The long sweep down the valley ahead is today one of Idaho's three principal agricultural areas.

Right from Rupert an unimproved road leads to the MINIDOKA DAM **15 m.** The Minidoka Reclamation Project involved the construction of a rock-filled dam across Snake River, together with a main canal and its tributaries and an elaborate pumping plant. This latter, operated by power generated at the dam, has three units, each lifting water twenty feet. The three of them require ten thousand horsepower of electric energy to operate. The diversion system and the pumping plant together irrigate about 116,000 acres at an initial cost of $6,500,000. The body of water impounded, now called Lake Walcott (in honor of a director of the U. S. Geological Survey), has a capacity of 107,000 acre-feet. There is such prodigal generation of current here that Minidoka County is said to be one of the most prolific rural patrons of electricity in the United States.

BURLEY 82 m. (4,240 alt.; 3,826 pop.) is the center of another reclamation project of 121,000 acres and 17,-000 homes. It is one of the two most thriving cities in this part of Idaho, but came into being only recently through the miracle of water and irrigation. Today it has an alfalfa-meal mill with a capacity of 125 tons, a beet sugar factory with a capacity of 800 tons, and the largest potato-flour mill in the world.

At Burley is the junction with U S 30 S to Ogden, Utah. Out of this city are side tours to unusual points of interest, though these lie at some distance.

1. Left from Burley on U S 30 S is DECLO 8 m. and then L on a side road is ALBION 6 m., the seat of one of the State's two normal schools. Though the campus here is lovely, of greater interest, perhaps, is the fact that Albion itself is a ghost town. It was once a county seat and on a main thoroughfare of travel into Utah, but today it is an assortment of decaying buildings that are precariously supported and kept out of complete ruin by the college upon the town's western flank. It is true, of course, as educators here declare, that most of these buildings are richly invested with fact and lore of a time now dead.

Perhaps the most beautiful spot in the Minidoka Forest is LAKE CLEVELAND at the head of Howell Canyon on Mount Harrison. This is just south of Albion over good road that climbs the mountain; and although the highway does not approach the lake, it is accessible by a short and easy trail. In this vicinity there are, in face, five glacial lakes. There are campsites throughout the length of Howell Canyon, fishing in adjacent streams, and magnificent views from Mount Harrison itself.

2. Left out of Burley over graveled road via OAKLEY 24 m. and thence over country road is the SILENT CITY OF ROCKS 38 m. This city covers an area of twenty-five square miles and lies almost six miles from north to south. In general this city is a weird congregation of eroded cathedrals and towers and shattered walls. Because formerly it was the junction of two famous trails—

the Sublette Cutoff and the California Road—it has recorded upon its walls one of the largest chronicles known of transcontinental travel. There are thousands of names and dates, as well as messages left for persons who were soon to follow; and it is evident that some of the more spectacular and foolhardy scribes must have been suspended by ropes from the tops of the cliffs, so high and remote from human footing are the records which they left.

Unlike the Gooding City of Rocks (see **Tour 5, Sec. b.**) this one has been carved by erosion from an enormous dome of granite which was anciently pushed up here into a mountain of its own. Because the weathered granite has become indurated or casehardened on the surface while its inner structure has often more rapidly disintegrated, the city presents the extremely bizarre aspect not only of mosques and monoliths and turrets but also of bathtubs and hollow cones and shells and strange little pockets and caverns. Bathtub Rock itself towers two hundred feet, and can be climbed to its summit whereon is a large depression that catches rainfall, in which, according to Indian legend, a bath before sunrise restored youth to the aged. Near the southern end are the gleaming turrets and fortresses standing upon a low saddle against the road. North from these are spires that rise two hundred and fifty feet from the floor of the basin and suggest from some distance the famous sky line of New York City. Others are rock brothers of the curious formations in Zion Canyon in southern Utah. Still others, fantastically grouped, look as if heathen temples had been rocked with dynamite and had rearranged their structure but had refused to fall.

Close scrutiny leads, for those anthropomorphically minded, to formations even more curious. A few stones look as if they had been sculptured by human hands and many so closely resemble one thing and another as to have been named. There are the Old Hen with Her Chicks, the Dragon's Head, the Giant Toadstool, the Elephant Rock, and the Old Woman. The upper surface of the Giant Toadstool has been hardened by arid winds and now has an overhanging cap, but the massive body below from cap to root is more rapidly disintegrating. Pedestal Rock is a casehardened boulder which rests upon a narrow staff. The whole chaotic, drunkenly fantastic region runs, indeed, through such a variety of erosive change that it is said to surpass in weird picturesqueness the famous Buffalo Rocks in the Buffalo Mountains of Australia.

For one not interested in strange formations of stone there are buried treasures to be searched for here. According to fact (or possibly legend) an overland stage from Kelton to Boise was accosted in this city in 1878, and $90,000 in gold was taken by the scoundrels. One of the bandits was slain, and the other subsequently died in prison; but before his death he told where he had buried the treasure among five junipers. Five cedars growing in the shape of a heart were found in the city long ago, and frantic excavations were undertaken, but it appears that the treasure is still undisturbed. Interesting, too, are the mountains roundabout.

MOUNT INDEPENDENCE, the highest peak in Idaho south of Hailey, rises 10,550 feet, and not far from it are the five lovely INDE-PENDENCE LAKES. Because few persons ever make this climb, the fish in the waters, an explorer reports, are apathetic from either starvation or boredom. The return via Oakley passes close to the OAKLEY DAM and the GOOSE CREEK RESERVOIR. The BOSTETTER PUBLIC CAMP, with accommodations for three hundred persons, is twenty miles west in the MINIDOKA NA-TIONAL FOREST. The setting is among lodgepole and aspen, gardens of wild flowers, and pure mountain streams.

This region abounds, at some distance from the city, in camping sites and in fishing and hunting. New roads have recently opened the natural beauty of the Minidoka National Forest on the south, and by way of Oakley the traveler can enter the mountains and canyons and make week-end camps among the evergreens by the streams. Deer have been protected throughout the year for a long while in this forest, and these animals, more abundant now, can often be seen from the roads. Within the hunting season, ruffled and pintail grouse are plentiful; and Chinese pheasants are common throughout the length of this and the Hagerman Valley to Bliss. In the streams are whitefish, perch, and trout.

At 96 m. is the junction with an improved road.

Right on this road is MILNER DAM 4 m. which, like Minidoka, is a structure of earth and concrete. It stands on the historic site former-ly known as The Cedars. Less impressive than some other dams in the State, it marks, nevertheless, the most successful large reclama-tion project in Idaho. Undertaken by the Twin Falls Land and Water Company in 1903, it was completed in 1905, and impounds upon Snake River enough water to irrigate 240,000 acres on the south side of the river and 32,000 on the north. The storage of 80,000 acre-feet is supplemented by a right to 98,000 acre-feet in the Jackson Reser-voir in Wyoming and 155,480 acre-feet in the American Falls Reservoir. The number of acres actually farmed under the South Side Milner Project is 203,000, and the number under the North Side is 128,000. Together these form the largest contiguous irri-gated acreage in the United States.

The benefits of reclamation in Idaho can be fully realized when it is remembered that thirty years ago this area was sagebrush terrain, worthless save for minor grazing, and that today the value of all holdings under the Milner Project with its eight hundred miles of canals, its thousands of miles of smaller laterals, its utilities and lands and railroads, is in excess of $75,000,000.

The present town of MILNER, just below the dam, is notable for two historic reasons. It was here on Snake River in 1811 that the Astorians under Wilson Price Hunt lost a boat and one of their members in the treacherous rapids. Because of the melodramatic behavior of the water here, Donald McKenzie named the spot Caldron Lynn, meaning water boiler or a boiling kettle. This spot also, because of a grove of cedar trees, was a favorite camping spot for immigrants over the Oregon Trail.

Right from Milner on a country road is the strange BURLEY WIND CAVE 3.5 m. It is a curious phenomenon, not because of its commonplace interior or the formation of its stone, but because tides of wind periodically flow into the cave or out of it. In the stone wall are numerous small holes no larger than a finger and through these the air everlastingly whistles, suggesting that there are remote and unexplored interiors with vents leading to the surface. This cave, too, like other phenomena westward, is evidence of the subterranean mysteries of central Idaho out of which came the volcanic pourings of the Craters of the Moon.

Paralleling U S 30, Snake River cuts a deep gorge through lava that is similar to that of the Colorado River across the Colorado Plateau. Because of varying degrees in the hardness of the stone and consequent variations in the ease and speed of erosion, the river has sculptured for itself several waterfalls, including Dry Creek, Twin, Shoshone, Pillar, Auger, and the Upper and Lower Salmon. Shoshone, and Twin, too, before the higher one was appropriated by a power company, have been outstanding among the waterfalls of the United States. U S 30 is now, in fact, entering one of Idaho's most picturesque wonderlands.

HANSEN 115 m. is the junction with country roads.

1. Left on country road is a historic spot, the first trading station west of Fort Hall, 7 m. It was a camping site, a pony express station, and then a settlement in 1863. The old store still stands.

2. Right from Hansen a country road leads to the HANSEN BRIDGE 4 m. which spans the Snake River gorge between Twin Falls and Jerome Counties. Formerly visited by many persons, this bridge is less an object of interest since the completion of the more impressive one west of it. Even so, this bridge, characterized in the *Scientific American* a few years ago as the highest suspension bridge in North America, is worth a visit. It is 345 feet high and 688 feet long and is suspended on enormous cables. The gorge here is narrower than below and offers from the bridge a beautiful summary of what time and a mighty river have been able to do with lava rock. In the sagebrush region three miles north of the bridge are the CLAY CAVES. Not so unusual by any means as many other caves in the State, these are nevertheless a curious object for many persons who enter them with gas lanterns and rubber boots.

The floor is of sticky clay. The caves have an aggregate length of about five city blocks, an average width of twenty to thirty feet, and a high ceiling studded in a part of it with stalactites. The entrance is little larger than a badger hole but even the portly visitor can effect a passage if he is willing to lie on his belly and exert himself.

A half mile down the river from the bridge is the ghost of SPRINGTOWN, dating back to 1870. It ran through six turbulent years, and today the mud huts of the Chinese (who usually followed to exploit what the whites scorned) are still to be seen.

TWIN FALLS 124 m. 3,492 alt.; 8,787 pop.) is the largest city and the metropolis of south-central Idaho. Three miles south of Snake River and on the bank of Rock Creek, it stands on a gently rolling watershed which was covered long ago by lava flows that are now the bedrock under the silt that has been blown in from surrounding mountains and old lake beds. Because there has been severe erosion and a plateau built up from a deep basin, the area from here to the Hagerman Valley forty miles westward is an unusually fertile field for the paleontologist. Covered anciently by a great sea and later by tropical jungle, this whole region has been discovered to be the repository of dinosaurs and ammonites, coral and sea shell. But the overlain soil in the Twin Falls country is also uncommonly deep, and in consequence of its richness has made this part of Idaho notable in crop yields. Twin Falls itself has sometimes been called the magic city, a characterization owing to the circumstance of its having risen so suddenly and swiftly after water reclaimed this arid valley. It was settled chiefly by families from the Middle West and is one of the few cities in Idaho that were carefully and enviably planned. It is not, unfortunately, on a railway trunk line, being served in this respect only by a somewhat inadequate side branch; but it has frequent motor coach service in all directions and air service daily making connections with points east and west. The municipal airport is five miles south.

Among points of interest within the city itself are several small museums. The CRABTREE (admission 25 cents), 211 Addison Avenue West, has an excellent collection of Indian artifacts, including an assortment of arrowheads from all parts of the United States. In addition to these are a few fossils and archaeological relics. The WEAVER MUSEUM (admission free), 149 Main Avenue West, has a collection of guns, fossils, curios, and mummified remains. WHITAKER'S TAXIDERMIST SHOP AND MUSEUM (admission free), 216 Second Avenue South, has in addition to Indian artifacts an interesting group of mounted game animals, wild birds, moths, and butterflies. The GASKILL BOTANICAL GARDEN (admission 15 cents), 266 Blue Lakes Boulevard, is a spot beautifully landscaped. Surrounded by trees, shrubs, and vines, the concrete pools within are stocked with water plants and fish. The GARDEN OF YESTERDAY (admission 25 cents) is just out of the city southeast: it is noteworthy for its miniature replicas of frontier life, including a tiny log house and a gristmill which is operated by water from a ditch. Another item of unusual historic interest is a natural cave in the wall of Rock Creek Canyon (R). This cave was the first jail in Twin Falls County, and prisoners were incarcerated here until Federal statute made it illegal to keep persons below the surface of the earth. Just south of the depot is a private fishery from which rainbow trout can be bought fresh from the ponds.

Twin Falls is at the junction with U S 93 (see **Tour 5, Sec. b).**

1. Three miles out on Blue Lakes Boulevard (R) is a left turn to a tollgate on the rimrock, where 25 cents admits the visitor to an area phenomenal in several respects. There is from the rim a magnificent view of the gorge, which here is seven hundred feet in depth on either side and almost sheer, and of the Twin Falls-Jerome bridge (see **Tour 5, Sec. b.**) Far below on the river is the famous PERRINE RANCH, which Douglas Fairbanks, Sr., once pondered buying before deciding to settle in England. From the rim it is one and one-fourth miles across to Blue Lakes and a narrow but safe road leads down and approaches the ranch through an incomparable corridor of poplars, and comes to the PERRINE MUSEUM, which contains Indian artifacts, fossil remnants, and antiques. *Admission to this was covered at the toll-*

gate. The Perrine orchard here is noted for its growing of rare fruits. The road leaves the ranch and crosses the river by bridge and proceeds to BLUE LAKES which are small lovely jewels as blue as the sky. They are in a tributary on the north wall of the main canyon. The head of this alcove is an amphitheater with walls three hundred feet high and with no stream entering from the surface or the plain above. The water boiling up from the springs in the amphitheater is clear but is blue and slightly opalescent because of fine siltlike materials held in suspension. These lakes, with bottoms of clear white sand, are well stocked with trout. The PERRINE COULEE FALLS, also in this tiny basin, is a small waterfall that drops 197 feet as an overflow drain of irrigated lands above the rimrock. It is most impressive for the person who drives behind it and looks up at the water descending in a slender deluging veil.

2. Because less impressive, TWIN FALLS 6 m. should be visited before Shoshone. North of the city is a right turn off U S 93 that parallels the power line. The twins are no longer twins: the larger one was taken over in 1935 by the Idaho Power Company; and though its plant here is notable for its compactness and beauty, it is hardly adequate compensation for the loss of the second mightiest waterfall in Idaho. For the larger of the twins was a plunge of 180 feet, with considerably more than half the river poured over a narrow escarpment into a terrific column that lost none of its concentrated power. Today only the north fall remains. Below the diversion dam the river now tumbles over wild cascades and delivers nearly its whole volume where formerly it spilled less than a third.

SHOSHONE FALLS is on the river three miles below, and can be reached by leaving the return road (R) at the sign or by turning off U S 93 (R) at the sign. First discovered by Wilson Price Hunt in 1811, and thereupon for many decades the chief attraction in Idaho for the thousands of immigrants passing through to Oregon, this waterfall is considerably higher than Niagara and is, when reservoirs do not vitiate its grandeur, in some respects more impressive. The river here plunges in a sheer drop of 212 feet over a great basaltic horseshoe rim nearly a thousand feet wide. Formerly the spectacle was, and sometimes still is, illuminated by flood lights. Idaho Power's diversion dam has produced a series of cascades which are an appropriate prelude to the falls below. The great plunge is against the south wall where the water goes down like a tumbling mountain of snow with a part of its body rolling in pale green veins. At the farther side over a wide and almost perfect arc the flood spills in an enormous foaming sheet. After viewing the falls from the lookout tower, the visitor should turn at the rimrock to the brink for a view at greater distance. A visiting newspaper editor once wrote: "Never anywhere else was there such a scene; never anywhere else so beautiful a picture hung in so rude a frame. But to feel all the awe and to mark all the splendor that

Snake River Gorge: the footprints of time

Perrine Coulee Falls

Twin Falls

Shoshone Falls (taken at night with the falls illuminated by searchlights)

comes of the mighty display, one must climb down the steep descent to the river's bank below."

But this is not the whole story of Shoshone Falls. It is one of Idaho's scenic losses that so much of the water of this river must be impounded for irrigation and that these waterfalls along here have to be robbed of their thunderous downpouring. During years of light snowfall upon the watersheds, about enough water goes over this wide escarpment in August to fill a teacup. After heavy winters, as in the spring of 1936, the reservoirs are soon filled, and the full flow of the river is delivered downstream. And so it is, then, that this spectacle varies a great deal from year to year. In May of 1936 Shoshone Falls were roaring mightily in their old splendor, and the circumstance was so unusual after many relatively dry years that persons hearing of the restoration came a long way to see them. In next year or the next, the flow may be too little to keep the escarpment wet.

It was inevitable that Shoshone Falls should have become a part of Indian folklore. The Shoshoni Indians called the falls Pah-chu-laka which means "hurling waters leaping." In the gloomy gorge above the falls there was, long ago, the trysting place of a deep-chested Shoshoni buck and the slender wild girl whom he loved. Their last meeting was here on a pile of rocks which overlooked the plunging waters. He went away to scalp with deft incisions and then to lift the shaggy mane of white men with a triumphant shout; and she came daily to stand by the thundering avalanche and remember him. That he would return unharmed she did not, with the ageless resourcefulness of women, ever allow herself to doubt. But time passed, and the moons that came and ripened were many, and she still came nightly to stand on the brink and watch the changeless journeying of the water. And it was here that she stood one black night above the roar of the flood when a warrior stepped out of shadow and whispered to her and then disappeared. As quiet as the flat stone under her feet, she stood for a long while, looking down into the vault where the waters boiled up like seething white hills to fill the sky with dazzling curtains and roll away in convulsed tides. For an hour she gazed down there two hundred feet to a mad pouring of motion and sound into a black graveyard of the dead. And then, slowly, she lifted her arms above her, lifted her head to the fullest curve of her throat, and stood tiptoe for a moment, poised and beautiful, and then dived in a long swift arc against the falling white background.... And the river at this point and since that hour has never been the same.[1]
Upon U S 93, northward a half mile, is Idaho's most beautiful bridge. (See **Tour 5, Sec. b.**) Up the northern bank of the river from this bridge to a point two and a half miles above Shoshone Falls is a gorge that opens off the main canyon of the river. It can

---

[1] This story was told many years ago to J. S. Harrington by a Shoshoni Indian on the Fort Hall Reservation named Quish-in-demi, and is used here with **Mr. Harrington's permission.**

be reached by country road or by boat up the river above the waterfall. In early days this terrifying rugged basin was used as a hideout by a gang of notorious horse thieves, and is today known as the Devils Corral. More than a hundred underground chambers have been discovered in or close by the Snake River Canyon along here.

West from Twin Falls on U S 30 is an unobstructed view on the right of Snake River clear to the Sawtooth Mountains. At 130 m. is the junction with U S 93 (L) (see **Tour 5, Sec. b.**), and at 132 m. is FILER, which can almost be regarded as the home of the famous Idaho white bean, inasmuch as nine bean plants operate here.

Right out of Filer by country road are AUGER FALLS 5 m. on Snake River. The water here pours through a partly obstructed channel over a series of escarpments, and twists and spirals strangely in its descent.

BUHL 142 m. (3,793 alt.; 1,883 pop.) is flanked by rolling country on the east that looks in June like Iowa. Named for Frank Buhl, an early empire builder, this thrifty, well-kept town is one of the most prepossessing in the State.

1. Left from Buhl over surfaced road south and west is CASTLEFORD 11 m., and thence 1 m. west, 1 m. north, and 3.5 m. west to BALANCED ROCK. From Castleford the traveler should follow the signs. He will come first to the gorge of a stream that goes under the name of either Salmon River or Salmon Creek. This gorge is entered and crossed, with a range of monuments on the farther side at the end of which Balanced Rock is the climax. It can be seen against the sky from the road, but for the fullest realization of the miracle of it the visitor should climb the mountainside and view it from all angles. The more closely it is examined at close range the more incredible it seems that this tower of stone should have weathered so many centuries on so small a base. But there it stands, in its precarious imperturbability, as a wonder for everyone who sees it. This balloon-shaped formation forty feet in height rested, before being reinforced by concrete, upon a small block of igneous stone that was only one foot by one and a half feet by three feet in dimensions. There are other marvels in the canyon of this stream. The colorful pillars and colonnades on either side look as if a section had been lifted out of Zion Canyon in Utah. Down the stream and accessible only to those willing to hike over rugged trails are the PHANTOM WALLS. Not far south of Castleford is BLOW HOLE, a recently discovered and still quite unexplored fissure in the earth. Alternate discharge and intake

Balanced Rock

Phantom Walls

Icicle Cove

Snowbank Falls

of powerful air currents suggest that the cavern is related to Salmon Canyon eight miles away. In a cliff near the historic Castleford crossing on the river is a formation known as the DEVILS KITCHEN, a room reached only by a somewhat hazardous descent down the chimney. For directions to any of these inquiry should be made in Castleford.

2. Right from Buhl over the Wendell-Buhl highway are CLEAR LAKES 4 m. in the Snake River Canyon. Sequestered on the north side of the river and obscured by high cliffs and bushes, these small beautiful lakes are accessible only by motorboat near Uhrlaubs Ferry. Though forty feet in depth, these lakes are as lucent as crystal, and the numerous jets clustered around a large central spring can be clearly seen gushing from the white sand of the bottom. Innumerable trout play among the clean floating particles of sand. These springs are, of course, related to Blue Lakes, to Thousand Springs, and to all the other water coming from the Lost Rivers far in the northeast and emerging on the walls of Snake River.

North out of Buhl on U S 30, Snake River Canyon is visible on the right at **150 m.**, and at **152 m.** some of the Thousand Springs can be seen on its wall in the distance. On the left is the mouth of Salmon Creek, the gorge of which is a fantastic wonderland through almost its entire length. The highway now drops down into the lovely Hagerman Valley. At **156 m.** (R) is the Thousand Springs (sometimes called the Minnie Miller) Farm, which is internationally known for its blooded Guernsey cattle. Just beyond the farm are the equally famous THOUSAND SPRINGS, though many of these have been appropriated and hidden by a power company. By the time commercial interests are done with Idaho's waterfalls and cascading springs there will be nothing to see, many Idahoans believe, except water mains and the roofs over turbines. Though long a source of mystery to both laymen and geologists, it is now believed that the Thousand Springs are the outlet of buried rivers that get lost in the lava terrain 150 miles in the northeast (see **Tour 4**). "In this stretch also occur a wonderful group of springs having a combined discharge of more than 5,000 second-feet, or enough water to supply all the cities in the United States of more than 100,000 inhabitants with 120

gallons a day for each inhabitant." The whole of central
Idaho, as a matter of fact, seems to be an area of subterranean rivers and possibly cavernous lake beds; and at
points through this valley a person can put his ear to the
ground and hear deep and troubled rumblings as if a
mighty ocean rolled far under. Across from Thousand
Springs is a ghost town. AUSTIN is still marked by a
cellar, a chimney, some stone walls, and fruit trees that
still bloom in a forgotten orchard.

HAGERMAN 164 m. is a small hamlet in the valley.
At 164.5 m. on U S 30 is a tablet (R) which commemorates
Marcus Whitman, the pioneer missionary who brought the
first wagon across what was to be known later as the Oregon Trail. In the high cliffs above Thousand Springs and in
other places throughout Hagerman Valley, marine fossil
remains are abundant. Besides luxuriant tropical vegetation, there are also survivals of mastodons, wild hogs, and a
rare species of ancient horse which seems to have been the
immediate forebear of the present beast. The discovery of
the latter was in what at one time was a boggy terrain, possibly a drinking place, for among the bones of the horses
were those of aquatic animals as well as remnants of frog
and fish. When, during investigations in this valley, dynamiting became necessary, a charge blew out the skull of a
mastodon that was buried at a level considerably above
that of the bones of horses. In the same neighborhood were
found the remains of a cat about the size of a cougar, and
this, it is surmised, may be a hitherto unknown species.
Since 1927 several expeditions have been sent into this
region. (See *Paleontology* in Sec. I, Ch. IX.)

Between Hagerman and Malad River 167 m. there
is a cave on the east wall of the Snake River Gorge which
contains interesting Indian petroglyphs. These have been
interpreted as a story of an Arapahoe massacre. MALAD
RIVER, crossed by U S 30, is said to be the shortest
river in the world; and it may be for it is only three or
four miles long. This river in springtime is a wild torrent

of considerable size that is fed from springs related to the series east of Hagerman and to the many small lakes sheltered in side canyons which open upon Snake River. The main source of Malad River is a huge spring which rises at the foot of a precipice and plunges down in a chain of cascades. An amazing summary of the subterranean nature of central Idaho is to be found in the fact that the Malad River "is the only stream in the whole of southern Idaho from Henrys Fork within 12 miles of the west boundary of Yellowstone Park, to the Idaho-Oregon line, a distance measured along Snake River of fully 450 miles, which, rising in the mountains in the north, reaches Snake River in the summertime." And Malad River, because of the demands of irrigation, is sometimes dry.

The highway now leaves the canyon. At the foot, just before the ascent begins, is the old Bliss Ranch where B. M. Bower wrote *Good Indian*. The evolution of the winding grade ahead from a crude pack trail through four different eras of travel is still discernible. At the top of the ascent is the village of BLISS **173 m.**, which received its name from an old-timer and not because its settlers regarded it as an especially felicitous haven. Bliss is the junction with State 24, which goes eastward to Gooding and Shoshone, where it forms a junction with U S 93. For side tours to the Gooding City of Rocks or to the Shoshone Ice Caves (see **Tour 5, Sec. b).**

1. Right out of Bliss a fair road leads to the interesting CLOVER CREEK SECTION 10 m. After crossing Clover Creek, a left turn goes one-fourth mile to hot springs which are scalding hot. The right turn goes one mile to the lakes, in which the water is so astringent that it will take the hair off a hog. These small lakes occupy old crater beds. They are known under various names but one of them is sometimes appropriately called LYE LAKE. Near the lakes are long tunnels, some with their ceilings tumbled in, some with natural arched bridges, and some remaining as subterranean caverns that are rarely explored. The hot springs were held in high esteem by Indians, who often journeyed far to bathe in the waters. The story is told of one buck who gambled so expertly that he left the others destitute; whereupon, in angry

council, they declared him a bad one but allowed him to accompany the tribe on its pilgrimage to the spring. He fell ill of spotted fever, and was thrust into the hot waters to effect a cure and was dragged out dead.

2. Right out of Bliss over State 24 4 m. to a right turn and thence over smooth road is the MALAD GORGE 14 m. Of ragged chasms there is none in the State that excels this one, and none more picturesque. Near its head is a blue lake about as large as a floor, fed by a waterfall, and below it is the river, cascading and bursting forth in springs and turning through all shades of pale green and blue; it is perhaps Idaho's loveliest stream. On the east rim of the gorge and running parallel is a deep rift and descents into it though hazardous are popular.

West of Bliss, U S 30 enters Elmore County, one of the chief grazing areas of the State, from which seventy thousand cattle and two hundred thousand sheep are shipped annually. KING HILL 190 m. is a historic spot. Just northwest is a landmark on an early trail from Utah to Boise; at the foot of the hill the old Overland stage station was burned by Chief Buffalo Horn in 1878; and on a flat above the village is the Devils Playground, a picturesque area of round smooth stones. At 198 m. is the historic THREE ISLAND FORD on Snake River, where emigrants headed for Oregon crossed on the Oregon Trail. An Indian trail still leads down to the river. Indians used to lie in ambush here by the crossing, and just south in the historic DEAD MANS GULCH, where an Indian massacre occurred. Buffalo Horn, an Indian scout with an honorable discharge from the U. S. Army, nursed a grudge and turned renegade, and on DEAD MANS FLAT he and his band killed three miners. Only one of the three graves has been found.

MOUNTAIN HOME 224 m. (3,142 alt.; 1,243 pop.) is a rather bleak town set upon a great plateau with sagebrush landscape rolling away from it on nearly all sides.

1. Right from Mountain Home State 22 provides a combination of points of interest, excellent fishing and scenery, and beautiful campsites. At 7.5 m. a right turn leads to one of the hottest springs 2 m. in the State, rich in sulphur and iron, and in favor as a medicinal drink. Formerly there were accommodations here, but now there are

Thousand Springs

Malad Gorge

Bruneau Canyon

Map of the United States—in Middle Fork of Boise River

only two old bathtubs available to anyone who wishes to take a bath. At 8 m. on the main road is a monument which marks the site of an old stage station. State 22 proceeds to CASTLE ROCKS 44 m., an area of granitic formations which have been called another Garden of the Gods. Though picturesque, these pinnacles and towers are hardly comparable with the Gooding or Cassia cities of rocks (see **Tour 5, Sec. b.,** and **Tour 3, Sec. b.).** At **30 m.** on the main road is the junction with the Atlanta road which goes northward to Sloan's Gulch and Fall Creek, past spongelike lava flows, past evergreen forests, and to a left turn **43 m.** which leads to lovely TRINITY LAKES **10 m.** RAINBOW LAKE at the head of the gulch is accessible by footpath. At **55 m.** on the main road is PRICE'S RESORT where outdoor pools and cabins are available. At ABBOT'S RANCH **61 m.** horses can be hired for penetrating to excellent fishing or to vantage points. TRINITY PEAK, perhaps the best of the latter, has an elevation of 9,473 feet. The hardy adventurer can proceed to Atlanta, a mountain-walled town and the end of the trail, and then go down the Middle Fork of the Boise River and the main river past Arrowrock Dam to Boise. Legend declares that there are fabulously large and interesting caves in this area north of Mountain Home, but sheepherders who know the region well look down their noses at the suggestion and profane softly.

2. Left from Mountain Home an improved road leads to another wonderland. At the bridge upon Snake River sturgeon fishing is a popular and most exciting sport. The equipment needed is several hundred feet of stout quarter-inch rope, a few feet of wire cable for a leader, and several strong iron hooks, baited often with raw beef. One end of the rope is tied to a tree on the bank and the other is anchored with a stone out in the river. When a sturgeon is hooked the fun begins. An old-timer here who captures sturgeon for a living usually hitches a team to the rope and after a long while of maneuvering drags the river-beast to the shore. Those who prefer fun that is more hazardous use a boat, manned, if the sturgeon is a large one, by several persons. The largest one ever taken from the river weighed nearly a thousand pounds but most of them are much smaller, and only those weighing less than two hundred pounds are of excellent flavor. Men fishing here perhaps ought to be warned of one danger; often a sturgeon when hooked will lead almost to the bank so gently that the one towing the line in will imagine he has no catch. But when one of these big fellows comes close enough to the bank to see his enemy, he turns with sudden and overwhelming power and speed, and many a man has had the flesh burned from his palms by a sizzling rope.

BRUNEAU **22 m.** is a few shabby buildings lost among lordly trees, with old-timers sitting in front of the solitary poolhall and spitting tobacco juice and swapping yarns. Those venturing from here to the magnificent BRUNEAU CANYON as well as to points of minor interest along the way should perhaps enlist the services of an old-timer as a guide. Of Bruneau Canyon it is frequently said that in its entire length of sixty-seven miles there is only one place where it is possible to take a horse down to water and only four places where a man can descend. This is an exaggeration: it depends on the man and the horse. But the gorge is, nevertheless, one of the deepest narrow canyons on earth. In places it is so narrow that a man can hurl a rock from rim to rim and so deep that it is two thousand feet to the river, with the walls almost sheer. Persons who like to have the breath taken out of them by lying on a rim and peering over into awful depth can probably find no better canyon anywhere. In the upper reach is a flanking canyon called Jarbridge, a Shoshoni word meaning devil. According to Indian legend, the devil claimed a sacrificial offering from the tribe when any member offended the Great Spirit. When angry cries of the devil were heard in the bowels of the earth, announcing his approach, a medicine man chose the prettiest maiden of the village and killed her and laid her body on the brink of the gorge. During the night, Jarbridge came to possess the offering. Rites to appease his wrath were held as late as 1890, when white men discovered that the infamous Jarbridge was a mountain lion.[1] It is in the Jarbridge area, too, that there is a remarkable natural bridge which spans the canyon at a height from the bottom of 186 feet. Because this bridge is difficult to reach, very few persons have seen it.

Left and east from Bruneau an unimproved road leads to Indian springs. At **5.3 m.** (R) is one of the oldest cemeteries in Idaho. At **6.8 m.** a side road leads (R) .25 m. to SETTLER'S TUNNEL. Sixty years ago, to escape from Indians who were on the warpath, settlers dug a tunnel into a bluff here and shaped it into a mountain home of several rooms, with vents to let out the smoke of the fires and with small holes to allow the thrust of guns against enemies. In this excavated home in hard clay no timbers were used, but the retreat is still in an excellent state of preservation. On the right at **7.5 m.**, is the PENCE RANCH, the oldest settlement in the valley, and out in its meadow is a swimming pool supplied from large hot springs. The man who first owned these springs was rather eccentric and declared that these springs must never be commercialized; and in consequence the swimming is free. A half mile farther the road forks; the left turn goes by poor road up the east side of the river and leads to a view of the Bruneau Canyon from the eastern rim. The other road, more commonly taken, crosses a bridge and then climbs the hills into the south. At **11.5 m.** a left turn leads **1 m.** to Hot Creek and the Indian Bathtub.

HOT CREEK alone is worth a visit. Springs boil out at the end of a ravine and flow for a mile down it in a large steaming stream to tumble over a fall into what is known as the INDIAN BATHTUB. The erosive action of the hot water has sculptured a tub that is about fifteen feet across, and was, until filled with sediment, about

---

[1] This legend was told to Lulu Lough of Buhl by Rock Creek Jim, a famous chieftain of the Shoshoni tribe.

ten feet in depth. Indians not only bathed here formerly but also drew pictographs on the stone walls. These are largely effaced now, but years ago visitors could swim in the tub and study Indian drawings at the same time. This tub is now owned by the United States Government, which has erected two sheds so that campers can undress here and bathe. The campsite, though both small and unimproved, is particularly attractive, inasmuch as a natural hot bath is on the one side, with a hot stream overflowing it, and a cold mountain spring is on the other.

From the turn to Hot Creek, the traveler who wishes to view the canyon can proceed southward as far as he pleases because the road roughly parallels the gorge. It is always, however, two or three miles from it, with no good roads leading across; and until one is built, the traveler who does not wish to abuse his car will do best to hike over the sagebrush terrain from the road to the gorge. It is breath-taking from either the eastern or western rim at any point south of Hot Creek, but is most impressive in its upper reaches. About seven miles south of the Hot Creek turn, the road climbs to a high flat tableland and it is across this to the left that visitors usually walk to the canyon, the outline of which is visible in the east.

West of Mountain Home on U S 30 the drive to Boise is over typical Western prairie with typical flora. The Owyhee Range is on the south, the Boise Mountains on the north. West of Pocatello the highway follows the Old Oregon Trail, and of the stories relating to early travel over it the following is typical. How much of this Sager story is legend and how much is fact nobody knows.

Nearly a century ago the Sager family left Missouri with a wagon train. In Wyoming the parents were stricken with dysentery, and the train deserted them and they made their way with their children to Soda Springs alone. Here both the mother and father died. The children went with a caravan to Fort Hall, and it was there that John, the oldest of the children, a lad of fourteen, listened to stories of the westward trek to Fort Boise and the Whitman Mission in Washington. He resolved to set out alone with his brothers and sisters, and is said to have approached the gates of Fort Boise weeks later, holding a babe of four months in his arms. There was no white woman in the fort, and John thereupon decided to push on to the Whitman mission. A month later the children appeared there: John had a starving infant in his arms, and behind him, perched on the back of an emaciated cow, were his sister of eight with a broken leg and his sister of five who had supported the leg mile after mile to keep it from swinging. When they descended from the cow she sank with an awful groan to the earth and a moment later was dead. These children (John, Francis who was eleven, three sisters ranging in age from three to eight, and an infant) traveled five hundred miles alone, feeding on the cow and wild fruits and roots, and arriving gray with hunger and distance in spite of hostile Indians and innumerable other dangers. John and Francis were slain three years later in the Whitman Massacre. There are those in Idaho who scoff at this story, declaring that Paul Bunyan never equaled it in tremendous farce. There are others who swear that it is literally true.

At **235 m.** (L) is CLEFT, a few deserted shacks on the railroad.

Left from Cleft are the CRATER RINGS (L) **3 m.**, regarded by some Idahoans as the most phenomenal spot in their State, but the roads running to them are nothing but cow trails, and until one of them is improved travel will be hazardous. These rings are two great volcanic cones that look like ancient amphitheaters from which all benches have been removed. Also here is a remarkable earthquake fissure: for five miles the surface was split open by some tremendous tremor in the past, and the crack, from five to ten feet in width, is in places of unknown depth. The rings themselves were doubtless caused by two gigantic eruptions of such force and volume that a cubic mile of lava was hurled into the air and blown into dust. Five hundred yards east of them in the fissure is an ice cave, a chamber about thirty-five feet deep.

At MAYFIELD **247 m.** is the junction with a road.

Left on this road is ORCHARD **6 m.**, a village of shacks in an arid region named for what was once a huge orchard but is now only a few stunted trees. South of Orchard are many caves, of which the HIGBY, six miles out toward Flag Butte, is best known. The road to it is difficult. But this whole area between Mountain Home and Kuna is one of caves, and in it more than thirty have been found, though a few, because of inconspicuous entrances, have been lost. None of those known are comparable to the Crystal Falls or Minnetonka caves, but many of them are interesting. Exploration here needs the service of old-timers.

U S 30 continues over semiarid region to Boise **268 m.**

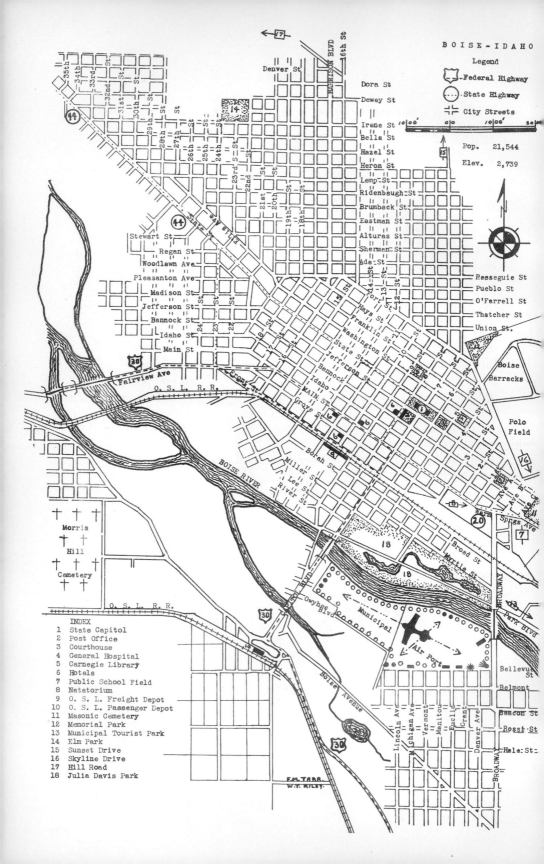

BOISE - IDAHO

Legend

⬡ Federal Highway
⬭ State Highway
✚ City Streets

Pop. 21,544
Elev. 2,739

INDEX
1. State Capitol
2. Post Office
3. Courthouse
4. General Hospital
5. Carnegie Library
6. Hotels
7. Public School Field
8. Natatorium
9. O. S. L. Freight Depot
10. O. S. L. Passenger Depot
11. Masonic Cemetery
12. Memorial Park
13. Municipal Tourist Park
14. Elm Park
15. Sunset Drive
16. Skyline Drive
17. Hill Road
18. Julia Davis Park

F.M.TARR.
W.T.RILEY.

Section c. Boise to Weiser, 72 m.

BOISE (2,741 alt.; 21,544 pop.).

Railroad station: Union Pacific, on the bench.
Bus station: Union Pacific Stages, 929 Main.
Airport, municipal: Off Broadway just south of Boise River.
Golf Courses: Boise Country Club, 3 m. southwest of city. Plantation, 4m. west on State 44. American Legion, at end of Eighth. All are nine-hole courses.

Boise, the capital of Idaho and its largest city, stands on the Boise River at the extreme upper end of the Boise Valley. It is primarily a city of trees and homes and enviable climate. Protected by great mountains on the north and lying in a belt of prevailing westerly winds, it and its valley are never outraged by the cold blizzards that sweep down from Canada and paralyze eastern Idaho and the States beyond. Its summers, though often hot, are nearly always dry, and its nights are usually cool. Its winters are mild. The city is supported chiefly by a few plants and factories within its site or adjacent and by a rich agricultural area given chiefly to hay and grain, vegetables, and fruits, of which the prune is famous. The valleys lying west of it to Oregon are the chief dairying section of the State. Like many other towns, it has an abundance of natural hot water, having tapped wells that flow 1,200,000 gallons daily at a temperature of 170 degrees F. Many of the homes, and especially in the eastern part, are heated from these flows; and the chief avenue, Warm Springs, takes its name from them. The large NATATORIUM and its playground are on this avenue at its eastern end.

Of the city's buildings, a few are in some degree noteworthy. The CAPITOL at Eighth and Jefferson is monumentally classical in aspect, with Corinthian columns supporting a Corinthian pediment. It is faced with Boise sandstone. In the rotunda is a remarkable equestrian statue of George Washington. This, the work of Charles Ostner, a soldier of fortune sojourning in Idaho, was carved by hand from a yellow pine tree at Garden Valley with the crudest of tools and with only a postage stamp to serve as a model. It was four years in the making, and was then carefully scraped with glass, sandpapered, gilded with paint, and later overlaid with gold leaf. It was presented to Idaho Territory in 1869 and dedicated to Idaho pioneers. In the basement of the Capitol is the STATE HISTORICAL SOCIETY (admission free), crowded into one room, with stuffed birds and beasts thrust out into the hallways, and with piles of materials shoved into drawers and vaults. Many valuable gifts and collections are being withheld until a suitable building is erected for housing them. On the Capitol grounds is the STEUNENBERG MONUMENT, designed by Gilbert Riswald, cast by Guido Nelli. Its legend declares that the former governor was "Rugged in Body, Resolute in Mind, Massive in the Strength of his Convictions." Frank Steunenberg, Governor of the State 1897-1901, was killed by a bomb in December, 1905, during the mine labor troubles of the period. The trial of those accused of causing his death was a court duel between William E. Borah, acting for the State, and Clarence Darrow of the defense.

Across from the Capitol is the HOTEL BOISE, a municipally owned structure of which Boiseans are reasonably proud. At the southern end of Capitol Boulevard, and facing the Capitol Building, is the beautiful UNION PACIFIC STATION. Set upon a hill, it overlooks the city, as well as the landscaped Howard Platt Gardens with their flowers and Norway maples, blossoming catalpas and weeping willows. These gardens, lovely under searchlights at night, were designed by Richardo Espino of Los Angeles. ST. JOHN'S ROMAN CATHEDRAL at Eighth and Hays was designed by Tourtellotte and Hummel of Boise, the architects of the Capitol. It is Romanesque in exterior and elaborately adorned with stained windows and marble altars inside. ST. MICHAEL'S EPISCOPAL CA-

THEDRAL (architects unknown) is of English Gothic and stands at Eighth and State.

Of buildings of historic interest the city has many. In JULIA DAVIS PARK, lying upon the north bank of the river just east of Eighth Street, is the COSTON CABIN. Built in the spring of 1863 by I. N. Coston, it was fashioned of driftwood gathered from the river and put together with pegs. Its original site was on the river seven miles above Boise, and there it served as a rendezvous for Indians, prospectors, freighters, and packers. In this park, too, is the PEARCE CABIN, built in the fall of 1863 by Ira B. Pearce of logs brought from the mountains by ox team. On the south side of the river near the Holcomb school is the BLOCKHOUSE, a two-story structure built in 1869 of heavy stones that were brought to the site by nobody knows what means. In early days this house served as a refuge against Indian attacks, and now reposes in legend as a haunted place. The DeLAMAR HOUSE on the southwest corner of Eighth and Grove was in its heyday the largest and most modern home in the town. It not only had the first mansard roof within the State but is said to have been the first home in the United States heated with natural hot water. In 1892, Captain J. R. DeLamar, the silver king, bought it for $35,000 and converted it into an exclusive club; in 1905 it became the home of Boise's first beauty parlor; and is today a Basque rooming house. The O'FARRELL CABIN, at Sixth and Fort, was built in 1863, and now has a tablet above the door which declares that this was the first home in Boise to shelter women and children. Within are the original fireplace and a teakettle which were used by the first occupants. At Fifteenth and Ridenbaugh is CHRIST'S CHURCH, erected in 1866 at Seventh and Idaho, and the first Protestant Episcopal church in Montana, Idaho, and Utah. Across from the Statesman building on Main is the HALLADAY STAGE STATION, whose history reaches back to early times. At 210 Main is the old U. S.

ASSAY OFFICE, built in 1870-71, and said to have received more than $75,000,000 in gold and silver bullion through its doors. It is now used by the department of forestry. Somewhere on Main between Eighth and Ninth a saloon operated a half century ago. Managed by James Lawrence and known as the Naked Truth Saloon, it advertised itself in most astonishing fashion.

Friends and Neighbors:

Having just opened a commodious shop for the sale of liquid fire, I embrace this opportunity of informing you that I have commenced the business of making:

Drunkards, paupers and beggars for the sober, industrious and respectable portion of the community to support. I shall deal in family spirits, which will incite men to deeds of riot, robbery, and blood, and by so doing, diminish the comfort, augment the expenses and endanger the welfare of the community.

I will undertake on short notice, for a small sum and with great expectations, to prepare victims for the asylum, poor farm, prison and gallows.

I will furnish an article which will increase fatal accidents, multiply the number of distressing diseases and render those which are harmless incurable. I will deal in drugs which will deprive some of life, many of reason, most of prosperity, and all of peace: which will cause fathers to become fiends, and wives widows, children orphans and a nuisance to the nation.

Boise has several candy factories that specialize in quality. The largest, at 412 South Eighth, welcomes visitors who wish to see how the famous Owyhee chocolates are made. Spanning the river on Capitol Boulevard is the Memorial Bridge, designed by Charles Kyle, and commemorating the pioneers who forded the river at this point. At 1301 Capitol Boulevard is a plant that specializes in "Oregon Trail" furniture, made exclusively from Idaho knotted pine. At First and Main is the URGUIDES LITTLE VILLAGE. In 1863, Jesus "Kossuth" Urguides, a frontiersman from San Francisco, established his freighting station where thirty one-room cabins now stand. These, built to house packers and wranglers, are today occupied by a little colony of old-timers who can still remember how the generous Urguides cared for them in sickness

A Boise sky

A view in Boise

Arrowrock Dam

Historic Table Rock

and health. Boise is said to have the second largest
Basque colony in the world. Its midsummer festival is a
genuine Romeria, similar to fiestas in Spain, with Basque
food, costumes, dances, and music. (See Sec. I, Ch. IX,
Emerging from the Frontier.)

Of recreation, Boise offers a small playground in JULIA
DAVIS PARK, with an art museum, picnic grounds, boating, and tennis courts. Close by the airport, and upon the
southern rim, there are small cabarets and clubs, modest in
size but still invested with much of the spirit of the old
West. Boise is small as cities go, but its interest in music
and its patronage of visiting musicians are enough to
inspirit a metropolis twenty times its size. Its music week,
born here in 1919 and held annually in May, has spread to
so many parts of the country that it has become almost a
national institution. But Boise is more the center of a
playground than it is a playground in itself, and it is the
side trips from here that offer the most in recreation.

1. Right from Boise up **Warm Springs Avenue** and then by road,
surfaced in part of its length, up the Boise River are the **ARROW-
ROCK DAM** and **RESERVOIR 24 m.** This dam is one of the State's
more noteworthy engineering achievements, and was, until more
spectacular construction followed, the highest dam in the United
States. Built by the Bureau of Reclamation and resting upon a
foundation of granite, it is 1,100 feet wide and 348.5 feet high
above bedrock, and contains 600,000 cubic yards of concrete. It
creates a reservoir 17 miles long, covering a maximum area of
2,890 acres and impounding 280,000 acre-feet. Especially impressive is the view here in late spring after a heavy winter when the
reservoir is full and the river is delivered to an overflow in a fall
twice the height of Niagara. The road has just been completed up
the river from here to **ATLANTA 66 m.**, a small mining town at the
base of the Sawtooth Range.

2. Right from Boise past the barracks, a safe but rapidly climbing
road leads to **TABLE ROCK 4 m.**, clearly visible from the city.
This huge flat table of stone, 1,100 feet above the valley, was
formerly used as a lookout by Indians, and from it today can be
seen the route taken by pioneers and their ox teams on the trail
south of the river. On this plateau is to be found the quarry from
which sandstone of unusual quality is taken. This is not only the
stone used in the Capitol but is also the stone that was demanded
by Yale University, by the Spokane cathedral, and by builders in

San Francisco and Hollywood. The view from this table is excellent
but is not comparable with that afforded by other points.

3. Right from the city on the road in side tour 1 to a left turn at **19 m.**
and then up Moore Creek through the Boise National Forest are
IDAHO CITY **45 m.** and the Boise Basin and its ghost towns (see
Sec. II, Ch. V, Ghost Towns). From Idaho City (which refuses
to be called a ghost, even though it is less than a handful of what
it used to be) is Lowman **82 m.**; and from here roads lead east, north,
and west into areas even more primitive. Above Lowman in a beautiful spot in the forest **4 m.** is the KIRKHAM HOT SPRINGS, where
free cabins are available. Right from Lowman on State 17 is the
GRANDJEAN HOT SPRINGS **30 m.** on the headwaters of the South
Fork of Payette River. When this Grandjean road is completed it
will lead into STANLEY BASIN **45 m.** and the area of the Sawtooth
lakes (see **Tour 5, Sec. a**). Westward from Lowman the road leads
through Garden Valley and to a junction with State 15 (see **Tour 6,
Side tour from Banks**).

4. Right from Boise up Eighth Street and past the water plant, a
road climbs for nine spectacular miles to PINE VIEW **9 m.** upon
one of the lower summits of the Boise Mountains. A few cabins
and refreshments are available here in a most unprepossessing inn;
and just beyond (R) is a free park with campgrounds. This is one
of the most popular and one of the most breath-taking drives in
the State, especially in the descent; but the most magnificent and
hair-raising side trip out of Boise is the next.

5. This trip can be reversed, with the beginning by way of Pine
View, but for an easier climb, for more impressive panoramas, and
for an appropriate climax, the journey should proceed west from
Boise over State 44 and 15 (see **Tour 6**) to the junction (R) **2.5 m.**
north of HORSE SHOE BEND **31.5 m.** The road from here around
the remainder of the loop is narrow and fairly smooth, and safe
only for experienced drivers. Unless the drive is made in cool
weather, three or four gallons of water should be carried. At
33.5 m. this tour takes the right turn past the schoolhouse and goes
up the canyon and climbs, sometimes steeply, for **13 m.** to the summit **46.5 m.**, where the right turn is to be taken. The road now proceeds up the backbone for a short distance and then drops over
switchbacks to lower ridges before climbing again to the rim of the
world where it follows the sky line of the Boise Ridge to SHAFER
BUTTE **62 m.** (elevation 7,591). After the Boise Ridge is gained, this
drive is breath-taking during the remainder of its length to Boise.
The road itself has so much mica in the sand that it looks under sunlight as if strewn with diamonds; the rock formations on either side
are very picturesque; and the panorama rolls away a hundred miles
in any direction. The most magnificent view, of its kind second to
none in the State, is to be had from the Shafer Butte Lookout: in
the northwest is a tumultuous kingdom of denuded mountains that

drop away to valleys and then lift to the Wallowa Range in Oregon;
in the south is the Boise Valley reaching to Snake River and walled
by the Owyhee Mountains; in the southeast is blue haze shimmering far and faintly clear to the Utah line; in the east is the blue
and golden empire of range upon range extending to the pale remote grandeur of the Sawtooths; and in the north are the Packer
John Lookout (see **Tour 6**) and the lookouts beyond. From Shafer
Butte the road winds upon the sky line and rims the world to Pine
View **71 m.** and then drops mile upon mile down the mountains
to Boise **80 m.**

6. Right from Boise over State 44 to the junction at **15 m.** with State
16, a surfaced road leads (R) to FREEZEOUT HILL **28 m.**, an
excellent vantage point for a view of Payette Valley, and thence
to EMMETT **31 m.** in the heart of a fruit area. This trip is especially
worth while in April when the loveliness and fragrance of the great
cherry orchards are unforgettable. Emmett has an annual cherry
festival later when the fruit is ripening, with a cherry queen pageant,
a rose show, and a carnival of floats and dances and parades. But
the heart of the festival is the display of the giant black luscious
Bings, the pride of this town. Right from Emmett on dirt road is the
BLACK CANYON DAM **4 m.**, a concrete structure 184 feet high.
At **8 m.** is the ROYSTON HOT SPRINGS with an outdoor pool.

U S 30 follows Main Street westward out of Boise.
MERIDIAN **10 m.** (2,650 alt.; 1,004 pop.) is the small
capital of a very fertile area, and is the largest shipping
point of its size in the State, and the home of one of
Idaho's largest creameries.

Left from Meridian on a surfaced road is Kuna **8 m.,** and a
poor road goes south from here to the KUNA CAVE **6 m.** This
latter road, at present unmarked by signs, swings southward past
the railway station; but two miles out there is a junction (R) with
a less traveled road that winds over sagebrush and lava terrain to
the cave which marks the end of this branch. The cave itself is by
no means so remarkable as several others in the State but is more
frequently visited because better known and easily accessible to a
large area. The most unusual thing about it is the descent: the
opening is a ragged hole in the surface of the earth and into this a
ladder is thrust for thirty feet to the bottom. The chambers, floored
with sand and distressingly dirty because of interior winds, are
excellent vaults without any striking formations. Many visitors are
impressed by the currents of air that move through them, sometimes, as in small openings, with perceptible velocity. It is said
that wind blows into this cave twelve hours and out of it twelve
hours in every day. The second interior can be reached by lying
prone in the dust and squeezing for ten feet under the low roof; and

the entrance to the third is also rather arduous. Persons entering
these chambers should wear rough clothing and expect to return to
the surface with dust in their ears.

NAMPA 20 m. (2,482 alt.; 8,206 pop.), seventh city in
size in the State, is said to have been founded by a wealthy
old-timer who, falling into a fury with Boise one day,
strode out of it swearing that he would make grass grow
in its streets. Neither his rage nor his wealth was able to
fulfill his threat, but he did help to bring into existence a
town that has been thriving ever since. Nampa takes its
name from a leader of the western Shoshonis who was one
of the most enormous thieves and murderers that ever
broke the back of a pony. Nampuh was so huge that the
vest of John McLoughlin, himself a giant of 315 pounds,
failed by fifteen inches to reach around him. This city is
the center of an agricultural and dairying area. Well known
throughout this valley is its LAKEVIEW PARK, seventy
beautiful acres at the eastern border of the city, with
golf courses, playgrounds, and a large swimming pool supplied from hot artesian water. On the north side is a
Spanish colony; just northwest of the city is a Bohemian
settlement; and the Scandinavian colony, largest of all,
indulges each summer in a huge picnic to which the fair-
haired come not only from these valleys but from neighboring States.

1. Left from Nampa State 45 leads into Owyhee County, a
picturesque and relatively unexplored area that has a population
of fewer than 4,000 but an acreage larger than Connecticut and
two Rhode Islands put together. Old-timers down here declare that
anything can be found in this county, including, they suspect, the
lost tribes of Israel. Just before reaching the bridge across Snake
River, a right turn goes down the north bank to the largest single
INDIAN PICTOGRAPH 6 m. that has ever been found. Here, upon a
great stone close by and to the right of the road, is carved a great map
which roughly defines not only the Snake River Valley but also Jackson Lake in western Wyoming and a few areas adjacent to both.
Vandals in recent years have broken off chunks of the rock and
carried away parts of the map.

The bridge on the river is at the site of the old WALTERS FERRY
which for fifty-eight years was an important link in the Boise-San
Francisco stage route. Today of the town only a few adobe huts

Jump Creek Canyon

A profile in Sucker Creek

remain, and of the ferry nothing. When building the bridge, work-men found arrowheads, rifle balls, and one poke of gold dust that had been hidden. South of the bridge are MURPHY 12 m., the present county seat, and SILVER CITY 44 m., patriarch of the ghosts (see Sec. II, Chap. V, Ghost Towns).

2. Left from Nampa on an unimproved road is LAKE LOWELL 6 m., upon which in August an annual motorboat regatta is held. This body of water, known also as the Deer Flat Reservoir, has a shore line of twenty-eight miles, and is fairly alive with perch, bass, and carp. There is no closed season on carp, and hundreds of sportsmen go to this lake to spear these fish, sometimes taking as many as three on a single lance. During spring spawning season, a fisher-man may catch as many as fifty in an hour, the largest of which are about thirty inches in length. There are also boating and bath-ing here but other accommodations are poor.

At **23 m.** on U S 30 is the junction with an improved road.

Left on this road is JUMP CREEK CANYON 26 m., one of the most beautiful spots in the State. At **14 m.** the highway drops down into a small lovely valley upon Snake River. On the left is LIZARD BUTTE, a historic landmark. The best view of it is to be had from the river bridge, where is to be seen its remarkable resemblance to an enormous stone reptile, lying prone upon the hill and clutching it with legs and tail while rearing its head. MARSING 16 m. is a wayside stop beyond the bridge. From here it is ten miles over poor road to the canyon, and only adventurous or very patient travelers should undertake the journey.

Jump Creek Canyon offers endless wonders to exploration. The road terminates at the mouth of it from which a trail leads up the stream. Along this trail are huge chambers under overhanging bluffs (in the first of which many campers eat their lunch); dark caverns running back into the ledges; vaulted archways where great piles of stone overshadow the creek and the trail; and high crags against the sky. A more inviting path it would be hard to find in Idaho. Less than half a mile from the beginning of the trail a climb should be taken to the left for the best view of the waterfall and the gorgeous backdrop beyond. The creek, if seen in spring or early summer, plunges like streams of snow down a black wall of lava for seventy-five feet. Beyond it the side of the gorge, stripped clean save for tiny gardens of moss, rises in enormous colored towers which range from blue gray and cobalt blue, from slabbed walls of burnt orange, through the old rose of façades and the somber red of columnar masses to patches of lemon yellow and delicate springtime green. If seen in early morning when the sun first strikes, this gorge is an indescribable riot of color. If, after sunrise no longer floods it with brilliance, it is brought close with powerful glasses, it is seen to be, and especially in the last terraced bluffs, a very rich mosaic, as if these walls had been inlaid with rough stone slabs of every color known. On some afternoons, when the ceiling is low, white clouds like floating islands asleep come drifting over the crags against the sky and spill gently into the gorge.

CALDWELL 29 m. (2,367 alt.; 4,974 pop.) has in the COLLEGE OF IDAHO, visible at the eastern edge of the city, the oldest institution of higher learning in the State. Across the highway from it is one of the largest feeding and shipping livestock stations in the Northwest. In ME-MORIAL PARK, beyond the campus (L) are playgrounds, a large outdoor pool fed by artesian water, and a cabin of historic interest. In the JOHNSON CABIN, three bachelor brothers lived in early days. At the west end of Main Street is the plant of The Caxton Printers, the regional publishers who in recent years have achieved a national reputation. Visitors are welcomed. But none of these items give the mental and spiritual flavor of this town which with its nineteen different churches and its some-what monastic quietness is quite unlike any other in the State. On U S 30 at the western edge of town is Canyon Ford Bridge upon Boise River, and just north of the bridge is the Dorion Monument, erected to Marie Dorion and as a marker upon the original Oregon Trail. The site of old Fort Boise is down the river one mile from its mouth.

Left from Caldwell on State 19 is Wilder 11 m. and Homedale 15 m. and from there over fair road is Sucker Creek 33 m. in Oregon just across the State line. SUCKER CREEK CANYON, accessible only or at least most easily by way of Idaho, is one of the beauty spots of the Northwest. This canyon, running for more than two miles in its more spectacular formations, is a stupendous area of monuments and monoliths, mounds and cones, faces and silhouettes, pedestals and spires, all gorgeously colored, with the dyes ranging from the yellow sulphurous walls, eroded and spilled, through great red and green bases to rich masses in which all colors are extravagantly har-monized. There is no more overwhelming view here than the one on the right at 37 m. where a hundred towers of varying heights and colors stand sharp and clean against the sky.

U S 30 goes north out of Caldwell through the Pay-ette Valley, the only part of the State that has more

available water for irrigation than is needed. NEW PLY-
MOUTH **54 m.** was conceived in the Sherman House in
Chicago by a chairman of a national irrigation congress;
and FRUITLAND **61 m.** is the center of one of the most
prolific fruit areas in the State.

PAYETTE **67 m.** (2,147 alt.; 2,618 pop.) has a well-
known shade-tree nursery which has developed a pink-
flowering and purple-bloom locust tree that blooms every
month. An apple blossom festival is an annual event here
when the orchards are burgeoned. Just west of the town
are the SHOWBERGER BOTANICAL GARDENS, an in-
ventory of which in 1934 showed 132 native plants that had
been identified, 100 that were still unnamed, and 1,500 wild
and cultivated varieties. These gardens supplied Hyde
Park in London with wild hollyhock after a long search
in Weiser Canyon to find it. Fifty different species of
pentstemon are grown here.

WEISER **82 m.** (2,119 alt.; 2,724 pop.) stands at the
confluence of the Snake and Weiser Rivers close by Oregon. It was named for Jacob Weiser, a German trapper,
and is pronounced Wee'-zer. The old town was for a time
called Weiser Bridge, and by 1890 had several stores and
hotels and barns and six saloons; but in this year a man
tried to take all of these saloons in a day's stride and
knocked a lamp over in a hotel, and the subsequent fire
almost wiped out the town. A new Weiser one mile westward was founded, and what remained of the first settlement moved over there. The town is today the gateway
of the fertile Weiser Valley with its huge orchards and
great belts of wheat fields. Of unexploited resources, this
region has an inexhaustible quantity of diatomaceous
earth, valuable in the manufacture of insulation.

There are several historic points of interest in or near
the town. At the eastern end of Twelfth Street is the old
immigrant crossing where wagon trains on the Oregon
Trail forded the river in early days. The old ferry boat
still stands on the Snake River crossing. Of historic

houses, the GALLOWAY and the HOPPER LOG CABIN are noteworthy, the first six miles up Weiser River, the second on the site of the old town.

At Weiser is the junction with U S 95 (see **Tour 7**). U S 30 crosses the Oregon line at **72 m., 65 m.** from Baker, Oregon.

TOUR NO. 4

Blackfoot—Arco—Junction with U S 93, **2 m.** south of Challis. **144 m.** State 27. Lost River Highway.

The Oregon Short Line Railroad parallels this route between Blackfoot and Mackay. Salmon River Stages use the highway between Blackfoot and Challis.

Accommodations throughout are less than average in hotels and tourist camps, and travelers who plan to spend some time in the region are wise to equip and provision themselves for an outdoor life.

State 27 proceeds out of Blackfoot (R) into the northwest, and soon leaves the fertile Snake River Valley to enter that enormous desolation of volcanic outpourings of which the Craters of the Moon are only a very small part. The contrast can be felt more deeply if it is remembered that State 39, which branches (L) at **5 m.**, turns south to SPRINGFIELD **20 m.**, in the vicinity of which is produced almost half of the Grimm alfalfa seed grown in the United States. State 27 soon reaches beyond all the irrigated luxuriance of this valley and lays its journey across apparently endless miles of the eastern slope of the great Idaho batholith. This Jurassic uplift underlies part of the State and is, with its innumerable folds and faults, its granitic gorges and basaltic buttes and cones, the most notable geologic feature of Idaho.

Right at **40 m.** are the TWIN BUTTES and on the left BIG BUTTE, famous landmarks for emigrants in early days. Two of them, BIG and EAST BUTTES, are rhyolitic volcanic cones completely surrounded by Snake River lava and are admirable examples of steptoes (islands formed in a once-molten sea of lava). MIDDLE BUTTE is an upraised block of stratified basalt. Middle Butte rises above the plain 400 feet, East Butte, 700; but Big Butte rises 2,350 feet as a deeply sculptured mountain and terminates in two ridges about a mile apart, with a deep depression between that apparently is the remnant of a crater. This mountain can be scaled but has unusual abruptness of ascent on all sides. It is composed chiefly of nearly white rhyolitic lava which varies in texture from firm-banded layers to light pumice and black obsidian. The basalt spilled at its base and spread into sheets is black. This formidable monument is a favorite haunt of certain wild animals, including bear and deer; and on its northern slope is a young and thrifty growth of fir and juniper. From the summit of Big Butte a broad vista presents the geologic record of the Snake River plains. Middle and East Buttes also rise abruptly. At the summit of the latter is the remnant of a volcanic crater. In the vicinity of both are many caves and underground passages, most of which have doubtless never been explored; and for any person seeking the unusual or wishing to venture into what has not within the memory of living man been seen, these three desolate sentinels are a terrifying playground.

At **54 m.** is the junction with State 29.

Right on State 29 are the LOST RIVER SINKS 20 m., where two rivers have long disappeared. As a matter of fact, not a single tributary reaches Snake River by surface travel from the high and rugged mountains lying west and north of its course between Malad River (see **Tour 3, Sec. b**) and Henrys (North) Fork, a distance of two hundred miles. In certain instances, as in the case of Big and Little Lost Rivers, the waters spread out in the marginal portion of the plain during the period of their greatest elongation and form shallow lakes. The chief reason these rivers are lost is the fact that the terrain across which they flow is rough and irregular, and evaporation and percolation in the lakes equal the influx. Big Lost River rises in the Sawtooth Range and flows ninety miles into this desert of stone to form a lake and vanish; and the Little Lost River emerges from the Pahsimeroi Mountains and flows eighty miles to disappear ten miles east of the other sinkholes. Both of these rivers were overland tributaries of the Snake before volcanic upheavals buried their channels and shook them out of their courses. Their outlet, as well as the outlet of other streams that vanish in this area, is thought to be chiefly the Thousand Springs which gush from the walls of Snake River Canyon a hundred and fifty miles in the southwest (see **Tour 3, Sec. b**).

ARCO 62 m. (5,318 alt.; 572 pop.) is the seat of Butte County and one of the loveliest of small Idaho towns.

From some distance it strongly resembles a village in Switzerland. The present site is its third since 1879, the first of which was called Junction; but the U. S. Post Office Department did not look with favor on so many Junctions, and the name was changed, though whether the present town was named for a visiting Count Arco or for Arco Smith, an early settler, or whether it was named because the town is on a bend in the river, seems not to be known. The Lost River Range terminates in the picturesque Wildcat Peak which is the backdrop of this town. The caretaker of the Craters of the Moon National Monument is stationed here and will provide guides if desired.

1. Left from Arco on State 22 is the CRATERS OF THE MOON NATIONAL MONUMENT 20.5 m. Martin's Ranch 18.5 m. (R) is a post office only. At the Hailey entrance accommodations are available. The panorama in this area at sunset is overwhelming, for at this hour the fields of lava are utterly black and strangely unreal; and in sharp contrast to them is the high and ghostly beauty of the Lost River Mountains in the east. Persons intending to leave the roads in the Craters region to explore should wear rugged clothing and very rugged shoes.

The Craters Monument, to which the buttes and the sinks with their surrounding country are an appropriate preface, is said to be unique upon the North American Continent. It was not explored save casually until recently, and was not set aside as a national monument until 1924. In Blaine and Butte Counties of Idaho, and resting upon the central lava terrain, the Monument itself is a newer part of a vast lava field that covers some two hundred thousand square miles and extends westward to the great Columbia Plateau. It is named Craters of the Moon because its caves and natural bridges, cones and terraces and weird piles of stone resemble the surface of the moon as seen through a telescope.

Three periods of eruption, the last of which probably took place 250 to 1,000 years ago, are recorded in the cones: the earliest in the cones of the Devil's Orchard and in the field of crags south of Big Cinder Cone; the next in the Sunset, Silent, Big Cinder, and their neighbors on the Great Rift; and the third by the North Crater and Big Craters, which formed the line of spatter cones southeast of Big Craters. The cones formed by the latter explosions are the most striking of the landscape.

The monumental area itself covers eighty square miles and is one of the largest national monuments under the National Park Service. Few spots on earth have such power to impress the human mind with the awful inner nature of the huge rock-planet upon which the human race moves at incredible speed through the universe. Anciently, and periodically thereafter, these eighty square miles and hundreds of square miles around them poured forth from thousands of steaming vents lava boiling at two thousand degrees F.; shuddered and heaved and cracked wide open in the granite depths; rolled over the miles in a great flood of molten rock, building grotesque caricatures; and then sucked downward through impenetrable black caves and were still. Today this area looks as if great seething cauldrons had poured from the sky upon this desolation, with the masses often cooling suddenly in the moving deluge, or stopping short as if flowing black or gray water had turned to stone. A person can spend days here and never see all that is to be seen or imagine the infinite variety of sculpturing and relief. Looking into a gigantic crack known as the Great Rift, and remembering not only that rivers disappear in the broad area eastward and flow in subterranean darkness, but also the strangeness of the whole region, the visitor can let his fancy build mightily and then fail to grasp the immensity of what once happened. Formerly several rivers came down off the watersheds and across this plateau to fall into the Snake where it was eroding its gorge far to the south. And then one day, a long time ago, the incalculable billions of tons of lava, running to what depth nobody knows, shook upward in boiling floods and poured over the plain for miles east and south and west. It came in such force and such volume that blocks of unmelted rock broke from the ceiling of the buried reservoirs and floated upward and were carried like driftwood on the mad tides. The torrents came out boiling, or gushed up in broad liquid floods that broke and fell in pouring terraces and swept out in great black tides that now lie like huge billowed carpets stretched to only half their length; or moved, half-congealed, in heavy slow motion out over the steaming landscape. Then for awhile there was peace; but other stupendous eruptions followed through the centuries, and the surface was torn apart in hundreds of vents and fissures, and outpourings built mile by mile the overwhelming picturesqueness of the region.

Strangely, there is but one type of lava, though this masquerades in several guises and assumes a variety of aspects. The dominant formation is basalt, rich in iron, which is the rimrock of the Snake River Gorge. In bright sunlight, some of the formations here look like blue glass; some like the half-deflated bodies of monstrous reptiles; and some like the transfixed waves of an ocean that had been caught running to high tide. There are many black buttes here, some with their tops blown off as if dynamite had scattered them to the winds; and some, rising several hundred feet above these, look as if they had been thrust up from the earth, inflated and ready to explode, but had cooled before explosion came. There are piles of solidified froth and foam that were blown out by fountains of fire; mounds of rock-clot that were soldered to one another under heat and collision after being thrown upward; and ribbons and spindle-bombs of stone that were shaped into beautiful symmetrical spheres during their moments of flight. There are dark musty caverns, dank and terrifying tunnels, and pits that are said to be bottomless. There are caves holding water that never

Monoliths at sunset and Volcanic Crater—Craters of the Moon

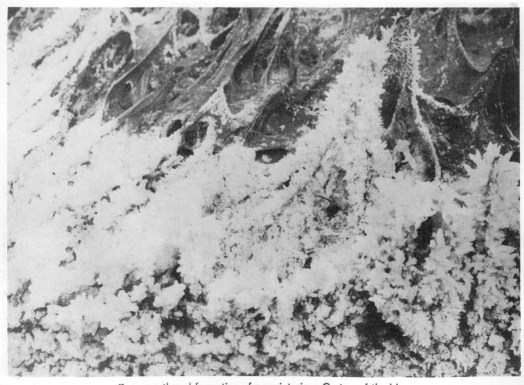

Cave mouth and formation of cave interior—Craters of the Moon

Indian Tunnel: entrance and corridor—Craters of the Moon

Lava flow—Craters of the Moon

Impression of charred log in lava—Craters of the Moon

rises more than two degrees above freezing even on the hottest days. And there are curious tree molds, because these eruptions buried a forest, and the lava in places flowed twenty feet in depth around trees, embracing the trunks within the boiling stone.

Perhaps the best view of this unutterably desolate region is to be had from Big Cinder Butte, which rises eight hundred feet above the adjacent plains. It is one of the largest basaltic cinder cones in the world. Lying eastward from it are broken pavements of black lava that unroll mile upon mile into the gray haze of the desert. Visible from this height is a strange yellow island of knolls, overgrown with grass, which were not inundated by floods. Southeast runs a series of volcanic vents reaching out into the black loneliness of lava for eleven miles and coming to a climax in Black Top Butte. Southward is an awful acreage of crags and domes; and over in the northwest lie the crater pits along the Great Rift. Some of these cones are brilliant red at noon and purple under twilight, and all of them together, when seen from Big Cinder Butte at dusk, are as weird a map of colors shimmering over a pattern of desolate waste as it is possible to see anywhere. Indians, indeed, held this spot in awe, and have handed down legends of that terrible time when the hills smoked and shouldered upward in their stupendous wrath and the whole broad reach of the desert trembled.

And this region, curiously enough, has wild animals living within it, as well as a few trees and many wild flowers. There are western junipers and limber pines and quaking aspens here; and among flowers there are red or yellow Eriogonums, blue pentstemons and larkspurs, purple lupine and red Indian paintbrushes, pink and white primroses; and loveliest of all, the most incongruous in the black wastes, are the white blossoms of the bitterroot, the yellow blossoms of the sand lily, and the gorgeous white sego lily, Utah's State flower. As if these were not enough, there are also cinquefoil and daisy and phlox, yarrow and aster and prairie pink. And a surprising number of animals make their homes here. There are several species of rabbit; gophers and chipmunks and porcupines; pack rats and rockchucks and skunks; and even coyotes and bobcats. In Moss Cave and Sunbear Cave there used to be dens of bears, and several grizzlies were slain in this area some years ago. Skulls show that mountain sheep and antelope and deer used to roam here. But there are no snakes in this region because the terrain is too rough and jagged for their journeying. Of birds there are woodpeckers and hawks and ravens and crows, larks and bluebirds and shrikes, sage grouse and mourning doves, and both the bald and golden eagle.

State 22 continues from the Hailey entrance into the southwest to its junction with State 23, which in turn proceeds to its junction at Shoshone with U S 93. Twenty-seven miles from Arco there is no longer a volcanic area on the right. On the contrary there is for many miles now the strangest contrast to be found on any Idaho highway. Upon the left is the ragged flank of the Craters area with long ridges running across like rifts of coal; and on the

right are denuded mountains so soft in color and texture that they
look in subdued light (in May or June) as if they were draped with
silk. At **30 m.** there is a broad view of the western reach of the
volcanic region, with the blue of Snake River Valley against purple
mountains in the southwest. Less than a mile after entering Blaine
County, the hills on the right are strikingly lovely in shades of
orchid and lilac, supplemented now and then by golden or blue
flanks and ravines. At **38 m.** the water on the left is a haven of
ducks, with lava piled like coal on the far side. A right turn **45 m.**
leads to Fish Creek and to excellent campsites in a canyon. Between
here and Shoshone there are intermittent patches of irrigated green
but for the most part the area still stands within possession of
volcanic landscaping.

CAREY **55 m.** and RICHFIELD **78 m.** are two small hamlets, each
the center of an irrigated oasis upon a pitted and rifted plateau
of waste. At SHOSHONE **96 m.** surfaced highways go north, south,
and west (see **Tour 5**).

2. Right from Arco a short distance on an unimproved road leading
toward Arco Pass a little-used wood road leads to the left toward
Beaverland Pass, and from the end of the road it is about a mile by
trail to the second most remarkable natural bridge in the State.
This arch completely bridges the canyon with a span of about 125
feet and a height of about 50 feet. Of irregular diameter, it spreads
into flanges at either end and is so rough on its surface that it is
difficult to cross it and not a little dangerous.

For the lover of beautiful mountains, the drive from
Arco to Challis is not comparable in massed splendor to
the distance between Challis and Salmon City (see **Tour
5)** or to the glittering imperturbability of the Sawtooth
Peaks west of Stanley Basin. But it is, nevertheless, a
minor feast, no matter whether in great rugged torsos or
in the low mounded extravagance of brown hills or in the
plump austerity of Mount Borah. From Arco, State 27
goes up the valley of Lost River, and attention is called
at **82 m.** to the contrast between the range on the left and
the one on the right. It is difficult to believe that almost
denuded mountains could be any lovelier than this Lost
River spur on the right, though the range across from it
is softer in contour and richer in color.

At **89 m.** is the junction with an unimproved road.

Right on this road is PASS CREEK GORGE **9 m.** on Pass Creek.
This canyon, too, it seems, is often called the Royal Gorge of Idaho,
and perhaps is worthier of the name than any other. This gorge, more

Mount Borah

Natural bridge near Arco

than a mile in length, is very narrow, and its sheer walls, rising more than two thousand feet, leave only a slender path of sky line above. Favored as a picnic ground, the bottom of the canyon is forested and is traversed throughout by a cold mountain stream. Fishing in this stream and in others here is excellent. The walls of the gorge are two thousand feet of strata, the lower depth of which is dark blue limestone which grades upward into shale. Like any other magnificent canyon, this one comes most fully to life at sunset when the upper ledges are luminous with glory and the shadows are banked depth upon depth in the lower reaches.

MACKAY 90 m. (5,897 alt.; 777 pop.) is another subalpine town in a lovely setting. It stands in a valley that once sheltered several boom towns, of which little or nothing remains, as well as gangs of lusty rascals who had things pretty much to their taste before the vigilantes came. Of minor indignities, the murder of Bill Noyes is still remembered. He was traveling with a friend whose name seems to have vanished beyond legend when the two men engaged in argument over a trivial matter and descended from the wagon to fight. Noyes was the huskier of the two, and after beating his friend in what a historian calls a "most barbarous manner" he waxed sardonically playful and drove the wagon over the prostrate body. But the now nameless one was tougher than he seemed. He came to his senses presently and sat up and shook both his fists and made horrible threats, all of which he later fulfilled by calling Noyes from his sleep one night and filling him with buckshot. Stories such as this still live within the memory of old-timers here and make a good part of the history of this valley.

At **92 m.** is the Cottonwood Grove dancing pavilion (R) ; and on the left at **95 m.** is a lake, either blue or green, depending on the light, which is the storage and diversion point of the river. South of here the old bed of Lost River is dry. CHILLY **107 m.** is a ghost town of a few deserted shacks.

Left from Chilly on the Trail Creek road is TRAIL CREEK SUMMIT and a fine improved campground 25 m. The distance to Ketchum is 43 m. (See **Tour 5.**) This road proceeds through a closed game preserve on the Lemhi National Forest, and deer are often visible to those driving across.

DICKEY **111 m.** still appears on highway maps but there is nothing here except a ranch on either side of the road. This is another ghost town. Mount Borah, straight east of it, is the highest known point in Idaho: though it stands at an elevation of 12,655 feet, it seems not to, perhaps because the tableland surrounding it is considerably more than a mile above the sea.

Right from Dickey a country road leads to the foot of the mountain, to the summit of which a few persons annually climb for the view afforded not only of much of Idaho but of parts of Utah, Wyoming, and Montana as well. Old-timers here say that only one woman has ever reached the top and they are dubious of her, surmising that her husband recorded her name there.

Much more impressive than Mount Borah itself in May and June is the incomparable mountain north of it with its colorful warm flanks and its deep and symmetrical ravines. This is Dickey Peak. Its lower slopes in spring and summertime look like a plush gray or green carpet, and its marvellously sculptured reaches look like golden velvet. Quite as beautiful is the range which runs north from it, visible as soon as the ascent is made out of Thousand Springs Valley.

At **123 m.** is a junction with a fair road.

Left on this road by way of STAR CANYON is CLAYTON **24 m.** on U S 93.

At about **130 m.** State 27 passes through the spectacular heaped ruggedness of GRAND VIEW CANYON, where the sheer walls are laid block upon block.

At **142 m.** is the junction with U S 93, and two miles north is Challis (see **Tour 5, Sec. a).**

TOUR NO. 5

(Missoula, Montana) — Salmon City — Ketchum — Sho-shone—Twin Falls—(Wells, Nevada). U S 93. Sawtooth Route.

Montana Line to Nevada Line, **365 m.**

The Oregon Short Line of the Union Pacific System parallels U S 93 between Ketchum and Shoshone, and the Twin Falls Stages follow the highway between Stanley and the Nevada Line.

This highway when completed will be one of the great transcontinental arteries between Canada and Mexico. This, from the Montana Line to either Arco or Hailey, is the most magnificent long scenic drive in Idaho. It is two hundred and forty miles of beautiful mountains, ranging from soft flanks voluptuously mounded to the lean and glittering majesty of toothed backbones. The lover of natural beauty who wishes to see most of what this tour offers will digress at North Fork over the side tour; and upon reaching Ketchum will take the road northeast over State 24 and then proceed to Shoshone by way of the Craters of the Moon. The additional distance will be less than a hundred miles.

Accommodations limited.

Section a. Montana Line to Hailey, 241 m.

U S 93 comes up the Bitterroot Valley in Montana and across the Bitterroot National Forest to enter Idaho over historic GIBBONS PASS (6,995 alt.) which was crossed by Lewis and Clark in 1805.

Left at the summit is a road that follows the Continental Divide to the ANDERSON MOUNTAIN LOOKOUT 7 m., from which is visible a large part of both Idaho and Montana.

South of the Montana-Idaho Line in Idaho is the Salmon National Forest with its densely wooded reaches. The road drops down into Idaho several thousand feet in the next twenty-five miles. This part of U S 93 between the Montana Line and North Fork is a winding drive through a wilderness of evergreens much like that to be found in many areas in Yellowstone Park. At **5 m.** after going down over a series of elbows the road eases at the first bridge over the North Fork of Salmon River. It was up the canyon on the right that Lewis and Clark went by mistake on September 3, 1805. The timber on the right or left during the first descent is chiefly lodgepole pine and Douglas fir with a little western yellow pine.

The SALMON NATIONAL FOREST of 1,723,872 acres is upon the western slope of the Continental Divide and is the chief watershed of the Salmon River and its forks, the Lemhi River, and of such large creeks as Panther and Horse, besides hundreds of smaller streams. Its principal trees are western yellow pine at lower altitudes, with lodgepole and Douglas fir higher up, and with limber pine and balsam still higher as valuable coverage on the watersheds. Engelmann spruce is abundant in the canyons and wetter areas. Its wild game is chiefly deer, mountain sheep, and goat, antelope, bear, cougar, coyote, and lynx. There are a few elk and moose and a few red deer. This region is a favorite with hunters from many parts of the world, not only for larger game but also for grouse, quail, pheasant, and, most notably, sage hens which are to be found in huge flocks. Natural campsites, unexcelled fishing streams, and roads and trails, often of poor texture, are all too numerous to be mentioned save in exceptional instances.

TWIN CREEK CAMPGROUND **9 m.** (R) is improved and one of the best in the forest. At **9.5 m.,** across the stream (R), is a marker to Lewis and Clark, for it was down this canyon they came on their historic journey.

GIBBONSVILLE **15 m.** offers meals and a few cabins.

This is a ghost town, and little remains of the thriving village that was once here.

Left from here an unimproved road leads to Montana and to good fishing and natural campsites on Dahlonega Creek in Idaho a few miles out. A distance of eight miles on this road leads to what some declare to be the finest vantage point in Idaho. From here on a bright day it is possible to gaze clear across the State to the haze of the Seven Devils Gorge upon the Idaho-Oregon line.

U S 93 continues to parallel the North Fork, with the valley widening enough to allow small meadowed ranches and with the lodgepole yielding at this elevation to aspen, birch, and willow along the stream, and to yellow pine and spruce on the flanks.

NORTH FORK 26 m. is only a store and a junction. Here is a fine monument to the Lewis and Clark Expedition and to Old Toby, the Indian who led them from here to the Bitterroot Valley.

Right from North Fork a road goes down the Salmon River and thence into primitive wilderness with return to U S 93 by way of Panther, Napias, and Williams Creeks to the junction five miles south of Salmon City. The road is narrow but fair to good.

Often called the River of No Return and a physical phenomenon in itself because it is navigable only downstream, and then never under any but expert guidance, the Salmon is the longest stream lying wholly within any of the States. In either its main channel or its middle fork, it journeys through a gorge that is deeper by a thousand feet than the Grand Canyon of the Colorado. It rises in its chief stream far in the southwest among the Sawtooth Mountains and flows eastward for forty miles before it swings northward for nearly a hundred, only to turn abruptly again, pick up the North Fork, and plunge westward for two hundred miles, dividing the State into its north and south halves and joining the Little Salmon at Riggins (see Tour 7, Sec. a). The Middle Fork, rising near the source of the main stream, goes northwestward and then north through a magnificent canyon of its own and through the heart of the Primitive Area. The road down the main river now goes almost to the junction with the Middle Fork (about 50 m.), and will eventually be completed all the way down the gorge to make one of the most picturesque scenic drives in America. J. B. Umpleby of the United States Geological Survey has declared that the canyon of the main Salmon is "one of the most magnificent gorges that nature ever produced." Boat trips down the river's length from Salmon City are arranged there; and for those with no taste or no money or time for so hazardous a journey, the highway can be followed.

A sign at the junction declares that the traveler takes this road at his own risk, but this warning need not alarm for it seems not improbable that he takes all roads at his own risk. On the left at 4.5 m. comes Dump Creek in wild haste down from the crags. Attention is called to the few rugged old-timers along the river, usually on the far side, and to the cables across which they coon when venturing out for supplies. Geologists with the recent National Geographic Expedition down the river have said that these pioneers are the most independent persons on earth. That is a slight exaggeration. The winters are relatively mild along this river, and these settlers are in touch through the year with the world beyond. If the traveler wishes to see persons living at the last reach of independence and remoteness, he can find them by pack trip into the hinterlands of this great forest.

A tiny MUSEUM 17 m. is left. It has a few heads of wild animals and a few Indian relics. Of greater interest is the enormous pile of antlers by the cabin south of it. Just beyond on the right is Indian Creek and a diversion road, built by the Forest Service, which climbs to the Bluenose, Beartrap, Oreana, and Long Tom Lookouts from any of which is offered a vast and breathless view of country. SHOUP 19 m. is a few unsightly shacks by the road. From here to the turn up Panther Creek, attention is called to the cascading haste of the river, especially in late spring when the floods are high. The road goes down the river several miles from the Panther Creek turn and leads to natural campsites and to almost unexcelled fishing.

At 27 m. the road turns (L) up PANTHER CREEK, which in June is a river in its own right. From this turn for more than twenty miles the road climbs an easy grade, and both the scenery and the water become increasingly impressive. At about 31 m. is HOT SPRINGS CREEK (L), of which the fountainhead is the mighty BIG CREEK HOT SPRINGS. Many of these pools constantly boil at a temperature hot enough to cook vegetables and meats, and all of them together discharge enough water to send down the canyon a steaming torrent of considerable size. Long used by remote settlers as a cure for rheumatism, these waters have never been commercially developed, and are held in reserve now by the Forest Service as the core of an eventual mammoth playground. Panther Creek at 39 m. is beyond all description impetuous in its haste. The traveler may be surprised and not a little appalled to find a tiny ranch now and then along this wild creek. These men are the last of the frontiersmen. With both time and tact, some of these recluses can be engaged in talk; but those engaging them are urged to lay aside their patronage because these independent folk are never in a mood for insolence and know how to rebuke it thoroughly. The beautiful trees with the golden yellow bark and deep black seams are western yellow pine.

At 47 m. on this creek is the junction with Napias and Upper Panther Creeks, two of the maddest streams that ever came down out of mountains. They come together in furious confluence to form Panther Creek, and at their junction is the LEACOCK RANCH, typical of the hermitages that were accessible only by horse or afoot until the Forest Service built roads here. The road at the right goes to Forney and the eastern entrance of the Primitive Area. The traveler taking the left turn up Napias Creek will probably reflect, especially if he leaves the road to look down upon it, that this is the wildest stream he ever saw. This creek, boiling down over indescribable cascades, does everything any stream can do and remain upon its bed. In one stretch (not visible from the road) it builds plunge upon plunge and goes under the name of the Napias Creek Falls. At **50.5 m.** an extremely difficult road leads left to the ghost town of LEESBURG, once a city of seven thousand but now a specter of twelve persons. The main or Napias Creek road takes the turn across the bridge (R) and climbs for several miles up a winding evergreen corridor to the summit. The elevation at the summit 57 m. is more than 8,000 feet, and for those who want a broader view there is a side road (R) leading to Lake Mountain.

A hundred yards down from the summit is an unobstructed view of the magnificent mountains in the east, ranging from the green and old-rose flanks in the foreground to the deep blue of the timbered crests far beyond. This winding descent for eleven miles is breath-taking, with vision intermittently obscured by dense forest or suddenly cleared to the sweep of distance where mountains look like lakes of cobalt blue. At **60.5 m.** is the improved Cougar Campground, and it is to be doubted that there is in Idaho a more beautiful site than this one. Far up here on this broad watershed, it overlooks a hundred miles of mountainous distance in the east and the Lemhi Valley below. The descending road goes down the Williams Creek Gorge with stone bluffs rising on right or left in amazing variety and beauty. This drive from the campground down to the valley is unsurpassed in Idaho. At **71 m.** is the junction with U S 93 5 m. S of Salmon City.

At **41 m.** is Carmen Creek where Captain Bonneville erected a temporary fort and log cabins in 1832. This was the first building done by white men along the Salmon River. U S 93 goes up Salmon River to enter a mountain valley.

SALMON CITY 48 m. (4,003 alt.; 1,371 pop.) is the industrial center of this valley. At the junction of the Salmon and Lemhi Rivers, it is the seat of Lemhi County, and except for Hamilton, Montana, is the largest city within the radius of a hundred miles. Few visitors enter this valley or this small subalpine town without commenting on the beauty of the one and the picturesque site of

the other. Its chief attraction is probably ISLAND
PARK, a timbered area of five acres in the river above
the bridge and a favorite campground.

1. Left from Salmon City on State 28 is an area with a dramatic historic background. At **17 m.** is a monument (L) to the memory of
Sacajawea, an Indian woman and sister of Chief Comeawait, who
came westward with Lewis and Clark and was restored to her people
in the Lemhi Valley. Midway between Tendoy and Lemhi (L) is a
monument to Chief Tendoy of the Lemhi Tribe. Tendoy was a full-
blooded Shoshoni Indian who befriended the whites during the Nez
Perce War and later when the Fort Hall Indians went on a rampage.
LEMHI **30 m.** (5,100 alt.; 25 pop.) was named, like the forest, county,
mountain range, valley, and river for Limhi, a character in the *Book
of Mormon.* Mormons were sent from Utah to colonize this valley in
1855. They built Fort Lemhi, irrigated on a small scale, and were
prosperous until driven out by Indians three years later. Remnants of
the old fort are still to be seen, and one of the irrigation ditches is
still in use. Later, gold was discovered in this region, and a stampede settled it, but today there is little save a few ranches and a
few ghost towns.

The story is told that during an Indian raid here one woman
became so excited that she leapt astride her horse facing its tail and
looked down in utter horror and cried: "Great God, they've shot
my horse's head off!" Whereupon, the legend goes, she remembered
that she had forgotten her daughter Hope and began to call "Hope!
Hope!" with anguished persistence, looking meanwhile at her head-
less horse. Her white friends heard her calling Hope, and, mistaking
the word for a battle cry, faced about and so completely annihilated
their foes that the only ones who escaped were 22,369 who jumped
into the river.

At **49 m.** is LEADORE, which has achieved some renown because of the distance its pupils travel to reach its high school.
The average distance covered daily by the seventy-seven boys and
girls enrolled in 1936 was thirty-one miles. Two sisters made a
round trip of ninety miles. In early days the stagecoach was held
up by two daring rascals on the summit south of Leadore and
$37,000 was stolen. The bandits barricaded themselves in cliffs
above the Hahn smelter and both were killed by infuriated prospectors who pursued them. The gold, said to have been hidden in
these bluffs, has never been found and is only one of the legendary
lost treasures that are regarded by some as a part of Idaho's invisible wealth.

2. Right from Salmon City is the Yellowjacket road which leads
to the eastern gateway of the Primitive Area. This road is in poor
condition and only the most adventurous undertake it. It proceeds
by way of LEESBURG **15 m.**, which once had a main street a mile
long and a large Chinese colony. FORNEY **32 m.** is another ghost
town, and YELLOWJACKET **44 m.** is the end of the trail. Here,

and at MEYERS COVE southward a few miles, guides and all necessary equipment are available for pack trips into the Area. On the summit (8,370 alt.) between the Panther Creek and Yellow-jacket watersheds there is a side road that takes a tortuous way over the mountains and along ridges to the HOODOO MEADOWS LANDING FIELD (L), which is on the margin of the Primitive Area at an elevation of 8,600 feet. This point offers a view of the BIG-HORN CRAGS, the most rugged range in the State.

3. Down the Salmon River by boat from Salmon City to Lewiston through 310 miles of the Salmon River and lower Snake River Canyon is a popular and adventurous excursion. This journey in flat-bottomed scows has been declared by a geologist who made it to be "a sporting and scenic event without equal." Arrangements have to be made far in advance to allow time to make the boats, and the trip is to be undertaken in any case only under expert guides to be found in Salmon City. For a journey down the Salmon River, see *National Geographic Magazine* for July, 1936.

U S 93 south of Salmon City runs across a mountain valley. At **52 m.** is a junction with a road.

Left on this road are the SALMON HOT SPRINGS 4 m., where swimming pools are available.

At **53 m.** is a junction with a good road.

Right on this road is the COUGAR POINT CAMPGROUND **10.5 m.** up Williams Creek. The turn is across a red bridge and then up a magnificent gorge over a series of switchbacks that rise several thousand feet. This camp is a large one with running water, shelter, stoves, tables, and a site that it would be impossible to excel. (See side tour from North Fork above.)

At **54 m.** U S 93 enters the upper gorge of Salmon River and follows it for more than a hundred miles. This canyon under different light is never twice the same and can be realized for what it is only in late afternoon or at sunset. It is not, for the most part, a gorge of sheer walls and overwhelming heights. It is remarkable rather in the variety of its mountains and in the exquisite coloring of its stone. There are ridges that sharply climb the sky with the sculpturing reaching from shoulder to shoulder; there are huge monuments set apart by time and erosion; and there are rounded brown bluffs with slide rock spilled smoothly at their base like tons of copper. There are picturesque collections of castles and towers, and in contrast with these are gently sloping flanks that look as if they were carpeted with green or golden velvet. There are magnificent solitary crags, and down below them, piled against the road, are weird gray formations so pocketed and cupped that they resemble cliff dwellings.

At **86 m.** is the lower end of the Pahsimeroi Valley, wherein ranges one of the largest herds of antelope in the world. The animals here and in adjacent regions are estimated to number five thousand, and if a person is alert he may catch sight of one while journeying through. Country roads go up the valley on either side of Pahsimeroi River and lead to natural campsites and excellent fishing.

At **93 m.** is the junction with the Morgan Creek Road.

Right on this road is MORGAN CREEK from which the road runs the full length of Panther Creek to FORNEY with a branch to Meyers Cove on Silver Creek. This is the best of the eastern entrances to the Primitive Area. (See side tour from North Fork above.)

At about **94 m.** is CRONKS CANYON, which is known as the Royal Gorge of Idaho, and it is here that the most beautiful coloring is to be seen. The rugged bluffs here standing as walls against the highway are stratified in red and yellow, green and dark blue, and even under morning sun are extremely rich. At sunset, when burning evening streams up this forge, this mountainside in its bewildering loveliness looks as if a thousand broken rainbows had been drawn into the stone.

CHALLIS **107 m.** (5,400 alt.; 418 pop.) is even more remarkable than Salmon City for the beauty of its setting. The mountains northeast of it are unusually picturesque under any light and in comparison with mountains anywhere. They are unforgettable when seen at sunset under a cloudy sky. The clouds lie low in blazing reefs and banks with the distant peaks thrusting up like golden crowns; and down under the great flaming panorama the colored bluffs upon the river look like a shimmering fog bank lost in an extravagance of colored mist.

The Sawtooth Mountains east of Stanley

The outlet of Redfish Lake

Stanley Lake

Roaring Lake

At **109 m.** is the junction of U S 93 with State 27 (see **Tour 4**). U S 93 turns to the right and enters the miniature grand canyon of the Salmon River with the walls sloping upward on either side for two thousand feet. Though the coloring is not so rich nor the formations so various as in the Royal Gorge, this canyon is, nevertheless, a mighty spectacle of splendor under the evening sun.

At **116.5 m.** is a junction with an unimproved road.

Right on this road up BAY HORSE CREEK are campsites and fishing.

CLAYTON **132 m.** (5,450 alt.; 106 pop.) looks as if a flock of terrified buildings had come down a strong wind to settle here in the gorge and were still troubled by loneliness and indecision. U S 93 continues up the river through beautiful country and over fast winding road. Wherever the highway has cut through the stone the coloring is exquisite. At **144.5 m.** is Torrey's (L), where cabins and meals are available.

At **151.5 m.** is the junction with a road.

Left on this road is ROBINSON BAR RANCH 1.5 m. This ranch on the mouth of Warm Springs Creek at an elevation of 5,883 feet is in the heart of the Salmon River Mountains and is fenced on all sides by great watersheds and wild streams. It is equipped with a lodge, two swimming pools, tennis courts, and horses for pack trips into the surrounding area. The fish in the streams here are Dolly Varden, rainbow, and cutthroat trout and three species of salmon.

At **153.5 m.** is the junction of U S 93 with an unimproved road.

Right on this road is the YANKEE FORK DISTRICT. This road, usually not open until early summer, leads to Bonanza and Custer, two picturesque ghost towns. The Yankee Fork has many beautiful campsites along its shores. At about **1 m.** (L) and at about **2 m.** (R) are improved campgrounds maintained by the forest. This road goes over Loon Creek Summit into the Loon Creek watershed, and on the far side demands very careful driving through ruggedly beautiful country. At the summit is another improved camp; and up the Yankee Fork from BONANZA **8 m.** there are three, the first right and the other two left, within a distance of a few miles. The last of these is about **30 m.** from U S 93. There are dozens of streams touching this

road or not far from it, and in every one of them of adequate size
the fishing is excellent. BOYLE'S RANCH, L from Bonanza, is on
Loon Creek 28 m. among the Salmon River Mountains at an elevation
of 5,785 feet with peaks standing from 9,000 to 11,000 feet around
it. This ranch specializes in hunting trips into the Primitive Area.
A good pack trail follows Loon Creek to the Middle Fork of
Salmon River, and en route over this trail a side trip can be taken
up Warm Springs Creek to the WARM SPRINGS and to the game
country or fishing areas in the wilderness of which Parker Mountain (9,128 alt.) is the center. The SHOWER BATH SPRINGS on
Warm Springs Creek are large hot streams that burst from the
cliffs.

U S 93 goes through the CHALLIS NATIONAL FOR-
EST, and this, like the Salmon, is a huge game preserve,
rich in wild life and countless unfished streams. Deer are
by far the most abundant of the animals, but black bear are
plentiful, and pack trips in pursuit of them are popular
with hunters. The trees, like those in the forest north,
are chiefly lodgepole, Douglas fir, yellow pine, and Engelmann spruce. There is an unknown number of hot springs
in this forest, but of these the most unusual are to be
reached only by pack trails.

STANLEY 166 m. (6,200 alt.; 154 pop.) is remarkable
for two reasons. The first is a feud which divided the
village against itself and sent a few of the residents
wrathfully two miles westward to establish a new townsite. The U. S. Government recognizes only the old settlement, the first entered on U S 93; but it looks pretty
shabby now and suffers strong intimations of becoming
another ghost, while the new Stanley looks down its nose
and continues to thrive. The second reason is the extremely beautiful country in which the Stanleys are remotely sheltered from the world. The Sawtooth Mountains westward are a magnificent backbone of blue spires.
And in addition to these are the lakes.

Right from Stanley a road goes through the Stanley Basin and
at about 4.5 m. branches (L) through the forest to STANLEY LAKE
3 m. In June the meadows here are golden with the mountain buttercup and blue with the camas. The setting of Stanley Lake is perfect.
On the far side is a mountain flank with evergreens as thick as they
can stand, and beyond rise for several thousand feet the streaked blue

Pettit Lake

Alice Lake

Imogene Lake

Galena Summit

domes of the SAWTOOTH RANGE. A mile and a half up the creek that flows into the lake is LADY FACE FALLS, a lovely cascade that has for many persons the profile of a woman against its descent. Northwest from here but still at some distance is the Primitive Area.

This side road proceeds from the turn to the lake to CAPE HORN RANCH 20 m. which has a lodge and cabins and a large outdoor swimming pool. This ranch, like Boyle's, equips hunting expeditions into the Area. The rugged picturesque Middle Fork country can be reached by pack train in one day from this ranch. This road continues to Beaver Creek and then over Vanity Summit into the Seafoam and Rapid River section, and here again pack trips are available in almost any direction. A poor road proceeds and emerges at Cascade on State 15, or turns southward by way of Lowman to Boise. This country is perhaps as virgin as any to be found in the United States.

U S 93 turns southward out of Stanley with the Salmon River on the left and the Sawtooth Mountains on the right.

At **170.7 m.** is a junction at the bridge with a dirt road.

Right on this road are BIG REDFISH LAKE 2 m. and LITTLE RED-FISH LAKE, which is about the size of Stanley Lake. Both, together with the large creek, are stocked with trout. Both are lovely in their setting but not so perfect as Stanley. The hotel and cabins on Big Redfish have never been opened (for reasons which seem quite mysterious), but boats can be rented and campsites are many.

At the bridge on U S 93, particularly in springtime, the beauty of the cascading water on either side is very impressive.

At **176 m.** is the junction with a dirt road.

Left on this road is the ROCKY MOUNTAIN CLUB 1 m., which is perhaps the most exclusive of the dude ranches in Idaho. At an elevation of nearly 7,000 feet, it faces the Sawtooth Mountains in the west and is famous for the view from its porch. It has a spacious clubhouse flanked by cabins, together with sulphur baths and hot plunges, and a lake for boating and swimming. This resort outfits for pack trips into the Area, to the more inaccessible lakes, or up the many canyon trails in its neighborhood. The rates here are high.

At **181 m.** the RUNNING SPRINGS RANCH, adjacent to the highway (R), offers pack trips to both hunting and fishing areas.

Over in the mountains on the right is the loveliest group of lakes in Idaho, in any one of which there are really too many fish rather

than too few. They can be reached only by trail. A favorite trip
from this ranch is one of seven days with a new lake fished in each
day. HELL ROARING LAKE is seven miles out on the trail. IMO-
GENE is eight miles, and TOXIWAY, ALICE, TWIN LAKES, and
YELLOW BELLY are spaced at short intervals beyond. All of them
are surpassingly beautiful. Another favorite trip from this ranch
is in pursuit of black bear.

On the ranges to the left here are mountain sheep and
on those to the right are mountain goats. At **195 m.** U S 93
leaves the valley and climbs over a series of spectacular
switchbacks for four miles to GALENA SUMMIT **199 m.**
which, at an elevation of 8,752 feet, is the highest point on
any Idaho highway. The view from this summit is one of
the most remarkable in the West. For fullest realization of
the distances as well as of the majesty of the Sawtooth
Peaks a clear day and good glasses are necessary. Even
more breath-taking than the climb is the descent, for this
highway drops almost a thousand feet in the next five
miles. At **205 m.** the stream leaving the wilderness in such
tremendous haste journeys under the unfelicitous name of
Wood River. Though shamelessly small in its beginning to
be masquerading as a river, it gathers its waters creek by
wild creek and emerges finally in respectable volume to go
down into Snake River Valley.

At **214 m.** is a junction with a road.

Right on this road are EASLEY HOT SPRINGS **.5 m.** These are held
by lease by the Baptist Church, and just south of them is a Baptist
camp. All attempts to build a lodge and cabins here have been
frustrated by the Forest Service, but there are natural campsites
adjacent and a large outdoor plunge.

U S 93 proceeds southward down this mountain valley. On the left is BOULDER PEAK (10,966 alt.) and on
the right **220.5 m.** are improved campgrounds. At **226 m.**
is a view in the north of the magnificent purple mountains
out of which the highway has come. GLASSFORD PEAK
(11,500 alt.) stands upon the summit in the north. At
227 m. U S 93 leaves the Sawtooth National Forest.

KETCHUM **229 m.** (5,821 alt.; 200 pop.) is being turned
into a resort town which, it is hoped, will compete with

Dog team on Wood River, near Hailey

Trail Creek near Ketchum

famous European winter playgrounds. There is a large, modern hotel here, as well as hockey rinks and ski slides. Summer visitors are served chiefly by the Bald Mountain Resort with accommodations in its rows of cabins for 125 persons. It has a large pool. Of excellent fishing streams near Ketchum, Trail Creek is only a few hundred yards out; Warm Springs Creek is westward a half mile; Lake Creek is 7 miles north, Baker Creek is 20, and Prairie Creek is 22. The East Fork of Wood River is 10 miles south. The head of Lost River and the East Fork of the Salmon are 15 miles into the northwest.

At **238.5 m.** is a junction with a dirt road.

Right on this road is the Aberdeen Hotel, where hot springs are available.

HAILEY 241 m. (see **Sec. b**).

Section b. Hailey to the Nevada Line, 124 m.

HAILEY (5,342 alt.; 973 pop.) is another lovely mountain town and does not seem to be, but is, surrounded by silver and lead mines. In the northwest, Red Devil Mountain is in summertime a huge garden of wild sweet peas. On other mountains here are crocuses and buttercups and blue and purple pansies together with other wild flowers less profuse, which make fragrant color of these hillsides. U S 93 still goes south between two mountain ranges, and attention is called in June and July to the loveliness of Lookout Mountain which is the backdrop southeast of BELLEVUE **5 m.** (5,170 alt.; 375 pop.). At **15 m.** the Sawtooth country to the north is left behind, and the sudden contrast upon entering the Snake River Plains is complete and overwhelming. The summit of Timmerman Hill offers on a clear day a broad rolling landscape of one hundred miles of valley reaching clear to the Owyhee Range.

At **23 m.** is a railroad crossing and the junction with a country road.

Right on this road is MAGIC LAKE RESERVOIR 5 m. The waters of this reservoir, with a storage of 193,000 acre-feet, are a bright blue when seen from distance and look in sagebrushed landscape like a huge sapphire in a massive setting of chromium.

At 25 m. is a bridge across Wood River, sometimes called the upside-down river because it is here that in one place it is a hundred and four feet wide and four feet deep, and in another, not far removed, it is a hundred feet deep in its gorge and four feet wide. The traveler should pause to view the amazing sculpturing in this gorge. Noteworthy is the river itself, boiling over waterfalls and down a canyon that a man can leap, but of greater interest are the fantastic carvings in the black rock. The picture looks as if an ancient potter had thrown his workshop into this little canyon. There are almost perfectly symmetrical cups and saucers and even big vats that hold many gallons of water after a rain. Especially smooth in workmanship but grotesque in configuration is the carving on the south wall just below the lower cascade. On the west side of the bridge the river pours downward in wild frenzy and on the east side, a few feet away, it is a gently swirling apathy that seems to have lost both its direction and life. Curious persons try to learn what happens to this river as it passes under the bridge.

At 25 m. (just south of the bridge and just beyond the black reefs that run out in a ragged spur to the highway) is the junction with a road.

Right on this road are the SHOSHONE ICE CAVES 1 m. Flashlight or gas lantern is necessary equipment for these interiors. These caves, by no means the most remarkable, are the only famous ones in Idaho.

The caves here are really a series of craters that cover a quarter section of land and lie against a rampart of volcanic lava that seems to have been comparatively recent. The open gorge was at one time a tunnel but its ceiling has fallen in, leaving a cavern at either end. The eastern one is unimpressive. The other is approached through a huge bowl full of enormous stones that lead downward to the entrance above which the roof is remarkable for both the coloring of the rock and the ragged precarious way in which it is sculptured. A little farther down are arches and natural bridges, huge pits with their ceilings tumbled in, and flanking alcoves. After going down over broken blocks of basalt, the descent comes to a platform of ice down which in early spring the water filtered from above flows backward to freeze. The ceiling hangs so low here that a person must stoop for a few feet until more head room is found. Hanging in picturesque indecision are the great stones above.

A descent is now made down a ladder frozen into a wall of ice. If the entrance is made in late spring, this huge corridor ahead will likely be barren and impressive only in the elemental strength of its arching. If the entrance is in the fall after water and freezing weather have worked their magic, this chamber will be a spangled fairyland of ice crystals as if a glass blower had been busy here exhaling millions of frozen petals and tiny spires. Just beyond, the floor descends again down a sort of long ice toboggan slide, but a platform has recently been laid the length of the cave. The corridor now is a long one with a high arched roof that looks eternal in the mighty imperturbability of its strength; and this, too, in the appropriate season, is flaked and garlanded down its ceiling and walls. The platform turns to the left past a carload of lava blocks and proceeds to the end of the cavern, a wall of ice. This is about forty feet wide and twenty feet high at the top of its arch, with a concaved surface of unknown depth. Tons of ice have from time to time been chopped off this wall in an attempt to sound its thickness or to penetrate it and enter chambers that possibly lie beyond.

The terrain in which these caves lie is called the Black Butte Crater District. Indian legends allude to many phenomenal caves and buried chambers in Idaho, but most of these have apparently never been found. This area itself is much more mysterious than it seems to be to the casual eye. It is a region of twisted and woven lava, fallen-in tunnels, arched bridges, potholes, and pits. Some of the pits are of considerable depth, and it is declared that at certain seasons water can be seen flowing in the bottom of them. Ice caves and walls, snow cellars, and tiny craters no larger than a dishpan hold water on the hottest summer days; and there may even be small pots of boiling water almost side by side with small depressions of ice. Or side by side out of fissures, it is said, both hot and cold water may run.

SHOSHONE **43 m.** (3,968 alt.; 1,211 pop.) is the seat of Lincoln County and of an irrigated farming belt and sheep-raising area. Pronounced both Shoshone and Shosho-nee, it is, of course, a corruption of Shoshoni, an Indian word meaning Great Spirit. This town, founded in 1882, was first called Naples. The interesting subterranean nature of central Idaho was again revealed twenty years ago when the owner of a hotel here drilled for water and at a depth of twenty feet discovered that his drilling tools had vanished. Investigation showed that there was

an enormous chamber under the town, apparently bottomless, because stones dropped into the hole that had
been drilled were heard to strike walls from side to side
on their way down until they reached such depth that
the echoing reverberation could no longer be heard. The
cavern thereupon was used for the hotel's sewage, but nobody yet has any idea of where the waste water ultimately
goes. Shoshone is the junction with State 23 (see **Tour 4**).

Right on State 24 is GOODING[1] **16 m.** (3,572 alt.; 1,592 pop.). Named
for a former Senator, it is, like Shoshone, the center of an agricultural
area. But Gooding, farther removed from the lava areas, is more lush
in its countryside, and closely resembles in June, like much of the
Twin Falls country southward, Iowa or Illinois. Right from Gooding
on State 46, oiled for **9 m.** and then graveled for 8 m. to the turn (L)
is the GOODING CITY OF ROCKS **25 m.** The complete distance from
Shoshone is forty-one miles. This city is about four miles long by
one and a half miles wide, with several main gorges and countless
tributaries running through it. The rock formations are of shale
and sandstone with no lava, and many of them are beautifully
colored. The stones, often rising to more than a hundred feet, are
of all conceivable shapes with strange pillars and columns, weird
terraces and façades, cathedrals and obelisks and spires. It is one
of the best known and most frequently visited of Idaho's wonderlands.
   The eastern entrance is remarkable chiefly for the great round
stones gorgeously colored that look as if they had been laid thin
slab upon slab. About a mile into the city is a sign on a rock
which indicates a canyon six hundred feet to the right; and from
here the view affords the best impression of sheer bulk, weight,
and eternity. Many of these colored piles show the stratigraphic
nature of the stone. At the bottom of this gorge is pure cool water
for those who are prepared to eat lunch here.
   But this is not a garden of the gods as is so commonly declared.
It is a garden of monuments that have been sculptured out of
eternity by the incalculable reaches of time. South, to the left, is
another deep canyon along which are innumerable curious formations. The most impressive view of the whole area is to be had
two miles from the entrance where upon the right is unfolded a
great ragged panorama of summits and gorges and ruins. The
aspect, seen from a distance, is almost overwhelming not in its
several items but in the indiscriminate way in which monuments
and towers and castles have been tumbled and spilled. Almost
every shape of stone is to be found here, from cones to pyramids,
from flat fortress walls to minarets, from balconies to stratified
stairways. The coloring though subdued is rich and satisfying with
reds and browns dominant. The city runs into the west still for a

---

[1] For side trip to the Malad gorge, river, lake and rift, see **Tour
3, Sec. b.**

Middle and third chambers, Shoshone Ice Caves

Gooding City of Rocks

Salmon Dam

Twin Falls-Jerome Bridge

considerable distance and though much curious work is to be found farther on, there is nothing quite so spectacular as this acreage of eroded and lonely masterpieces of weather and wind. In fact, the more a person looks at the assemblage of thousands of separate items, the more he is likely to fancy that some ancient sculptor of enormous size and restless ambition worked here for a century and left his dream unfinished.

Those who spend only an hour here, looking casually and seeing nothing perfect in itself, go away disappointed; but those who explore and examine at close range the amazing variety, are speechless before the miracle of what wind and sand can do. Especially intended to silence the sceptic is a descent into either gorge and a view of the monuments against the sky line.

JEROME 62 m. (3,660 alt.; 1,976 pop.) is the seat of Jerome County and the center of a large Carey Act irrigation project. In contrast with the volcanic areas north and east, this countryside is burgeoned like a garden in summertime and is enviably situated between the purple mountains north and the luxuriant Twin Falls country south. Out of it U S 93 now suddenly approaches the canyon of Snake River and crosses the gorge on the only toll bridge in operation in the State. Formerly, before this and the Hansen bridges were built, the deep gorge of the river was an impassable barrier between the fertile regions north and south, and Twin Falls, in consequence, was almost as remote from Jerome as it was from Boise.

THE TWIN FALLS-JEROME BRIDGE 73 m., the most impressive one in Idaho, has a cantilever span of 1,350 feet, a distance between towers of 700 feet, and a height from water level of 476 feet. It is the third highest bridge in the West. Completed in 1927, it has done more than to facilitate travel between the two irrigated areas. It offers, too, the finest perspective to be had on one of the most beautiful sections of the gorge. Persons who frequent this bridge for the view declare that a casual glance does not in any degree summarize what is to be seen. Superficially, there are two walls here five hundred feet in height and dropping in most of their distance sheer to the slide-rock or the river; and there is a river which, having just come over Shoshone Falls, seems no longer to be in any haste; and there is some vegetation upon the shores. A closer scrutiny discovers much in addition to these.

After crossing the bridge, U S 93 proceeds to TWIN FALLS **76 m.** at the junction with U S 30. (For this city, as well as for the points of unusual interest in its environs, see **Tour 3, Sec. b.**) U S 93 follows U S 30 westward out of Twin Falls and at **82 m.** turns southward. Adventurous persons with the time and a wish to explore may find the country south of Twin Falls to their taste, for across this sparsely settled area there is probably more to be discovered than is yet known.

At **85 m.**, or **3 m.** south of the departure from U S 30, is GODWIN SIDING (L), and at **86 m.** is a frame house sheltered by tall trees. This was the home of Lydia Trueblood Southard, Idaho's notorious female Bluebeard, who vented her emotions over a period of years by poisoning a baby daughter, a brother-in-law, and five husbands. She is now in the penitentiary at Boise. HOLLISTER **96 m.** is the junction with a dirt road.

Left on this road the NAH SUPAH HOT SPRINGS **3 m.** afford a very large swimming pool, supplied by natural hot water, together with camping and recreation grounds. The name (spelled also Nat Soo Pah) is an Indian word meaning living or life-giving water. A mile southwest of here is a famous landmark and early watering hole called WILD HORSE SPRINGS.

AMSTERDAM **101 m.** is the junction with an unimproved road.

Left on this road are HOT CAVES **4 m.**, a mile and a half southeast of the Goat Springs Ranch. It was here in 1885 that a prospector and two companions were boring a tunnel into the mountain when the prospector suddenly and unexpectedly disappeared from sight. His companions discovered that he had quite literally fallen into the mountain and into a stream of hot water that flowed through a subterranean tunnel. Years later, after artesian wells had been sunk at Goat Springs, this flow of hot water ceased, and today the interiors are dry. Six underground chambers have been explored, and doubtless many more remain unseen. Stalactite and stalagmite formations cover the floor, walls, and ceiling, ranging in length from a few inches to twenty feet. Because the tunnel entrance is now caved in and because numerous rattlesnakes have taken a fancy to the caves, no attempts have recently been made to enter.

Adventurers interested in exploration can enlist the assistance of Ora Jones, one mile west of the Goat Springs Ranch, who knows of another entrance.

Possibly it was in this region that Hy Conner, an old-timer, suffered his most humiliating experience. One night he was sitting by a campfire, listening to the melancholy of wind in the pines and to the complaints of his companions, one of whom was telling of a hard-boiled foreman who docked his men if they were off the job. Said one: "If a man was offen his job only a minute, why that-there foreman, he out with his watch and looked hard at it and docked the poor bugger for that much lost time." It was then that Hy yawned and put a fresh quid in his mouth and spoke. "Boys," he said, "you ain't heard nothing, not a plumb belly-guzzled thing. You should a-known the foreman I worked under when we was a buildun the Oregon Short Line. That man wouldn't take no excuses. That man was tough. I remember one time I was runnun in a cut with a single jack and drill and I drilled into a missed hole and the powder went off and blowed me high in the air. The boys, they looked up and watched me and they said first I looked like a little bird and then I looked like a bee and then I went plumb out of sight. In about ten minutes they seen me coming back and at first I looked like a bee and then I looked like a bird and down I come right where I was a-settun before I left. I still had the hammer in one hand and the drill in the other and I set right to work. But, say, you know what that son-of-a-buzzard of a foreman did? He docked me for the fifteen minutes I was gone!"

ROGERSON 106 m. (4,803 alt.; 280 pop.) is a tiny hamlet, but the largest town, nevertheless, in this part of the State. It stands on the historic site formerly known as Deep Creek Meadows.

1. Right on a dirt road is SALMON DAM 8 m., one of the largest concrete structures in the State. It is 220 feet high, 450 feet long, and 119 feet thick at its base; it impounds a reservoir with a capacity of 180,000 acre-feet; and on this artificial lake swimming, boating, and fishing are popular. There are campsites but no improved grounds. Five miles above the dam on the Salmon River is the BRACKETT RANCH, and three miles west of it is BROWNS BENCH, a flat mesa, near which, in the canyon (now inundated), occurred a famous robbery. A stage, crossing the river here in 1888, was held up by a lone rascal, but before he had gone far with his loot he was overtaken by cowboys and shot from his horse. He escaped, even so, by crawling into a cave, and the furious cowboys, after waiting several hours for him to appear, closed the entrance and fancied that they had entombed him alive. Upon returning a few days later, they were astonished to find the entrance open and the dead robber lying inside with a map which he had apparently drawn during his last spasm. This map gave the

location of his buried loot, and this for many years has been searched for but never found.

2. Left from Rogerson is a junction of two roads **14 m.** in the MINIDOKA NATIONAL FOREST. The right turn goes south about **10 m.** to the MAGIC HOT SPRINGS, where there are a small hotel, thirty-four cabins, a restaurant, and hot baths. Rates are very nominal. These waters, strongly charged with radium, were also a favorite with Indians, who made pilgrimages to bathe in them in both the fall and spring. The left turn leads into the forest, where there are seven improved campgrounds within a distance of a few miles. The Pentstemon Camp is named for the beautiful blue flower which during its season completely covers the camp area. Leading off the road into the forest right or left are branches that proceed up streams to fishing and to natural campsites against a background of evergreens. The ranger station is **18 m.** from Rogerson, and **5 m.** beyond it is a summit at an elevation of 7,600 feet, from which is visible Mount Borah in the north or the Humboldt Mountains in Nevada or the Great Salt Lake in Utah. Two miles down from the summit is Camp Pettit in a thicket of aspens and pines, with trails leading out to beaver dams or to fishing streams. Because of the congestion of game on this forest it is not uncommon to see, and especially in morning or evening, herds of deer ranging in number from few to as many as two hundred.

At **124 m.** U S 93 crosses the Idaho-Nevada Line, **65 m.** north of Wells, Nevada.

STATE OF IDAHO
MAP OF
SECTION IV
1936
TOURS
6
7B
8

SECTION IV

TOUR NO. 6

New Meadows—McCall—Cascade—Boise. State 15 and 44. Payette River Route.

New Meadows to Boise **122 m.**

The Oregon Short Line of the Union Pacific System parallels State 15 between McCall and Horse Shoe Bend. Scenic Stages follow the route throughout.

Accommodations limited. This, a mountain route over improved road, is one of the most attractive drives in the State. Between Boise and northern Idaho it is usually the highway followed to its junction at New Meadows with U S 95.

State 15 from its junction at New Meadows with U S 95 goes southeast through a forested canyon.

At **4 m.** is a junction with an unimproved road.

Left on this road are GOOSE and HAZARD LAKES **22 m.** This whole area between New Meadows and McCall is being developed as a recreational center, and no part of it is more attractive than Hazard Lake, not only for its good fishing but also because it is a beautiful body of water with perfect campsites and a magnificent background. The road to it is fairly steep and winding and fairly rough, but it is passable, and without its difficulties this lake would not be the enviable retreat that it now is.

At **9.5 m.** is a junction with a fair road.

Left on this road is BRUNDAGE LOOKOUT **8.2 m.**, to which the grade is easy except in the last mile. There is nothing spectacular in the view from this lookout: it is one of soft loveliness rather than of grandeur. Blue lakes lie upon the south, surrounded by forested slopes, with McCall in plain view and with the valley beyond it reaching to Cascade. In the west is a meadowed basin framed by dense growth that is as blue as the lakes when the sun is right; and in the east is a denuded backbone of peaks. The distance south or west is blue, with the farthest ranges looking like color without substance, and with very nebulous form.

At **10.5 m.** is the junction with a fair road.

Left on this road is a long journey, with return by Cascade, that is so adventurous that it demands tolerance of fair or poor roadbed and the fortitude necessary in exploring a vast wilderness. The terrain is so vast that it is impossible to grasp the extent of it, even from the highest peaks. Off the main route countless digressions are available. This side trip, not open to travel until June, can be made in a day; or for those with time and taste for the primitive it can be made in a month or a summer, with almost no repetition of road and with no monotony of scene. The Middle Fork of the Salmon River in the Primitive Area is accessible by pack trip from strategic points on the loop, or the remotest reaches of the Thunder Mountain region and the last zeniths of Chamberlain Basin. The topography in general is of rugged mountainous landscape, heavily blanketed with forests, laced with thousands of streams, broken open by canyons more than a mile in depth, and topped by summits that stand two miles above the sea. The wind moves gently here, or falls into a skyful of lazy breezes, each burgeoned with the fragrance of wild flowers and evergreens and a clean sky.

The road at first parallels a river to UPPER PAYETTE LAKE **17 m.**, where there is a campground. From here it proceeds, with GRANITE MOUNTAIN on the left, over SECESH SUMMIT. At **28 m.** is the junction with the Burgdorf road (L). At BURGDORF **2 m.** are natural hot springs, a swimming pool, campsites, and fair accommodations. The Burgdorf road runs northward to FRENCH CREEK HILL and drops down over spectacular switchbacks through deep forest to the main Salmon River (see **Tour 7, Sec. b, side tour from Riggins**).

The main route proceeds from the Burgdorf junction to WARREN **43 m.**, a small mining town in a canyon. From the air (see A Trip into the Area, Sec. II, Ch. III) the dredgings here look like a carpet of magic. The road, turning southward at Warren, follows in turn Warren Creek and Elk Creek to the South Fork of the Salmon River. The road has now entered the PAYETTE NATIONAL FOREST, the entire area of which is a primitive wilderness of hunting and fishing. Leaving Elk Creek, the road now climbs the ELK CREEK SUMMIT (9,000 alt.), the highest vantage point on the main route. The trees here are chiefly limber pine. From this summit the road goes down Government Creek to EDWARDSBURG **70 m.**, where there are a post office and a landing field. The road now climbs again to cross PROFILE GAP (8,500 alt.) and then descend by way of Profile Creek.

At **88 m.** is the junction with a dirt road. The main route takes the right turn here. Left on the other road is STIBNITE **11 m.**, another small mining village and one of the western jumping-off-places into the Primitive Area. The main route proceeds (R) to YELLOW PINE

South Fork of Payette River

Payette Lake

91 m., another ghost in this huge area. South from Yellow Pine the main route follows Johnson Creek. At **94.5 m.** is the GOLDEN GATE CAMPGROUND. Riordan, Hanson, Bear, and Trapper Creeks, as well as innumerable others, now come down from the zeniths; and on every side and from every summit is an uninhabited wilderness as far as human vision can reach. At **105 m.** is the junction with another branch road (L). This, the old Thunder Mountain road, leads into the THUNDER MOUNTAIN AREA of early mining days. The region was named for the rumblings of great landslides that came down the mountains during the days of the gold seekers. The ghost town of ROOSEVELT is in this area, though it is now a lake because a landslide buried it; and RAINBOW PEAK is also there, an unusually beautiful mountain when sunset strikes the naked colors of its stone.

The main route turns right at the Thunder Mountain junction. Along the way now are Halfway, Coffee, Rustican, Trout, Park, Pid, Sheep, Lunch, and other creeks. Forest signs indicate various points of minor interest right or left from the main road: Big Baldy, Chilcoot Pass, Thunderbolt, and the Knox Trail. At **117 m.** is LANDMARK, and it is hardly more than that. South from Landmark the main route proceeds to a junction at **122 m.** with a poor road (L) that leads deeper into the wilderness.

This branch road goes southward and at **15 m.** forms a junction. The right turn leads to the DEADWOOD DAM AND RESERVOIR **10 m.**, a favorite spot in this wilderness for fishermen. The left turn proceeds to a junction at **13 m.** The right turn here goes to LOWMAN (see **Tour 3, Sec. c., side tour from Boise**), and the left turn goes through Bear Valley and down the Stanley Basin to STANLEY **35 m.** (see **Tour 5, Sec. a**).

The main route turns right at the Deadwood junction. At **132 m** is the junction with a road (L) that leads to WARM LAKE **1 m.**, a favorite spot in this Forest. Covering about six hundred acres, it offers excellent fishing, campgrounds, hotel and cabins, and a large outdoor swimming pool, maintained by the Forest, **2 m.** south. The road along the west side of the lake continues for a few miles and then terminates in trails just beyond the South Fork Ranger Station. Many forest campgrounds are being prepared in this region.

West from the Warm Lake junction, the main route proceeds to KNOX **134 m.**, another village in this huge Forest. The main route goes southwestward from Knox. At **134.5 m.** is the junction with a road (L) to Warm Lake. At **135 m.** there is a free campground on the South Fork of Salmon River. The main route now follows Trail Creek and climbs to BIG CREEK SUMMIT **142 m.** (6,608 alt.), and then drops to follow Big Creek and enter Scott Valley. The flora along here is chiefly yellow pine, lodgepole, and fir.

At **157 m.** is the junction with State 15 at Cascade.

State 15, going southward around Payette Lake, takes
its way among matured yellow pine trees.

McCALL 13 m. (5,025 alt.; 651 pop.) is upon lower
Payette Lake in the heart of one of the State's chief
recreation areas. The town itself is rather unprepossessing, but the lake is as blue as water can be, with shades
varying from delicate pallor to depth that is almost purple. McCall outfits for pack trips into the surrounding
area. Of many available, only two are suggested here.

1. The first, demanding three days or more, is from upper Payette
Lake by way of Twenty Mile Creek south to Duck Lake and then
down the North Fork of Lake Fork to the Lake Fork Ranger Station. Both fishing and scenery are excellent.

2. The second begins at Roy Shaw's ranch and goes via Boulder
Lake, Buckhorn Creek, the South Fork of Salmon River, Fitzum
Creek, and the East Fork of Lake Fork to the above station. The
time required is four days or more.

South of McCall State 15 goes down a meadowed valley
that lies between a river and a forest.

CASCADE 42 m. (4,800 alt.; 726 pop.), the seat of
Valley County, is a microcosm of Idaho's past and present.
All the industries, including lumbering, mining, agriculture, and stock raising, are apportioned to this town and
its valley as perhaps in no other part of the State; and so
in miniature is afforded a composite picture here of most
of what Idaho has to offer. Northward is one of the principal resort areas; roundabout are a rich valley, a tremendous forest, and outlying mines; and eastward is a
vast playground.

State 15 S of Cascade goes through a narrow valley
which in summertime is meadowed with wild flowers,
with the blue camas unusually conspicuous; and then
along the North Fork of Payette River, lazily serene in
this stretch.

At 60 m. is a hamlet called SMITHS FERRY, left
across the river.

Out of Smiths Ferry southward down the river on an improved forest road is the PACKER JOHN LOOKOUT 8 m., from which at an elevation of more than 7,000 feet is afforded a view which of its kind is second to none in the State. The circumference swings around a microcosm of Idaho, with timber as dense as meadow grasses, with mines in the whole domain east of the Payette River, with agriculture in the valleys, with cattle and sheep in the grazing areas of the forest, and with a natural playground lying unbroken clear around the compass. Everything that Idaho offers is summarized here.

In all directions this tower overlooks a tumbled mountainous terrain, with human vision reaching far and faltering and coming to an end in the cloudy uncertainty of the remotest peaks. Southwest is Garden Valley with crests serrated in row on row beyond it to the Boise Basin and all its ghost towns. Eastward in the foreground are low forested flanks, but vision lifts to Scott Mountain, highest zenith on a far-flung arc, and then breaks suddenly a hundred miles to the far pale majesty of the Sawtooth Range. Northward are Round and Long Valleys, with Cascade visible in the distance against the farther backdrop that frames the Payette Lakes. In the northwest densely wooded slopes fall down to the river; and beyond is the stupendous hulk of blue shadow piled upon the eastern wall of Snake River Canyon. Westward is High Valley, a subalpine meadowed basin, with dark hills flung like arms around it; and farther the mountains run north and south in sharply sculptured backbones with the Crane Creek Reservoir like a jewel among them. Far in the west is the nebulous wonder of the Wallowa Mountains in Oregon, and far in the south is the Owyhee Range.

Sunsets here, no two of which are ever the same, run from a vast and flaming acreage of molten towers and burning reefs to the soft lilac witchery of sky pastures in which long lines look like golden brooks and outlying reaches are a purple tangle of cloudy fern. The eastern mountains lie under veils of blue air and vanish into such depth and softness that the forests shimmer like black carpets; and the ridges westward are slopes of delicate light with each crest drawn like a purple line across the sky. The one at the left, catching the fires more remotely, deepens into piles of shadow that melt and merge with the sky; and the Seven Devils Peaks far in the north fade into an amorphous kingdom of mist and are indistinguishable from the clouds around them. The reservoir awakens to a sheet of yellow light and then becomes an exact image of the sinking sun, with the streamers of its flame like the upper half of an enormous golden star. As the sun itself sinks behind its burning reefs, the western foreground comes out black, and the stupendous sweep beyond it burns low to blue draperies; and the eastern terrain rolls away in piles of dusk.

State 15 now follows the North Fork of Payette River which in springtime rolls furiously in white cascades with few interruptions, with dense evergreen growth carpeting the walls down to its edge. The trees here are chiefly yellow and lodgepole pine. At **74 m.** is an improved campground (R).

At **78 m.** is the junction with an unimproved road, State 17.

Left on this road is GARDEN VALLEY **9 m.** This road enters the Payette National Forest and penetrates the enormous wilderness adjacent on the west and south to the Primitive Area. At **12.6 m.** is the junction (R) with the road leading southward to the ghost towns of Placerville, Centerville, and Idaho City. At **13.6 m.** the road enters the forest and proceeds by creek and peak and valley to the junction at **20.6 m.** (L) with a road that leads up the Middle Fork of the Payette River. This diversion road, going up the river about twenty miles, is a lovely trip for those who wish to camp at its end and proceed by trail to such excellent fishing streams as the upper reach of this river or to its larger tributaries beyond the end of the road.

East of this junction State 17 goes to Lowman **35 m.**, and from here a road leads northward along Clear Creek in the Boise National Forest and then enters the Payette Forest and proceeds by way of Cache, Sack, Elk, and Pole Creeks to a junction **(34 m.** from Lowman) with another road that leads eastward through Bruce Meadow to Stanley Basin in the Sawtooth area **(Tour 5, Sec. a),** or westward to a left turn that goes south to the Deadwood Reservoir and unsurpassed fishing, or to a left turn that goes north to Landmark. Once a person has penetrated this huge central Idaho terrain he can vanish into utter wilderness over several forest roads or by innumerable trails. The whole region is National Forests, and all the turns are in consequence well marked.

At **91 m.** is a junction with an unimproved road (for this spectacular drive, see **Tour 3, Sec. b, side tour 5 out of Boise).**

From HORSE SHOE BEND **93 m.** State 15 leaves the valley of the river to pursue a devious course over numerous elbows and climb to a summit. Very beautiful in June or July are the denuded mountains on the left. The highway drops down over curves and switchbacks into the

Boise Valley, with the breadth of it southward to the Owyhee Range.

At **115 m.** is the junction with State 44 which turns leftward into BOISE (see **Tour 3, Sec. c)** on U S 30 (see **Tour 3, Sec. c).**

TOUR NO. 7

(Canada)—Bonners Ferry—Sandpoint—Coeur d'Alene —Moscow—Lewiston—New Meadows—Weiser. U S 95. North-South Route.

Canadian Line to Weiser **494 m.**

This, the only N-S highway in western Idaho, and only recently completed, is one of the most picturesque scenic routes in the West. Following rivers, skirting National Forests, or climbing mountains in spectacular switchbacks, it unfolds in one panoramic vista after another, and offers side trips which penetrate excellent hunting and fishing areas or lead to mountainous depths and heights of unusual grandeur.

No railroad parallels this highway, but the buses of various motor coach lines serve sections of the route.

Customary accommodations, with improved campsites from time to time.

Section a. Canada to Lewiston, 241 m.

In EASTPORT (2,600 alt.; 25 pop.), Idaho's most northern town, the Forest Service maintains a free tourist camp for those held up while clearing the customs. From here U S 95 goes down the valley to COPELAND **16 m.** at the junction with State 1, and then continues through the diked lands of the Kootenai Valley, which stretches from Canada to Bonners Ferry as flat as a floor. This valley, once a series of lakes and tiny islands, was not reclaimed until 1922. Because of its deep deposits of silt it has proved to be an agricultural wonderland. The river itself is a wide and lazy stream, usually muddy and always moving gently. In the west are the high peaks of the Selkirk Range.

At **31 m.** is the junction with U S 2.

Left on U S 2 is MOYIE RIVER 5 m. Of waterfalls in Idaho there are some with more grandeur and might but there is probably none lovelier than the Moyie. Upstream from the bridge the river is visible for a considerable distance, cascading from plunge to plunge and swirling its green pools after each fall. It comes down then black and leisurely to the power dam and pours over it like pale green ice and churns at the bottom in a gorgeous foaming picture that looks like steam. But for a few feet only: after bursting into white violence and losing its direction, the water rolls downward again, green in its body but covered over with backwashing ridges that look as crisp as celery. Under the bridge it is a very dark green that revolts in indecision before taking its way below the bridge in a great plunge. Seen from the bridge, the color varies with the sun and the sky, but a common aspect is of a stupendous spraying of millions of white and green and orchid gems. This picture is made more remarkable by the huge beautiful stone formations on either side that draw the river in and confine it and force it to deliver itself through two narrow channels. In the chief one of these the green water plunges over a stone escarpment and then leaps into a wide spread that falls, not like water but like tons of colored glass crystals. From the rocks below it boils out in incomparable beauty. At the very bottom is a white seething mass like lace that rolls away as if the river here were full of green slush. Farther below are cascades and another plunge before the stream goes serenely between its narrow walls. U S 2 crosses the Montana Line (1,819 alt.) at 24 m.

U S 95 drops to cross the deep Kootenai River over a handsome bridge.

BONNERS FERRY 33 m. (1,779 alt.; 1,418 pop.), the seat of Boundary County, is the center of an agricultural and lumbering area. It is at the foot of forested slopes and on the Kootenai River, which from here is navigable to Nelson in British Columbia. Fishing is excellent in the river east of the town. Bonners Ferry has its own municipal power plant, as well as the air of a place that is thriving and knows it.

South of Bonners Ferry, U S 95 follows the narrow canyon of Deep Creek to Naples 45 m., which stands between the two halves of the Kaniksu National Forest. The Bitterroot Range in the east is usually obscured by haze that looks like deep blue smoke, but in the west the mountains are stark and strangely barren for northern Idaho. The whole aspect changes soon to more softness of scene, to a lush excess of flora, and to beauty without that grandeur which touches these far northern mountains. Some peaks here lift naked shoulders above the timber line, and now and then there are rock formations of bald granite. The mountains of northern Idaho generally, except in parts of the Bitterroot Divide, are densely wooded, softly obscure in haze, and do not thrust up in the majestic spires found in the central part of the State.

SANDPOINT 67 m. (2,086 alt.; 3,290 pop.), the seat of Bonner County, is enviably situated on LAKE PEND OREILLE which is fourth or fifth in size of the fresh-water lakes lying wholly within the United States. Formed by the drainage from Flathead Lake in Montana through the Clark Fork River, it has a shore line of 125 miles and an extreme depth of 1,800 feet. It abounds in trout and whitefish and affords attractive campsites along its shores. This city, served by three railroads, is also the junction of U S 195 and State 3 (see **Tour 11**). Of unusual interest is the SANDPOINT BRIDGE upon U S 95 at the southern extremity of the city. Though not spectacular in comparison with the great bridges of the world, it nevertheless spans the lake for a distance of two miles.

Southward from Sandpoint, U S 95 is in summertime a wilderness of flowering syringa upon its borders.

At COCOLALLA 81 m. is the junction with an improved road.

Left on this road 7 m. are beautiful views of Lake Pend Oreille. They are the best views upon the west shore line.

At GRANITE 89 m. is the junction with an unimproved road.

Right on this road is an extraordinary area of swamps and lakes, as well as what is said to be one of the best duck-hunting regions in the Northwest. GRANITE LAKE .5 m. (L) is a small body of water that looks almost black because it is walled in by ledges. KELSO LAKE 1 m. (L) is considerably larger and is surrounded by mountains and meadows. There are unimproved campsites here

Spirit Lake

Forest trail from Hayden Lake to North Fork

Hayden Lake

Surf-riding on Lake Coeur d'Alene

and swimming is popular. North of it **2 m.** over poor road is BEAVER LAKE, and still farther are HOODOO VALLEY and the HOODOO LAKES to which ducks come by tens of thousands.

At ATHOL 93 m. is the junction with improved roads.

1. Left on a road is BAYVIEW **8 m.** on the beautiful southern extremity of Lake Pend Oreille at the base of Cape Horn Peak in the north and of Bernard Peak in the south. There are accommodations in Bayview. There are also regular excursions by boat to Clark Fork, Sandpoint, and eleven other stops on both sides of the lake. Fishing in this water is unusually good.

2. Right on the road is SPIRIT LAKE **10 m.** Out of the small town of Spirit Lake a road goes westward and drops down a hill to pass a huge lumber mill and proceed to the shore of beautiful SPIRIT LAKE **1.5 m.**, named for an Indian legend. This lake is a perfect gem flanked by high mountains, and is unusual in having a solid rock bottom that holds the water as an enormous bowl. The road past Silver Beach goes over the mountains to Spokane. This lake, like others in this region, has little to offer in developed beaches but much in its own calm loveliness.

From the town of Spirit Lake, the road goes **12 m.** southward to TWIN LAKES **22 m.**, which are right from the highway **.5 m.** REST HAVEN BEACH, rather deceptively named, is owned and managed out of Spokane. The lower of the Twin Lakes is small but perfect in the pure clarity of its water and in its wooded shore lines and forested backdrop. LUGER PARK is north (R) with private cabins; and beyond it a left turn leads to ECHO BEACH across from which, and accessible only by boat, is EXCELSIOR BEACH. From Echo Beach a right turn leads to the upper lake. Though both of these lakes are becoming more popular with visitors, they have been exploited very little, and offer only poor accommodations or none at all.

From the lower lake the road proceeds southward to RATHDRUM **27 m.**, a shipping point for farm products, and turns eastward to U S 95 **34 m.**

At CORBIN 96 m. is the junction with an improved road.

Left on this road is WHISKEY ROCK LODGE **6 m.** on the east shore of Lake Pend Oreille and in the heart of an attractive fishing and hunting area. Available here are cabins, boats, bathing, and pack trips. This place was named for a legend. Two old-timers were going by boat up the lake when darkness forced them to make camp. Taking with them only their bed and a gallon of whiskey, they discovered on the next morning that their boat had vanished; and for three days they devoted themselves to their jug and meditation before rescue came.

At **105 m.** is the junction with an improved road.

Left on this road are HAYDEN CREEK 7 m., the HUDLOW
MOUNTAIN LOOKOUT 9 m., and MOSKINS CREEK 13.5 m.
This road also proceeds to Elmore and Rockaway Beaches on Hay-
den Lake, where cabins and boats are available.

At **107 m.** is the junction with an improved road.

Left on this road are HAYDEN LAKE 1.5 m., and the COEUR
D'ALENE COUNTRY CLUB, a well-kept 18-hole golf course, and
the BOZANTA TAVERN, a popular resort. This lovely little lake,
framed by mountains, looks as if it were an offspring of Lake
Coeur d'Alene. It has a clean unmarred shore line shadowed by
evergreens that afford numerous campsites; and it has so many
bays that its shore line is five times in length what would be expected of a lake of its size. Sheltered by mountains, the water is
usually as serene as a cloud in a windless sky.

At **112 m.** is the junction with U S 10 (see **Tour 10**).
Left is the COEUR D'ALENE AIRPORT, the first municipally owned in the United States.

COEUR D'ALENE **114 m.** (2,158 alt.; 8,297 pop.)
stands on the site chosen by General Sherman for a fort
that was built in 1878 and abandoned in 1901. This
beautiful city, the seat of Kootenai County, got its first
impulse to growth from mining and lumbering industries; and though these are still important, Coeur
d'Alene's more recent development has been steadily in
the direction of horticulture and dairying, and as a playground. Enviably situated on the beautiful lake of the
same name, and the hub of a huge area of lakes, Coeur
d'Alene stands on U S 10, the northern highway artery,
and draws from all adjacent territory, including Spokane
in the west. It is in consequence a city of homes first,
and only secondarily an industrial and commercial center.

A long promenade follows the lake, with bath houses,
water slides, diving towers, and other facilities for water
sports. Annually on the third, fourth, and fifth of July,
Coeur d'Alene holds its water regatta, which includes
speedboat and sailboat racing, water skiing, surfboard
riding, log rolling, and swimming.

Coeur d'Alene

U S 95 through the pines of northern Idaho

A campus view

The Lewiston Hill

Out of the city in any direction are scenic drives, the most important of which are covered in other tours. Most beautiful is that along the eastern side of the lake (see **Tour 9),** or eastward through the Fourth of July Canyon (see **Tour 10)** or northward to other lakes **(this tour).** The Coeur d'Alene National Forest lies eastward from the city and can be penetrated over a number of roads.

A boat leaves daily for a trip down the lake and up the St. Joe River, and offers not only unusual beauty of water and landscape, but leads also to excellent fishing streams. Accommodations are available along the route, and cabins and cottages can be rented.

U S 95 skirts the lovely city park (L) and crosses a bridge on its way southward from the city (for alternate route to Moscow, slightly longer but the loveliest drive for its length in Idaho, see **Tour 9).** After passing a huge mill, U S 95 swings around the lake and climbs over a fine piece of highway architecture, with farms below looking like gardens. For many miles now the country has been logged or burnt over, with most of it restored to beauty by fields or young growth. From time to time signs indicate roads which lead (L) to Lake Coeur d'Alene; but this body of water, though never far away, remains invisible from U S 95. (For a description of Lake Coeur d'Alene, see **Tour 9.)**

PLUMMER 149 m. (2,650 alt.; 346 pop.) is on the edge of the Coeur d'Alene Reservation, which was officially set aside in 1873. These Indians, like the Kutenais, are primarily engaged in agriculture. The agency for this reservation is in Moscow, but the subagency is west of Plummer **3.5 m.**

Left on improved road from Plummer is HEYBURN STATE PARK 7 m. This park, occupying a basin and looking from the mountains around it like a sunken garden, covers 7,838 acres, of which 2,333 are water, with most of the remainder heavily timbered. The park strongly suggests that a part of all that is loveliest in northern Idaho's lakes, mountains, and trees had been taken to build the perfection of this playground. The lakes are the CHATCOLET, HIDDEN, BENEWAH, ROUND, and a part of COEUR D'ALENE, of which the first is one of the most beautiful in the State, cupped as it is like a huge bowl in a mountain with evergreens reaching down to its edge. Upon it is a floating hotel as well as boats. There is also boat service at ROCKY POINT. Fishing is good in all the lakes and in the St. Joe River which winds among them; but the only hunting allowed is for ducks within season. There are two good beaches, and both swimming and boating lure as many visitors as fishing. More than 150,000 persons visited this area in 1935 and the number is rapidly increasing.

Just S of TENSED is DESMET **164 m.** (and little more than a name). In Desmet is the SACRED HEART MISSION which was founded by Father De Smet in 1842. Another of Idaho's historic buildings, the Father's house, built in 1881, was burned to the ground in 1936, and only a few of its more valuable possessions were saved. Among these was a communication from Pope Pius IX in 1871, believed to be the only papal brief ever addressed to an Indian tribe. Fronting the Mission, also partly destroyed by fire, is a group of one- and two-room shacks which are occupied only over week ends when Indians come in from the countryside for the Sunday services. Around Desmet is an area cultivated by the Kutenai Indians. Comparing favorably with those of white men in both their manner of operation and in living conditions, these farms suggest the progress that these Indians have made.

U S 95 crosses the western end of the ST. JOE NATIONAL FOREST and takes its way through an idyl of farms and the changeless loveliness of cultivated hills. Westward is the mounded plumpness of eastern Washington, and eastward is the misty wilderness of virgin timber.

At **184 m.** is the junction with U S 95 Alt. (see **Tour 9**). U S 95 now climbs or descends through evergreen hallways, looks over great cultivated vistas, or passes through villages, each of which is an incongruous homeliness on the landscape.

MOSCOW **203 m.** (2,564 alt.; 4,476 pop.) is the seat of Latah County, the home of the STATE UNIVERSITY, and the center of the pea industry of northern Idaho. The campus, overlooking Paradise Valley, and unusually attractive in its landscaping, lies upon an eminence (R) in the southwest part of the city. Its farther grounds slope down into a natural amphitheater which has been laid out as an athletic field; and to the left are the university's flower gardens and forested slopes, a part of the Department of Forestry's arboretum. The campus covers 685 acres.

The town itself is in the heart of the prolific Palouse country, with its rich soil of black volcanic ash and its unusually heavy yields of grain and peas. On B Street in the eight-hundred block is the site of old Fort Russell, now commemorated in a monument. Until a few years ago some of the stumps of the old stockade could be seen, but now all have been removed save a few which remain buried in the earth.

South of Moscow, U S 95 proceeds over landscape that in summertime is a pastoral of farms, with almost no interruption of the solid pattern of hay and grain. This rolling prairie is green in June, golden in August. GENESEE 221 m. (2,677 alt.; 555 pop.) is the heart of it. At some distance south of Genesee, U S 95 swings westward into Washington to connect with U S 195, and returns to the summit of the famous LEWISTON HILL (2,750 alt.). The descent is two thousand feet in the next ten miles.

Lewiston Hill, unlike the White Bird or Gilbert, is relatively barren, and the road lies below like the segments of an enormous boa, with each loop hugging a denuded brown mound. In the foreground below is the Clearwater River with its bridges, with Lewiston on its far bank. To the right is Snake River and west of it, in Washington, is Clarkston, beyond which the flanks ascend to the vast rolling watershed of eastern Washington. Running into the south is the deep canyon of Snake River, dividing State from State and lifting away to the high blue remoteness of the Seven Devils area. Leftward from the canyon the mountain range is almost a perfect line upon its backbone.

At the foot of the Lewiston Hill, U S 95 crosses the mighty Clearwater River to enter Lewiston (see **Sec. b**).

Section b. Lewiston to Weiser, 253 m.

LEWISTON (741 alt.; 9,403 pop.), the seat of Nez Perce County and the lowest spot in Idaho, stands at the junction of the Snake and Clearwater Rivers. At its western end it is connected with Clarkston in Washington by a steel bridge across Snake River. Lewiston was the first incorporated town in Idaho, the first capital of Idaho Territory, and is today the largest city in the State north of Salmon River. It is the center of a grain and fruit belt, of mining and lumbering interests; and is Idaho's only "seaport." Annually about five hundred carloads of fruit are shipped from here, and one thousand of livestock, as well as considerable quantities of minerals and lumber. The city is served by three railroads, by river launches, and by air.

Lewiston, standing on a most unusual site, flanked by great mountains in all directions, and bounded by two mighty rivers, is the most picturesque city in the State. Its one long street, with a river on the north, with an upland table of beautiful homes and orchards on the south, is strongly reminiscent of many small European cities, and especially of those down in canyons in which the main street feeds off to a water front or to a terraced hillside. Upon the rolling terrain south is the attractive campus of one of the State's two normal schools. Roads lead out of the city to points of interest, and excursion and freight boats go by water up Snake River to the beautiful Box Canyon.

1. Right from Lewiston are various surfaced roads leading to its more than four thousand acres of orchards, of which three fourths are given to cherries. Visitors can see the picking, packing, and shipping of cherries as they ripen in the latter part of June; and if fortunate enough to be in Lewiston in May they can witness the Cherry Blossom Festival, the chief gala event of the year, not excepting the fall fair and rodeo in September.

2. Right from Lewiston up the south bank of the Clearwater River is the gigantic plant of the POTLATCH FORESTS, INC. 1 m. This is (1936) the second largest sawmill in the world, the first in size being upon the Omar River in Russia. Visitors are welcomed to this

mill. At the gate a card of admission is given, together with a
map of the plant and directions. Most impressive is the fetching
of logs out of the pond, the huge band saws with their miraculous
precision of machinery, and the box factory and planing mills.
Sawdust here is now converted under enormous pressure into logs
for fireplaces.

The major plant, covering 360 acres, employing 850 men,
powered by 1,200 electric motors, protected by 21,000 automatic
sprinklers, and running night and day in three shifts, turns out
1,200,000 feet of lumber in every 24 hours. This is enough lumber
to build 200 five-room houses complete, or to make a pile 1,000
feet high and 10 feet square, or to lay a board walk 4 feet wide
for 56 miles. The sawdust used in Pres-to-Logs is laid under a
pressure of 165 pounds to the inch, and is packed to a greater
density than that of the hardest coal. The machines operating in
the Pres-to-Log plant are entirely automatic.

U S 95 goes up the north bank of the Clearwater
River. The valley on all sides climbs away into rolling
distance. This part of Nez Perce County is very fertile
and supports many orchards, chiefly cherry, as well as
extensive grain and dairy farms. Formerly, tens of thousands of logs were floated in springtime down this river
from the great white pine forests eastward, but the log
booms here will be for some time to come largely a thing
of the past.

At **11 m.** is the junction with State 9. (See **Tour 8).**

At this junction is SPALDING, now little more than a
tiny museum and a historic spot. It was here in 1805 that
Lewis and Clark pulled their dugout canoes upon the
shore of the river and traded with the Nez Perce Indians.
An early settlement was made in 1836 by the Reverend
Henry Spalding, a missionary whose influence among the
Nez Perces was largely responsible for their friendly attitude. It was in or near Spalding that the first school and
church in Idaho were established, the first seed planted, the
first gristmill operated, the first printing press installed,
and the first blacksmith shop built. Although neither the
first nor the second home of the Spaldings is standing today, several of the trees which he planted can still be seen.
Land has recently been purchased in this area for a
Spalding National Park, and it is intended that this will

include the ancient Indian burial grounds where the bodies of the Spaldings now lie. The site of the old Lapwai Mission is one of the most historic spots in Idaho. It is now commemorated in an eighteen-ton boulder, bearing a bronze tablet, at the bridge over the Clearwater River.

Here, too, is the SPALDING LOG CABIN MISSION AND INDIAN MUSEUM, now privately owned by a descendant of the Nez Perce Chief Timothy. A small admission fee is charged. The owners, supported by certain affidavits, claim to be in possession of the cabin built by Spalding in 1836, as well as several relics, including a Lewis and Clark canoe. Some authorities, denying these claims, believe the cabin is the one built by John Silcott in 1861 to be used as an office for the Lapwai Agency. In any case, even if the eagle feather ceremonial bonnet was not worn at the signing of the William Penn Treaty in 1682, or even if the buckskin dress and necklace were not worn by Sacajawea, the Indian woman who accompanied Lewis and Clark on a part of the journey, it is admitted, nevertheless, that this cabin contains a fine collection of Indian exhibits, many of which were passed down from generation to generation by Nez Perce Indians.

LAPWAI 15 m. (970 alt.; 416 pop.) is an Indian subagency and has the sanitarium of the Fort Lapwai Reservation, which was set aside for members of the Nez Perce tribe. The Indians on the reservation number fourteen hundred; their holdings consist of fifty-six thousand acres of land. To the Indian dances here, said to be inferior to the Hopi Snake Dance or the Navajo Rain Dance, the public is only rarely admitted. SWEETWATER 17 m. is the home of a State game farm devoted chiefly to the rearing of Chinese pheasants. The barren country westward is unusual in lush northern Idaho: it is neither mountain nor prairie but an obstinate hybrid.

The WINCHESTER (sometimes called the Culdesac) HILL 17 m. is one of the most impressive pictures in the State. Like the Lewiston, Gilbert, and White Bird Hills,

White pine lumber

Winchester Hill

Along the Salmon River

The Salmon River from the North-and-South Highway

it offers a remarkable panorama, but it cannot be fully appreciated until the summit is reached and vision turns back and downward. Down this mountain, farms are picturesquely landscaped for miles, lying steeply on either side of the highway from elbow to elbow. This is doubtless the best area in the State to show how completely cultivation has possessed many of the more difficult slopes, as well as to suggest the great unirrigated wheat belts common in the West. From the topmost reach of the farms it is still three miles to the summit.

WINCHESTER 38 m. is typical of many small northern towns. Its unprepossessing aspect is enhanced by the pastoral midsummer loveliness around it. If this town were in southern Idaho against a background of bleak hillsides or the gray of sagebrush or the yellow of alkaline wastes, it would not seem so incongruous. In sylvan northern Idaho, where even the cows in distant pastures look fragrant, some of the villages appear to have been blown out of mining areas.

Much of this rolling landscape is in summertime a garden of wild flowers. The blue and purple flowers in such profusion are lupine; the flowering bushes are the syringa. Upon the farms of this vast tableland there are innumerable tiny forests of evergreen, chiefly fir; and fir trees and wild flowers make fragrant wilderness of every untilled pasture and every roadside.

GRANGEVILLE 79 m. (3,323 alt.; 1,360 pop.) is upon the south side of one of the most beautiful valleys in the State. In 1898 rich gold ore was found in the Buffalo Hump Mountains southward, and inasmuch as Grangeville was the main gateway to these mines, the town boomed for a considerable while. After the mines were exhausted it became the industrial center of a large agricultural area that had been developing meanwhile. On the second, third, and fourth days in July, and for three days in September, Grangeville has annual rodeos and festivals. Primitive regions are accessible from here (see **Tour 8).**

Right on unimproved road through virgin country in the NEZPERCE NATIONAL FOREST is FLORENCE 32 m., once regarded as the richest gold camp in the State, and now, after long years of slow dying, showing renewed activity. There are excellent fishing streams throughout this area. On this road to Florence are the Cold Springs and Sheep Springs improved campgrounds.

The WHITE BIRD HILL 84 m. (5,430 alt.) is almost as famous as the Lewiston Hill, but its northern approach is unimpressive, save for the luxuriance in summertime of the wild flowers. This ascent to the summit at 89 m. is only five miles by easy grade. On the summit the flora is chiefly white fir with a little Douglas fir and pine. The vista from here is breath-taking. Far southward, and flanking out east and west, are canyons blue with mist, backbones reaching high in purple obscurity, and the nebulous zeniths of the Seven Devils Peaks. The descent from this hill drops over a series of elbows twenty-eight hundred feet in the next twelve miles, with the view closing in, as the road falls down, and releasing first the vast canyons southward and the forested backbones; dropping next to the immense low foreground of brown and green foothills; and finally closing the shutter to the narrow canyon and the village of White Bird. Unlike the Lewiston Hill, this mountainside in summertime is a continuous garden of wild flowers, and especially at the higher levels. Most conspicuous are wild rose and fireweed, crowsfoot and ocean spray, wild geranium and blue pentstemon, all of them laying loveliness upon the acres and fragrance upon the miles.

WHITE BIRD 100 m. is only a small sheltered village and the center of a grain area that unfolds over the southern hills and rolls out of sight. It was here in White Bird Canyon that the first battle in the Nez Perce Indian War was fought in 1877, with a complete victory for the red men. When in 1919 a steam shovel excavated the skeleton of an unknown soldier, Idaho County erected a granite shaft to commemorate the dead of this historic fight.

U S 95 follows White Bird Creek for a short distance and then proceeds up Salmon River (for a description of this impetuous stream, see **Tour 5, Sec. a**). At **112 m.** cabins and campground are available (L). The mountains up this river are bleak in arid colors, with the rock of their torsos naked and eroded, with their flora usually baked like brown parchment. At **121 m.** the steep mountainside is picturesquely terraced with tiny farms. It is only **10 m.** from the highway here over to the mighty gorge of Snake River, with the mountains standing high between the two streams. Though the westward canyon is the deepest, the one which U S 95 now follows is one of the deepest in North America.

RIGGINS **132 m.** (1,800 alt.; 25 pop.) is only a village in an extremely deep canyon. (All of Idaho south of here is on Mountain Time.) Visible from Riggins is a trail across the river which climbs the mountain to Chair Point, an excellent lookout.

At **133 m.** is the junction with a fair road.

Left on this road is the gorge of the main. Salmon River, which forms its junction with the Little Salmon at Riggins. This lower part of the canyon of the River of No Return is no more spectacular than that of the Little Salmon which U S 95 follows: the more magnificent reaches lie farther eastward and are not available by highway. But there is a remarkable picture at **8 m.** in the river's cascades, with the dark green water plunging under a stone wall that rises several hundred feet. The stone here is beautiful in both color and stratigraphy, with some of it like veined marble, with some like rounded walls over which colored paint has been spilled. At **10 m.** a right turn crosses the river to the RIGGINS HOT SPRINGS **.5 m.** with accommodations for forty guests. At **10.5 m.** there is a campground (L), and at **13.5 m.** the rock walls are black except where dynamiting has shaled them off to uncover huge white or red slabs. A little farther the suspension cables of the Manning Bridge are anchored in these ledges of granite. At **19 m.** wild French Creek comes down on the right, and up this canyon is a good road that climbs over breath-taking switchbacks through dense forest to reach the summit and proceed to Burgdorf (see **Tour 6, side tour E of McCall).** The road up Salmon River does not go much farther, but is being slowly built mile by mile into the vast primitive area that lies between here and eastern Idaho (see

Tour 5, Sec. a). When the highway is finally completed up this river, it will doubtless be one of the finest scenic drives in the State.

At POLLOCK **141 m.** (hardly more than a name) is the junction with a fair road.

Right on this road is a RANGER STATION **6 m.**, from which is offered at present the easiest point of access by pack trip to DRY DIGGINS LOOKOUT. No accommodations are now available here, but inquiry should be made, as it is intended by the Forest Service to build a road along the backbone between the Snake and Salmon Canyons, with branches off to U S 95. The view from this lookout is worth almost any extreme in hardship for a person who seeks a view which of its kind is said to be unequaled. Vision here drops down for more than a mile over the shelved and terraced eastern wall of the Grand Canyon; to the river which, though broad, looks from this height like a very narrow path of snow because of the cascading waters; to the steeply descending forested reaches in the foreground or the mighty western wall that climbs away to the peaks in Oregon; or to the blue timelessness of mountains which on all sides vanish into distance. Few persons except miners and forest rangers have ever stood on this lookout; and one of the latter, a man who has seen all the major grandeur in North America, says this is the only sweep of depth and distance that ever left him profoundly shaken.

At **145 m.** are cabins and free campground (L). At **147 m.** FALL CREEK is a sudden foaming descent on the right; and at **149 m.** BOULDER CREEK (R) comes down from the heights. At the Black Bear Inn **156 m.** meals are available, as well as outfitting for pack trips into the surrounding area.

Right from here on good road is the SMOKY CAMPGROUND **6 m.** on Boulder Creek. This is one of the best and most popular campgrounds in the forest.

At the MEADOWS VALLEY HOT SPRINGS **162 m.** is a free campground (R).

U S 95 continues to follow the canyon of the Little Salmon River, but now leaves the broad view, the barren mountains set like great piles, each a solitary mound of its own, and with no pattern or meaning in the indiscriminate arrangement, and enters a forested area. Still farther south, the canyon widens, spreading now and

Typical National Forest Lookout

Rapid River Falls

then enough to allow a tiny ranch as large as the palm of a giant, and less frequently closing to the width of the river and the highway. At sunset, shadows fall down from the ledges with almost the cool depth of night and make magic of the cascading river which in nearly every mile of it is in frantic haste.

NEW MEADOWS 167 m. (3,850 alt.; 220 pop.) is in a beautiful round meadowed valley. The site of the older town is eastward on State 15 (see **Tour 6).**

Between New Meadows and Council the distance is a gradual transition from the mountainous landscapes of northern Idaho to the valleys and plateaus of the south. U S 95 now winds through a forest of yellow pine, one of the most beautiful of the conifers.

At **175 m.** is the junction with an unimproved road.

Right on this road is the LOST VALLEY RESERVOIR 6 m., where fishing (trout and catfish) is unusually good.

At **180 m.** is the EVERGREEN CAMP (L), an improved site. This reach of U S 95 is in the WEISER NATIONAL FOREST.

STARKEY 187 m. is nothing but a small resort (R). It has a hotel, cabins, and an excellent large outdoor pool supplied by hot radioactive water. The flow from more than twenty hot springs here is so large that only a few are diverted to the pool. The others are used for a hydroelectric plant. The management proudly declares that this is one resort in Idaho where beer is not served, and declares that it is very popular with Idaho teachers. In any case, the water is refreshing and the mountain air is redolent with yellow pine. There is fishing here in the Weiser River, and especially in Lost Creek, three miles over the hill westward.

COUNCIL 197 m. (2,914 alt.; 355 pop.) was once a spot where Indians gathered for huge powwows.

Right from Council a fair road goes up a narrow valley, entering at **14.5 m.** the Weiser National Forest, which lies like a horseshoe around the head of Weiser River. It is a relatively primitive area with good hunting and fishing in its less accessible parts. At **15 m.** is the HORNET CREEK RANGER STATION (R). The road now climbs easily through a logged-off area in which solitary stately yellow pine trees remain; and at **31 m.** forks. The right turn leads into a fisherman's paradise. BLACK LAKE **15 m.** and EMERALD LAKE **3.5 m.** north of it by trail are popular; and besides these there are many other lakes, all small and lovely, and hundreds of streams. On Bear Creek and on Black Lake are improved campgrounds. Roads lead east and west into wilderness.

The left turn goes to CUPRUM **39 m.** (from Council), the ghost of an old mining town. Here there is a small hotel (and practically nothing else); and away from it roads and trails radiate in nearly every direction. The hotel outfits pack trips. A hair-raising road goes downward from Cuprum (L) into Snake River Canyon **8 m.**, and thence down the river for **12 m.** to bring into view some of the more majestic reaches of the gorge. A bridge crosses to Homestead in Oregon.

North out of Cuprum a road climbs **10 m.**, sometimes sharply, to KINNEY POINT and to SHEEP ROCK, an overhanging shelf. Of all points accessible by highway, this rock affords the best view of the Grand Canyon.

This Canyon of Snake River, known variously as Hells Canyon, the Seven Devils Gorge, and the Grand Canyon, is the deepest on the North American Continent. Idaho highway maps give its depth as 5,500 feet. As a matter of fact, the depth from He Devil Peak, 7 miles east of the river, is, according to the U. S. Geologic Survey, 7,900 feet, whereas the depth from Bright Angel Point, an equal distance from the Colorado River, is 5,650. This is also the narrowest major gorge on this continent. The phenomenal aspect of it is matched only by the fact that it is comparatively unknown and rarely visited. Parts of the canyon are richly colored in shades of red, orange, and yellow, and parts are densely bedded with timber. Downstream from Homestead, both the river and the gorge narrow gradually, and near Kinney Creek the stream enters Hells Canyon. "Aside from the impressive boldness and height of the steep walls, perhaps the most striking feature of the canyon is the extreme roughness of the solid rock faces."[1] The river in this section often narrows to less than 100 feet and drops almost 13 feet to the mile. After **38 m.** the canyon widens to 400 feet at a height of 300 feet above the river; but soon the walls close to form the well-known BOX CANYON upstream from Lewiston. From Brush Creek past the mouth of Deep Creek there is a stretch of four miles of perpendicular walls rising 2,000 feet to a bench and then reaching sheer and high to a second shelf. Boats can go through by portaging the Steamboat, Deep, Hells, Brush, and Granite Creek Rapids. The worst of these

---

[1] *Water-Supply Paper 657.*

is the latter. The volume and gradient of the river are comparable with those of the Colorado in Cataract, Marble, and Grand Canyons, or of the Green River between Hells Half Mile and Disaster Falls.

This Seven Devils area N of Cuprum, named for seven serrated peaks standing in a semicircle and reaching thousands of feet into the sky, is thought to be potentially one of the richest mineral regions in the world. The chief mineral is copper, of which no one has tried to estimate the enormous deposits, with a rich content of silver and gold. But there is no transportation into the canyon, and all the surveys that have been made have discouraged the undertaking of either railway or highway.

MESA 205 m. (2,900 alt.; 25 pop.) is the center of one of the largest apple orchards in the world. Upon the rolling hills here are twelve hundred acres which in harvest time demand a crew of six hundred persons. The orchard is equipped with two huge cellars, each of which can store one hundred and fifty thousand bushels of fruit; and with an elaborate irrigation system which brings the water over the hills by means of a network of syphons and flumes. The fragrance of this orchard in bloom drenches the air for miles.

CAMBRIDGE 220 m. (2,651 alt.; 336 pop.) is at the junction with an unimproved road.

Right on this road is HEATH 19 m. at the upper reach of the long Snake River Canyon that lies between Weiser and Lewiston. This side tour is only for careful drivers. The road going up the river is now and then cut out of great overhanging walls of stone, but the gorge here is only a small preface to the overwhelming proportions farther north.

U S 95 southward from Cambridge leaves the blue haze of mountains and forested slopes. It now lies through a fertile area that has given to Washington County a leading place in the production of rye, alfalfa, and peas, and in dairying.

MIDVALE 230 m. (2,544 alt.; 203 pop.) is at the junction with an unimproved road.

Left on this road is the CRANE CREEK RESERVOIR 16 m. where natural campsites are available. Ducks and geese are abundant here in season, and there is fair fishing.

At **241 m.** is the junction with an unimproved road.

Right on this road is the SPRING CREEK CAMPGROUND **15 m.** on Mann Creek. The Kiwanis Club of Weiser has established several camps along this road, each with excellent water and improvements. The popularity of the area has depleted the fishing in Mann Creek.

At WEISER **253 m.** is the junction with U S 30 (see Tour 3, Sec. c).

TOUR NO. 8

Spalding— Orofino— Nezperce— Kooskia— Grangeville.
State 9 and State 7. Clearwater Route.

Spalding to Grangeville **108 m.**

A branch line of the Canadian Pacific Railroad remotely
parallels this route.

This alternate loop between Spalding and Grangeville is
38 m. farther than the distance between the two cities
over U S 95, but is a much more beautiful route. It is especially attractive to those seeking side trips into huge virginal areas where both scenery and fishing are excellent.
Valley-and-mountain route over improved road. Accommodations less than average.

State 9 branches E from U S 95 at Spalding (see **Tour
7, Sec. b).** From this junction State 9 goes up the broad
and mighty Clearwater, with the prairies, feeding westward to Lewiston, yielding to flora that steadily becomes
richer and more abundant. The mountains along here are
striking pictures in the way farms hang down slopes so
steep that it looks as if animals would lose their footing
and roll into the river.

At **33 m.** is the junction with State 7.

Left across the river is OROFINO (1,031 alt.; 1,078 pop.), the seat
of Clearwater County and the gateway to one of the greatest
forested areas in the Northwest. This town, built in a canyon, and
confined on all sides by mountains save where the Clearwater enters
and leaves, still thrives lustily, being supported by both timber and
mines. Three miles down the river (L) is AHSAHKA, the site of
a Lewis and Clark camp in 1805.

The junction to Orofino is at the junction also with
State 11.

Left on this road is the CLEARWATER NATIONAL FOREST.
The distance of this side trip to its farthest reach is **102 m.,** but the
road is being extended year by year, and inquiry should be made in
Orofino. This Forest lies between the St. Joe on the north and the

Selway on the south, where its boundary is the historic Lolo Trail over which Chief Joseph and his Nez Perce warriors made their phenomenal retreat. Inasmuch as most of this area is ruggedly mountainous with few roads, it offers unusual attractions to both the hunter and fisherman. State 11 proceeds straight into the heart of it.

It is 8 m. to GREER, and here the road swings eastward, leaving the river and climbing 2,370 feet in 10 miles. It then levels off into a rolling mesa that extends clear to the Bitterroot Mountains. The ascent E of Greer is one of the finest in the State, with the massed mountain ranges expanding and lifting and flowing away in vast evergreen carpets pooled with green fields. To the east or west as far as the eye can see runs the Clearwater River, with its canyon narrowing to blue haze and with the river itself vanishing in a path of silver. The motorist usually expects to descend after reaching the summit but there is no descent. The terrain rolls away to purple horizons with almost no suggestion of valley or canyon, but with the tilled foreground as a sweeping prelude to the forested reaches beyond.

WEIPPE 26 m. is one of the largest producers of lumber in the State. After leaving it, the road enters deepening forest, chiefly of yellow pine and fir. Millions of feet of dead logs, felled but never removed, lie scattered for miles in every direction. After ten miles the forest closes in, with white pine showing now, straighter and taller and cleaner than the other trees. PIERCE 45 m. was founded in 1860 after the first discovery of gold in Idaho and is still active. The road forks here, the right turn going to the BUNGALOW RANGER STATION 28 m. and the left turn leading to HEAD-QUARTERS 14 m. and to the end of the road 42 m. beyond. So immense have lumbering activities been in this area that a person unused to such scenes is likely to be startled. Headquarters is unusual in the arrangement of the houses: they stand in a circle after the manner of early wagon trains when attacked by Indians; and are built to facilitate movement and communication in winter months when the snow lies from twelve to fifteen feet in depth. Nine miles farther is the ghost of HOLLYWOOD, a town built in 1936 for the sole purpose of photographing a moving picture. The traveler has now penetrated a wilderness of forested country that is the delight of everyone who has seen it. There is good fishing in all the streams, there are thousands of big game animals in the adjacent terrain, and there are accommodations for pack trips available at several points. Not a mile of this long side tour will be regretted by the most exacting seeker of wild and beautiful country.

State 7 now ascends for 8 m. over a mountainside so luxuriant in its small flora that it is often impenetrable.

This is the beauty of landscape when it is not, as so often in southern Idaho, devastated by sheep. From the summit of the GILBERT HILL (3,350 alt.) is a view in north or east over forested mountains with farms scattered and almost lost among them, even to the highest summits; and beyond is the purple Bitterroot Range on the Continental Divide. Far down in the canyon below is Orofino. The highway goes southward out of this wooded region and crosses another panorama of green and golden hills.

NEZPERCE 57 m. (3,142 alt.; 444 pop.), on the edge of the Kamiah Valley, is the seat of Lewis County and the industrial center of this rich agricultural area. After leaving Nezperce the road overlooks mile after mile of rolling tilled hills that are a part of the great agricultural wealth of Lewiston; and if there were corn here instead of wheat, it could easily be imagined that this countryside was Missouri. From the summit (3,250 alt.) the highway descends through gardens for seven miles. Landscape could hardly be lovelier in summertime, no matter whether it is the bronzed hills westward or the green and lavender slopes southward or the valley below.

KAMIAH 74 m. is a richly flowering village that does little to shame its picturesque environs. The road swings to the right over a long bridge out of Kamiah and enters a long narrow valley that is very beautiful, with its farms hanging like pictures framed with evergreen against the soft witchery of the hills. The Clearwater River offers a strange sight in early summer as it gradually separates itself into two streams. On the far side is the yellow South Fork and on the near side is the lucent green or silver of the Middle Fork, the two streams flowing side by side as one river with the yellow now and then penetrating like smoke. Up the river a few miles they cascade, the one rolling in yellow, the other in green, and still go side by side without interfusion. Just below their junction they are almost as separate in their identities as they would be with a wall between.

KOOSKIA 82 m. (1,261 alt.; 411 pop.) is a village in a canyon here at the junction of the Middle and South Forks of the Clearwater. It may seem to be quite remote from the comforts and amenities of civilized life, but a road from here penetrates the Selway area.

Left from Kooskia on State 9 is the MIDDLE FORK. This drive up the river is through a canyon, with ranches laid like pictures on the gentle slopes. The flora here is chiefly white and lodgepole pine, Douglas and alpine fir, western red cedar, and Engelmann spruce among the trees; and among the shrubs the dogwood, syringa, snowberry, mountain laurel, thimble-, huckle-, and elderberry, wild rose and currant, and mountain ash. The fern which grows in such luxuriance is the brake (bracken), and with it are the sword and maidenhair ferns. The almost countless species of wild flower include hellebore, violet, yellow bell, paintbrush, geranium, hollyhock, lupine, pentstemon, wind flower, camas, snapdragon, Clarkia, and lily.

LOWELL 23 m. is only a post office at the junction of the Lochsa and Selway Rivers. The Middle Fork is a broad and unhurried and dimpled stream, but these two rivers, as much alike as twins, are swifter in descent, and fall in cascading loveliness in their upper reaches. The left road up the Lochsa River will, when completed, connect with Missoula in Montana. Two improved forest campgrounds are available a few miles up, and others will be established. One mile from Lowell there is a left turn from the Selway road that leads to the COOLWATER LOOKOUT 1 m. and to two lovely alpine lakes that are heavily stocked with trout. Up the Selway River at 19 m. is the SELWAY WATERFALL (R), visible from the road. Unspectacular, this descent of water is, nevertheless, one of the loveliest in the State. Two miles farther on Meadow Creek is an improved campground. The road goes south here up Meadow Creek and climbs to the summit and a magnificent view and proceeds to Elk City. It crosses a wilderness of county and streams.

The Middle Fork of the Clearwater is a study in color. In its lower reach it may be almost black depth with white manes streaming from the boulders, or it may lie broad and shallow in dappled brown over its stones. Farther up it varies from pale green at its edge and darkens to blue, running through every possible shade. Or along a stretch it may give thousands of white intimations of cascading but never do more than to stir its surface into jewels.

The highway proceeds along the South Fork to STITES 86 m., which is little more than a name. Just N of HARPSTER 95 m., the mountains on the left are very

The Lochsa River

Pierce City, one-time capital of Idaho Territory

Through the Clearwater National Forest

Government pack string on the Selway River

beautifully terraced in golden brown with narrow alternating gardens of pale green.

At **97 m.** is the junction with State 14.

Left on this improved road is a drive up a river that is flawless. The canyon walls are densely wooded above an inextricable tangle of underflora; with wild flowers in extravagant gardens mile after mile; and with the river in springtime rolling in a torrential flood. In June its water may look like coffee pouring down the cascades; or over the diversion dam at **6 m.** it may look like a waterfall of liquid gold. In autumn the mountainsides are aflame with color, and the river is as clear as a journey of melted glass. A right turn at **17.5 m.** crosses a bridge and climbs the Hungry Creek road to the MARBLE CREEK LOOKOUT **14 m.** A sensory part of this journey comes from the sound, especially when the stream is rampant; for in one moment it is hushed and in the next it swirls and gathers its power to plunge. At **23 m.** it loses its temper completely and cascades wildly; and the lush flora yields for a short distance to blue-black ledges of stone. Many side streams enter, and upon the mouth of some are attractive campgrounds. These streams all come down in spring and early summer as if they had been thrown over precipices and enraged, and the river itself churns down the miles with uninterrupted gusto. And a sensory part of this journey is in smell, for the fragrance of water, wild flower, and evergreen and fern all mix into a floating bouquet that fills the canyon.

CROOKED RIVER enters at **43 m.** (R) and over the hill from it is the village of ELK CITY **46.5 m.** The road proceeds from it eastward and forks at about **56 m.**, the left turn leading to RED RIVER HOT SPRINGS, where hotel and cabins are available, and the right turn penetrating forest to connect eventually with Hamilton in Montana. At the Crooked River junction the right turn goes southward and leads in **20 m.** to improved campgrounds and lovely lakes in a virginal wilderness.

CRYSTAL LAKE is especially unusual because it is framed in a rockbound depression and is wild of aspect. A trail leads from it to FISH LAKE. Other lakes are the WILDHORSE, RAINBOW, DEER, and RUBY, all accessible by road or trail, and some, like the Wildhorse, equipped with a campground maintained by the Forest. This is part of one of Idaho's great primitive areas, and is in the center of the Nezperce National Forest.

No forest in Idaho holds a greater diversity of scenery and interest. Elevations vary in parts of it several thousand feet within a few miles, and while in some areas flowers are blooming, other regions are buried invisibly under snow. Much of the wild game has never been disturbed, and many streams have rarely been fished. Of its hot springs, the Red River is becoming a popular summer resort. Principal among its larger trees are yellow pine, larch, lodgepole, Douglas fir, western red cedar, white and alpine fir, and Engelmann spruce.

The highway goes westward from the junction, and rises out of the canyon of the South Fork of the Clearwater River for ten winding miles among white fir. These miles in summertime are perfect, with every farm a pastoral loveliness of green hills, forested coves, and crests, and burgeoned fragrant meadows.

At Grangeville is the junction with U S 95 (see **Tour 7, Sec. b).**

TOUR NO. 9

Coeur d'Alene—St. Maries—Potlatch. U S 95 Alt. Lake
Coeur d'Alene Route.

Coeur d'Alene to Potlatch **110 m.**

This is perhaps the loveliest drive for its length in Idaho.
Accommodations are less than average.

U S 95 Alt. follows the route of U S 10 for eleven miles
(see **Tour 10)** E of Coeur d'Alene before turning south
along the eastern shore of LAKE COEUR D'ALENE.
After crossing the bridge the highway follows the shore
line and passes BEAUTY, SQUAW, TURNER, and CAR-
LIN BAYS, the first of which is usually calmly blue when
the main body of the lake is rolling in high waves. From
Beauty, Turner, and Carlin, paths lead (L) to the summit
of Mount Coeur d'Alene, following streams or passing
through heavy evergreen growth. This summit (5,200
alt.) is the highest point in the range and offers a fine view
of the surrounding country. Branching from these trails
are other trails leading to Elk, Killarney, and Red Horse
Mountains.

For a considerable distance the highway follows close
to this body of water, which the *National Geographic* is
declared by legend to have called the fifth loveliest in the
world. Entirely surrounded by low wooded hills, it lies for
mile upon mile, serenely blue with pale acreages of light
falling upon it in broad fields or trembling upon it in silver
paths. The view afforded will depend on the position of the
sun for this lake is not the same at morning, noon, and evening, nor when looking away from the sun or against it.
If the wind is very gentle, the surface wears a pattern
like that of fern leaves, and if the wind is a little stronger,
then it is like a dappled blue pavement of glass. If the
wind is stronger still, the dark blue miraculously opens
into white crests as if flowering, and the tiny valleys are
ridged in bloom. There are areas where upon the blue a

deeper blue seems in shadow to have been poured or in
sunlight to lie like a veil of silk; or it may seem as if the
depth is golden yellow above a buried sun, with lilac
mists trembling on the surface; or it may look as if
liquid light has been spilled on the water. In afternoon
there are reeflike paths that look like solid gray ice, with
the water on either side like dimpled prairies of cobalt
blue. In early morning sun, golden sheens seem not quite
to touch the surface but to lie close against it like a mist
of butterfly wings. At sunset, especially under a cloudy
sky, the wooded hills are purple or black fog and the
shadowed water is like condensed darkness; but the water
touched as the flame of the sunset dies looks like a meadow of soft white bloom. There may be lovelier lakes in
the world. Some who have seen Coeur d'Alene under
varying light in all its moods from utter deep blue
serenity to whitecapped perturbation would like to know
where they are.

Continuing southward, U S 95 Alt. follows the shore
of the lake or cuts back over forested hills. It finally
enters a canyon, and for two miles the lake is eclipsed,
but the mountainsides here in summertime are a continuous garden of wild flowers, with the syringa drench-
ing the air in June. Almost immediately south of the
canyon, the highway reaches the point where the Coeur
d'Alene River empties into the lake.

Left on a road up this river is a chain of ten lakes scattered within
a distance of six miles. Taken together, these offer an ideal spot
for both sportsman and vacationist who demand little in accommodations, though upon four of them, to which branch roads lead,
there are cabins and campgrounds. These ten lakes are a series
of lovely mountain jewels, and those to which no road leads are
available by path or from the river by launch or rowboat. Anderson, Black, Cave, and Medicine Lakes are south of the river;
Thompson, Blue, Swan, Killarney, Hidden, and Rose are north.
Killarney Lake with its two small islands at the upper end is perhaps the most picturesque of all.

On the right, north of HARRISON 39 m. (2,207
alt., 493 pop.), a ghostly hybrid of a resort and milltown,

Marble Creek

The St. Joe River

Beauty Bay, Lake Coeur d'Alene

Sunset on Lake Coeur d'Alene

are the remains of a deserted mill; and contrasting here
with the ugliness is the lake beyond. Mills and log booms
have done their best to deface the lake along here, and
beauty lies far out beyond the homely industry of human
hands. Harrison, terraced up a mountainside, is, surprisingly enough, the center of a farming area. Picturesque in its site, uncertain in its appearance, it once
flourished, too, before the mill here was abandoned to
decay. At one time it had nine mills along its water front.
Today it has none.

South of the scabbed southern extremity of Harrison
and the serene blue loveliness of Lake Coeur d'Alene, the
highway enters a rich agricultural area where river bottoms have been diked. These great dikes, running for
twelve miles, are so built that they form roadbeds as well
as dams to control flood waters. The soil here is extremely rich in its silted deposits. The highway itself
proceeds by wooded hill and cove to rise over a distance
of ten miles to HARRISON FLATS, a burnt-over region
now possessed by young growth, wild flowers, and a few
ranches. Vegetation is so lush that this tiny valley looks
tangled and choked by its own thrift. The highway climbs
gently out of the Flats and then makes a forested descent
which leads by way of a canyon to the meadowed valley
of the shadowy St. Joe River. The road follows the valley
for about eight miles before it crosses the river.

ST. MARIES 58 m. (2,145 alt.; 1,996 pop.), the seat
of Benewah County, is sprawled on hills and almost lost
to itself. The older part of the town, first entered by
train from the east or U S 95 Alt., once roared with gusto
and then declined as the adjacent timber was largely exhausted; and just west of it a new town made a fresh
start. The streets, in consequence, run without design or
reason up or around the hills which reach away to the
south. It is on the main line of the Chicago, Milwaukee,
and Puget Sound Railroad, and is an important junction
for the shipping of pine timber. St. Maries is the southern terminus of both freight and passenger boats on Lake

Coeur d'Alene, with the St. Joe River, said to be the
highest navigable river in the world, connecting the lake
and the town. Westward (R) is a shallow lake which
is really the upper end of LAKE CHATCOLET, and this,
together with five miles of what is known as the COEUR
D'ALENE SLOUGH along the St. Joe River, comprises
some of the best bass-fishing and duck-hunting area in
the State. The bottoms between the St. Maries and St.
Joe Rivers cover about seventy-five thousand acres of
very rich soil, especially adapted to fruits and vegetables.
This area is smooth and green, with clusters of willows
bordering small pools that are fed by springs. The whole
scene has the appearance of a great sunken garden.

At the junction of the St. Maries and St. Joe Rivers,
U S 95 Alt. swings to the right over a bridge and then
climbs through mile after mile of beautifully wooded
country. It goes up the St. Maries River Canyon, which
steadily widens and lengthens in an unfolding blue and
green panorama of mountains, with occasional small
tablelands opening to the river. Two areas running beyond vision and over backbones are still stark and ugly
under the devastation of former fires. The road descends
through the canyon, crosses the St. Maries River, and
swings right to its junction with State 7 at **73 m.**

Left on State 7 is CLARKIA 17 m., which is noted not so much
for itself as for its surroundings; for it is situated in a forest of
immense trees from one to three hundred years old. Out of Clarkia,
a side trip can be taken (L) to MARBLE CREEK 12 m. upon
which is the largest single stand of matured white pine remaining
in America. It covers about 136 square miles between the creek and
the St. Joe River.

From the junction, U S 95 Alt. continues southward to
SANTA CREEK **74 m.** which is indicated by a sign on
the right. Here not long ago a channel was dynamited to
change the stream, and down in the rock gorge was exposed one of the most unusual deposits of carbonized trees
yet found in the State. Below, in the rock wall, are
twenty-two trees which remain just as they were dis-

covered. The logs, varying in diameter from eight to twenty-seven inches, are extinct species of oak, redwood, beech, and bald cypress, none of which are now native to this region. These seem to be a remnant of a Middle Miocene forest that perhaps covered two hundred thousand square miles of the Pacific Northwest before it was buried by lava flows from a few to more than five thousand feet in depth. These logs still show growth rings, medullary rings, and the minutest of cell structure.

EMIDA 80 m., on the edge of the St. Joe National Forest, is hardly more than a name on the map. Westward from it the deeper forest rolls away in massed ranges on which the growth is broken only by canyons or by small areas cleared by fire.

South of Emida, U S 95 Alt. passes through a logged-off and burnt-over forest area before entering a corridor whose high cool beauty stands in striking contrast to the devastation left behind. The highway winds for nine miles through this magnificent corridor of matured juniper and white pine, the former easily identified by its lacy foliage and its stately shaft which often for a hundred feet is without a limb. Other trees here are lodgepole, fir, and spruce, with some hemlock and larch. The luxuriant shrubbery is chiefly elder, ample, syringa, dogwood, grape, huckleberry, heath, laurel, and hawthorn. The commonest ferns are the brake (bracken), maidenhair, and sword. The varieties of wild flower are almost countless: among the loveliest are the syringa, lilies, lupine, violet, shooting star, hollyhock, fireweed, queencup, and monkey flower.

The beautiful ST. JOE NATIONAL FOREST is one of the smallest in the State, with an area of only two hundred thousand acres. In 1910 it was severely gutted by fire, and some large stands of mature white pine were destroyed. Much of the forest, therefore, is of young growth, though large bodies of pine still stand in the center of it; and it is chiefly in this region that deer and bear are plentiful, with mountain goat in the Sawtooth

Peaks. Much of the interior of this forest is very rugged, and inasmuch as it has few roads, fishing is excellent for those willing to go by trail.

A few miles S of the edge of the forest, U S 95 Alt. enters HARVARD **98 m.** and leaves it to cross a valley and enter an area of scattered rolling farms.

POTLATCH **108 m.** is typical of small towns which, almost entirely supported by a single industry, thrive with it and then move into the realm of ghost towns when the industry has exhausted its resources. This town will doubtless steadily decline, like so many others in the State, until it is little more than a store and a gas station serving its countryside.

South of Potlatch, U S 95 Alt. runs past a game preserve and passes the Potlatch lumber mill, formerly said to have been the largest in the world but now less active.

At **110 m.** is its junction with U S 95 (see **Tour 7, Sec. a).**

TOUR NO. 10

(Missoula, Montana)—Wallace—Kellogg—Coeur d'Alene
—(Spokane, Washington). U S 10. Mullan Road Route.

Montana Line to Washington Line, 82 m.

The Union Pacific Railroad parallels this route between
Mullan and Cataldo, and the Spokane, Coeur d'Alene, and
Palouse between Coeur d'Alene and Post Falls. The Intermountain Transport Co. buses follow the highway. Usual
accommodations.

U S 10 is the chief artery of travel across northern Idaho
into the Northwest. Formerly known as the Yellowstone
Trail, it follows the Mullan military road that was built
by Captain John Mullan in 1861 between Fort Benton in
Montana and Walla Walla upon the Columbia River in
Washington.

U S 10 crosses the Montana-Idaho line over Lookout
Pass (4,738 alt.), 111 m. west of MISSOULA, from
which is afforded a view of a large part of two National
Forests, the St. Joe on the left and the Coeur d'Alene on
the right, as well as a part of the Coeur d'Alene Mountains, whose flanks late in every summer are blue with
ripe huckleberries. The chief trees are Douglas fir, white
and yellow pine, larch, cedar, western hemlock, Engelmann spruce, and lodgepole. The principal shrubs are
dogwood, huckleberry, thimble-, snow-, service-, and elderberry, ocean spray and mountain ash, Oregon grape, alder,
and wild cherry. This descent for six miles to the Coeur
d'Alene River (South Fork) is beautiful save for the
scars which remain from one of the worst forest fires in
history. This epic of devastation wrote its record in a
flood of flame that lighted the sky for a hundred miles
and in mountains of smoke that obscured the sun over a
huge area—as well as in thousands of acres of charred
trunks and blackened landscape. But even so, these first

miles offer little foretaste of what is to be found in the Coeur d'Alene mining district. At the foot of the descent is a lovely lucid river, but a half mile farther a group of scalded red buildings suggest the area ahead.

MULLAN 6 m. (3,245 alt.; 1,891 pop.) is not, as mining towns go, wholly without its prepossessing aspect. Founded in 1884 between two silver-lead mines, and shaken since by strike after strike, it has managed to evade in some degree the complete and pitiless homeliness that usually falls like a blight on towns in such regions. The MORNING MINE, still operating here, is the third largest lead producer in the United States and sustains most of the population of the town. Its developed area reaches for almost thirty-eight miles. On the right is a monument to Captain Mullan. On the right, too, as the highway leaves the W end of town, is the river, but it is not the lucid stream of a mile ago. It has been diverted to the mines here, impregnated with poison, and turned free. It now looks like a river of lye. Or, better, it looks as if all the dirty clothes in the world had just been washed in it.

WALLACE 13 m. (2,728 alt.; 3,634 pop.), standing in a triangular valley in which many streams enter the main fork of the Coeur d'Alene River, is the seat of Shoshone County and the distributing center of this large mining and lumbering area. The great fire of 1910 partly destroyed this town, since rebuilt and quite picturesque, with its better homes terraced on the mountainside, row on row. In its lovely little park at the western end is another monument to Mullan. Perhaps the most notable thing about Wallace is its stores, which, at least in regard to food, cater to the most exacting of epicures and offer a greater variety of exotic delicacies than most cities a hundred times its size.

1. Right from Wallace on a paved road is BURKE 6 m. (3,741 alt.; 500 pop.). Its only street is a narrow gulch occupied by a railway and lined with stores and shacks. This town seems to have been resourceful: finding itself cabined, it has spawned down the canyon

clear to Wallace a flock of imitations, some of which almost excel the parent in scabbed aspect. GEM, however, midway between the two towns, is a ghost, having been founded in 1886 and having had a saloon in every building of any consequence. Burke still thrives. The Hecla Mining Company has its million-dollar plant here, said to be very modern and complete. This mine is fifth among the lead producers.

2. Right from Wallace on an unimproved road is the COEUR D'ALENE NATIONAL FOREST. The road follows Ninemile Creek for 3.5 m., then crosses Dobson Pass (4,179 alt.), and then turns over elbows for 2 m., follows Dudley Creek for 1 m., Two Mile Creek for nearly 4 m., and rejoins U S 10 at Osburn. This loop circles Dago Peak.

A longer journey continues through Unknown Gulch (R), Pony Gulch (R), Alder Creek (L), White Creek (L), and Cleveland Gulch (R) and along Beaver Creek to DELTA 3 m. Turning right at Delta, the road now follows Trail Creek and goes over Kings Pass to MURRAY 8 m. on Prichard Creek, the center of rich gold placers. Close by is the ghost of EAGLE CITY (see **Ghost Towns**). As a matter of fact, ghost towns and deserted camps are now to be seen in nearly every direction. For 26 m. now the road winds through a forest of white pine, crossing dozens of streams, and returning to U S 10 just east of Cataldo.

At **14 m.** is the SUNSHINE MINE (L), the largest silver producer in the United States. High above in the St. Joe Mountains is STRIPED PEAK (6,388 alt.).

KELLOGG **25 m.** (2,305 alt.; 4,124 pop.) is a famous mining spot, with the Bunker Hill and Sullivan, the largest lead mine in the United States, located here. Below it the river bottoms look like a caricature of a graveyard, and above it the denuded mountains declare the potency of lead. The Sullivan Mine here has a development of sixty-four and a half miles and (with 560 men) the largest payroll of any mine in the State.

Left on a fair road from Kellogg is WARDNER 4 m. (2,960 alt.; 903 pop.), another mining town. It is the location of the famous stockade referred to locally as the Bull Pen, in which a thousand men were kept under heavy guard after the strike in Kellogg in 1899. In this feud many lives were lost, including that of Idaho's governor, Frank Steunenberg; and following the destruction of property, martial law was maintained for more than a year. During this period of strife, several hundred miners seized a car of explosives and blew up the mill. Those placed in the stockade were forced to repudiate the union before they were allowed to return to work.

West of Kellogg with its miracles of machinery, there is still to be seen a poisoned and dead or dying landscape. Trees slain by the invisible giant still stand with lifeless limbs and with roots still sucking the poisoned earth. But gradually the blight thins, the flora looks up to new strength, and the drive becomes increasingly lovely.

CATALDO 35 m. (2,143 alt.; 110 pop.) is of note only because it was near it that the famous Cataldo mission was built in 1848 by Father Ravalli, chiefly with the aid of unskilled Indians. The mission was abandoned in 1887. It rapidly fell into ruins and was largely forgotten until the citizens of Wallace, Kellogg, Coeur d'Alene, and Spokane in 1930 restored it and set it apart as a historical monument. The chapel is interesting not only because of its age and former associations but also because of its structure. After stones and logs were brought on trucks drawn by Indians, wooden pegs were used for nails, and mud from the river was spread over the walls. Inside there were three altars and a baptismal font. Of the paintings on the walls done with Indian dyes, two still hang, the one a representation of heaven, the other of hell. The restored mission is visible on a hill (L) just west of Cataldo.

U S 10 now enters Kootenai County in which lumbering and mining are diversified with farming and dairying. Leaving Coeur d'Alene River on the left, the road skirts Mission Flats and at the confluence of Fern and Mission Creeks enters the beautiful and historic FOURTH OF JULY CANYON. It was here on July 4, 1861, that Captain Mullan and his men were encamped while building the Mullan Road. They raised an American flag to the top of the tallest white pine, and from this circumstance the canyon has taken its name. The highway now climbs for a thousand feet to the summit.

Right from the summit on a dirt road is the MULLAN TREE .1 m. Standing in the center of a fifty-acre park, this tree still bears the date, 1861, and the initials M. R. (Mullan Road).

The Sunshine Mine

Coeur d'Alene National Forest

The Mullan Tree

Fernan Lake and beyond

At **50 m.** is the FOURTH OF JULY SUMMIT (3,290 alt.), marked by a tunnel 394 feet in length.

Right from here a side trip much in favor goes to COPPER MOUNTAIN 5 m., which is a lookout station.

West of the summit, U S 10 enters Wolf Lodge Valley, descending over seven miles of broad fast highway.

At **55 m.** is the junction with a road which runs into the Coeur d'Alene Forest.

Right on this road is the RUTHERFORD RANCH 2 m., the home of a once well known trapper and hunter who from this point used to run his numerous trap lines for bear, beaver, marten, and lynx. Beyond the ranch the road follows Wolf Lodge Creek and then, turning right, follows Searchlight Creek up a narrow canyon through beautifully wooded area with countless mountain streams. From the HONEYSUCKLE RANGER STATION 10 m. the road climbs more sharply to LIEBERG 15.5 m., where there are improved campgrounds. The right road here follows Lieberg Creek to its source, crosses the divide, and drops down to Tepee Creek, the peer of all fishing streams in this area. The seventeen miles between Lieberg and the McGEE RANGER STATION 32.5 m. are intersected by twenty-one streams. From McGee, hiking and pack trips are available, including Grizzly Ridge, McDonald Peak, Grassy Mountain, Lookout Peak, McGee Peak, Elkhorn Peak, and Cathedral Buttes. These are all in the heart of the Coeur d'Alene National Forest.

At the W end of Wolf Lodge Valley and E of Lake Coeur d'Alene, U S 10 passes a solitary surviving monarch of the white pine forest that formerly stood here. This tree is 216 feet in height and 8 feet in diameter at the bole.

At **57 m.** is the junction with U S 95 Alt. (see **Tour 9).** To the left is the eastern extremity of Lake Coeur d'Alene, with a long wooden bridge spanning Wolf Lodge Bay. To the left also is Beauty Bay, to the right of it is Blue Creek Bay, and these with the Wolf Lodge Bay form a three-leaf clover design. The highway now climbs for some distance and overlooks the lake, only to drop down a canyon and climb again for two miles to a deep forest; and drop again to follow the lake into Coeur d'Alene.

At **67 m.** is the junction with a road.

Right on this road is FERNAN LAKE .5 m., which is navigable for small fishing crafts and is an excellent resort for bass and perch fishermen. In wintertime there are ice skating and hockey here, with the Coeur d'Alene Eskimo Hockey Club sponsoring carnivals in which all the more popular winter sports are featured.

COEUR D'ALENE 68 m. is at the junction with U S 95 (see **Tour 7, Sec. a**).

U S 10 goes W out of Coeur d'Alene at the N W corner and after a little follows the Spokane River through forests of jack pine. At **75 m.** is the junction with a surfaced road that goes (R) into one of Idaho's richest wheat belts and from there to some of its loveliest lakes (see **Tour 7, Sec. a**).

At **76 m.** is the plant of the OHIO MATCH COMPANY (L), one of the industrial giants of the Northwest. Equipped with the most modern of machinery, this plant cuts the finest of straight-grained white pine into match blocks and ships these to Spokane. The working conditions in this factory are said to be very good.

POST FALLS 77 m. (2,147 alt.; 509 pop.) is a small lumbering and fruit-packing town on the Spokane River. A half mile south of it (L) is the Post Falls Dam, which impounds the river and delivers power to the eastern part of the Inland Empire.

At **78 m.** is the junction with an improved road.

Right on this road is HAUSER LAKE 7 m., a beautiful jewel in a deep forest of evergreens. Inasmuch as it is close to both Spokane and Coeur d'Alene, this lake is a favorite resort in northern Idaho. Fishing in the lake is fair; and large flocks of wild ducks, making their summer home here, remain late enough in the fall to be caught by the hunting season.

At **82 m.** U S 10 crosses the Idaho-Washington Line over the Spokane Bridge **18 m.** E of Spokane.

TOUR NO. 11

(Missoula, Montana)—Clark Fork—Sandpoint—Priest River—(Spokane, Washington). State 3 and U S 195.

Montana Line to Washington Line, **62 m.**

The Northern Pacific Railroad parallels this route between Cabinet and Sandpoint, and the Great Northern between Sandpoint and Newport. The Deering buses follow the highway between Priest River and the Washington Line.

Accommodations less than average except in Sandpoint. This, the northernmost artery across the Panhandle, is a river-and-valley route.

State 3 enters the State over the Bitterroot Range of the CONTINENTAL DIVIDE (2,400 alt.; **173 m.** N W of Missoula, Montana) at a point where the mighty CLARK FORK RIVER has eroded its gorge. This is one of the wildest and most picturesque streams in the West. Having found itself imprisoned by mountains after the retreat of the glaciers, it has done some amazing sculpturing in cutting a path to the sea, and often, because of the invincible toughness of its walls and beds, has to turn up on its edge to pour through chasms, and sometimes its canyons are so narrow that they can be spanned by logs. It has many waterfalls and boxed gorges; and in the last fifty miles of its journey its haste is so wild that it cascades almost continuously. Its entrance into Idaho is marked by the Cabinet Gorge with its sheer narrow walls; and through here in time of spring floods the river is so white and thunderous in its journey that persons travel for many miles to see and hear it. The water goes through here with such force that logs, caught in the boiling violence, are sometimes broken into kindling; or they may be sucked under and held for many minutes before they are released and hurled back to the surface. It seems probable that the river is to be tamed by a dam and a reservoir. On the left at **1.5 m.** is a sign which indicates the village of CABINET across the river, accessible from here only by a suspension footbridge.

The Cabinet Gorge can be seen by crossing this bridge and proceeding a half mile up the river on the far side to the gorge, or by driving up the south side of the river from Clark Fork.

State 3 proceeds down a beautifully wooded drive to cross Mosquito Creek and enter Clark Fork.

CLARK FORK **8 m.** (2,081 alt.; 432 pop.) is chiefly the home of the Whitedelf Mine, a lead and silver producer.

1. Right from Clark Fork an unimproved road goes up Lightning Creek. Five miles out a trail leads (L) to Bee Top Mountain. At RATTLE CREEK **18 m.** is an improved campground. The road goes past Porcupine, Mad, Sheep, Fall, Deer, and other creeks to LAKE DARLING **25 m.** This lake is in the heart of the PEND OREILLE NATIONAL FOREST, an area of 874,000 acres of which nearly a fourth is privately owned. Mt. Pend Oreille (6,785 alt.) is just north of the lake. The trees in this area are chiefly yellow pine (with the long needles hanging in pale green bouquets), cedar (with its lacy luxuriance of foliage), Douglas fir, larch, hemlock, and white fir.

2. Left from Clark Fork on a dirt road is the site of the old THOMPSON TRADING POST **10 m.** David Thompson and his men, representing the Hudson's Bay Fur Trading Company, arrived at Pend Oreille Lake on the eighth of September, 1809, and while searching for a canoe route to the Columbia River, they made, five days after their arrival, the first recorded business transaction in Idaho, with the Pend d'Oreille Indians, by trading for about one hundred and twenty-five furs. They had come into Idaho from Canada by way of the Kootenai River, crossed a pass in the Cabinet Mountains, and traveled down the Pack River to the lake. They built their trading post, the Kullyspell House, two miles from the mouth of the main channel of the Clark Fork River and one-half mile from the Memaloose Island because of the proximity of this point to all other points on the lake by canoe. They built two houses of logs, one for the trading of goods and furs, and the other for the men to use, and named their post Kullyspell House, probably a different spelling for Kalispel, the native name of the Pend d'Oreille Indians. The following year David Thompson moved the post to the Spokane House near the present site of Spokane, Washington.

One authority says that the Kullyspell House was located on the shore of the lake near the present town of Hope, that it was abandoned two years later, and that it was destroyed by a forest fire about 1834, leaving two stone chimneys which stood for twenty years longer. In 1923 the exact site was located through the memory of a blind eighty-year-old Indian, Klai-too, who had seen the chimneys when a small boy. Following his instructions, two piles of even-sized rocks were discovered overgrown with brush and vines. In one of them searchers uncovered a regular cavity resembling a fireplace, and in it traces of ashes. The citizens of Bonner County erected a monument over the site in 1929, commemorating not only the first house ever erected in the State of Idaho, but also its builder, David Thompson.

At **10 m.** LAKE PEND OREILLE comes into view and the highway now follows it almost to Sandpoint. This, the largest of Idaho lakes, with a shore line of 125 miles and an extreme depth of 1,800 feet, sometimes rolls in waves thirty feet high but usually is quite serene and is rapidly coming into favor as a playground area. The Clark Fork River flows into it and out of it. To the left of the highway on the left side of the lake are four islands, the Warren, Cottage, Pearl, and Memaloose, which were used by the Pend d'Oreille Indians as a cemetery. These Indians instead of burying their dead suspended them from trees.

HOPE **17 m.** (2,078 alt.; 111 pop.) is a village along the lake shore and the home of a small mine. On the left is a monument to David Thompson, and just below it on the shore is the David Thompson Park. At **19 m.** can be seen the peaks of the SEVEN SISTERS in the west; and at **20 m.** is TRESTLE CREEK, a popular area for camping, huckleberrying, and fishing. The flowering bushes along this drive in midsummer are chiefly syringa and elderberry.

At **26 m.** is the junction with an unimproved road.

Right on this road are junctions with several other roads, each of which leads to its own attractions. Pack River itself rises at Harrison Lake and winds for thirty miles before emptying into Lake Pend Oreille. A fair motor road, following the river most of the way and intersecting more than forty tributaries, leads into densely wooded regions, but WALSH LAKE **13 m.** is the chief objective, with return to Sandpoint easy over U S 95. Or the river road may be followed to its end from which trails proceed to Chimney Rock or Harrison Lake or to the Roman Nose Lookout (7,264 alt.), all of them within hiking distance.

CULVER 28 m. is at the junction with an unimproved road.

Right on this road are LIGHTNING CREEK 10 m. and a notable stand of virgin white pine.

BOYER 29 m. is at the junction with an unimproved road.

Right on this road is the heaviest growth of western yellow pine to be found in the Pend Oreille National Forest.

SANDPOINT 34 m. (2,086 alt.; 3,290 pop.) is the seat of Bonner County and the junction with U S 95 (see **Tour 7, Sec. b**).

State 3 now becomes U S 195 and westward from Sandpoint parallels the Clark Fork, lying between hills that are covered with pine, hemlock, cedar, and fir. The river here is deep and wide and is navigable for small boats from Lake Pend Oreille to Albini Falls west of Priest River. The highway passes through DOVER 37 m., a ghost town with a smokeless factory and rows of identical empty shacks; through WRENCO 43 m., from which is visible JOHNNY LONG MOUNTAIN on the right; and LACLEDE 48 m., another ghost that was once a prosperous mill town. At Laclede the highway leaves the W end of the Pend Oreille Forest and approaches the Kaniksu and the most popular playground in the northern part of the State.

PRIEST RIVER 56 m. (2,080 alt.; 949 pop.) at the junction of the Pend Oreille and Priest Rivers is the gateway of the Priest Lake country. This town has an Italian colony, noted for its weedless gardens; a sawmill which specializes in white pine lumber of exceptional quality for interior woodwork, and a tourist traffic that is rapidly increasing.

1. Right on an improved road is COOLIN 20 m. at the southern end of PRIEST LAKE, and NORDMAN 38 m. at the western side of the lake. This body of water, regarded by some Idahoans as the loveliest lake in the State, lies upon the eastern boundary of the Kaniksu National Forest. It is about twenty-four miles long and from one to

Lake Pend Oreille

Priest River country

Priest Lake

Chimney Rock near Priest Lake

fourteen miles in width and is a perfect huge sapphire against a forested backdrop that is almost as dense as an evergreen area can be. The forest is, in fact, almost a phenomenon in itself, and only the more adventurous go far into it without a guide. Lying half in Washington and half in Idaho, it covers 444,593 acres, and lifts its great shoulders under the southern spurs that reach down the Selkirk Mountains of Canada. Besides its larger flora of pine and fir and spruce, it has a luxuriant undergrowth that is often impenetrable, with fern and shrub and wild flower matting the earth and lifting tropical gardens shoulder-high. Nearly any part of it will meet the most exacting tastes of those seeking wild beautiful retreats; and most of it offers fine hunting and fishing. Besides Priest Lake, in which fishing is always good, there are smaller lakes and countless streams, some of which are rarely fished at all; and the wooded regions have thousands of deer, bear, elk, and goats. Both native and blue grouse are abundant.

The right-hand road from Priest River (often called the Coolin Road) is bordered on both sides by large evergreens of such maturity that they give the appearance of a tunnel through the forest. At **16 m.** the PRIEST RIVER EXPERIMENT STATION (R) .5 m. is interesting for its variety of research related to the welfare of the National Forests. From here a drive of six miles leads easily to the LOOKING GLASS LOOKOUT, where a forty-foot tower affords an excellent view. Right on this branch road **1 m.** up the East River are campsites and excellent eastern brook trout fishing. COOLIN **25 m.** is a small resort town on the southern extremity of the lake. Accommodations are available here; and at the PAUL JONES BEACH **25.5 m.** north and the SHERWOOD BEACH **27 m.** north there are boats and cabins. At **27.5 m.** a right turn leads up SOLDIER CREEK, in which there is excellent native trout fishing. But the most exciting trips from Coolin are by both water and land. One of them is a boat trip from Coolin to INDIAN BAY 10 m., and then by trail up INDIAN CREEK to its fork 3 m. and from there 6 m. up the south fork to the end of the trail. To reach CHIMNEY ROCK it is necessary to cross the creek and make a stiff climb for a half mile eastward. Chimney Rock, rising about 200 feet, is triangular in shape and was formed by three glaciers that backed in toward the divide. A goat trail leads along the north side of the chimney to a narrow escarpment extending about a half mile eastward. Goats are often seen in this vicinity. The rock itself can not be scaled without elaborate mechanical apparatus. HARRISON LAKE 5 m., north as the crow flies, can be reached from here. This, a beautiful glacial cirque of deepest blue, framed in a rock-bound setting, is by far the loveliest of all the numerous high lakes along the Selkirk Divide.

2. The west side of Priest Lake can be reached by the west branch road by way of Nordman or by a crossroad south of Coolin. From the town of Priest River a right turn at 28 m. leads (R) to PRIEST LAKE .5 m.; to LUBY BAY at 31 m. (1 m. R); and to KALI-

SPELL BAY at 34 m. (1 m. R). To reach points farther up the lake it is necessary to travel by boat or trail. Boats, motors, cabins, and other accommodations are available at Coolin, Outlet, Luby Bay, Kalispell Bay, and on the mouth of Granite Creek at the head of the lake. At Luby and Reeder bays are improved forest camp-grounds. The drive between Outlet and Kalispell by way of Luby Bay is quite as beautiful as any drive could be. In addition there is a variety of side trips into the forest, both by road and trail; and one of the easiest of the latter turns off the west branch road just south of its junction with the Luby Bay road and proceeds for three miles to an eighty-foot steel lookout tower that gives a magnificent view of the lake and its background. The Granite Creek road penetrates deep into the forest. Four miles from Nordman a right turn leads to the river, upon which is a modern fish trap, recently completed, and popular with visitors when the fish are being impounded and stripped.

U S 195 crosses the Washington line at **62 m.**, **49 m.** N E of Spokane, Washington.

II

THE PRIMITIVE AREA

THE PRIMITIVE AREA

THE Primitive Area, almost in the geographic center of Idaho, is a compact but slightly elongated unit of 1,087,744 acres. It is bounded on the north by the main Salmon River, on the east by the Bighorn Crags, Yellowjacket Range, and Sleeping Deer Mountain, on the south by a line just south of and paralleling the Middle Fork of the Salmon River to Rapid Creek, and on the west by a divide that is the western limit of the watersheds of Marble, Monumental, Beaver, and Chamberlain Creeks. It is a wilderness of mountains and streams with a few upland meadows, a handful of ranches, a little grazing, and a few mines. All but a few thousand acres of it lies within four of Idaho's National Forests.

Its topography is extremely varied. It ranges from high rolling plateaus and ridges as found in the Chamberlain Basin, Cold Meadows, and Thunder Mountain regions to precipitous bluffs and deep gorges upon the rivers. Mt. McGuire, its highest point, with an elevation above ten thousand feet, is on the east side at the head of Roaring Creek. Many other peaks, accessible by trail to their summits, have altitudes above nine thousand feet, and of these, Cottonwood Peak in the northwest probably overlooks more territory than any other. Its climate is also extremely varied, and a few hours of travel in July can easily range through forty-five degrees of temperature. There is, strangely enough, little snowfall upon the main Salmon and its Middle Fork, but upon parts of the area the snow is piled many feet in depth. More than 90 per cent of this huge playground is forested. The commonest trees are lodgepole pine and Douglas fir, both of which occur in dense stands at higher elevations, together with some Engelmann spruce and limber pine. At lower altitudes are forests of matured western yellow pine, especially upon Big Creek and the Middle Fork of Salmon River. Difficulties in building either highway or railway lines place nearly all of this timber indefinitely beyond commercial reach. The underflora is typically the subalpine varieties found in this latitude, and the wild flowers are unusually lovely and numerous.

There are about fifty lakes in the Area, varying in size from ten to a hundred acres. Located for the most part at the heads of streams, these are fed by melting snows, and the water in any of them is clear and cold in all seasons. Most of their shore line is timbered. From a historic point of view the most interesting lake in the region is that called Roosevelt on Monumental Creek. The small mining town of Roosevelt just above Mule Creek awoke one day to the realization of a landslide and found itself buried under nearly thirty feet of water before the next sunrise. The mountain of earth that came down here covered two miles of distance in a few hours but at no time moved with haste, and gave the settlers time to flee with everything but their pianos. Hundreds of small streams head in the higher country and pour in cascading frenzy to the rivers far below. There are many hot springs, most of which are mineralized and most invigorating to tenderfeet after they have spent a few hours in the saddle. Of the several meadows that are ideal natural campsites, the most popular are Crescent, Cold, Moose, Hand, Chamberlain, and the Meadow of Doubt. Adjacent to these and to countless others are cold pure water, forage for beasts, and an abundance of wood. Inasmuch as this is a primitive area, it is not planned to equip these sites with stoves and air conditioners and bathtubs.

Middle Fork of Salmon River

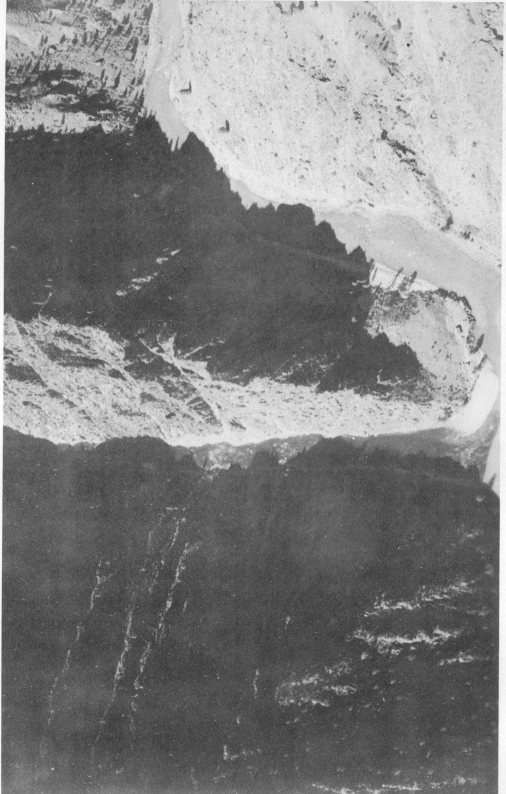

Junction of Middle Fork and main Salmon

Submerged town of Roosevelt—Thunder Mountain area

A Monument on Monumental Creek

There are no unusual natural phenomena. The Bighorn Crags on the eastern border are distinguished by being set upon a high divide, and rise perpendicularly from it for hundreds of feet to resemble huge monuments. Southwest of these is Rainbow Mountain, named for its colored mists and formations, and especially beautiful under sunrise. There are a number of caves along Big and Camas Creeks and upon the Middle Fork. Used formerly by Indians, their walls are often covered with paintings and pictographs and innumerable hieroglyphics. A group of caves in the upper end of the boxed canyon on Big Creek suggest that they were used as a stronghold in years past. The gorges of the main Salmon, the northern boundary, and of the Middle Fork are two of the deepest in North America. The Middle Fork stream itself is utterly impassable to any manner of travel now known.

The Area has not been and will not be improved save as may be necessary for protection against fire. There are no roads. There are about two hundred miles of trail, and other trails are being constructed, and a few more bridges will be laid across the streams. "The construction of roads, trails, or other improvements will not be allowed to mar the landscape or interfere with its primitive characteristics." Campgrounds will not be improved. Signs have been and will continue to be placed until even the most terrified dude will be able to retrace his path and find his way back to his automobile.

This is the largest and the most unvisited of all Idaho's huge game preserves. The chief big game animal is the deer, of which the Area contains more than thirteen thousand. Most of these are Rocky Mountain mule deer, although some white-tailed deer have entered the region from the north. The annual increase of deer is estimated at 3,250 head, but they suffer a loss, perhaps not to exceed 10 per cent, from predatory animals. There are probably five hundred elk, chiefly upon the Chamberlain and Disappointment Creek watersheds. Sometimes herds of thirty or more are seen on Cold and Cottonwood Meadows, but during the open season this beast ranges far back and is not often taken by the hunter. There are a few moose, but for the most part this country is too rough for them. Of bear there may be a thousand, and these, like the deer, are quite evenly distributed over the whole area. Now and then a grizzly is killed and possibly there is still quite a number of grizzlies in the more inaccessible reaches. Of mountain goat and mountain sheep there are about a thousand head. The goats roam the bluffs of the larger streams and remain high up until midwinter. The sheep inhabit lower and flatter areas. Of predatory animals the cougar is the greatest menace, and doubtless these huge cowardly cats slay more deer, sheep, and goat in a season than all the other predatory animals combined. A few timber wolves may exist. Coyotes are common. The red and gray fox are to be seen, the lynx rarely at high altitudes, but the bobcat is abundant in the rougher sections. There are also marten, mink, otter, badger, wolverine, porcupine, and beaver.

This Area is an interesting bird refuge because there is a mingling of northern Rocky Mountain and Coast species. Blue grouse are plentiful in the more isolated parts and especially in the Rush Creek country; and ruffled grouse are common along the streams. Franklin grouse (known also as fool hens) are found chiefly in the extensive lodgepole pine areas. There are a great many golden eagles, now believed to be destructive of young game, and a not inconsiderable number of bald eagles and ospreys. Of smaller birds a great many species are found in large numbers. Geese and ducks occur as migrants.

No part of Idaho is more prolific in fish, and it can be declared without exaggeration that every stream of fishing size is well stocked, and some have never been fished. There are great runs in winter and early spring of steelhead trout, some of which weigh fifteen pounds. Dolly Varden or bull trout are widely distributed, and so are the white fish known as mountain herring. The only salmon occurring in these waters is the Chinook, and these, coming from the Pacific Ocean, are abundant in early fall. There are also native and rainbow trout, the former of which, often called black-spotted or cutthroat, is the commonest of all. Two excellent fishing streams are Big Creek and the Middle Fork, with a road up the former and a mountain trail going down the latter to Mormon Ranch. Fish Lake, Flossie Lake, and Roosevelt Lake are well stocked.

The chief use made of this Area is by hunters, with fishing as a casual pastime of their journey. The whole region is open to hunting except two hundred and fifty thousand acres upon the Middle Fork State Game Preserve. Because the hunter has to penetrate a considerable distance, pack trips are necessary, and horses and equipment and guides for these are available at all points of entrance. For persons wishing to pack in during the summer months when hunting is forbidden, arrangements can be made at a great many places upon all but the northern border; or foot journeys can be provided with guides for those who wish to penetrate any of the hundreds of places that can be reached only by foot travel. Some who could afford it have flown in to land on the meadowed fields, particularly in the Chamberlain Basin, but sportsmen are in general opposed to the flight of aircraft over this Area. "If auto travel is not to be condoned, surely entrance by air should also be discouraged."

Though the Area is accessible on all sides, the northern entrance is extremely difficult and is only for those who are willing to proceed afoot for a considerable distance. This entrance is by boat down the Salmon River from Salmon City (see **Tour 5)** and strongly appeals to sportsmen who like a somewhat hazardous journey down the magnificent gorge. Return by boat up the river is out of the question; but adventurers choosing this approach to the region can climb out of the canyon and be met at appointed places by pack strings; or if they prefer to ape the hardy frontiersmen they can take their way over the great mountains afoot and with provisions on their back and emerge at some automobile terminal south or west. Or they can return to the river and proceed by boat to Riggins or Lewiston.

The eastern entrance is by way of Salmon City over the Yellowjacket road, or over the Morgan Creek road between Ellis and Challis, both of which lead to Yellowjacket or Meyers Cove, favorite jumping-off points into the Area (see **Tour 5**). The southern entrance is by way of Stanley (see **Tour 5**) or out of Boise by way of Lowman (see **Tour 3, Section b**). The western entrance is by way of Cascade into Bear Valley (see **Tour 6**), or by way of McCall and Burgdorf to Edwardsburg (see **Tour 6**). For a typical pack trip hunting expedition into the Area, see the next chapter.

III
A TRIP INTO THE AREA

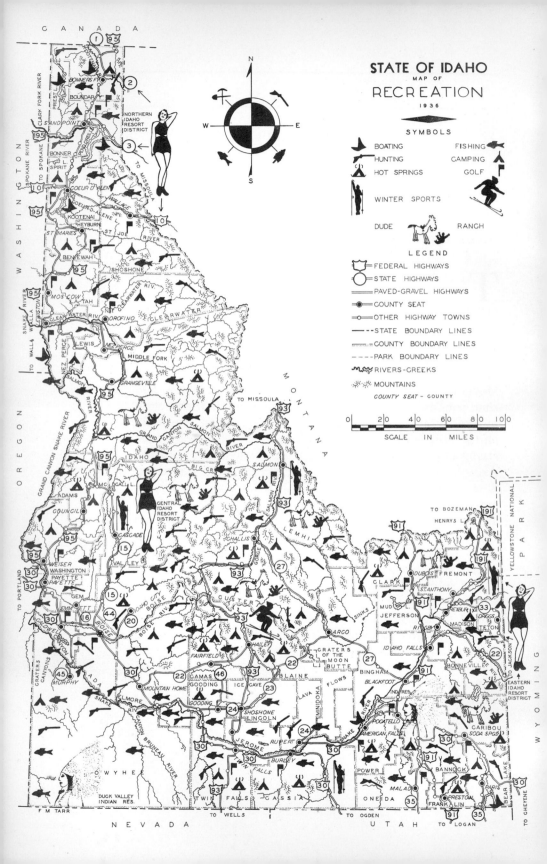

A TRIP INTO THE AREA

THE PRIMITIVE AREA is entered within season (July-November) by pack strings which are outfitted from many points on the eastern and southern boundaries (see **Tour 5, Sec. a)**, or from many points on the western boundary (see **Tour 6, side tour from McCall)**. Ordinarily, persons desiring to enter the area drive by automobile to such outfitting spots as Forney, Meyers Cove, Cape Horn, Landmark, or Stibnite, and then pack in; but some prefer to fly to a dude ranch close by the Area, inasmuch as from these ranches, especially on the Middle Fork of Salmon River, the journey by pack string is much shorter. Most of the expeditions into the Area are in the fall when the season is open on big game. Some persons, however, seeking primitive wilderness, enter during July or August, when both flora and streams are at their loveliest, and the weather is less severe. This chapter will attempt to suggest, rather than to give in explicit detail, an autumn journey by air and by pack string after big game.

Of points of departure by air, McCall (see **Tour 6)** is perhaps the best. Adventurous persons, desiring the fullest measure of beauty, like to leave Boise two hours before daylight and learn what an undertaking in magic the coming of morning can be upon Payette River and the mountains that stand like enormous shoulders on either side. There are only valleys of darkness at first, with the highway looped from summit to summit, and with ravines looking like black sunken reefs from the Craters of the Moon. When day breaks, the peaks emerge into golden light, and the world melts into the soft glory of morning dusk. The black water of the river becomes luminous flowing shadow; the night withdraws under pale veils of light; and the leaves of barberry and maple make gardens of flame upon the mountainous backdrops.

The take-off from McCall is no less appropriate. Below is the deep blue serenity of Payette Lake, and on all sides is the delicate lucid green of its streams. Mountains adjacent look like mounds of chalk, or like slabs of granite adorned with golden furze and tiny subalpine mirrors. Ranges now swim into vision, with backbones serrated in row on row, with forested depressions and altitudes stretching to the farthest reach. The enormous landscape eastward is not only a wilderness of peaks and canyons and streams. It is also a wilderness of legend, of doings both fabulous and real, with the truth of them deferring to drama and getting lost in the telling. The few mining towns here, each lonely and isolated in the vast sweep below, have strange histories that most likely will never be told. There is Warren, looking from the air like an incredible carpet of magic: a hundred unchronicled volumes sleep there, each of them as perfect in its fact and fable as the tale of China Sam. For many decades, this gentle and whimsical Chinese gentleman was custodian of the town's property and morals, and came to be known, indeed, as the Mayor of Warren and the most honest man in Idaho. He was not only watchman-in-chief, the alert guardian of residence and mine; he was also tender of babies and chopper of wood for overworked housewives, mail carrier to prospectors and trappers in outlying canyons, and nurse to the sick and distressed. North, south, and east were persons no less charitable or strange.

Some of them, it is true, were not so gentle as Sam. This great Area has known women who could could pick a deer up by its heels and antlers and throw it down cellar, or murder a husband with an iron skillet and bury him and never lose a night's sleep. It has known men whose only law was the law of survival, whose only belief was the cogent one that it is better to be alive than dead. Far eastward in that misty acreage of canyons is a man whom, Forest Rangers declare, nobody would be fool enough to approach—or lucky enough to approach and emerge alive. This hermit never bathes except when he falls into a river, and never lays eyes on another human being if he can help it. He is bearded and wild and tameless. In some hour, years ahead, his bones will be found in his shack, and it will be told of him only that he died alone and unconquered, with his gun at his side. Years ago there was a wild family here, and none of them, legend declares, had ever bathed in all their years of life. One of them, a fiercely beautiful girl, was on a pretext lured from the wild hermitage of her home and threatened with a bath. The Supervisor of a National Forest summarizes the picture: "I shall never forget it. She withdrew to the farthest room of the house and stood in a corner, trembling like a fawn, her nostrils distended and her dark eyes terrible with fright and scorn. In the majesty of her terror and contempt she was the most beautiful thing I have ever seen." But not all of the persons living in this remote jungle are indifferent to the refreshing kindness of water and soap. There are, for instance, John and Jim (the names are disguised), two old-time gamblers: their house, immaculate inside and out, and with everything fastidiously in its place, is one of the many miracles in Chamberlain Basin.

The plane will probably set down in this Basin, for it is, with the possible exception of the watersheds west of Jackson Hole in Wyoming, the greatest elk country on earth. If, on the way here, a digression is made southward, the site of Roosevelt will come into view. Once a lusty town, it is now a lake; and it is said that adventurous and thirsty men still dive down to the submerged saloon and swim around among the beaver, searching for the whiskey that is supposed to be there. But Chamber-

lain Basin, for the wanderer on the trail of buck and bighorn, deer and elk, is the first objective. Pilots declare
that elk here are so abundant that now and then they
have to be scared off the landing field before the plane can
set down; deer are so many that the only rancher in an
area of three hundred thousand acres has to build a nine-
foot fence around his garden; and trout in Fish Lake
westward are scooped up by the pailful. And Miles Howard, an old-timer with eyebrows as big as shrubs and a
beard like barbed wire, declares that blue grouse so infest
the region that he no longer bothers to use a gun. He
merely takes a cudgel and knocks their heads off. Just
north of this field is the Reeder Ranch.

It is possible, of course, to fly directly from McCall to
such a ranch as the Flying W or Double O, but direct
flight would disregard some most impressive vistas. If,
from Chamberlain Basin, the plane heads eastward, in
a few minutes it will be above a magnificent depth of
spilled peaks and sheer walls where two great rivers join
their waters. Here, at the junction of Salmon River with
the Middle Fork, the sculpturing that has been achieved
by time and erosion is overwhelming. Not far southward
are the Bighorn Crags, said to be the most rugged range
in the Northwest. These are really a huge garden of
granite monuments and turrets, with the highest of them
reaching an altitude of more than ten thousand feet, with
most of them as stripped and lonely as the stones in a
graveyard. Ship Island Lake is an enormous jewel among
them.

In going up the canyon of the Middle Fork, one of the
three deepest gorges in North America, anyone who has
ever heard of him will want to make the detour by way
of Big Creek to look down upon the remotely silent shack
where Cougar Dave lived. Famous as a lion hunter, and
until his death possibly the most remarkable person in
Idaho, Dave Lewis was a small and unconquerable kingdom of his own. Here in the utter loneliness of Big Creek,
with nothing around him for half a century except peaks

Packing in

Mountain goat country

Cougar Dave and his dogs

Journey's end

and wild streams, wild animals and a blue ceiling of sky, he lived with his guns and his dogs. He killed many men during his time, but he always carefully explained that he had to kill them—meaning, but meaning it gently, remorselessly, that he preferred the long end of the draw. His eyes were as cold as the back of a lizard, his skin was like leather thrice tanned, and his walk had the stealth of the cougar itself. Dave was not something that hunted adventure: he was adventure itself. Nor was hunting lions a theatrical matter with him; it was only the unexciting routine of making a living, of keeping his guns oiled and his dogs fed. In July of 1936, at the age of ninety-three, he felt a little ill—possibly for the first time in nearly a century. Alone, he hiked out of this deep dark canyon for more than twenty miles and asked a distant friend to take him to Boise. The next day he was dead.

Just up Big Creek from his shack is the Soldier Bar landing field, a small narrow table nearly a thousand feet above the stream. Plains land here, and take off, too; but most passengers, after looking down on this tiny white strip of land, prefer to continue southward. Southward is the barren rocky gorge of the Middle Fork, with a farm now and then hugging the river and looking no larger than a tennis court, with a winding pack trail, the only way out, following the stream. The Blackie Wallace, or Flying W, Ranch has a part of its history recorded in murders, the most picturesque of which concerns a gentleman who killed another man with a hay knife, and then saddled the assassination on the horns of a bull. Blackie Wallace is almost a legend himself, with one of the more spectacular of his eccentricities lying in the fact that his only son is named Bill Borah. Along this river are the Mormon Ranch, the Jones Ranch, the Ramey Place, and a few others, each so far from the end of a road, each so completely isolated in a canyon more than six thousand feet in depth, that persons flying far above and looking down are likely to be amazed to learn that women and children live there. Around them is the

largest solid expanse of blue peaks and nebulous mountainous distance in the United States. In any direction
for a hundred miles, and in some directions for a much
greater distance than that, there is only an ocean of thousands of zeniths, each high and imperturbable in a misty
blue integrity of its own; of thousands of lakes, each cool
and fragrant and perfect; of tens of thousands of wild
animals hiding below among the millions of trees. From
peak to peak, from backbone to backbone, the landscape
lifts and falls until it shimmers in mist and distance and
withdraws to the far purple horizons that look like
neither mountain nor cloud. In the far southeast are the
Sawtooth spires; in the far northwest is the tumbled blue
cloudland of the Seven Devils.

The plane will descend to some landing field upon this
river, and at some dude ranch the expedition will be outfitted and a pack string will take its way to the country of
deer or elk, goat or sheep. No matter which direction is
taken, there will be incalculable wonder north, east, south,
and west. The path will skirt towering mountains upon
which the evergreen timber will be so dense that it will
look like solid growth; past blue lakes so numerous that
nobody has ever counted them; through deep canyons and
up high ridges from which the streams below will look
like white strings of beads; across torrents coming in
tumultuous foaming journeys down from the moraines;
through autumn gardens aflame with leaf and with flowers smoking and fragrant under recent frosts; and along
rocky flanks where stone, spilled in millions of tons, defies
everything but sheep and goat or the agile mule.

Around campfires at night, if the guides have been
well chosen, there will be many a tall tale. There may be a
Dave Lewis story of a cougar, skulking, cowardly, and
waiting for a deer, that was so frightened by the sudden
screech of a horned owl that it slipped in flight and fell
a thousand feet down a precipice to break its neck. There
may be a story of how Dave grunted with scorn at the
statement that he was a brave man because he climbed

trees and shoved mountain lions off a limb to the fury of
his dogs. It may be a Sam Cupp story of an old-timer who
once homesteaded one of these precipitous slopes and fell
off his ranch so many times that he gave up in disgust
and returned to Alaska. Or it may be the story of a
Missourian who boasted of his coon dog:

"I remember it was along about 1855 and I set that
dog on a coon track. Well, he tracked him for two or
three miles through the woods until he came to a piece
of ground that had just been plowed and he lost the scent
because the coon went over that-there ground before the
plowing. Well, the farmer raised a good crop that year.
I waited and when he plowed the ground again, what do
you think happened? Why, he turned that coon track up
and that old dog, he just picked up the scent and caught
that coon in no time. And that was the biggest coon I
ever saw...."

Around campfires, too, there will be much that any
man, once he has known it, will wish to return to, or
that any man, never having known it before, will take
to his heart. There will be the smell of pine and cedar
boughs on a friendly fire, fragrance of bacon in a hot
skillet, and of coffee steaming. There will be the smell of
old cones and leaf depths, aspen hillsides, mahogany
reaches, and landslides of stone. Persons who pack into
this area know the smell of bear or rockchuck, of elk beds
or beaver slides, goat and golden eagle. They know the
feel of bridle rein and of gun and saddle horn, the sound
of cascades, the flavor of mountain trout; the smell of
wide clean landscapes, the smell of health. They sleep on
the earth and breathe of it and walk on it all day, remembering the hard pavements of city streets. They
breathe the fragrance of blue sky, and of winds that
travel down over evergreen valleys from the fields of snow.

Persons who pack into this jungle of mountains and
streams nearly always get their big game: a bighorn if
they want one, a mountain goat—and a deer and an elk
with no trouble at all. But the intangible possessions are

for many of greater importance than those. They learn that joy can be deep, a man's appetite ravenous; they discover how sweet a crust of bread can be at the end of a day's hard journey; and they discover the depth of untroubled sleep. Instead of a ragged and anguished weariness of heart, they know the tiredness of muscles hungry for nourishment, the deliciousness of food flooding the mouth. With wolfish appetites, they search the camp for signs of food and wonder if there is food enough. Far from a beauty-rest mattress, they fall to earth on a blanket or on no blanket at all, and sink into dreamless sleep.

And after the pack string returns to headquarters, with the mules staggering under their burden of wild flesh, the return by air is usually made under the clear candor of sunlight. The landing fields in the Area are short and a little hazardous, and cautious pilots demand an untroubled ceiling and far vision. The more adventurous, of both pilot and hunter, prefer to return by moonlight; because at nighttime this almost infinite wilderness wears a different beauty. It is an especially dramatic experience to climb out of the canyon of the Middle Fork after dark, with the plane going round and round its orbit and wheeling like a great bird from shadow to moonlight, with the plane climbing more than a mile before it can clear the lowest peaks and look out over the terrain homeward. The daylight journey is one of broad plateaus of distance; the journey under the lazy melon of a moon is one of incalculable sorcery, with everything below softly and indescribably unreal.

Canyons now are only deep dark valleys of shadow; mountainsides are pale golden fairylands; and peaks are obscurely solitary with the glory of night. Lakes flash like mirrors and fall backward into gloom, and rivers and creeks appear and vanish like highways of gleaming silver. Forest lookouts are utterly lost in their high and remote desolation. A village or a mine, a ranch or a landing field, is only a momentary wonder upon the rolling carpet of distance. Westward the Seven Devils Peaks are less real than the sky above them; and in the southeast the bluish monuments of the Sawtooth Range look as if they reach halfway to the moon. And upon the ragged horizon clear around the compass, stars are tangled in tree tops, and clouds are banked like blue cotton upon the peaks.

IV

BURIED TREASURES

BURIED TREASURES[1]

ALL WESTERN States have buried treasures, some beyond all question actual, some legendary, with the two often indistinguishable in folklore. A few of many have been chosen from Idaho for summary here. All of them have been searched for by many persons and for many years, and in all cases there is good reason to believe that they really exist, even though tradition may have exaggerated their sums. Obviously no attempt can be made to localize them, even if all the maps, both fabulous and real, were available: it is intended only to suggest by a few instances the nature of the treasure-hunting industry of the State; for hundreds of persons have spent thousands of dollars and a good part of their lives in attempts to find buried loot. In some cases (not included here) the loot has been found.

Off U S 191 (Tour 1). In former years the Jackson Hole area of Wyoming was a favorite hide-out for rascals of all breeds, and four of these men once engineered a robbery that netted them $150,000. When a posse pursued, two of the robbers were killed, a third was wounded, but the leader escaped with the plunder and fled to unfrequented mountain trails. Near Rea upon Snake River in Fremont County the wounded man died and was buried, and the leader hid most of the loot near the grave. In Montana

---

[1] This essay is indebted chiefly to J. A. Harrington, who probably knows more than any other man about the hidden treasures of the State.

he was captured and wounded and thereupon gave directions to the hidden money. The chief factors in this story for gold seekers are an old trail, a ford on the river, and a grave; but the area is a large one and though many persons from time to time have searched here, none of the loot has been found.

Such escapades as this one inspired a man living in Teton Basin in the days when horse-drawn coaches took visitors to and from Yellowstone Park. With a handkerchief over his face and a sawed-off shotgun in his grasp, he waylaid coaches again and again until he had considerable quantities of money and jewels. Some while later a part of the stolen jewelry was found in his home in the Basin, but he had buried the money and it has never been found. The circumstances are hardly definite enough to impel gold seekers to action, but the next case, much better known, is more promising.

Off U S 91 (Tour 1 b). This pilfering occurred at what is known as Robbers Roost, three and a half miles north of McCammon. It was in 1865 that the southbound stage was halted and $100,000 was taken after four passengers had been killed and the driver wounded. The robbers fled, but it has always been argued that the amount of gold was too heavy for quick flight by horse and that in consequence a large part of it must have been buried near the scene of the crime. One of the thieves, a man named Updyke, was tracked down by vigilantes the next year and hanged to a tree in Alturas County. The exact site of this robbery is definite. The question is whether the men buried a part of the loot or took all of it with them.

A man (disguised here as Red) had respectable parents and an evil temper and joined the army only to desert and cast his misfortunes with a notorious band of outlaws. After two of them were killed, Red discovered that a reward was placed on the head of any member of the gang, and so cunningly shot his partner and started to flee. He had one pack horse loaded with gold, and the weary nag refused at the mouth of Camas Creek in Jefferson County to travel farther. Red shot the beast and with a small sum of gold went his way and eventually reached his childhood home, where necessity and not wish forced him into an honest life. Years later, when an Idahoan visited the town, Red told him he knew where a huge store of gold was hidden and offered to return to Idaho and find it; but at the last moment he weakened and refused to budge. He did, however, tell the story of his life and give directions to the cache; and died a few days later, appropriately penitent and destitute. This buried treasure is estimated at $150,000; and though the area of its concealment is known, there are no definite clues to the spot itself.

Glowing tales of gold in Idaho in 1863 brought a tenderfoot out of Montana and led him to the lower canyon north of Spencer, where he met a man who was freighting by pack horses into the mines. This freighter was in a hurry and in consequence engaged the young man to take the pack train to Virginia City in Montana. But the young man got lost and wandered for several days; and one morning, while hunting for his horses, he stumbled upon a rich ledge of gold and gathered samples and proceeded on his way. Upon reaching his destination, he displayed the ore, and great excitement prevailed among men who were not easily excited. The tenderfoot, however, was unable to retrace his journey to the ledge, and it doubtless awaits rediscovery.

Near the present town of Camas in Jefferson County the old stage road crossed Camas Creek. Upon a time the stage, carrying a large amount of gold, was held up near the old Camas station, and the robbers turned south with their loot and buried it on the east side of the creek near a small lake. A little later they were surprised and a running fight ensued. Later, one of the scoundrels committed a crime for which he was sentenced to a penitentiary in the East; but before his death he drew a map for a fellow prisoner to show where the gold was hidden.

During the year of 1909 and for several years thereafter this man appeared with teams and scrapers and a crew and excavated here, declaring that he was building an irrigation canal. After he became discouraged a crystal-gazer came and stared into a glass ball and instructed the men as they drove their teams. After plowing up half the countryside here, the former jailbird gathered up his maps and vanished; and the treasure remains.

One day a stage carrying gold approached a rock (since known as Hold Up Rock) in Beaver Canyon a short distance above Spencer in Clark County. Four heads appeared, two on either side of the rock, and shots were exchanged; but the robbers got possession of the gold and were almost at once hotly pursued. Two of them were wounded and captured and hanged to a tree. The other two hid the gold just east of the railroad Y in Beaver Canyon near the old town of Beaver, and fled. Captured later, they described where the loot was hidden, but the officers were unable to find it; and while they were deciding to force the robbers to guide them, the vigilantes swung into action and hanged these two members of the notorious Plummer Gang to the beam of a log cabin.

Off U S 30 (Tour 3 b). Six miles above Boise on the south side of the Boise River there was formerly a section covered with brush and willows that was a favorite early hide-out for plunderers. Near this spot the east-bound stage from Boise was once stopped by a lone robber; and though he got possession of the strongbox containing $50,000 in gold, he was wounded by a passenger and only with difficulty dragged the box after him into the shrubbery as he fled. On the next day a posse from Boise found him dead in the willows not far from the scene of the robbery but they were not able to find the box. It has been supposed that the man buried the loot before he died.

Near Oakley occurred a robbery that has since become well known. Upon the narrows at the head of Raft River another lone bandit robbed the stage and escaped, though an alarm was later sounded in Strevell and a posse started in pursuit. They tracked the robber to the City of Rocks, and he was there captured and sentenced to jail; and though officials of the insurance company which protected this route often visited him in jail, he persistently refused to tell where he had hidden the gold. A cattle thief later occupied a cell with this robber, and after an inquisition by officials the latter confided in the former, declaring that upon his release he would return and recover the plunder. But the robber was stricken with consumption and died. Though he never divulged the spot, it has been assumed that the gold, estimated at $150,000, must have been hidden in the rocks of the city; and many persons have explored here and some still explore.

Off State 27 (Tour 4). Well known in and around Blackfoot was a freighter called Blackie who was a good judge of whiskey and liked a stiff game of poker. His associates, wanting in foolhardiness themselves, persuaded him to rob the stage on its way to Blackfoot from the Salmon River mines. After watching the loading of the gold, the confederates sent word to Blackie, and after fortifying himself with several drinks and taking with him a bottle from which to sip courage, he took up his vigil west of the town and waited. Unable after the robbery to make off with the heavy box, he buried it among the lavas near the road and returned to Blackfoot; and on the next day he and his more timid pals got as drunk as lords and rode out to get their loot. They were met by officers and a barrage of gunshot and fled into darkness; and on the next day Blackie was found dying. He told as well as he could where the $40,000 in gold was hidden, but it still remains in the lava fields.

In early days before machinery was brought into Custer and Lemhi counties, the rich gold ore was freighted from the mines by pack train. Across the arid region between Blackfoot and Arco a freighter was proceeding with a six-horse load of rich ore when he decided to upset one of the wagons and hide the wealth for his own use in a small cave near by. In Blackfoot he reported that his horses had run away and scattered the ore over the desert, but the owner of the outfit, after following the wagon tracks, became suspicious and had the driver arrested. He was acquitted. But he was also closely watched, and after several unsuccessful attempts to return unseen to his cache, he apparently gave it up and later died while working in the mines of northern Idaho. The ore which he hid is said to have been worth $2,000 a sack.

In the late seventies gold bars were regularly shipped from the Custer Mine in Custer County. One of these shipments was stopped by a lone highwayman on Root Hog Divide a few miles east of the Big Butte stage station in Butte County. He was tracked northward up Little Lost River but was not overtaken, though later he was surprised in a gambling den in Salmon City. He admitted that he had five thousand dollars of the loot on his body and happily agreed to lead officers to the remainder, which he had buried in the lava beds near the spot where it was taken. Upon arriving at the scene, he cunningly maneuvered until dark, pretending that he was seeking his landmarks; and then put spurs to his horse and rode out of sight and was never again seen here. Thirty years later a young man came from New Mexico with a map on which was marked a cave near the old stage road by the Root Hog Divide. The stranger declared that the map was made and given to him by the robber who was afraid to return; but the New Mexican went back home without the gold.

Off State 28 (Tour 5 a). On the Birch Creek watershed of the low range west of the junction between State 28 and State 29, in the extreme southwestern corner of Clark County, is a rich ledge of silver ore which assays from eight hunded to twelve hundred ounces per ton. In 1888 William Tyler and Sam Goddard were on a bear hunt. When they came upon silver quartz here they forgot about bears and remembered the lost Texas Jack Mine which had been found in 1885. Texas Jack had died in

Salmon City but he had drawn a map of his lost mine and was very explicit in his directions. The Richard Ranch was ten miles southeast, Rattlesnake Point was fourteen miles northeast, and a high peak east of Nicholia was twenty-five miles north. Among Texas Jack's effects after his death was ore that assayed one thousand ounces of silver to the ton. But Goddard and Tyler, also finding their samples rich, proceeded to harvest their crops and upon returning the following year discovered their mine to be as lost as Texas Jack's.

In the summer of 1890 an elderly man applied at the Lidy Hot Springs for a job and devoted his spare time later to the rolling foothills north. After several months he announced that he was unable to find an old pine tree that used to be near the springs and asked old-timers if it had been cut down; and said further that when he was a guard in a penitentiary he had been given by one of the prisoners a map which exposed the location of a buried fortune in gold. The map showed a dry gulch north of the springs, with a pine tree near; but trees had been scarce and had all been felled, and the fifty thousand in gold buried at the foot of one of them may still be there.

During the gold rush south of Gilmore in Lemhi County a small smelter was erected and a town established under the name of Hahn. While mining lime rock to be used in the smelter, one of the workmen uncovered several bars of gold and quickly recovered them, intending to return later undetected. But winter set in and deep snow covered the mountain; and in the next spring the smelter ceased operations and the workmen moved away. The man attempted to find his gold and failed and thereafter searched for it annually. Its site is north of the spring on the old Davis ranch.

Two highwaymen named Sy Skinner and Bob Zachery were hanged by vigilantes at Hell Gate in 1864. Among other robberies, they were charged with that of the stage west of Birch Creek in Lemhi County. Of the four robbers, two were slain at the scene, and their graves are still to be seen near Horse Thief Trail, which goes north-ward into Montana. The other two, fancying they would draw a lighter sentence, told the vigilantes where they had hidden the gold, declaring that the spot was near the old pack trail skirting Spring Mountain on the gravel bar at the mouth of the longest dry gulch running eastward. The spot was marked by a circle of round water-sculptured boulders. But treasure seekers have found more than one gravel bar, each with its round boulders, and have spent a good part of their time sitting in doleful meditation, wondering which is the right one.

Off State 22 (Tours 4 and 1). On the northern edge of the Craters of the Moon and a half mile east of State 22, a large black volcanic rock stands some fifteen feet above the surrounding flow. Looked at from the right direction, the rock shows as the profile of an Indian chief adorned with headdress. In the late seventies the immigrant road known as Tim Goodale's Cutoff passed near this rock, and stolen gold was hidden in a cave of which the Indian head is the chief landmark. The directions given to officers by members of the gang follow: on the twenty-first day of June, mark the spot where the rising sun casts a shadow from the Indian head to a mound of lava westward. Using this line as a base, proceed directly from the head south-ward one half the distance between the first two spots and here a cave will be found which outlaws used as head-quarters and in which they hid their gold. Instructions so explicit ought to invite any gold seeker to be at Indian Head annually on the twenty-first of June.

In Kelley Canyon just above Heise Hot Springs $50,-000 in gold dust is buried. It was on a cold evening in September that Jim Kelley was overtaken by a posse and hanged near the bank of the river for his indiscreet part in a robbery near Mud Lake the previous evening. The bandit who fled with the box got out of Idaho by way of Bear Lake and had a look at several Eastern States before returning. But upon his return he was unable to find the gold and, feeling illness, went to Spokane for attention.

During the ensuing winter he realized that he was dying and thereupon gave to his landlady a map of the canyon with the loot indicated, and this excited woman thereafter annually pitched her tent in the gulch and gave her summer to study of the map and vain attempts to find the wealth. As with so many others, it seems unreasonable to doubt that the buried gold is still there.

Off U S 93 (Tour 5). During the placer days of the Boise Basin, there were two robbers who had preyed busily on miners and had resolved to get out of the country. They had reached a point on the road known as the Cottonwoods on Big Wood River in Lincoln County near the Shoshone Ice Caves when they were overtaken by a posse that shot their horses from under them. The robbers took to the lava fields. At some distance eastward they erected a barricade but were surrounded and shot, and it is supposed that their loot, estimated at $75,000, must have been buried not far from the spot where their horses fell.

A prospector with the unfortunate name of Swim found gold quartz on the south side of Salmon River near Robinson Bar and the mouth of Yankee Fork where a storm had unearthed a huge tree. Beneath the roots was exposed a ledge of honeycombed quartz that assayed $18,000 to the ton; and the claim was staked and recorded at Challis. Having no money to prosecute his claim, Swim allowed winter to overtake him, and by the time the deep snow had melted in the following spring his story had traveled far and he was followed by enough gold seekers to fill a town. When the party reached Stanley Basin in June, a parley was held, and Swim declared to the multitude that he preferred to go alone and stake some claims for his financial backers. There was vigorous protest. Swim thereupon said he would not proceed except alone, and the gold hunters yielded and he went down the Salmon River. When, after several days, he did not return, the others followed him and discovered that his horse had entered the river but had not emerged, and later its bones were found in a log jam. Swim's ledge of rich ore is still unclaimed.

When placer mines were profitable in the area of Idaho City, robbers were almost as numerous as woodpeckers, and three of them raided the stage as it swung around a bend near the confluence of Grimes and Moore Creeks. They took $90,000 in gold dust and fled, but the messenger had left and doubled back by way of the next canyon east and surprised the rascals by shooting them off their horses. But they had hidden the strong box, and it remains hidden.

Around Boise. In early winter another stage was speeding northward from Silver City when a lone highwayman asked for the express box. The remainder of the story is less credible. It declares that as soon as the stage had vanished the robber brought forth his horse, attached a rope to the strongbox, and dragged it across the prairie after him as if he had roped a calf. Tiring of so heavy a cargo, he shot the lock off the box and disappeared with its contents into Kuna Cave. Meanwhile, a number of men had started chase and surprised him as he entered the cave and then established a vigil at its entrance; but during the night he escaped. It is supposed that he buried most of the gold after taking it from the box.

Dave Levy was a prosperous and secretive man who had a drinking place in Boise. One time when a new sidewalk was being laid around his dwelling, he astonished the workmen by asking them to raise a part of the walk and thereupon lifting out a pot of gold. From this and from the circumstance of his riding often in Rocky Canyon north of Boise came the legend that he had buried most of his wealth; and when, following his murder in 1902, the administrator of his estate was unable to find the money which Levy had been known to possess, it was suspected that most of it had been hidden in the canyon. Since then many persons have spent their Sundays exploring there, and even today a favorite pastime with some is a day spent in Rocky Canyon searching for Levy's gold.

Off U S 95 (Tour 7 b.) During the period of heavy production of gold from the mines in and near Florence, pack outfits carried the mineral to shipping points. Doc Noble was paid a dollar an ounce to guard and transport gold to Lewiston. When one of his trains was attacked and the beasts stampeded, a running fight ensued, the horses were frightened beyond control, the guards were momentarily overwhelmed, and the highwaymen got their hands on $75,000, which they hid in the rocks near the trail. The scene of this robbery was on the east side of the old pack trail along the Salmon River south of White Bird. After concealing the gold, the bandits headed for the rough Seven Devils area, but all of them were eventually overtaken and slain before returning to find their cache. There can be little doubt that this fortune still remains among the rocks in the canyon.

Among mines that have been most persistently hunted is the Lost Cleveland on the Middle Fork of Salmon River. A man named Cleveland followed a rich float up the mountainside a half century ago and uncovered a ledge of very rich ore. He gathered all that he could carry and sold it to the mint in San Francisco and then returned to his home in Missouri to reflect on his good fortune and to visit his relatives. The next year and thereafter he was unable to find his ledge of gold and he died while still searching and today his body lies near the Yellowjacket Mine in Lemhi County. The Lost Cleveland Mine has lured many prospectors into the wilderness of the Primitive Area but has never been found.

V

GHOST TOWNS

GHOST TOWNS

MUCH OF Idaho for the sensitive person is lonely today with memory of the vigorous and turbulent life of towns and cities where there is now only desolation and a handful of ruins. Where once there were thousands of persons there may now be only a few shacks, or there may be nothing but a stone or a tree and the indefinable loneliness of something that is dead. For Idaho in one perspective is an area of ghost towns or of spots where not even the ghost remains. In mountain basin or on hillside or in valleys of sunlight and sage there were towns, more than half a century ago, that leapt into being in a night or a week and sometimes ran their destiny within a year. Nor in this State was their number few. There were dozens of them, and today they are housed in a dilapidated and aging handful of what they used to be, or their former existence is commemorated by a weedy cemetery and a ruined wall, or they are as dead and gone and as forgotten as the men and women who made them. Some of them, of course, took on a more extravagant importance and not only grew to considerable size but were the metropolises of large areas. Others, less spectacular, came into being so quickly and precariously that a wind could have blown them down; and vanished almost without leaving a sign.

There is what once was Springtown just west of the present Hansen Bridge. In the eighth decade of the last century it sprang into existence on the rim of the Snake

River Gorge. Today there are only the ruins of some
mud huts in which Chinese miners are said to have lived
while they feverishly panned gold. There was Bullion a
few miles west of the present town of Hailey: it had two
general stores, a post office, a hospital, many dwelling
houses, and nobody knows how many saloons. Today
nothing remains. Or Oro Grande, situated on the west
side of Loon Creek, had as many as five stores and a
saloon for every store. The gold here was exhausted in
about a year, the gulch was abandoned and sold to the
Chinese who trailed the more enterprising hordes and
reworked what they left; and now the site of this town
is indistinguishable from the country which surrounds
it. Vienna at the base of the Sawtooth Range had almost
a thousand persons in it and was the largest of the mining
towns in this region. The last resident left it in 1892.
One of its competitors, Sawtooth City, flourished for
many years, but when, in 1897, the postmaster resigned
there was an exodus, with only five persons remaining in
possession of everything in sight. These weathered one
more season and then left Sawtooth City to loneliness and
the snow. Up north in the Panhandle, Eagle City was
once the capital of the Coeur d'Alenes and so thriving and
ambitious a place that extensive improvements were
made, and town lots, inviting newcomers, lay almost the
length of a mile. Today Eagle City is not even shown on
a map. And there were Galena and Kingston, Florence
and Gem—or Moose City which once had nine thousand
persons. Today it can be reached only by horseback in
a journey of three days over the Bitterroot Divide, and
where once was a city of nine thousand, only one decaying
log cabin stands now.

But not all of these cities of a half century ago per-
ished so completely as these. Many of them are still on
the maps and have a handful of survivors living in memory among the ruins. There is Leesburg a few miles west
of Salmon City: first settled by immigrants from the
Southern States and named for General Robert E. Lee, it

The old hotel at Florence

Grave of an old-timer

was once a city of several thousands, had a main street a mile long, and even a Chinatown. Now, with twenty-five inhabitants, it is only a lapful of wretched shacks and haunted streets. Leesburg still appears on highway maps, but Nicholia, in the same area, has suffered greater indignities and has only a half-dozen buildings smelling of age and ruin, and a population of fewer than ten. More impressive in its history, if not in its present appearance, than either of these two is Mount Idaho, the first town built on the Camas Prairie. In 1876 it was not only the county seat of Idaho County; it enjoyed such prestige that the first Republican convention in Idaho Territory was held here, and the city dreamed obscurely of becoming the capital of an empire. In 1922 its post office was discontinued because no one among the few persons remaining could be induced to apply for the job. Comparable in its former glory and in its present stubborn yielding to decay and silence is Pierce City, which blossomed out of a gold stampede as early as 1861. It was a county seat, too, and had a Chinese population of nearly a thousand and a joss house which rivaled the courthouse in splendor. The courthouse was sold some while ago for fifty dollars, to the astonishment of the residents of Pierce City, who could not understand how this once famous building could be worth fifty cents. This historic building, the first of its kind in Idaho, was turned by its purchaser into a private residence.

All of these many ghost towns have had a colorful and dramatic past, and it is of interest to look more sharply into the history of a few of them. Silver City is today the most picturesque of the lot of them and the patriarch of the ghosts. Set high in the Owyhee Mountains of southwestern Idaho, its history began in 1863 with the discovery of gold in Jordan Creek upon the headwaters of which it stands. A few miles down the creek from it was Ruby City, a town of eight hundred persons and the county seat of Owyhee County, and the two entered at once, in the way of frontier towns, into bitter competition, and it was clear from the start that one of the two would destroy the other. Because of its proximity to spectacular mines and because of its geographical protection from the high and violent winds, Silver City triumphed, drew Ruby City's population to its breast, and became the county seat. It so completely annihilated its rival that the exact spot of Ruby City is not today known, though it has in an unfenced cemetery on the northern side of Silver City its memorial and the sleeping place of many of its dead.

The discovery of gold and silver in this area was more than ordinarily spectacular. Ore from the Poorman Mine assayed between four and five thousand dollars to the ton, and a mass of solid ruby-silver crystals weighing a quarter of a ton was discovered at a depth of a hundred feet. Some of these crystals won a gold medal at the Paris Exposition of 1866, and Silver City in no while at all became internationally famous. The city reached its peak a half century ago: it had a newspaper then; a Catholic Church was dedicated to "Our Lady of Tears"; a barber shop was advertising baths as a specialty ("Call and be convinced") with a photograph of an actual bathtub in the advertisement, and it had barrooms with impressive mirrors and polished interiors. Silver City needed only a fire engine to make it the undisputed rival of Boise. And because another of its competitors, the thriving town of Fairview on War Eagle Mountain, was without such a gadget, everything in it except its cemetery burned to the ground in 1875, and Silver City absorbed its population.

And in other respects, too, Silver City became famous clear to the parlors of Boston. Almost in Silver City's dooryard two mining companies recruited thugs and engaged in desperate warfare; and it was in front of its chief hotel that one of the feudists was shot to death. The hotels themselves were more than usually interesting, even in a country where a hotel might be anything from the haymow of a livery stable to an enterprising den of harlots. The Idaho Hotel was the more magnificent of the two, but like the War Eagle, it was a crazy aggregate of buildings, varying in height from one to three stories, and put together, at least in the case of the second, around a small cabin that had been built by an early pioneer. The War Eagle, haunted by the ghost of a young girl who had died there, was deserted many years later, and in 1917 it gave up its precarious and despairing existence and collapsed. This city, similarly with so many others, boomed and receded like the tides; suffered periodic depressions or glories; and took its way steadily toward desertion and ghosts. But as late as 1898, long after its chief triumphs had expired, it had six general stores, two hardware stores, a tin shop, two meat markets, two hotels, four restaurants, a photographer's gallery, a brewery and a bottling plant, a jeweler, a newspaper, two lumberyards, a tailor shop and three barber shops, four lawyers, two doctors, and eight saloons. Since then many of its buildings have been torn down, though it still has an Episcopal Church looking down from a rocky eminence, a Masonic Hall spanning Jordan Creek, a deserted county courthouse and several deserted saloons, and a hotel. It suffered its most crushing blow in 1935 when the county seat was moved to Murphy. Today it lives hopefully from year to year, scanning the horizon, meditating on its dead glories, and watching its buildings sag and fall. It would be impossible to convince the fifty people now living where several thousands used to be that Silver City will not someday make the grass grow in the streets of Boise.

Dewey, only five miles away, was earlier called Booneville and came into splendor of its own only after a wealthy man took a fancy to it and tried to build it into a monument to himself. It was in 1896 that Colonel W. H. Dewey bought a mining property and with it the deserted town of Booneville. He spent lavishly and was not content until he had made Booneville one of the most attractive towns in the State and had renamed it after himself. His Dewey Hotel, with its cupola and double portico, was for a considerable while the pride of Owyhee County; pictures of the hotel and of its caretaker's house appeared on postcards, cream pitchers, china cups, and souvenir spoons. This hotel was steam heated, electrically lighted, and given every advantage of sanitation that the Colonel had ever heard of. Whereupon, still ambitious and still endowed with funds, he built stores, a steam laundry, a barber shop, an elaborate house for his superintendent of mines, a water system with fire plugs that were declared to secure for the town an "almost perfect immunity from fire," and a livery stable more impressively prosperous than most hotels of the period. But for all the town's immunity, the Colonel's gaudy hotel burned to the ground, though the superintendent's house, with its elaborately carved gables and its porch railings, "white-crusted and as untouchable as a wedding-cake," stood for many years. When its steps rotted away and its railings sagged, an enterprising person in Silver City removed the bannister and stairway to a house there. And today, of all Colonel Dewey's costly memorials to himself, only a few deserted buildings remain and not a single permanent resident. A few sheepherders get their mail here during the summer months.

Dewey is five miles from Silver City, De Lamar is nine, and their history in some respects has been much alike. The latter was once called Wagontown because it was only a stopping place on a stage line; but when Captain De Lamar bought the Wilson Mine and adjacent claims in 1888, he built a hotel and even a schoolhouse and changed the name of the place to honor its benefactor. In 1891 he sold his interests to an English company, and there was an influx of Cornish miners, "a small, dark, energetic people, quick of speech and lively of wit" who "marked the little town with the peculiar pungency of saffron cakes, seedy bun and black tea." By 1898 there were a hundred and fifty pupils in the red brick schoolhouse. There was a spicy and entertaining newspaper called the De Lamar *Nugget*. Today the town is deserted,

though down the long winding main street many of the
buildings still stand, smelling of emptiness and death. In
the second-story parlor of the hotel, the piano strings have
been taken by rust; and upon the window ledges of the
assay office there are dusty bottles and the smell of acid.
The footprints upon the streets now are those of the
rabbit and the coyote.

Such are three of the ghost towns in that picturesque
and relatively unexplored region known as Owyhee County. With an area greater than that of Connecticut and
two Rhode Islands put together, it has a population of a
few more than four thousand and no town in it appreciably
larger than the ghost towns themselves. Not very different from it is the Boise Basin, still another part of
Idaho where many a thriving city is now almost less than
a wraith of its former self. Pioneerville, New and Old
Centerville, Placerville, and Idaho City are a few of these,
with the last two pre-eminent over all others in the lusti-
ness of their past and the landmarks of their present
existence. More than any of the others, they were rich in
murders and hangings, feuds and melodramatic deaths,
cemeteries and saloons.

Placerville is a miracle of persistence because it has
survived not only desertion but also several destructive
fires. As late as 1931 a great forest fire came in a deluge of
smoke and flame across this part of the State, consumed
Quartzburg and many mines close by, and fell in a roaring
yellow flood to the edge of Placerville and almost made
this town curl up like a sheet of paper on a hot lid. It
burned the trees in the cemetery and poured huge burning cinders upon the post office and hotel and made the
whole place look as if it had been drawn half cooked out
of a gigantic oven. But Placerville has always clung dog-
gedly to its life. The town was built around a square
which, strangely enough, was called the Plaza, and its
chief saloon, the building of which still stands, went
under the fragrant name of Magnolia. In front of it is
the old well, still with rope and bucket, that was so im-

portant a part in tragedies of early days: it was here that a man, stopping his mule train while he drank from the well, was accosted by a villainous gambler who wished to amuse his friends who sat on the Magnolia's porch. He first threw a bucket of water into the wanderer's face; and then, while the astonished man was half choked and sputtering and reaching uncertainly for his gun, he shot him dead. The murderer was acquitted, of course, on self-defense, inasmuch as in those days it was less trouble to acquit a man than to cart him off many miles to a jail.

Not far from this town occurred a slaying that is today known as the murder of the fiddlers of Ophir Creek. These musicians, called fiddlers in those days, were on their way to Centerville when they were shot in their backs by nomadic thugs and robbed. The bodies were found at Ophir Creek with the fiddles at their sides and were buried, two by lodges and one by the county, in the Placerville cemetery. Their graves are now marked by four pine trees, with one in each corner of the lot. But these were dark and dangerous times. Gold dust was legal tender, and a glass of whiskey was worth a pinch of it, though a cat, in early days, was worth a whole jug. An epidemic of mice sent a thoughtful man on a journey, and when he returned he brought a whole wagonload of cats and sold them for ten dollars apiece. Before 1864 mail was brought into the town by horseback at a price of fifty cents or a dollar for a newspaper or a letter, depending perhaps on the number of thugs patrolling the highway. In this year Placerville got a post office, a school, and three stage lines. By 1870 the placers were exhausted and the boom was over. Today the Magnolia still fronts the Plaza, which rests in peace under its weeds and tin cans.

But of all the ghost towns, perhaps Idaho City has had the most dramatic and interesting history. It has run through the cycles of triumph and defeat, with its population flowing in or out by thousands, with its destiny

moving uncertainly from year to year. At the zenith of
its power it is said to have been a city almost as large as
Boise today. It was, beyond all dispute, the metropolis
of a huge area and one of the centers of activity and
growth of the entire Northwest. Now it has only two
hundred persons; and if it still clings to the odds and
ends of a former glory, it does so chiefly because it is the
seat of Boise County and a spot of unusual interest less
than an hour's drive from Boise itself. The turbulence of
its former life, the violence of its ways, is to be inferred
from the statement of old-timers that only twenty-eight
of the two hundred persons buried in its cemetery in
1863 died natural deaths.

Its jail was the first in the large territory once called
Idaho, and this jail, used until 1870, was the scene of
some stirring episodes. It had two sturdy rows of cells
and a doughty stockade that enclosed a whole acre of
land, but long ago it fell under decay and erosion and disappeared. During its life, it and the cemetery were an
inseparable picture because not only were the rascals
hanged within the stockade and buried there but the
vigilantes commonly met in the graveyard to plot the
death of scoundrels who still lived. There was Ferd Patterson, for instance: gambler, gunman, and murderer, he
killed the captain of a boat in Portland, scalped his ex-
mistress, and climaxed his playfulness by slaying the
sheriff of Idaho City. Ferd was, records declare, a pulp
villain of the first water: he affected high-heeled boots,
plaid trousers reinforced with buckskin, a fancy silk vest
spanned by a heavy gold chain of California nuggets,
and a frock coat of beaver cloth trimmed with otter. But
the sheriff whom he killed is described by an early historian as one of "nature's noblemen," and not fewer than
a thousand men awaited Mr. Patterson's return with a
deputy who sailed out to capture him. The mob was bent
on lynching, but the deputy outwitted them and got his
prisoner safely into the jail; whereupon the vigilantes
met in the graveyard, went to Boise and got a cannon,

and resolved to attack. But the deputy, a man who apparently was remarkably nimble of wit, got a cannon also, cut portholes in the jail wall, manned his fortress with a bunch of desperadoes, and waited. And he won. It is not recorded that he almost died of chagrin when Patterson went to trial and was freed.

This episode is typical and it is only one of many. After a shyster named St. Clair was hanged within the stockade, the rope was to be seen for many years in a lunchroom with this legend under it: *This is the rope that hung St. Clair.* The Chinese here, of whom there were several hundred, also helped to keep monotony out of this town. Their Fan-tan Hall was a noted gambling resort, and every evening at sunset a lantern was hung in front of its door and an attendant bellowed in Chinese that the game was open. After the placers were worked out, most of the Chinese left, but a few remained, living alone and dying off, one by one.

And today Idaho City is as picturesque and interesting a spot as can be found in the State. Like Placerville it has suffered the outrage of many fires, and most of its historic buildings have, in consequence, been lost. It has been disfigured by dredging and decay, but its little white Catholic Church still stands on a hill, and its streets are still vivid with memory of a time when Idaho City was as melodramatic a spot as ever came out of frontier life.

A considerable distance north of Idaho City and just west of the Middle Fork of the Salmon River is the Thunder Mountain district, one of Idaho's most inaccessible and remarkable areas. In early mining days this region had two unusual towns, Roosevelt and Thunder City, with a population together of nearly five thousand. Roosevelt itself had many substantial buildings, including a post office and laundry, and every saloon had a piano in spite of the circumstance that everything had to be freighted in on muleback. The boom in this region was as short-lived as it was sensational, though Roosevelt years later sprang again into dramatic relief. At a time when a former governor of Kansas was fleeing from the wrath of his State, with William Allen White hot on his trail, he was caught and killed with a companion known as Hot-foot. Roosevelt, White declared, was "a log town with one street and no society," and soon thereafter it was not that much. A capricious mountain delivered upon it all in one blow a landslide and a flood and so completely buried the town that only two or three buildings remained visible. The residents escaped, but one enterprising matron of a bawdy house lost her piano and profaned mightily at the men who, in full flight with their hair standing on end, refused to come to its rescue. Today the beaver have taken possession of Roosevelt (which is a small lake) and have built their home in the attic of a house that was not wholly buried. Thunder City, too, was distinguished at one time by severe winters, fabulous riches, and the number of its saloons. Escaping sudden burial, it has vanished piece by piece off the landscape; and today the Thunder Mountain area is very quiet.

The Yankee Fork district in Custer County is almost as rich in ghost towns as it formerly was, and still may be, in minerals. There were Bay Horse and Clayton and Crystal, Custer and Bonanza, with the latter two probably the most widely known. These are only a few miles apart, and the truth of one is the truth of the other, save that Custer never afforded the luxury of a cemetery. This fact assumed considerable importance a few years ago when a miner in Custer was blown up with dynamite and had to be carried through ten feet of snow to Bonanza for his burial. Gold in this area was discovered in 1870, the city of Bonanza was laid out in 1877, and two years later it had grown so impressively that it had five lawyers and nine saloons. It had a newspaper, too, the Yankee Fork *Herald,* and a laundry whose owner advertised in this fashion:

Celestial laundry, Charlie Bumboo, Prop.
Shirts nicely starched and beautifully polished.

One of the leading gambling houses, the Classy and Hogle, is said to have had as much as thirty thousand dollars on its tables at one time.

But the only item of interest in Bonanza today is the cemetery. Of one grave, far removed from the others and fenced off within its own loneliness, the following story is told. A woman of infamous flavor was found shot to death in a dance hall, and the respectable folk of Bonanza did not want to bury her in their brand-new cemetery which they had proudly fenced; nor did they fancy the custom of Silver City which interred beyond the fence the persons whom it scorned. Bonanzans compromised by burying her off in a corner of her own and erecting a high fence around her; and there she is today, asleep under the legend:

Agnes Elizabeth King, a native of London, England
Died July 26, 1880

Bonanza and Custer have no more than fifty persons between them now. Bay Horse is even less fortunate, but it got used to adversity many years ago when the Federal Government refused to allow it the privilege of the name it had chosen and rechristened it Aetna.

And these are only a few of many.

VI
A FEW TALL TALES

A FEW TALL TALES

EVERY Western State has its tall tales, a few of which are indigenous but most of which belong to the folk-lore of the world and reappear with variations as something new under an old name. Of the few given, it is not known how ancient their ancestry may be or in how many countries and times they have been born anew; but only such fables have been chosen as seem likely not to have been trademarked by too much use. The first was told by Fay Hubbard, one of the first sheepherders in the State.

FAY HUBBARD'S DOG

Soon after the Oregon Short Line Railway was laid, Hubbard went to Omaha with sheep, and after he had squandered all his money but five dollars he decided to buy a dog and ride the blinds back to his home. But the only thing he had ever ridden was a horse and he got by mistake on the observation platform, taking his hound with him, and was accosted by an angry conductor who told him he didn't mind a hobo but he hated a pooch. Hubbard said he would tie the dog behind and let him follow the train on a leash; and did so, and at the end of the first fifty miles the dog was hardly panting. Whereupon, more annoyed than ever, the conductor yelled for more steam, swearing that he would drag the beast to death; but at eighty miles an hour the dog trotted serenely, sometimes on three legs, sometimes on two, and with a philosophic eye on his master. At Grand Island the conductor ordered more speed, and from there to North Platte the train did a hundred miles an hour and the dog never tightened the rope, though the telephone poles alongside looked like the teeth of a fine comb. Seeing with what nimble ease the hound followed, the conductor fell into a great fury and the train was whipped up to incredible speed; and though the dog now had to use four legs, he did so with grace and without perturbation, with the rope sagging like a clothesline between him and the train. At a hundred and eighty miles the conductor looked out and saw that the dog had vanished.

"And where is your gad-dinged pooch now?" he asked.

Hubbard said to look ahead, and as he did so the train came to a crashing stop with the boxcars telescoping one another like a bunch of egg crates hit with a pile driver. For the dog had broken the rope, had taken the red flag from the cowcatcher, and had run ahead to flag the engineer for a washout. And from here the dog rode to Idaho, and dogs have been free passengers on Union Pacific trains through the State ever since.

LONG TOM

Thomas Wickersham was an old-timer who as a lad was so thin that for two years he traveled with a circus as a living skeleton. After he had taken so many reducing powders that he rattled when he walked, he invested his savings in oil and went out to see his property. But he was unable to find it and after many miles he climbed to the top of a derrick the better to see and became dizzy and fell off. He came down headfirst and went headfirst into an eight-inch gas pipe and was swiftly on his way underground when it occurred to him to press out with his knees and elbows to check his descent. Nevertheless, he traveled at lightning speed through the pipe and was shot like a cannonball into a vast underground cavern of gas where, with unusual presence of mind, he knew he would soon suffocate. He wiped his eyes until vision cleared and then perceived an opening that led to a still larger chamber; and he entered and followed this tunnel and it spread to incalculable dimensions, but after several miles he came to an underground river which proved to be of kerosene. This he swam down for a mile or more before he left it to sit on the bank and have a smoke; and the match he carelessly threw into the river. The whole enormous underground region awoke and burst into a sheet of flame, the heat of which was disconcerting; and Wickersham took to his heels down the bank. He ran for a long time, noticeably distressed by the river of fire at his back, before he came to a tunnel which proved to be as round and smooth and almost as small as a gun barrel. This he entered upon hands and knees. Behind him there was a stupendous explosion which fired him out into a long parabola and set him down on the front porch of 218 San Francisco Street in Boise. There were only three Indians in Boise then and two coyotes and one of the Territory's absconding governors.

To Tan a Hide

His name was John Shipton but in the Hood River country he was known as Happy Jack. He came to Boise Basin during the gold rush, bringing with him his fiddle and its three strings upon which he could make better music than other fiddlers on a full set. One day he left his mountain retreat to hold the farmers' harvest. Most of the ranchers on Silver Creek were Missourians, and Happy Jack was an Arkansan with a quaint drawl, and both Jack and his native State were held under sarcastic summary.

"They tell me the women in Arkansas chaw terbacker and go barefoot and eat tree mice. Is that so, Jack?" "Hey, Jack, and does the men go barefoot, too?"

"I guess so," said Jack. "And we made the shoes ourselves. Hey, I remember one time back in 1840 and pap, he sent me out huntin to git a hide for to make a pair of shoes. He counted the bullets and measured out the powder and I had to fetch a hide for every bullet or I got a tannun. Well, I hunted all day and didn't see nothin to shoot at except a few squirrels. So long about sundown I reckoned I'd kill a squirrel but every time I'd go to shoot at them dad-burned things they'd hide behind a tree and I couldn't see nothin but the head and I didn't want to shoot the head for pap warned me to bring the brains of anything I killed to tan the hide with. Well, I finally got mad and shot one in the head and I just about blowed all the brains out. That made me feel pretty bad. Well, I was in for a wallopun when I happened to remember there was a settlement of Missourians over the hill just about as far as I could see and twice as far as I could holler. Well, so I decided to go down there and shoot one them-there Missourians for some brains to tan that squirrel hide with."

"Oh, the heck you did," said one of the men.

"Yes, and I did," said Jack. "But that ain't the worst of it. Say, you know I had to kill nine of them-there Missourians to get enough brains to tan that hide?"

THE DEATH OF SAM RICH

Sam Rich was brought up in Cassia County. After he got his first spurs he was riding the lava beds in southern Idaho when he saw a bunch of painted savages following him. And they were beyond all question savage. They crowded close upon him and he raced pellmell for the roughest lava fields and the arrows fell around him like confetti on New Year's Eve and he was forced to leave his horse. He jumped into a narrow rift and fled down it, and behind him came thousands of Indians whooping like mad and slicing the air with their tomahawks and biting their fingernails; and then suddenly the crevice came to an end. There was a deep waterfall in front of him, a straight wall on either side of him, and so many Indians behind him that the earth was shaking with their enthusiasm.... When Sam Rich reached this point in his story he always paused and looked forlorn and abject and nodded his head with triumphant unreason. And when the silence was broken with an anguished whisper, "My God, Sam, what did you do then?" Sam looked around him with awful woe and dropped his voice to a pouting falsetto. "They killed me," he said.

IDAHO'S BOOM

An insurance salesman, down at heel and scurvy of disposition, was sitting in unspeakable melancholy one morning, wondering how he could make a living now that no one in Boise ever died, when he had a thought. He leapt to his feet and kissed his wife, a circumstance sufficiently strange, inasmuch as no one in Boise had kissed his wife in months. He remembered that a wealthy man had come from the East to buy land, and with him he vanished into the lava domains, not stopping for blowouts (of which there were none) and running over several pedestrians, all of them from California. "Now here," said the salesman, "is the chance of your life—of a dozen lives like yours, in fact. Are you from Boston? Anyway, you're looking at the greatest unexploited stretch of land on earth—on any earth, and I don't care where your earth is. In fact, you're looking at ground that is practically worth its weight in gold—and it's heavy ground. Will you lift a hunk of it? Try that pile of basalt. Try that hill. Or don't you Easterners lift hills any more?"

"But what," asked the wealthy Easterner, "would I do with this ground? What could a man grow on land like this?" And he fell to his knees and looked with singular earnestness into the lidless gaze of a horned toad. He rose and knocked a pile of basalt from his knee. "What?" he said.

"Anything. Cocoanuts and bananas and avocados, grapes and oranges, melons and grapefruit and pecans. Or orchids. Or even wheat. The question is: what do you want to grow?"

"Well, now," said the Easterner cannily, "anything that will make money."

"Very well. Up there is a reservoir to irrigate it. There is the sun. You need only sun and water to make anything grow. And it never freezes here."

"Not here?" said the Easterner, politely amazed. "Not in this land," he said, looking around him, "which I should judge to be in Idaho?"

"Never. It never freezes and it never thaws."

"I don't understand," said the Easterner urbanely. And he sneezed. "Pardon me," he said.

"It's a secret. You see all these piles of lava? Or what," asked the salesman, "are you looking at? Now this lava absorbs the heat from the sun in the daytime and holds it all night and when it's fifty below in Boston it's like the middle of June here."

"I can't believe it," said the Easterner, and sneezed again.

"Place your hand on that rock." And the Easterner did, and it curled up like a bacon rind on a hot stove.

"It is rather warm," he said. But to make sure he sat on a stone and his flesh began to steam, and he added: "It is very comfortable here. How much do you want for this land?"

"A thousand dollars an acre—and that includes fifty boulders to the rod. A hundred boulders to the rod will cost you more."

The Easterner rose and looked around him happily for he had never seen such a bargain. He bought two hundred acres and set to work, and before he had plowed up the first acre of stone he uncovered $125,000 in gold that was buried here by Bitch Creek McDade and his gang after they had robbed the Arco stage. He averaged thereafter a buried treasure to the acre and started drilling and in the second month sank a shaft right through the center of the Lost McElmore Mine.[1] He turned up the

---

[1] See the essay on Buried Treasures.

John R. Rudd mine next, a very rich vein that had vanished in 1871 and had never again been heard of; and then took the Lost Bonanza, the Lost Gilpin McCreary, and both Lost Rivers in turn. A town, the Winnie Mae,[1] sprang up over night and within a year had a population of fifteen thousand. Lost mines were yanked to the surface all over this terrain, and buried treasures stood around as thick as bags of potatoes in a field in October. Winnie Mae is a ghost town now between Shoshone and Arco, but persons still go to the area and dig up minor treasures, though they usually do not average more than fifty thousand dollars to the pot.

WHY IDAHOANS ARE CAREFUL WITH FIRE

Sam Strickland was a member of a threshing crew when the men lit their fags and Sam gave his lecture. "Careless smoking," he said, "leads to a sad experience. I'll tell you. When I was a kid and didn't know any better, I was working in a Du Pont powder mill. I was making rifle powder and I had my pipe full of Durham but it wouldn't burn and I lit it a dozen times and it wouldn't burn and then I got me a hickory coal and laid on the pipe. That coal must have rolled off when I didn't know it because when I went to the grub house for dinner I saw a big smoke rolling up from the mill and I just about knew that mill was on fire. I finished my dinner as quick as I could and then the gang of us went over but we dallied along too much. I lost my job that time. For twelve tons of the best powder we had burnt up before we could put that fire out."

A CRACK SHOT OR TWO

Carl Buck of eastern Idaho was a crack rifleshot. He could trim the whiskers off a cat at a hundred yards or shoot between the legs of a hummingbird at fifty. One

---

[1] Named for Winnie Mae Spooner, the mistress of Deadshot McDoodle.

morning he saw a coyote out in a field and seized his gun and at just a little over half a mile blazed away. The coyote did not budge. It was strange, Carl reflected, that he had missed so easy a shot; and after approaching a hundred yards nearer he fired again. And still that coyote stood there beyond the sagebrush and looked at him. Carl examined his gun and approached another hundred yards and again fired—and again drew nearer and fired and drew nearer. When he was only fifty yards away, he sat and took a dead rest and delivered six shots—and still that beast stood without batting an eye and stared at him across the sagebrush. At this point Carl began to have a weird sense of unreality, and for perhaps an hour he wiped his brow and looked at the coyote and the coyote looked at him. He thereupon decided to approach without firing, and learned to his amazement that he had with his first shot struck the beast exactly in the center of the forehead and had put twenty-six more bullets through the same hole. The coyote's chin had caught in the fork of a sagebrush and there the villain had hung as dead as a doornail while its body from its neck clear to its tail was being shot completely away.

The On and Off Country

Much of the country in northern Idaho is so precipitous that old-time prospectors and trappers there always had to level the ground for a spot to rest their bed on. A few years ago three gentlemen from Minneapolis came out to invest in fruit lands, and were accompanied from area to area by two real-estate agents. They had not gone far when a great boulder fell at their feet, and while they were staring up at the mountains and the sky around them, a whole cargo of stones came down and spilled around them. Amazed and apprehensive, they proceeded; and a little later a tree came down and crashed into splinters across their path, followed after a moment by a pig, seven chickens, and a team of mules. They waited in horror, wondering if the sky was coming after the mules, when a man came down with an awful bang and rose in fury to his feet and shook himself. "Confound this country!" he roared. "This is the third time today that I have fallen out of my fruit ranch!"

SNAKE MEDICINE

The cowpunchers of the Salmon River country grew tired of their sowbelly and doughgods and resolved on a change of fare. With spades they dug for earthworms and filled a tobacco can, and the next morning bright and early they saddled their nags and set out to fish the Middle Fork of the Salmon. On arriving, they learned that they had forgotten their worms, and while looking around for bait one of them saw a bull snake that had partly swallowed a frog and was resting in his labors. The cowpuncher massaged the snake's throat and worked the frog upward and released it but the snake looked up at him so reproachfully that he said, "That's a devil of a way to treat a poor snake what has been out earnun his livun just like us." So he drew his flask of whiskey and opened the snake's mouth and gave the reptile about a half a finger. The snake stuck out its tongue and looked very benign in its eyes and then began to wiggle its tail and roll over as if exceedingly happy. The cowpunchers used the frog for bait; but after awhile one of them was attracted by something that tapped insistently on his boot. He looked down and there was that bull snake, gazing up at him hopefully and holding another frog in its mouth.

PAUL BUNYAN WAS HERE TOO

And of course all old-timers in Idaho remember the night when Paul Bunyan drank nine kegs of rum in Idaho Falls and started for Seattle with his blue ox. It was a black wet night full of rain, and Paul wandered stupendously in a great drunken stupor, with his crooked trail behind him filling with water. The trail since that time has been known in all geographies as Snake River.

TRUTH IS STRANGER THAN FICTION

But legends in Idaho are in many instances no taller
than the truth itself. Of authenticated but almost unbelievable stories of actual events, the following is typical
of many. William Howell and Andrew Morrison were once
accosted by Indians in early days, and when the red men
learned that the two invaders were unarmed they let off
a terrific whoop and two confederates came to the scene.
Howell wanted to run but Morrison swore that he would
never run from an Indian. They strove, in consequence,
to make peace, but one of the Indians declared that a
white man had killed an Indian on Battle Creek and they
were on the warpath to avenge the murder. The white
men offered their team but it was their scalps that the
Indians wanted. They then persuaded the Indians to go
to town with them and mounted their load and started,
but the wagon got stuck in a crossing and while Howell
and Morrison were laboring to get it out, they were attacked. Morrison was struck by an arrow. He shouted
to Howell to flee and Howell did so, escaping the flying
arrows. Morrison was struck twice, one arrow lodging
below his collar bone and the other below his heart. The
arrow below his collar bone he pulled out but the head
of the other broke off. Howell, meanwhile, sounded an
alarm and the Indians fled. A messenger went all the
way to Salt Lake City with a team of mules and the front
half of a wagon and returned with a doctor, but the doctor said the spike of the arrow was too near the man's
heart. He said Morrison could live only a few days at
most. But Morrison lived for twenty-seven years with
the spike lodged near his heart and his spine.

VII

ORIGINS OF NAMES

ORIGINS OF NAMES

MOST of the names of places and things in Idaho have been derived from Indian words, from some geologic or topographical aspect, or from animals and persons. Those have been omitted in which the derivation is obvious; all the goose and elk and sheep and bear and deer creeks, or such names of counties as Washington or Jefferson, or such names of towns as Fairfield and Cascade. The following list does not affect completeness: it includes the Rees investigations to which are here added about a hundred more.

ADA: For Ada Riggs, the first white child born in Boise.

ADDIE: For Addie Greenway, wife of an old-timer.

AGENCY CREEK: For the Lemhi Indian Agency, established in 1872.

ALBION: Named because an old-timer thought the word meant mountain lion.

ALMO: Named because of the cottonwoods there.

ALTURAS: A Spanish word meaning mountainous heights. Still the name of a lake, it was also once the name of a county.

AMERICAN FALLS: These falls on Snake River were called American for a party of trappers of the American Fur Company that ventured down in canoes and was unexpectedly pitched over the cascade.

ARCO: Rees says this town was named after a city in Austria, but another authority declares it was named for a visiting Count Arco. Possibly neither was right. The original settlers called the town Junction, but the U. S. Post Office Department decided it had too many Junctions already.

ARIMO: An Indian word (air'-i-mo) which means that the uncle bawls like a cow.

ASHTON: Named for one of its founders.

ATHOL: For an Indian chieftain.

ATLANTA: For a battle in the Civil War.

BEAR LAKE: The river under this name was first called Miller, but the Indians called it Quee-yaw-pah, meaning the stream along which the tobacco root grew. The lake was given its present name by McKenzie in 1818.

BENEWAH: Ben'-e-wah: for a chieftain of the Coeur d'Alenes.

BISUKA: Bee-soo'-ka: Indian for not a large place.

BITCH CREEK: An unhappy corruption of Biche Creek. The French word means doe.

BITTERROOT: Named for the bitterroot, the State flower of Montana. The root of this plant, though edible and formerly used for food, is extremely bitter.

BLACKFOOT: Uncertain. The Blackfeet Indians called themselves Siksika because their feet are said to have been blackened by wading in ashes.

BLISS: Named not because of the town's happiness but for one of its settlers.

BOISE: Named by French Canadians who, after a long journey through semiarid regions, exclaimed Les Bois! upon seeing trees. In pronouncing this word, Boiseans today neither anglicize the word nor retain the French. Some call it Boy'-see and some, Boy'-zee.

BONNERS FERRY: For E. L. Bonner who built a ferry on the Kootenai River here in 1864.

BONNEVILLE: For that indefatigable explorer, B. L. E. Bonneville.

BOVILL: For Hugh Bovill.

BRUNEAU: The river, canyon, and town, all in Owyhee County, were named by French Canadians. The word means brown or gloomy water.

BUFFALO HUMP: This name was given to the volcanic cone by Indians. Their word was see-nimp.

BUHL: For Frank Buhl, an early empire builder.

BURGDORF: For Fred Burgdorf who discovered the springs.

BURLEY: For an agent of the Union Pacific Railroad.

CACHE: From the French *cacher* meaning to hide.

CALDWELL: For a Senator from Kansas.

CAMAS: This is from the Chinook and means sweet.

CANFIELD: For one of the few survivors of the Whitman massacre.

CARMEN: For an early settler.

CASSIA: Named for the cassia plant along the creek.

CATA: Cah'-tah: Indian for hard ashes or cinders.

CAVENDISH: For the town in Vermont.

CENTERVILLE: This ghost town was first called Hogum because some of the settlers wished to declare their contempt for the greed of their neighbors. Outraged patriotism later threw Hogum away and called the place Centerville because it was midway between Placerville and Idaho City.

CHALLIS: For A. P. Challis who founded the town.

CHILCO: Uncertain but probably of Indian origin.

CHINOOK: An "aspirated, gutturalized, sputtered, and swallowed" jargon widely used by both whites and Indians in early days. It was a dialect of French, English, and Indian.

CLARK FORK: Named, of course, for the explorer, this river has been called Bitterroot, Deer Lodge, Hell Gate, and Missoula.

CLEARWATER: This river was called Kookooskia by Indians. The word means clear water.

COCOLALLA: Indian for cold water.

COEUR D'ALENE: The origin is still uncertain. The best authority seems to favor heart of an awl, a derisive term applied (in Indian language, of course) to greedy trappers from Canada, who thereupon applied the epithet to the Indians themselves.

COLTKILLED CREEK: When oppressed by hunger, Captain Clark was always unfelicitous in his choices.

CONANT: This creek and valley are called Coonard by those who live there. They were named for a man who came within an inch of losing his life in the stream.

CONDA: A diminutive of Anaconda.

COOLIN: For an early settler.

CORBIN: For an early settler.

COUNCIL: It was in or near the present town that Indians gathered for powwows.

CRAIG: For William Craig, a comrade of Kit Carson.

CULDESAC: Meaning literally in French the bottom of a bag, the word more loosely indicates a place with only one outlet.

CUPRUM: From the Latin meaning copper.

DEARY: Not intended as an endearment, this town took its name from an early settler.

DECLO: Dek-lo: for two pioneer families, *De*thles and *Cl*oughly.

DENT: For one of its founders.

DOLBEER: For an early settler.

DRIGGS: For an early Mormon.

DUBOIS: For a former Senator, Fred Dubois.

EDEN: A former Senator named this town (but not facetiously) from the Bible.

EMIDA: After the surnames of the first three families to settle there: *E*ast, *Mi*ller, and *Da*wson. E-mi'-da.

EMMETT: For Emmett Cahalan, the first white boy born there.

FILER: For Walter G. Filer.

FIRTH: For one of its founders.

FORT HALL: For Henry Hall.

FRANKLIN: Named for the leader of the Mormons who settled it.

GEM: This county was perhaps named gem because it has been supposed that Idaho means gem of the mountains.

GENESEE: For the town in New York.

GILMER: For John T. Gilmer.

GOODING: For former Governor Frank Gooding.

GRANITE: Named for the stone formerly quarried here.

GUYER: These springs were named for Captain Henry Guyer.

HADEN: Named for a man named Hayden.

HAILEY: For John Hailey.

HAMER: For Thomas R. Hamer.

HARPSTER: For an early settler.

HAWLEY: For former Governor James H. Hawley.

HEISE: For Richard Clamor Heise, an old-timer.

HOPE: Like Bliss, this town was named for a man and not because the settlers were depressed.

HYNDMAN PEAK: This, the second highest peak in the State, was named for Major William Hyndman, a veteran of the Civil War.

IDAHO: The name, pronounced I'-da-ho, is a contraction of Shoshoni words "Ee-da-how," which have been translated with utter disregard of accuracy as "gem of the mountains." The first Indian syllable is intended, as nearly as we can tell, to convey the idea of coming down, and is the generic root in such Shoshoni words as raining and snowing. The second syllable is a root for either sun or mountain. The third is almost precisely the equivalent of the English exclamation mark. Bearing in mind, therefore, the way language evolves and the manner in which words become either more or less pregnant with meaning, it seems reasonable to suppose that for the Indian mind, Ee-dah-how once declared that the sun was coming down the mountain, and that this recognition of morning was so pleasant to the Indian that he made it exclamatory. Later, however, in the way of language, the expression came to mean both more and less, to become emotionally nebulous in content on the one hand, and on the other to become more definite and exact in its actual symbolism. Thus Ee-dah-how seems quite certainly to have been an exclamatory greeting equivalent to *It's sunrise!* or *It's morning!* and to have indicated to the Indian mind the circumstance of another day and the need to arise and go to work. But any expression of that kind, either in the Indian or in any other mind, is also, of course, invested emotionally beyond the reach of definition; and precisely or even obscurely what the exclamation meant to the Indian beyond the fact of sunrise we do not and can hardly hope to know.

Idahoans of the past, taking their lead from poetic fanciers who suggested the matter, have persisted in translating the term as gem of the mountains, indifferent to the enormous incongruity of calling an empire resting upon a granite batholith two hundred thousand square miles in area a gem. There is, of course, more poetry in the simple cry, "It is morning!" with its investment of eternities and awakening and renewal than in all the gems in existence. One Idaho historian says that the Indians "beheld a lustrous rim of light shining from the mountain top. This radiant mountain crown or diadem was likened to a gem glittering from a snowy peak." If the notion of a gem glittering from a snowy peak had been in the Indian's mind, it seems unreasonable to suppose that he would have characterized the vision in words which declare the sun is coming down the mountain.

It is said that the name was first used in 1859 when Idaho Springs, the first permanent settlement in Colorado, was founded, and that the word was familiar to these settlers through their contact with the Comanche Indians whose dialect was much like that of the Shoshoni tribe. In the autumn of 1860 the name was given to a steamboat launched at Victoria by a man who had lived in Soda Springs. In 1862 the Washington legislature gave the name to a county which is now the largest in Idaho. When in 1863, the Idaho Territory was established, United States Senator Henry Wilson of Massachusetts thought Idaho the most appropriate of all the names suggested, possibly because a colleague from Oregon declared that the word meant gem of the mountains. It is thought that the spelling was changed to its present or to very similar form by Joaquin Miller.

INKOM: Ink'-um: an Indian word meaning red hair.

JEROME: Named for Jerome Hill.

JOSEPH: For that brave warrior, Chief Joseph of the Nez Perces.

JULIAETTA: For Julia and Etta Snyder.

KALISPEL: Indian meaning canoe or boat people. Kullyspell is a corruption.

KAMIAH: Kam'-e-eye: from Kamiakan, a chieftain of the Yakima tribe.

KANIKSU: Ka-nick'-su: an Indian name for a priest who was buried in what was once Kaniksu but is now Priest Lake.

KELLOGG: The original name of the famous mining town was Milo but it was changed to honor Noah Kellogg who discovered the Bunker Hill Mine.

KENDRICK: First called Latah, the name was changed to honor an engineer.

KETCHUM: Once called Leadville, this town was changed to honor David Ketchum.

KEUTERVILLE: For Joseph Keuter, a pioneer farmer.

KIMAMA: Kee'-mah-mar: an Indian word meaning butterfly.

KOOSKIA: A shortened form of Kookooskia (see Clearwater).

KOOTENAI: A corruption of Kutenai, the Indian name for themselves. The word means water people.

KUNA: Indian meaning green leaf or good to smoke.

LACLEDE: Apparently for an engineer of the Great Northern.

LAPWAI: Nez Perce Indian word meaning place of the butterflies.

LATAH: First syllables of two Nez Perce words: la-kah meaning pine tree and tah-ol meaning pestle.

LEESBURG: Soldiers from the Civil War quarreled over the naming of this mining town and finally had both a Leesburg and a Grantsville, the latter of which was absorbed.

LEMHI: A corruption of Limhi, a character in the *Book of Mormon.*

LOLO: Named by the Flathead Indians for a man named Lawrence. Loulou was as near as they could come to pronouncing his name.

MALAD: Named for French Canadians because they became ill here.

MALTA: For the island of Malta.

MENAN—An Indian word meaning going home.

MIDAS: Named for Midas in the hope that the feverish touch of prospectors would turn the place into gold. It did not.

MINIDOKA: A Shoshoni word meaning broad expanse.

MONTOUR: Named by a woman who sought a word expressive of the beauty of the mountains.

MONTPELIER: Named by Brigham Young after his birthplace in Vermont.

MORA: Moo'-rah: Indian for mule.

MOSCOW: Said to have been named by a Russian with the unbelievable name of Hogg.

MULLAN: For Captain John Mullan.

NAMEKO: Nam'-e-ko: Indian meaning drive away.

NAMPA: Two Shoshoni words *namp* and *puh* meaning bigfoot and referring to a chieftain who is said to have had a foot six inches wide and seventeen inches long.

NAPATA: Nah-pah'-tah: Indian for by the hand.

NAPIAS: A Shoshoni word meaning money.

NEZ PERCE: Means pierced nose, of course, though inasmuch as these Indians never pierced their noses it is probable that *nez presse* (flattened nose) was intended.

NOTUS: Indian for "it is all right."

OAKLEY: Named for a stage superintendent.

OMANI: Oh-mah'-nee: Indian meaning to walk or travel.

OREANA: This word seems to mean an unbranded yearling.

OROFINO: Spanish words *oro* and *fino* meaning pure gold.

OWINZA: Oh-ween'-zah: Indian meaning to make a bed of or use for a bed.

OWYHEE: A corruption of Hawaii.

PAGARI: Pah'-gah-ree: Indian for lake or pond.

PAHSIMEROI: From the Shoshoni words *pah* meaning water, *sima* meaning one, and *roi* meaning grove. This one grove of evergreens by a stream in the Pahsimeroi Valley was miles from any other trees.

PALOUSE: a French word meaning grassy spot or place.

PAYETTE: For Francis Payette, a Hudson's Bay trapper.

PEND OREILLE: Whether the name was given to the Indians because of their earrings or because in shape the lake is said to resemble an ear is not known. The first seems more probable.

PETTIT (LAKE): For Tom Pettit.

PICABO: This Indian word, commonly pronounced peek'-a-boo, means come in, and is correctly pronounced pee-kah'-bo.

PINA: Pee'-nah: Indian for sugar.

PINGREE: Named for its founder.

POCATELLO: From the Shoshoni words *po* (road), *ka* (not), and *tello* (to follow). Though some residents of Pocatello strenuously object, it seems nevertheless that this Indian chieftain was a shifty fellow who refused to follow the road. Or perhaps he lived his name down.

PORTNEUF: Uncertain. Perhaps the ninth gate or the river of nine gates.

POTLATCH: From Chinook, it means giving. The story is told of a Nez Perce Indian who ferried prospectors across the river on a cayuse. One time the pony stumbled and a huge Irishman was thrown into the stream, whereupon the Indian yelled, "Potlatch quarter! Then drown if you want to!" Most likely the Irishman swam out.

PRICHARD: For one of the discoverers of gold in this area.

RAFT RIVER: So named because early settlers had to cross its mouth on rafts inasmuch as beavers had filled the river with dams. Why the settlers did not cross on dams seems not to have been declared.

RATHDRUM: Named after Rathdrum in Ireland.

REXBURG: A corruption. Named for Thomas Ricks.

RIDDLE: For an early family. "There were so many Riddles that it was riddle-riddle everywhere."

RIGBY: For William Rigby, a Mormon.

RIGGINS: For R. L. Riggins, an old-timer.

RIRIE: For a Mormon bishop.

RUPERT: For a reclamation engineer.

ST. ANTHONY: Named for St. Anthony Falls, Minnesota.

ST. MARIES: Named by Father De Smet.

SAMARIA: "Ever since the first ones settled here, and even to this day, those who come among us are always taken care of so well that we have always been called The Good Samaritans."

SELWAY: A Nez Perce word meaning stream of easy canoeing.

SHELLEY: Named for an old-timer.

SINKER: A creek so named because settlers used gold nuggets for sinkers on their fishing lines.

SKELETON BUTTE: The skeleton of Lew Landers was found there.

SNAKE RIVER: The name Snake was loosely and incorrectly attached to Bannack, Paiute, and Shoshoni Indians. The origin of the name is disputed. One says the name means inland; a priest has declared the Indians were so named because, like reptiles, they dug food from the earth; and a third says these Indians ate serpents. A fourth declares that when an Indian was asked the name of his tribe he made a serpentine movement, intended to suggest not snakes but basket weaving. The last seems the most probable. The Shoshonis themselves called the river Yam-pa-pah, the stream where the yampa grows; though later after the Oregon Trail followed it they called it Po-og-way, meaning river road.

STITES: For one of the founders.

SWEET: Not intended as raillery, the town was named for an early settler.

TAKAB: Tah-kawb: Indian for snow.

TARGHEE: From a Bannack chieftain. Correctly spelled Tygee.

TENDOY: For a chieftain of the Lemhis. Unten-doip: he likes broth. Tendoy was very fond of coagulated blood in boiled meat.

THUNDER MOUNTAIN: Indians called it yag'-gi, meaning clouds crying.

TICEKSA: Tee-chay'-shak: Indian for top of a tent or house.

TIKURA: Tee-koo'-rah: Indian for skeleton of a tent.

TOPONIS: To'-po-nis: Indian for black cherries.

TUNUPA: Too'-nah-pah: Indian for boy.

TYHEE: From Indian tee-hee, meaning like a deer.

USTICK: Named for a doctor.

VICTOR: Named for an old-timer.

WAHA: An Indian word meaning beautiful.

WALLACE: For Colonel W. R. Wallace who established the townsite.

WAPELLO: For a town in Iowa.

WARDNER: For James Wardner.

WEISER: Wee'-zer: named for a Hudson's Bay trapper.

WILDER: For an author of that name who once tried to write there.

WINSPER: For an old-timer.

A SELECTED BIBLIOGRAPHY

CHAPTER I

BAILEY, ROBERT G., *The River of No Return*, Lewiston, Idaho, 1935. A history and travelogue containing interesting facts and legends.

BANCROFT, HUBERT HOWE, *History of the Pacific States of North America*, San Francisco, 1890. A summary of Idaho from 1862 to 1889, with general accounts of Indians, topography, resources, and development.

BIRD, ANNIE LAURIE, *Boise, the Peace Valley*, Caldwell, Idaho, 1934. A history of the early days and later progress of the Boise Valley.

BROSNAN, C. J., *History of the State of Idaho*, New York, 1935. An elementary textbook.

BROWN, JENNIE BROUGHTON, *Fort Hall on the Oregon Trail*, Caldwell, Idaho, 1932. A trustworthy source of information based largely on letters, narratives, and diaries.

DEFENBACH, BYRON, *The State We Live In*, Caldwell, Idaho, 1933. A history of Idaho.

DRIGGS, B. W., *History of the Teton Valley*, Caldwell, Idaho, 1926. A history of Pierre's Hole drawn largely from recollections of early settlers.

ELLIOTT, WALLACE W., AND COMPANY, Editors, *History of the Idaho Territory*, San Francisco, 1884. Interesting only as a historical document.

ERWIN, RICHARD P., *Indian Rock Writing in Idaho*, Twelfth Biennial Report of the State Historical Society, Boise, 1929-30.

FRENCH, HIRAM T., *History of Idaho*, Chicago, 1914. 3 volumes. The first is history, the other two are biographies.

GREGG, HERBERT C., *Idaho, Gem of the Mountains*, St. Paul, 1893. The official souvenir book of Idaho's exhibit at the World's Columbian Exposition.

HAILEY, JOHN, *The History of Idaho*, Boise, 1910. A history of Idaho Territorial days based largely on personal experiences of the author.

HEBARD, GRACE R., *Sacajawea*, Glendale, California, 1933. A scholarly treatment of the printed and unprinted material relating to Sacajawea.

HOSMER, JAMES K., *Journals of the Lewis and Clark Expedition*, Chicago, 1904. 2 volumes.

IRVING, WASHINGTON, *The Adventures of Captain Bonneville*, New York, 1868. A romantic account of the explorer.

JUDSON, KATHARINE B., *Myths and Legends of the Pacific Northwest*, Chicago, 1910. An interesting source book.

MCCONNELL, WM. J., *Early History of Idaho*, Caldwell, Idaho, 1913. The author's reminiscences.

MEEKER, EZRA, *Ox Team: or the Old Oregon Trail*, 1908. An account of Meeker's journey over the Trail to mark historic sites.

PARKMAN, FRANCIS, *The Oregon Trail*, New York, 1931. Treats chiefly of Indian life and character.

REES, JOHN E., *The History of Lemhi County*. An unpublished manuscript in the State Historical Society.

————————————, *Idaho Chronology, Nomenclature, Bibliography*, Chicago, 1918. A valuable but very incomplete source.

SCHULTZ, JAMES W., *Bird Woman*, New York, 1918. Sacajawea's story as she is supposed to have told it to others.

SMYTHE, WM. E., *Conquest of Arid America*, New York, 1905.

WALGAMOTT, CHARLES S., *Reminiscences of Early Days*, Caldwell, Idaho, 1935.

CHAPTERS II and III

ARNOLD, R. R., *Indian Wars of Idaho*, Caldwell, Idaho, 1932.

HEBARD, GRACE R., *Washakie*, Cleveland. An account of Indian resistance of invasion of their territory.

MCBETH, KATE C., *The Nez Perces Since Lewis and Clark*, New York, 1908.

HOWARD, O. O., *Nez Perce Joseph*, Boston, 1881.

See also under Chapter I; and various reports and publications of the Bureau of American Ethnology (notably the 45th) and of the Smithsonian Institution (notably Bulletin 30).

CHAPTER IV

ELDRIDGE, GEORGE H., *A Geological Reconnaissance Across Idaho*, Washington, D. C., 1895. Pp. 217-282.

IDAHO BUREAU OF MINES AND GEOLOGY, Pamphlets 10, 12, 27, 40; and Bulletin 3. U. S. G. S. Bulletins 430, 620, 713, 62, 199, 530, 580, 528, 732, 774.

STEARNS, HAROLD T., *Guide to the Craters of the Moon*, Caldwell, Idaho, 1930.

CHAPTER V

FRYE, T. C., *Ferns of the Northwest*, Portland, Oregon, 1934. Information both scientific and popular.

HASKIN, L. L., *Wild Flowers of the Pacific Coast*, Portland, Oregon, 1934.

HOTTES, A. C., *The Book of Trees*, New York, 1932. Trees from the point of view of the horticulturalist.

KEELER, HARRIET L., *Our Native Trees*, New York, 1900. Trustworthy and fairly complete.

LONGYEAR, BURTON O., *Trees and Shrubs of the Rocky Mountain Region*, New York, 1927. A scientific study of Rocky Mountain flora.

PARSONS, FRANCES T., *How to Know Wild Flowers*, New York, 1900. A guide to names, haunts, and habits.

PIPER, C. V., AND BEATTIE, R. K., *Flora of the Northwest Coast*, Pullman, Washington, 1915.

ROGERS, JULIA E., *The Tree Book*, New York, 1905. A popular guide.

RYDBERG, P. A., *Flora of the Rocky Mountains*, New York, 1917. The standard source.

SAUNDERS, C. F., *Western Wild Flowers*, New York, 1933. A popular discussion, limited largely to California.

ST. JOHN, HAROLD, *Flora of Idaho*. An unpublished manuscript in the possession of The Caxton Printers, Ltd. The only exhaustive treatment of Idaho flora.

CHAPTER VI

BAILEY, FLORENCE M., *Handbook of Birds of the Western United States*, Boston, 1921. A standard source.

BLANCHAN, NELTJE, *Birds that Hunt and Are Hunted*, New York, 1905. A popular treatment.

DAGLISH, ERIC F., *The Life Story of Beasts*, New York, 1931. The habits and peculiarities of the better-known mammals.

DITMARS, RAYMOND L., *The Reptile Book*, New York, 1907. A scientist's popular presentation.

ELIOT, WILLARD A., *Birds of the Pacific Coast*, New York, 1923. An account of distribution and habits of 118 species.

MATHEWS, F. S., *Field Book of Wild Birds and Their Music*, New York, 1921. Literal transcription of bird song.

MILLS, E. A., *In Beaver World*, Boston, 1913. Besides a study of the beaver, it contains some data on the trapping era in the Northwest.

SETON, ERNEST T., *Lives of Game Animals*, New York, 1929. 4 volumes. A popular account.

U. S. BUREAU OF ORNITHOLOGY AND MAMMALOGY, *Bulletin 5.* A Biological Reconnaissance of South Central Idaho. Washington, D. C., 1891.

CHAPTER IX

GIDLEY, J. W., *Hunting Fossils on the Old Oregon Trail*, Smithsonian Institution, pp. 31-6.

——————————————, *Continuation of the Fossil Horse Round-up, ibid*, 33-44.

Idaho Digest and Blue Book, Caldwell, Idaho, 1935.

LUKENS, FRED E., *Idaho Citizen*, Caldwell, Idaho, 1925.

MILLER, H. H., *Democracy in Idaho*, Caldwell, Idaho, 1935.

ROSE, C. E., *Civil Government of Idaho*, New York, 1919.

U. S. G. S., *Professional Paper No. 140*, "Flora of the Latah Formation," Washington, D. C., 1926.

ACKNOWLEDGMENTS

Grateful acknowledgment is made to the following for materials used in this book:

K. D. SWAN, United States Forest Service, Missoula, Montana, for pictures titled: Timber; Power Plant at Moyie Falls; Rapid River Falls; The Lochsa River; Pierce City, one-time Capital of Idaho Territory; the St. Joe River; Coeur d'Alene National Forest; The Mullan Tree; Priest River Country; Priest Lake; Grave of an Old-timer; the Old Hotel at Florence; Typical National Forest Lookout.

BISBEE STUDIO, Twin Falls, Idaho, for pictures titled: Snake River Gorge: the Footprints of Time; Idaho's Big Potatoes; Sego Lily: Utah State Flower; A Row of Onions; Twin Falls; Icicle Cove; Snowbank Falls at Blue Lakes; Perrine Coulee; Balanced Rock; Phantom Walls; Malad Gorge; Salmon Dam.

JOHNSON AND SON, Boise, Idaho, for pictures titled: White Bark Pine: Two Grotesques; Hunting is Good in Idaho; The Limit: Cutthroat and Rainbow; Snake River Sturgeon; Wild Geese and Ducks; A Boise Sky; A View in Boise; A Profile in Sucker Creek; Alice Lake; Imogene Lake; Payette Lake; The Salmon River from the North-and-South Highway; Journey's End; A Monument on Monumental Creek; Frontispiece: Idaho State Flag; Pettit Lake; Government Pack String on the Selway River.

M. S. BENEDICT, Forest Supervisor, Caribou National Forest, Montpelier, Idaho, for pictures titled: Roaring Lake; Panning for Gold; Twin Falls-Jerome Bridge; Mount Borah; Crystal Falls Cave: Crystal Falls; Crystal Falls Cave: a backdrop; Crystal Falls Cave: a corridor; Crystal Falls Cave: a ceiling; Corridor of the Kings; Cavern of the Idols; The Bride; Shoshone Falls; Galena Summit; Dog Team on Wood River.

ROBERT JEWELL, Boise, Idaho, for pictures titled: Junction of Middle Fork and Main Salmon; Submerged Town of Roosevelt.

LEWIS LONGTEIG, Boise, Idaho, for picture titled: White Pine and Cedar.

E. L. FULLER, Boise, Idaho, for picture titled: Deer on Moore Creek.

NOEL STUDIO, Lewiston, Idaho, for picture titled: Elk in Winter.

CHARLES J. BELDEN, Pitchfork, Wyoming, for picture titled: Antelope in Flight.

IDAHO STATE CHAMBER OF COMMERCE for picture titled: Mountain Goat.

SHIPLER, Boise, Idaho, for picture titled: Thousand Springs.

UNITED STATES FOREST SERVICE, for pictures titled: Matured Yellow Pine; Sheep.

STANDAR'S STUDIO, Idaho Falls, Idaho, for pictures titled: Jim Marshall; three studies of Fort Hall Indians; Balsam and Lupine; Along the Salmon River.

D. F. DAVIS, U. S. Department of Agriculture, Salt Lake City, Utah, for picture titled: Upper Mesa Falls.

U. S. DEPARTMENT OF AGRICULTURE, Soil Conservation Service, for picture titled: A Lava Field Near the Craters of the Moon.

INTERMOUNTAIN AERIAL SURVEYS, Boise, Idaho, for pictures titled: Looking Northeast Toward Atlanta from Arrowrock Dam; An Aerial View of Boise.

JOHN W. GRAHAM, Spokane, Washington, for pictures titled: Winchester Hill; Surf-riding on Lake Coeur d'Alene; Hayden Lake; Spirit Lake; Beauty Bay, Lake Coeur d'Alene; Sunset on Lake Coeur d'Alene; Lake Pend Oreille.

THE 15TH PHOTO SECTION, AIR CORPS, U. S. ARMY, for picture titled: Teton Peaks.

GROVE STUDIO, Boise, Idaho, for pictures titled: Arrowrock Dam; South Fork of Payette River.

H. C. SHELLWORTH, Southern Idaho Timber Protective Association, Boise, Idaho, for pictures titled: Cougar Dave and His Dogs; Mountain Goat Country.

HAROLD T. STEARNS, U. S. Geological Survey, Washington, D. C., for pictures titled: Indian Tunnel: Entrance—Craters of the Moon; Lava Flow—Craters of the Moon; Impression of Charred Log in Lava—Craters of the Moon.

RINKER'S STUDIO, Kellogg, Idaho, for picture titled: The Sunshine Mine.

W. M. IRVINE, Seattle, Washington, for picture titled: Syringa: Idaho State Flower.

TED CRAMER, Boise, Idaho, for pictures titled: The Outlet of Redfish Lake; Stanley Lake; Trail Creek near Ketchum.

HILL STUDIO, Gooding, Idaho, for picture titled: Gooding City of Rocks.

HODGINS, Moscow, Idaho, for pictures titled: A Campus View; The Lewiston Hill.

FRANK PALMER, Spokane, Washington, for picture titled: Forest Trail from Hayden Lake to North Fork.

DR. A. E. WEAVER, Boise, Idaho, for pictures titled: Map of the United States; Historic Table Rock; Bruneau Canyon; Middle Fork of Salmon River; Packing In.

LYMAN MARDEN, U. S. DEPARTMENT OF THE INTERIOR, for picture titled: Natural Bridge Near Arco.

NATIONAL PARK SERVICE, U. S. DEPARTMENT OF THE INTERIOR, for pictures titled: Aspen; Tag Alder; Mountain Ash; Elderberry; Kinnikinnick.

WILDLIFE DIVISION, NATIONAL PARK SERVICE, San Francisco, California, for pictures titled: Indian Paintbrush; Marsh Marigold; Colorado Blue Columbine.

BURNS STUDIO, Lewiston, Idaho, for picture titled: A Lettuce Patch.

BURNS, Coeur dAlene, Idaho, for pictures titled: Trainload of Logs; Sluicing Logs; U S 95 Through the Pines of Northern Idaho; Fernan Lake and Beyond.

THE 116TH PHOTO SECTION, 41ST DIVISION AVIATION, WASHINGTON NATIONAL GUARD, for pictures titled: Sawtooth Mountains West of Stanley; Bayview on Lake Pend Oreille; Lewiston; The Seven Devils; The Sawtooth Mountains East of Stanley; Coeur d'Alene; Chimney Rock near Priest Lake.

WESLEY ANDREWS, Portland, Oregon, for pictures titled: Rocky Mountain Sheep: Beginning of a Battle; Elk: Finish of a Fight; Monoliths at Sunset and Volcanic Crater—Craters of the Moon; Cave Mouth and Formation of Cave Interior—Craters of the Moon; Indian Tunnel Corridor—Craters of the Moon.

RAINIER NATIONAL PARK COMPANY, Tacoma, Washington, for pictures titled: Bear up a Tree; Come on Down!

J. F. ANDERSON, Lewiston, Idaho, for pictures titled: White Pine Lumber; Through the Clearwater National Forest; Marble Creek.

INDEX

A

Academy of the Immaculate
    Heart 188
Agate 175
Agriculture 165
Ahsahka 319
Albion 236
Alder, white (tag) 99
Alpine beauty 109
American Falls 232
Amethyst 176
Amsterdam 290
Antelope, description 123
    number 123
    range 155
Arco 266
Arrowhead 112
Ash, Rocky Mountain 98
Ashley, General William 21
Ashton 201
Ashton dog derby 201
Aspen, quaking 98
Athol 303
Atlanta 257
Austin 246

B

Badger 126
Balanced Rock 244
Bald Mountain Resort 285
Balsamroot 116
Baneberry 101
Basque, colony 187
Bay Horse 389
Bays, Beauty 325
    Carlin 325
    Indian 341
    Kalispell 342
    Luby 342

    Reeder 342
    Squaw 325
    Turner 325
    Wolf Lodge 335
Bear, Black, description 120
    Grizzly, description 119
    range 155
Bearberry 101
Bear grass 115
Beaver 124
Beavertail Point 225
Bellevue 285
Big Springs 199
    Inn 199
    Lookout 199
Bilberry, dwarf 100
Birch, red 99
Bittern 139
Blackbird 143
Blackfoot 211
Black Bear Inn 314
Bliss 247
Bloodstone 175
Blow Hole 244
Bluebird 147
Boa, rubber 129
Bobcat 121
Bobolink 149
Boise 253
Boise Basin 32, 34, 385
Bonanza 281, 389
Bonners Ferry 301
Bonneville, Captain B. L. E. 23
Borah, W. E. 37, 254
Boyles Ranch 282
Bozanta Tavern 304
Bracken 105
Bridges, Hansen 239
    Manning 313
    Natural 250, 270

Sandpoint 302
Taylor Toll 209
Twin Falls-Jerome 289
Bridger, Jim 23
Bruneau 249
Brutality, white instance .. 24
Buckbean 112
Buckbrush 114
Buhl 244
Bungalow 320
Burgdorf 294
Burke 332
Burning bush 103
Buttercup, western 107
Buttes, Big 265
   Big Cinder 269
   Black Top 269
   Lizard 261
   Menan 206
   Middle 265
   Twin 265
Buzzard (see vulture)

C

Cache National Forest 218
Caldwell 262
Camas, blue 107
Cambridge 317
Campgrounds, Bostetter 238
   Buffalo 200
   Cold Springs 312
   Cougar Point 279
   Evergreen 315
   Golden Gate 295
   Meadow Creek 323
   Pentstemon 292
   Pettit 292
   Sheep Springs 312
   Smoky 314
   Spring Creek 318
   Torrey's 281
   Twin Creek 274
Canyons, Box 316
   Bruneau 249
   Cronks 280
   Fourth of July 334
   Grand View 272
   Jump Creek 261
   St. Charles 219
   Star 272
   Sucker Creek 262
Cape Horn 81
Cape Horn Ranch 283
Carey 270
Carey Act 37
Caribou National Forest 218

Cascade 296
Castle Rocks 249
Cataldo 334
Caves, Burley 239
   Clay 239
   Crystal Falls 203
   Formation 224
   Higby 252
   Hot 290
   Ice 226
   Kuna 259
   Minnetonka 219
   Shoshone Ice 286
   Sunbear 269
Cedar, Giant Arborvitae 94
   ground 104
   Rocky Mountain Red 94
Centerville 385
Chamberlain Basin 355
Challis 280
Cherokee Bob 31
Cheyenne 35
Chickadee 144
Chief Joseph 31
Chilly 271
Chimney Rock 341
Chinese (see Racial Elements)
Chipmunk 128
Chokecherry 99
Clark Fork 338
Clark, William 19
Clarkia 111, 328
Clarkston 308
Clayton 272, 281
Clearwater National Forest 319
Cleft 252
Cocolalla 302
Colleges, Gooding 188
   Junior 188
   Northwest Nazarene 188
   of Idaho 188, 262
Columbine 107
Conda 224
Coolin 340
Coot 141
Coral root 108
Corbin 303
Cormorant 137
Cottonwood 98
Coeur d'Alene 304
Coeur d'Alene Lake 83
Cougar, description 120
Council 315
Cowbird 138
Cranberry 102
Crane 138

Crater Rings 252
Craters of the Moon Na-
    tional Monument........267 ff.
Creeper 145
Cuckoo 148
Cuprum 316
Currant 102

D

Dams, American Falls 232
    Arrowrock 257
    Black Canyon 259
    Deadwood 295
    Milner 238
    Minidoka 86, 235
    Oakley 238
    Post Falls 336
    Salmon 291
Daisy, mountain 107
Darrow, Clarence 37, 254
Deer, description 123
    number 123
    range 154
DeLamar 384
De Smet 26, 306
Devil's club 101
Devils Kitchen 245
Dewey 383
Dewey, Col. W. H. 383
Dickey 272
Dogwood, red-osier 101, 103
Downey 213
Dover 340
Driggs 205
Dubois 216
Ducks, kind 156-58
    range 156-58
Dunes, Sand 202

E

Eagle 133
Eagle City 333, 380
Eagle Rock 209
Eastport 300
Education, status 188-90
Egret 142
Elderberry 101
Elk City 323
Elk, description 122
    number 123
    range 154
Emida 329
Emigrant Rock 235
Emmett 259

Experiment Station, Priest
    River 341
    U. S. Sheep 217
Exports 177

F

Fairy bell 113
Fairy slipper 109
Falcon (see hawk)
Falls, Auger 244
    Cave 201
    Mesa 200-01
    Moyie 301
    Perrine Coulee 242
    Selway 322
    Shoshone 86, 242
    Twin 242
Farms, experimental 189
Ferns 104-05
Festival, Cherry Blos-
    som 259, 308
Filer 244
Filipino (see Racial Ele-
    ments)
Finch 148
Fir, Alpine 97
    balsam 96
    Douglas 93
    white 96, 97
Firewood 113
Fish, enemies (see fauna)
    kinds 158-62
    range 158-62
Fish Haven 222
Fleabane 110
Flicker 144
Florence 31
Flycatcher 144
Forney 278
Fort Boise 20
Fort Hall 21, 212
Fort Henry 204
Franklin 25, 214
Fruitland 263

G

Galena Summit 80, 284
Game Laws 152
Garnet 176
Geese 158
Gems 175-76
Gentian 108
Gibbonsville 274

Goat, mountain, description 124
    number 124
    range 155
Goldenrod 113
Goldfinch 149
Gooding 288
Gopher 127
Gopher snake 130
Gooseberry 103
Gorges, Cabinet 337
    Malad 248
    Pass Creek 270
    Royal 280
    Seven Devils 317
    Williams Creek 279
    Wood River 286
Goulder, W. A. 26
Grace hydroelectric plant.... 226
Grand Canyon (see Seven
    Devils)
Grandview Point 200
Grangeville 311
Granite 302
Grape, Oregon 113
Grass, blue-eyed 108
Greenleaf Academy 188
Grebe 139
Grosbeak 146
Groundsel, morning 109
Grouse 155
Grouseberry 100
Gull 142

H

Hackberry 102
Hagerman 246
Hailey 285
Hansen 239
Harebell 113
Harpster 322
Harrison 326
Harrison Flats 327
Harvard 330
Hawk, kinds 134-35
Hawley, James H. 34
Hawthorn 99
Headquarters 320
Heath 317
Heather 103
Hecla Mine 333
Heise Hot Springs 207
Hellebore 112
Hell's Half Acre 210
Hemlock 97
Henry 225
Henry, Major Andrew 21

Henrys Lake 198
Heron 138
Heyburn Park 305
Hills, French Creek 313
    Gilbert 321
    Lewiston 307
    Timmerman 285
    White Bird 312
    Winchester 310
Hollister 290
Hollyhock 111
Hooded tresses 108
Hooper Spring 223
Hope 339
Horse Shoe Bend 298
Horsetail, swamp 104
Hot Creek 250
Hot Springs, Bear Lake 222
    Grandjean 258
    Ha-wah-Na 227
    Heise 207
    Lava 226
    Lidy 217
    Mud Bath 227
    Pincock 205
    Red River 323
    Riggins 313
    Royston 259
Huckleberry 100
Hudson's Bay Company 19
Hummingbird 147
Hunting, areas .... 154 ff.
Hyacinth 110

I

Ibis 142
Idaho, batholith 76
    climate 74
    from the air .... 73 ff.
    game department 153
    game laws 152
    geology 77
    name first used 409
    origin 408
    original boundaries 73
    racial elements 185-87
    territory 35
    topography .... 74 ff.
    university 188
Idaho City 258, 385-88
Idaho Falls 208
Idaho Hotel 33, 383
Imports 178
Indian Bathtub 250
Indian Pipe 112
Indian Springs 233, 250

Indian, artifacts .... 63 ff.
    celebrations 67
    legends .... 68 ff.
    music 66
    pictograph, instance 260
    tribes 41-52, 57-70
Information, general for
    tourists 194
Inkom 228
Island Park 200, 278

J

Jackson Hole 207
Jasper 175
Jay 148
Jerome 289
Julia Davis Park 255
Junco (see snowbird)
Juniper, mountain 94

K

Kalispel House (Kully-
    spell) 19, 338
Kamiah 321
Kellogg 333
Ketchum 285
Kildeer (see plover)
Kingfisher 137
Kingbird 147
King Hill 37, 248
Kinglet 146
Kingston 380
Kinnikinnick 101
Kinport Peak 229
Knox 295
Kooskia 322

L

Lakes, Alice 284
    Alturas 80
    Bear 221
    Benewah 305
    Big Redfish 283
    Black 316, 326
    Bloomington 219
    Blue 242, 326
    Chatcolet 305
    Clear 245
    Cleveland 236
    Cocolalla 302
    Coeur d'Alene 83
    Crystal 328
    Darling 338
    Deer 323

Duck 296
Emerald 316
Fernan 336
Fish 323
Granite 302
Goose 293
Grays 211, 225
Harrison 341
Hauser 336
Hayden 304
Hell Roaring 284
Hidden 305, 326
Hoodoo 303
Imogene 283
Independence 238
Kelso 302
Killarney 326
Little Redfish 283
Lowell 261
Lye 247
Market 217
Mud 217
Payette 294, 354
Pend Oreille ..20, 83, 302, 339
Priest 340
Rainbow 248, 323
Roosevelt 355
Rose 326
Round 305
Ruby 323
Spirit 303
Stanley 282
Swan 326
Thompson 326
Toxiway 284
Trinity 249
Twin 284, 303
Walsh 339
Warm 295
Wild Horse 323
Yellow Belly 284
Lakota Resort 222
Land 165
Landmark 295
Lapwai 310
Larch 93, 97
Larkspur 107
Laurel, mountain 97
Lava Hot Springs 226
Lavas, the 210
Leadore 278
Leesburg 278
Lemhi 278
Lewis, Meriwether 19
Lewiston 25, 87, 308
Lewiston Orchards 308

Lily, kinds 111, 114-15
Lily of the valley 108
Lincoln 209
Livestock, kinds 168
Liza Manuel 21
Lizard, kinds 131
Logan, Utah 215
Lolo Trail 320
Lookouts, Anderson Moun-
   tain 273
   Bear Trap 276
   Big Springs 199
   Blue Nose 276
   Brundage 293
   Coolwater 322
   Dry Diggins 314
   Hudlow Mountain 304
   Long Tom 276
   Looking Glass 341
   Marble Creek 323
   Oreana 276
   Packer John 297
   Roman Nose 339
Loon 139
Lowell 322

M

Mackay 271
Mack's Inn 199
Malad City 213
Maple, mountain 98
Marion More Tragedy 33
Martensia 109
Martin's Ranch 267
Massacre Rocks 235
Massacre, Whitman 27
Mayfield 252
McCall 296
McLoughlin, John 20
Meader trout farm 230
Meadow lark 150
Meridian 259
Mesa 317
Mesa Orchards 317
Meyers Cove 279
Milner 238
Minerals, kinds 171
   range 172-77
Miners, history .... 31 ff.
Miners' lettuce 114
Mines, Bunker Hill and
   Sullivan 333
   Hecla 333
   Morning 332
   Sunshine 333

Minidoka 37
Minidoka National Forest.. 236
Mink 126
Missions, Cataldo 334
   Spalding Log Cabin 310
   Whitman 25
Missouri Fur Company 21
Mockingbird 149
Mole 128
Monkey flower 111
Montpelier 219
Moose, description 122
   range 154
Moose City 380
Mormons 25
Moscow 306
Moss 104
Mount Borah 80, 272
   Hyndman 80
   Idaho 381
   Independence 238
   Sherman 224
Mountain Home 248
Mountain lion (see cougar)
Mullan 332
Mullan Tree 334
Muskrat 125

N

Nampa 260
Nampuh, Chief 17
Negro (see Racial Elements)
New Meadows 315
New Plymouth 263
Nezperce 321
Nicholia 381
Nordman 340
North Fork 199, 275
Northern Pacific 35
Northwest Nazarene Acad-
   emy 188
Nutcracker 145
Nuthatch 145

O

Oakley 236
Ohio Match Company 336
Old maid's hair 116
Onyx 176
Opal 176
Orchard 252
Orchards, Lewiston 308
   Mesa 317
Orchid, phantom 108
Origins of names 405-413

Oriole 148
Orofino 319
Oro Grande 380
Otter 125
Our Lady of Lourdes
    Academy 188
Ouzel 146
Owl, kinds 135-37
Owl Clover 116
Owyhee County 84

P

Pack rat 128
Paintbrush 113
Paleontology 190-92, 246
Palouse Country 28
Panhandle 82
Parker, Samuel 26
Paris 219
Pass, Chilcoot 295
    Gibbons 273
    Lookout 331
    Targhee 197
Pass Creek Gorge 270
Payette 263
Peaks, Boulder 284
    Dago 333
    Dickey 272
    Glassford 284
    Rainbow 295
    Seven Devils 89, 316
    Wild Cat 267
Pearly everlasting 114
Pelican 138
Pentstemon 107
Perrine Ranch 241
Phalarope 140
Phantom Walls 244
Pheasant, Chinese 155
Phosphates 222
Pierce 320, 381
Pierre's Hole 21, 205
Pincock Hot Springs 205
Pine, kinds 94-95
Placerville 385
Plantain 112
Plover 141
Plummer 31, 305
Pocatello 213, 228
Pollock 314
Pond's Lodge 200
Population, elements 185-87
Poplar 207
Porcupine 121
Post Falls 336
Potato 78

Potlatch 330
Preston 214
Price's Resort 249
Prickly Pear 116
Primitive Area, boundaries 345
    entrances 350-53
    facilities 347
    natural phenomena 347
    typical expedition .... 353 ff.
    topography 345
    wild life 348
Pussytoes 114

Q

Quartsburg 385
Quail 142, 156

R

Rabbit 129
Racial Elements 185-87
Rail 140
Ranch, 4S 224
Rathdrum 303
Rattlesnake, kinds 130
Ravalli, Father 334
Raven 146
Reclamation 165
Redstart 147
Reservations, Indian 51-52
Reservoirs, American Falls 232
    Arrowrock 257
    Blackfoot 224
    Crane Creek 317
    Deadwood 295
    Goose Creek 238
    Lost Valley 315
    Magic Lake 285
Resources, natural .... 165 ff.
Rexburg 206
Rhododendron 110
Richfield 270
Rigby 206
Riggins 313
Ririe 207
Rivers, Bear 222
    Bechler 201
    Big Lost 77
    Bruneau 85
    Clark Fork 83, 337
    Clearwater 30, 32
    Coeur d'Alene 83
    Crooked 323
    Kootenai 83
    Little Lost 77

Lochsa 83
Malad 246
Moyie 301
Palouse 83
Potlatch 83
Portneuf 227
Priest 340
Red 323
Salmon 77, 80, 275
Selway 322
Snake .... 76, 79, 230 ff.
Spokane 83
St. Joe 83
St. Maries 83, 328
Warm 202
Wood 75
Robber's Roost 225
Roberts 217
Robin 143
Robinson Bar Ranch 281
Rockchip 130
Rockchuck 129
Rocks, Gooding City 86, 288
    Silent City 86, 236
Rocky Mountain Club 283
Rogerson 291
Roosevelt 295, 388
Ruby 176
Ruby City 381
Running pine 104
Running Springs Ranch 283
Rupert 235

S

Sacajawea 19
Sack's Cabin 199
Sacred Heart Mission 306
Sage hen 155
Sager family 251
Salmon, kinds 161-162
Salmon City 277
Salmon National Forest.... 274 ff.
Salmon River, description .. 275
Salmonberry 102
Sandpiper 141
Sandpoint 302, 340
Santa Creek 328
Sapphire 176
Sapsucker 145
Sawtelle Peak 199
Sawtooth City 380
Sawtooth Mountains 283
School, for deaf and blind .. 188
    Industrial Training 188
    Normal 188

Scouring brush 104
Sego 108
Serviceberry 99
Settler's Tunnel 250
Seven Devils 89, 316
Shafer Butte 258
Sheep, mountain 124
    range 155
Sheep Rock 316
Shelley 210
Shootingstar 114
Shoshone 287
Shoup 276
Shrew 128
Shrike 137
Silver City 84, 381
Sinks, Lost River 266
Siskin, pine 145
Skunk 127
Skunk cabbage 112
Smiths Ferry 296
Snake, water 131
Snake River (see Rivers)
Snipe 141
Snowberry 102
Snowbird 144
Snowbunting 144
Soda Point 226
Solitaire 149
Solomon's seal 109
Sorrel, mountain 108
Southard, Lydia 290
Spalding 309
Spalding, Rev. Henry H. ..25, 26
Sparrow 143
Spencer 216
Springtown 240, 379
Spruce, Engelmann 96
    Blue 96
Spud Day 210
Squirrel 128
Stampede Park 224
Stanley 282
Stanley Basin 81
Steamboat Springs 223
Stibnite 294
Stilt 141
Stites 323
St. Anthony 202
St. Joe National Forest 329
St. Maries 327
Swallow 143
Swan 142
Swan Valley 207
Syringa 106

T

Table Rock 257
Tall Tales 393-402
Tanager 146
Targhee Pass 197
Tendoy, Chief 278
Tern 140
Teton Peaks 84, 200, 202
Thimbleberry 100
Thompson, David 19
Thompson Trading Post 338
Thousand Springs 245
Thrasher 150
Three Island Ford 248
Thrush 150
Tiger lily 111
Timber 169-71
Transportation 183-85
Trapping, history .... 19 ff.
Trillium 111
Trude 200
Twin Falls 86, 240
Twinberry 101
Twinflower 104
Twisted-stalk 112

U

Umbrella plant 111
Union Pacific 36, 98
University of Idaho 188
Ursaline Academy 188

V

Vale 128
Valleys, Bear Lake 218
  Boise 82
  Garden 297, 298
  Hoodoo 303
  Hagerman 245
  Long 297
  Pahsimeroi 280
  Paradise 306
  Round 297
  Snake River 37, 75
  Weiser 263

W

Valley View Ranch 197
Vetch 104
Victor 206, 207
Viola 216
Violet 110
Vireo 150
Vulture, turkey 134

Wallace 332
Wapato 112
Warbler 149
Wardner 333
Warm River Inn 201
Warren 294
Water, irrigation 166
  power sites 167
  resources 166
Waxwing 147
Weasel 126
Weippe 320
Weiser 263
Whiskey Rock Lodge 303
White Bird 29, 312
Whitman, Marcus 246
Willow 99
Willow Creek 209
Winchester 311
Wolf 121
Woodchuck 129
Woodnymph 109
Woodpecker 144
Wren 148
Wright, Col. George 28
Wyeth, Nathaniel 20

Y

Yankee Fork 281
Yellowbell 110
Yellowjacket 278
Yellow-legs 145
Young, Brigham 20, 25, 214
Young Ranch 201